Health and Family Planning in Community-Based Distribution Programs

Westview Special Studies

The concept of Westview Special Studies is a response to the continuing crisis in academic and informational publishing. Library budgets are being diverted from the purchase of books and used for data banks, computers, micromedia, and other methods of information retrieval. Interlibrary loan structures further reduce the edition sizes required to satisfy the needs of the scholarly community. Economic pressures on university presses and the few private scholarly publishing companies have greatly limited the capacity of the industry to properly serve the academic and research communities. As a result, many manuscripts dealing with important subjects, often representing the highest level of scholarship, are no longer economically viable publishing projects--or, if accepted for publication are typically subject to lead times ranging from one to three years.

Westview Special Studies are our practical solution to the problem. As always, the selection criteria include the importance of the subject, the work's contribution to scholarship, and its insight, originality of thought, and excellence of exposition. We accept manuscripts in camera-ready form, typed, set, or word processed according to specifications laid out in our comprehensive manual, which contains straightforward instructions and sample pages. The responsibility for editing and proofreading lies with the author or sponsoring institution, but our editorial staff is always available to answer quiestions and provide guidance.

The result is a book printed on acid-free paper and bound in sturdy, library-quality soft covers. We manufacture these books ourselves using equipment that does not require a lengthy make-ready process and that allows us to publish first editions of 300 to 1000 copies and to reprint even smaller quantities as needed. Thus, we can produce Special Studies quickly and can keep even very specialized books in print as long as there is a demand for them.

About the Book and Editors

The authors of this book address the major issues involved in developing and evaluating community-based delivery (CBD) health-care services administered by nonmedical workers in developing countries. Ranging from a general discussion of integrated community-based programs to the prescription of dose regimens that nonmedical personnel can use in field situations, the contributions cover such topics as nutrition intervention, antihelminthics distribution, oral rehydration therapy, and the efficacy of existing programs designed to train those who administer these services.

Maria Wawer is assistant clinical professor, Center for Population and Family Health, School of Public Health, Faculty of Medicine, Columbia University. Sandra Huffman is associate professor, Department of International Health, School of Hygiene and Public Health, The Johns Hopkins University. Deborah Cebula is a consultant for the American Public Health Association. Richard Osborn is a professor with the Department of Preventive Medicine and Biostatistics, University of Toronto.

Health and Family Planning in Community-Based Distribution Programs

edited by
Maria Wawer, Sandra Huffman,
Deborah Cebula, and Richard Osborn

Routledge
Taylor & Francis Group
LONDON AND NEW YORK

First published 1985 by Westview Press, Inc.

Published 2018 by Routledge
52 Vanderbilt Avenue, New York, NY 10017
2 Park Square, Milton Park, Abingdon, Oxon OX14 4RN

Routledge is an imprint of the Taylor & Francis Group, an informa business

Library of Congress Cataloging in Publication Data
Main entry under title:
Health and family planning in community-based distribution programs.
(Westview special studies in social, political, and economic development)
Papers from a conference sponsored by the Johns Hopkins School of Hygiene and Public Health and the U.S. Agency for International Development.
1. Community health services--Developing countries--Congresses. 2. Birth control--Developing countries--Congresses. 3. Health services administration--Developing countries--Congresses. I. Wawer, Maria. II. Johns Hopkins University. School of Hygiene and Public Health. III. United States. Agency for International Development
RA441.5.H426 1985 362.1'0425 84-7527
ISBN 13: 978-0-367-01645-6 (hbk)

Contents

PART SEVEN
OTHER THERAPEUTIC INTERVENTIONS

PART EIGHT
TRAINING ISSUES AND STRATEGIES IN CBD PROGRAMS

PART NINE
EVALUATION AND RESEARCH

Tables

Figures

Preface

International efforts to improve access to family planning and health services in urban and rural areas of less developed countries have led to a great increase in the number of community-based distribution (CBD) projects over the last ten years. The extension of services through such programs reduces the reliance on clinics and broadens service delivery, frequently by employing health professionals who are not highly trained. While this model permits coverage of larger populations, it also presents project planners with special challenges in selection of services, implementation, and monitoring.

Recognition of the special characteristics of CBD programs has resulted in efforts by a number of agencies to summarize experience to date and to determine future directions. The current proceedings emanate from a Workshop focused on the Selection of Health and Family Planning Components in CBD Programs, organized by the Population Center of The Johns Hopkins School of Hygiene and Public Health, and funded under a contract with the U. S. Agency for International Development (USAID), Office of Population. The papers represent an important effort to define a broad range of CBD strategies, their potential and problems, and to discuss future opportunities for CBD family planning projects, many of which will be integrated with health. Previous activities under the Johns Hopkins/USAID contract have included: the preparation of the Comprehensive Review of Field Experience: Community Based Distribution of Contraception; a Workshop on Cost-Effectiveness and Cost-Benefit Analysis and subsequent publication of the proceedings entitled, "Evaluating Population Programs: International Experiences with Cost-effectiveness Analysis and Cost-benefit Analysis," and several other in-depth monographs regarding worker selection, training and supervision in CBD programs.

This workshop was designed to provide a forum for a discussion of issues, activities, and strategies in the selection and field use of common primary health and family planning services. It brought together planners, scientific experts, and program directors from a wide range of donor agencies and host countries to exchange experience and insights from CBD projects in Latin America, Africa, and Asia. The goals of the workshop were:

to define major issues in selecting and implementing services for CBD projects. Such issues included selection criteria, worker training, program evaluation, research directions, and questions pertaining to categorical versus integrated programs. Methods of selecting services in order to avoid program overload constituted a major point of discussion.

to discuss specific, important services (oral rehydration, nutrition, immunization, antihelminthics, contraceptives, and other selected therapeutic interventions) and to consider their suitability to the CBD setting, delineating technical and management strategies to ensure successful implementation.

The Workshop resulted in a number of recommendations concerning the specific services discussed, and provided information regarding broad CBD issues. The authors trust that the mix of theory and field experience contained in the proceedings and compiled in the Editor's Overview will provide a theoretical and practical guide to both future CBD projects and those attempting to improve or expand present activities.

We would also like to take this opportunity to express our appreciation to the Operations Research Division of the Office of Population, U.S. Agency for International Development who provided support for this endeavor, and to our editorial assistant Pamela J. Burdell whose attention to detail and perseverance made this final product possible.

Maria Wawer, Sandra Huffman,
Deborah Cebula, and Richard Osborn

Editors' Overview

INTRODUCTION

Increasing numbers of countries are establishing delivery systems outside the traditional clinic mold as they struggle to provide health services to all that need them. The Workshop on the Selection of Health and Family Planning Components for Community-Based Distribution (CBD) Projects marshalled the expertise of field planners, donors and the scientific community to discuss the advantages and problems associated with the community-based implementation of important primary health and family planning interventions. CBD programs offer planners a flexibility and outreach capacity rarely found in other delivery systems. However, the possibility of overextending current resources exists in the majority of such programs, given that the availability of these resources, including manpower, is relatively fixed. Thus, it is, important that CBD projects be judiciously used to disseminate those services of greatest benefit, and that care be taken not to overload any single project with an unrealistic assortment of services.

Managerial constraints are common to many health systems in LDCs; CBD programs, however, offer specific challenges. Lacking the base afforded by clinical programs, CBD programs must pay special attention to the programmatic requirements of using widely dispersed, lay distributors. These concerns include: the number and types of services workers can deliver effectively, the frequency and content of their interactions with clients, methods of training and supervision suitable to the needs and educational level of the workers, and program evaluation which takes into consideration worker recordkeeping capacities and the geographical dispersion of much of the fieldwork. Additional important considerations shared with other primary health care/ family planning delivery models, include the need for selecting services with proven health effects and choosing appropriate methods of introducing them to the community (Parker, Wawer). Despite the great potential of CBD programs, the problems encountered in their successful implementation and expansion are myriad.

Discussion during this workshop focused around service selection, implementation, and management requirements given the above constraints. Issues included goal setting for CBD projects, the assumptions and constraints underlying the delivery of multiple services, and methods of ensuring adequate training, supervision, and evaluation.

Discussion of specific services presently being incorporated into CBD projects focused upon their suitability, health effects, and other implementation issues. The interventions considered were:

- Oral rehydration (ORT)
- Antihelminthics
- Nutrition
- Immunization
- Contraceptives, and
- Other therapeutic interventions, including antibiotics, anti-malarials, obstetrical activities, and first aid.

SELECTING MIX

Given the extensive health needs of communities, CBD projects have been responding to a growing demand to provide a broader mix of services. Such demand has arisen at both the community and governmental levels (Reinke, Mangani, Ladipo, Gillespie). It has frequently been suggested that integration of service, with its greater comprehensiveness in addressing health and family planning needs, reinforces the effectiveness of any one intervention and increases service efficiencies (Reinke). Evidence supporting the thesis that delivery of health services in conjunction with family planning leads to increased family planning acceptance is inconclusive. However, community acceptability of integrated programs, their potential cost-effectiveness, and the reality that they may offer the only means of providing needed health and family planning services (Gillespie), ensure the continuing expansion of the integrated CBD service delivery model.

ISSUES IN INTEGRATION

In designing integrated CBD projects, or in enlarging the scope of existing ones, it is important to consider potential constraints to the combined service approach. Integration, which can occur at the administrative level, service level, or both, may confront problems of pre-existing administrative compartmentalization within the central government or regionally. Individual ministries and services may be reluctant to see budgetary, personnel, or logistical functions (which they control or wish to control) taken over by an integrated entity. In addition, very few health systems within LDCs presently have the infrastructure to provide the large array of services implicitly proposed in statements such as that emanating from Alma Ata. Additionally, donor agencies frequently are organized to favor concentration on specific services rather than on primary health infrastructure building. Given economic and infrastructural limitations, a selective approach to service implementation deserves consideration. In such a selective framework, major causes of mortality and morbidity are identified, and an assessment is made of the effectiveness of the various interventions in treating or preventing the identified conditions.

Selection of appropriate services is made on the basis of these criteria and the relative ease and cost of introducing the interventions (Gillespie). Although, as Gillespie points out, a selective strategy frequently results in difficult compromises, it does provide a basis for resource allocation, planning, and analysis. Overall, selection of services should take into consideration regional health priorities and goals, but in addition separate goals should be set for each intervention.

Further considerations in CBD intervention selection include:

- the reaction of legal and professional groups to service implementation by lay individuals or minimally trained health workers;

- simplification of therapeutic regimens, training, and supervision, in accordance with CBD worker schedules and capacities;

- and the logistics of distributing supplies to scattered personnel.

Every intervention puts certain stresses on a CBD delivery system. Some, like oral rehydration and oral contraception, require substantial client learning and participation. Others, such as immunization, make intensive demands on logistical and transport systems. Workers' technical abilities are of great importance in activities such as the administration of injections or obstetrical procedures.

When interventions are to be combined in a CBD project, it is important to consider the different program demands each will place on the system. Services which simultaneously stress a particular program segment (worker training, logistics, the clients' ability to learn and remember a relatively large amount of information) should not be implemented simultaneously unless sufficient resources are available to reinforce the "weak link" (Wawer). The implementation of multiple services can potentially dilute program effect at the expense of an important intervention (Gillespie). This possibility must be considered in planning, field supervision, and ongoing program evaluation.

IMPORTANT FACTORS IN CBD PROJECT ORGANIZATION

Training

The importance of developing a well-trained cadre of workers, prepared to deal with unexpected situations and with the demands of their outreach role, cannot be overemphasized and is stressed throughout this volume. CBD workers range from health personnel to housewives in the community. Geographical dispersion and irregular work schedules are common factors in CBD projects, and daily or even regular supervision is impossible. These factors all conspire to increase the importance of initial training and subsequent retraining.

Training for CBD fieldworkers must be based on a clear understanding of the goals and technical activities of the program, and take into account existing worker proficiencies. It must be practical and prepare workers to deal with actual field situations, to react to new problems without recourse to immediate help, and to recognize their limitations. Role plays and practice which duplicate field conditions are essential components of a training course. Extraneous theoretical material and terminology should be avoided, especially given the short duration of most CBD courses (El Tom, Golden et al.). Attempts to increase the length of training courses beyond one or two weeks have encountered difficulties due to increased training costs and the inability of some trainees to leave their homes for longer periods (Ladipo, Mangani). Thus, it is important during the brief training period to stress only material and techniques essential to fieldwork .

Experience from the Sudan Community-Based Health and Family Planning Project indicated that younger literate workers had fewer difficulties than did older illiterate workers, in remembering course material and using their knowledge in the field. This observation was made in spite of the fact that most of the teaching methods did not require that they be literate (El Tom). On the other hand, the Zaire PRODEF project experienced difficulty in recruiting the relatively highly educated women (auxiliary nurses, schoolteachers) it originally hoped to attract, and has since scaled down its educational requirements to include female high school students (Mangani). Compromises in personnel selection may thus have to be made in many projects, and training courses and teaching materials must be designed to reflect the different manpower levels available.

Trainer selection is important. Field personnel who are senior to designated CBD workers, but who perform or have performed work similar to that of the workers, have proven to be well suited to the teaching role; they understand field conditions and can express concepts in a manner comprehensible to the students. Such trainers must be introduced to technical aspects of the program and to active, competency-based training methods (Golden et al., El Tom). Further research is needed regarding innovative training methodologies, including the use of self-learning modules versus traditional course work, as is currently being tested by the PRINAPS project in Guatemala.

Supervision

The indispensibility of effective regular supervision, whether the delivery contemplated ranges from oral contraceptives to oral rehydration, is repeatedly stressed in the chapters that follow (Cash, de Quadros, Wawer, El Tom, Mangani). Ideally, supervisors should have had field experience in the type of fieldwork being performed, and be accessible on a regular basis.

Supervisory models can very widely. The Sudan Community-Based Health and Family Planning Project provides supervisory training for the Health Assistants based in rural dispensaries. Due to their close proximity to the project midwives, the Health Assistants can be contacted at any time by the project midwives who conduct home visits. The project also has designated a number of its central staff to visit the Health Assistants and the midwives on a regular basis to ensure that the system is working smoothly. In turn, the central staff, in their role as overall field supervisors, have been asked to observe Health Assistants carrying out activities in the field.

In the Zaire project, a supervisor travels continuously with the team of home visitors. The supervisor is expected to observe home visits, and using a supervisory checklist, determine their comprehensiveness and clarity. On-the-job retraining is administered on the basis of the observations.

Daily supervision of workers is particularly difficult in nonresearch CBD projects, which are less likely to allocate sufficient manpower and financial resources to this task. Nonetheless, the need for regular, active supervision remains paramount. Supervisors need to visit the field to observe the quality of the work carried out at the household or village level: perusal of CBD worker records alone is insufficient to provide the needed information for process evaluation; and service statistics lack specificity and timeliness.

Logistics

Well-planned worker schedules ensuring regular contact with clients are obligatory for several reasons. Certain interventions, such as immunization, need to be delivered at predetermined points in time for optimal effectiveness (de Quadros). Others, like ORT and contraception, may require repeat visits to guarantee that clients have mastered correct usage and to provide ongoing motivation and improved continuation (Wawer, Gray). Given field realities in most LDCs, adherence to fixed schedules is difficult if not impossible at times. Alternate forms of transportation for supplies and personnel, and reliance on local supply depots (such as the village depot run by matrones (local midwives) in the PRODEF project in Zaire) become important.

The PRODEF project underscored some of the problems of organizing transportation for field personnel. The project operates in an area with no public and virtually no private transport, and relies on its one Land Rover. To facilitate logistics, workers travel as a team; however, this results in inevitable waiting for the project vehicle. Careful scheduling is necessary to minimize such costly delays. Prohibitive fuel and maintenance expenses render full-time use of two vehicles impractical (Mangani). Where means of local transportation are available and relatively reliable, workers can use public transport, for which they receive reimbursement (Ladipo).

The importance of establishing a secure supply system cannot be stressed too much. Project experience indicates that breaks in supply can occur due to in-country shortages of drugs and commodities, delays in international shipments, and national customs regulations at the point of entry (Mangani). Such supply breakages can lead to loss of client confidence (Ladipo). Wherever possible, previous stockpiles, backup supply sources, or alternative implementation strategies should be available, a principle which is well illustrated in the case of ORT (Cash).

ONGOING EVALUATION

Most projects operate in areas with inadequate census and vital statistics, resulting in a lack of baseline information. Many projects are also of short duration and unlikely to result in dramatic changes in maternal, infant, and child mortality and morbidity. If, in addition, community agents are illiterate or semi-literate, these combined factors render evaluation and assessment of project impact difficult indeed (Ladipo). Much of the regular evaluation will depend on routine service statistics, on determination of the amounts of health commodities and contraceptives distributed, and the results of regular supervision.

In cases where agents are illiterate, color-coded cards with symbols can be devised to assist workers in keeping track of the number and type of services rendered, and in keeping a tally of results (such as acceptance, number of supplies distributed [El Tom]). In the Nigerian CBD project, commodities carry a small monetary value, part of which is to be returned to the project. This, plus a system of close personal supervision, is expected to decrease problems of overreporting of field activities (Ladipo). Regular meetings between fieldworkers and supervisors (monthly or more frequently) can serve a number of purposes, including the assessment of performance.

RESEARCH AND EVALUATION IN OR PROJECTS

Operations Research (OR) projects discussed here serve to test new delivery strategies and provide information on many aspects of distribution. Evaluation and research frequently overlap in CBD-OR projects: one of the most important goals of operations research is the improvement of service delivery and the identification of problems which hinder cost-effectiveness, in one project or across projects. Attempting to separate the concept of evaluation from that of practical, field-oriented research may be unnecessary and counterproductive (Gray). Operations Research techniques can be simplified to make them suitable for use in nonresearch CBD projects, and regular data collection can be designed to serve a research function (Heiby).

Objectives of evaluation cum research vary from project to project. Descriptive evaluation can provide valid, valuable information on project development. Operations research can systematically explore the advantages and disadvantages of variations in the service delivery model. Evaluation can also serve a quasi-political purpose, illustrating a point for the benefit of a ministry, for example, or consolidating prior experience.

Given the lack of accurate baseline data on morbidity, mortality, and contraceptive use in many areas, CBD-OR projects frequently conduct a baseline survey in the project region to determine problems and set goals. Data from simplified surveys (minisurveys) can be supplemented by existing local data (health records, government estimates, and records from other programs) for use in goal setting and to provide a baseline from which to judge future project impact.

The four separate aspects of ongoing evaluation (input, process, output, and impact components) were given consideration by discussants.

Input evaluation consists of quantifying and describing the types and quantities of services and supplies to be delivered, and the resources necessary to fulfill these goals. Selection of services will affect all other aspects of evaluation, and the opportunity costs of selecting one service over another should be considered at this stage.

Process evaluation may be the most important type of evaluation for CBD projects. Detailed descriptions of the number of services delivered and accepted, of the quality of client-worker contact, and of support services (training, supervision, supplies, transportation, physical plant, etc.) provide the most timely, concrete, and appropriate information for feedback to project managers. Process evaluation performs a useful monitoring function, facilitating the rapid detection of difficulties either in the overall organization of the system, or with individual workers or clients (Gray, Heiby, Rohde).

The extension of process evaluation beyond the point of service delivery to include training, supervision, and logistics is of great importance. For example, training programs frequently fail to evaluate the actual activities that occurred during the course. Information regarding the course plan is usually available, as are final student evaluations, but no data are gathered on whether the course syllabus was actually covered, the amount of time spent on practical versus theoretical activities, or on student participation. If training is ultimately deemed inadequate in preparing workers for field activities, it is important to know which aspects of the materials and teaching were unsuitable (Golden et al.). Process evaluation to describe supply and cash flows, and how and where delays occur, is of prime importance if supply interruptions are to be avoided and distribution of supplies improved in a project.

Output evaluation denotes analysis of the number and type of services actually distributed in a project. If summary counts are unduly low or high, further examination of the underlying process may be warranted: Are workers performing an inappropriate number of home visits? Are they stressing certain medications instead of others, regardless of importance? Has some problem arisen which makes clients reject a specific service? The interaction between output and process evaluation is obvious. Output evaluation is also fundamental in the determination of the number of workers, the volume of supplies, etc., that are necessary for ongoing and future projects.

Impact or outcome evaluation is frequently difficult to perform, requiring long follow-up periods, a large study population, and comprehensive data on morbidity, mortality, fertility, and child development. Such data are expensive to collect, and unless their quality control is high, may be impossible to interpret against the background noise of other factors. Unless a project has adequate resources in funds, personnel, and time, attempts to gather long-term outcome measures may not be advisable.

Another form of evaluation, the cost-effectiveness study, has been frequently discussed. Such a study is difficult to perform, since it requires the disaggregation of activities by functions, detailed recordkeeping of costs, and follow-up activities to determine outcomes. Cost-effectiveness studies can be important in policy making, but caution must be exercised in their interpretation, particularly if the data are incomplete. Although such studies are unsuitable for use in the bulk of CBD projects, the information gathered from those that are designed to specifically collect such data will be vital to the design of future projects, particularly in times of diminishing financial resources.

IMPLEMENTATION ASPECTS OF SPECIFIC INTERVENTIONS

The health effects and feasibility of specific interventions are analyzed in the expert papers, as well as methods of simplifying their implementation for CBD settings, without compromising safety and utility. Both the advantages and the limitations of the interventions are summarized below.

Oral Rehydration

Oral rehydration is an effective, technologically appropriate treatment for diarrheal dehydration (Cash, Wawer). Although physiological and technical aspects of the intervention are reviewed, emphasis is directed toward implementation issues. The expert paper by Cash reviews different delivery strategies, such as the use of imported or locally produced packets versus home preparation of sugar-salt solution. The former strategy ensures uniformity in the quantities of ingredients used, and simplifies preparation of the solution in the home (only the quantity of water need be measured). On the other hand, sugar-salt solution reduces reliance on an organized ORT delivery system and may reduce costs. The choice depends, however, on the availability of both sugar and salt in local markets. Training for clients must reflect the extra complexity of measuring ingredients other than water.

Whatever the technology used, worker training and the quality of the worker/client interaction remain central to the success of a program. Agents who distribute oral rehydration and teach its use to others must first understand its purpose themselves, know how it is to be prepared, and be able to transmit the information to mothers or other caretakers. The BRAC project in Bangladesh has prepared a list of 10 points that workers must transmit to clients and that the mothers must remember thereafter (Cash). It is essential that workers (during their training) and mothers (during home visits or group meetings) be given practical training with the opportunity to practice the multiple skills demanded of them (Cash, Wawer, El Tom). Field supervision must reflect the need to adequately test both worker and client knowledge. If clients can indeed prepare ORT correctly and have adopted it for use during diarrhea, this implies that workers have successfully carried out their tasks. If direct or indirect supervision (observing client/worker interactions and performing supervisory visits to the client after the worker's visits) reveals incorrect preparation or lack of acceptance, worker activities (including worker training) must be reexamined. The quality of the worker-client interaction will be influenced by the number of home visits scheduled, and work quotas determining the time spent per client. Outside influences on mothers including family members and other health practitioners need to be explored to determine if they act as barriers to knowledge acquisition and acceptance.

Data regarding ORT acceptance can be acquired from baseline and post-service surveys and can provide a global indication of project impact on ORT usage. Regular supervisory visits, however, permit immediate management decisions if problems are detected during the course of the work.

The need for multiple contacts with clients is noted in the paper by Tekce. The lack of impact in the Menoufia ORT project resulted in part from the use of workers who were perceived as young and inexperienced by village women, a lack of repeated contact with mothers for motivational purposes, and insufficient initial efforts to promote ORT among local health professionals.

Evaluation of ORT programs to measure long-term effects on mortality, morbidity, and growth is difficult. Such assessment requires complete, careful follow-up of cases of diarrhea; ascertainment of whether and how ORT was used; and, optimally, selection of controls to determine whether changes are indeed due to ORT or to other factors. Many projects have a time span of one to three years and are of an inadequate duration to clearly determine trends in morbidity and mortality. Given such problems, and the fact that ORT has proven effective as a means of treating dehydration in many clinical trials, it is not necessary for CBD projects to reaffirm ORT's potential benefits. Evaluation should focus on ascertaining whether ORT is used consistently and correctly. As in the case of penicillin and other known therapies, it can be assumed that correct application of the technology will be beneficial in cases where it is indicated.

Major points to emerging from the discussions are:

- ORT is an effective, safe therapy if prepared and used correctly.

- ORT workers need to understand its preparation and use, and be able to transmit this information to clients.

- Repeat contacts with clients (individually or in groups) are an essential ingredient of an ORT program: the time allotted per contact must be enough to transmit the 10 or more key points about ORT. Workers must be taught how to test their clients' comprehension and ensure that they have learned the necessary information. The importance of repeat visits is heightened in a CBD project since the worker may not be present continuously in the village (some CBD projects use mobile teams); mothers must be confident that they can prepare ORT independently. Criteria for referral must also be made explicit to the worker and the mother.

- Supervisory visits should include observation of client/worker contacts, as well as repeat visits to clients, to assess how well they can prepare and administer ORT after a worker's visit, and whether the clients have used it or plan to use it. Supervisory data can be used to restructure worker training, increase the number of client contacts, or increase the time spent per contact, if deemed necessary. The local health establishment (private physicians, pharmacists, etc.) needs to be informed about, and, wherever possible, incorporated into the program. This is particularly important in CBD programs where the community agent may not immediately enjoy the confidence of other health professionals.

ORT program evaluation should emphasize immediate process evaluation including: client knowledge and acceptance of ORT, the amount of supplies expended, and whether supplies are adequate and continuous. Long-term mortality, morbidity and growth analysis are beyond the scope of most CBD ORT projects.

Antihelminthics

Antihelminthics have been used in CBD family planning projects to fulfill two major goals: to decrease morbidity associated with intestinal helminths; and to improve acceptance of other project services, notably contraception. The use of the drugs in CBD settings has generally been on a mass treatment basis for target groups such as all children under five. The expert paper by Keusch discusses the existing evidence for the health impact of worm infestation on health and development. Current experience would indicate that this impact is marginal, and that few individuals have worm-related symptoms, except in cases of heavy worm loads. In those relatively infrequent cases in whom loads are heavy, hookworms can provoke iron deficiency anemia, Ascaris lumbricoides may occasionally lead to intestinal blockage, and Trichuris trichuris has been known to result in rectal prolapse. Evidence regarding the effects of Ascaris and Trichuris on nutritional status is inconclusive, but suggests that direct effects are infrequent unless concurrent diseases are also present.

Thus, the public health relevance of problems caused by helminths is not great. In addition, improvements in health and growth indices after deworming are likely to be marginal unless diet is also improved. Alteration of nutritional states is frequently beyond the scope of emerging CBD programs. Iron supplementation alone, in cases of hookworm infection, results in more rapid improvements in hemoglobin than does deworming without iron supplementation. Given the environmental sanitation conditions in most LDC villages, reinfection is frequently rapid, so that the effect of a single treatment will be relatively short-lived, and repetition of treatment may be required on a regular basis.

Selection of a target group for mass antihelminth treatment can be complex. Although CBD projects have frequently concentrated on maternal and child health, the epidemiology of helminths indicates that maximal exposures and loads occur among adult agricultural workers in the case of hookworm, or older children in the case of Trichuris. This discordance further reduces the health and nutritional impact of antihelminthics used in family planning/maternal and child health CBD projects. The point was made, however, that antihelminthic treatment of symptomatic individuals merits consideration.

The feasibility of implementation is not in question: antihelminthics fit fairly easily within the CBD framework. Ideally, treatments should be repeated three or four times yearly in order to decrease worm loads and transmission, but even treatments twice a year will reduce loads in most individuals and cure a number of others. Antihelminthic drugs are generally safe and easy to administer; and clinical testing has indicated that single doses of piperazine (the drug of choice for Ascaris), pyrantel/oxantel (used for hookworm and Ascaris), and mebendazole (Ascaris, hookworm, and Trichuris) will cure or substantially decrease worm loads in most recipients.

The papers by Gomez and Rodrigues et al. indicate that implementation of antihelminthics is feasible in CBD projects, but that the health effects of the intervention are difficult to measure under field conditions. Antihelminthics represent a program activity which is frequently popular with both workers and clients, and may improve acceptance of a CBD project at governmental and political levels. However, in both the Brazilian and Colombian projects, antihelminthics were not found to have a discernible impact on improving family planning acceptance. The Gomez presentation pointed out that the popularity of antihelminthics waned over the life of the project: few large, visible worms were expelled in individuals who had been previously treated, and clients lost confidence and interest in the therapy, and by association with the treatment lost confidence in the worker.

Although the use of antihelminthic drugs is relatively easy in a CBD project, the opportunity cost of implementing this service on a mass basis (worker time, cost of supplies) as compared to that of an activity with proven public health benefits, must be carefully weighed before any such therapy is instituted.

Immunization

Immunization offers recognized and substantial public health benefits: the Expanded Program of Immunization (EPI) has the potential to reduce morbidity and mortality from measles, tetanus, diphtheria, pertussis, polio, and tuberculosis. More limited activities, such as those directed at neonatal tetanus (described by Bhatia), can also have desirable, measurable effects.

As outlined in the de Quadros and Huffman papers, however, a large-scale immunization activity is complex, requiring extensive resources - personnel, supplies, transportation, storage facilities, and scheduling - beyond the capacity of most CBD projects. The Matlab activities, directed toward provision of a single immunization, were possible within the context of a large, well-organized CBD project capable of providing intensive worker training and close supervision.

An approach to immunization which may be feasible in a larger number of CBD projects consists of cooperation with ongoing EPI activities or with other organizations or agencies already involved in an immunization program. For example, the Sudan Community-Based Health Project shares vehicles with local EPI teams, refers mothers to the immunization program, and in turn receives referrals from the EPI workers (Mubarak).

Major points emerging from the discussion of immunization are:

- Immunization, if properly performed (vaccines stored correctly to ensure potency, injections administered by competent individuals at the correct time) can have major public health impact.

- The resources necessary to mount an immunization activity are complex and costly.

- Given that the activity is beyond the scope of most CBD projects, community-based workers can nonetheless play a valuable role by cooperating with any existing immunization program: they can refer mothers to the immunization team, motivate and remind clients to attend, explain the need for multiple injections, and, potentially, since they remain in the village after the team has departed, be taught to deal with minor side effects of the immunization.

Contraception

Offering a mix of contraceptive methods within one program allows the CBD worker and the client to determine which contraceptive is best suited to the latter's requirements, and provides alternative methods if the contraceptive originally selected proves not to meet changing needs.

While there are some risks associated with the use of contraceptives (as is true with most medical interventions) the balance of incidence indicates that the benefits of contraceptives, including orals and injectables, outweigh the potential risks in populations of fertile women in less developed countries.

Screening of clients, via simple checklists, can serve ethical and health functions, and may increase project acceptance among the medical establishment in a given country. Screening should not be so stringent as to disqualify women unnecessarily, and thus potentially deprive them of contraception. The preparation of screening lists should be based on known health risks in a given population, but should also take into account the available alternatives if a woman fails the test: is either referral or another method available to her? Workers need appropriate training to master the simple screening lists, to accurately interpret findings, and to direct clients to appropriate alternatives.

Oral contraception is relatively simple to deliver. Still, workers must be trained to understand and teach correct usage, and to reassure women in cases of minor side effects. The provision of multiple dosages of pills is not warranted given existing project data: it is difficult to predict which dosage is optimal for which woman, and the switching of pills complicates worker activities without necessarily improving compliance. The use of progestogen-only minipills during lactation may be a potential exception to this rule.

Estrogen administered in the early post-natal period can reduce milk volume in lactating women. The effects of estrogen transfer to the infant by breast milk are not known. For these reasons, oral contraceptives containing estrogen should not be prescribed to fully lactating women for at least six weeks after delivery. In societies where women breastfeed fully for prolonged periods, and where average lactational amenorrhea is also prolonged, the inception of estrogen-containing oral contraceptives can be delayed for six months or even longer.

Injectable contraceptives (Depo Provera, Norigest, etc.), while not presently provided by AID funds, are highly effective and convenient for the majority of women. Although animal studies have raised questions regarding potential carcinogenic effects, the relevance of the findings to humans remains unclear, and no increase in relative risk has been noted in carefully conducted studies in less developed countries. Injectables may have great applicability in those CBD projects where workers can be trained and supervised to maintain the drugs and equipment and to give injections. Mobile teams which contact clients every three months offer another mode of delivery. In each case, women require contact with a village level worker who can answer questions regarding side effects and refer the client when necessary (as in cases of prolonged menstrual bleeding during early use, or infection at the site of injection).

CBD workers also can be trained to provide barrier methods, and to refer clients for IUD insertion and sterilization. The number of contraceptives offered by a program will influence the duration of worker training, the complexity of the logistical system, and the intensity of supervision. The availability of multiple methods will also increase the required client education.

Those in attendance at the workshop pointed out that:

- Method mix is an important factor in increasing contraceptive acceptance, and particularly continuation.

- It has been repeatedly demonstrated that CBD workers can serve as effective distributors of oral contraceptives and barrier methods, and as a referral source for IUD insertion and sterilization. The provision of injectable contraceptives by a CBD system is also feasible, employing either traveling teams (who would ideally work in conjunction with permanent workers in the village) or permanent workers themselves, if the latter receive the necessary training. Supervision is essential to ensure proper techniques and recordkeeping.

- The introduction of additional methods of contraception should be reflected in an increased duration of training.

- Field supervision is an important component in worker motivation and in verifying that the technical and educational aspects of contraceptive provision are carried out correctly. These visits can also serve to enhance the status of the worker in the eyes of the community. Clients' knowledge of correct usage should be ascertained via indirect supervision.

Nutrition

Nutrition supplementation programs to combat protein-energy malnutrition are technically complex, require large inputs of manpower and financial resources, and are difficult to evaluate. Indeed, because of the multiple factors which influence nutritional status (including birth order, sex, parental knowledge, and illness), the results of food supplementation programs have generally been inconclusive. Nutrition activities in CBD programs should be directed to interventions with simpler resource requirements, greater measurable public health benefits and an increased potential for replicability.

The potential benefits resulting from improved nutritional status among infants and mothers cannot be disputed (Lechtig). What is far less clear is the ability of most CBD projects to mount such programs. Huffman describes three nutritional supplementation activities which can be adapted to CBD programs: supplementation of a target group with iron and folate, vitamin A, and iodine. In areas where dietary deficiency in any one of these nutrients is common, CBD distribution of the supplement in question will result in public health benefits (reduction of iron and folate deficiency anemia, of xerophthalmia and blindness, and of goiter and cretinism, respectively). In the case of iodine, a decrease in the size of many goiters will occur within months, potentially increasing client acceptance of the CBD program. Visible improvements in vitamin A deficiency eye conditions among children are also likely to occur. The benefits of iron and folate supplementation are less likely to be obvious to the community, although they are no less important from a public health perspective.

Specific target groups can be identified to receive each of the supplements. In general, pregnant women represent the highest priority for the distribution of iron and folate. Preschool children are prone to vitamin A deficiency, and develop severe sequelae most rapidly. Iodine administration to women of childbearing age will have an important effect on the reduction of congenital cretinism. Depending on project resources, the identification of target groups can be expanded to include other individuals at risk.

Except for the case of iron and folate, which are most effective if taken daily, administration occurs approximately every six months (vitamin A) or every few years (iodine). Thorough records to ensure full coverage of target groups, and to avoid overdosing (particularly in the case of vitamin A in children) are essential. Since distribution schedules are fairly simple, they can be introduced into other CBD activities. Conversely, visits to deliver the supplements can be used as an entree to discuss other health issues and the CBD program in general. Iron distribution to pregnant women, for example, can be used as an occasion to discuss pre- and post-natal care.

Recognizing the limitations of protein-calorie supplementation programs which rely on food sources external to the area, Rohde and Soejatni describe another approach to the problem of infant and childhood feeding which is currently being tested in Indonesia. Women in the UPGK program are taught to make optimal use of foodstuffs available in the region. Mothers of children whose development is faltering are paired with women whose children are growing normally: participants learn proper feeding techniques from each other. Mothers are also taught to monitor their children's growth through monthly weighings. Results are plotted on clear, simple growth charts, and if a child is seen to be faltering, the mother is given additional support, education, and, only if necessary, food supplements to use on a temporary basis.

Program costs per child are low, parental interest appears to be substantial, and the replicability of the system is probably greater than that of classical supplementation programs. The largest program resource requirement is manpower. Personnel must be available for monthly weighing sessions, parental education, and follow-up where necessary. Project results are not yet available, although ongoing evaluation is currently being undertaken.

Other Therapeutic Interventions

Additional potential interventions for a CBD program include antibiotics, antimalarials, obstetrical interventions, treatment for simple skin conditions and conjunctivitis, and first aid. These interventions are reviewed by Parker and Wawer. All of the therapeutics discussed are popular among clients, and a number have the potential for a substantial public health impact (for example, antibiotics for lower respiratory tract infections, antimalarials and obstetrical interventions). A number consist of simple regimens, but some, such as antibiotics or obstetrical activities, require relatively substantial training, supervision, or logistical provisions.

The selection of interventions from this group depends in part on the type of worker available. A program that utilizes the services of traditional birth attendants, or midwives, may implement simple obstetrical care more easily than a program that uses sanitation workers. As in the case of any intervention, the inclusion of one of the services above will have to be calculated into the sum of program inputs and weighed against opportunity costs.

CONCLUSION

The CBD model represents an important, timely, and efficient mode of service delivery, be it of health or family planning. The combination of multiple services within any one project must, however, be accomplished in a manner so as not to overextend resources and dilute the impact of important interventions. Training and supervision must be adapted to the complexity of each task, and process evaluation is essential to assess the functioning of components necessary to perform each activity.

To prevent the displacement of effort from interventions having the highest project priority, it is essential to maintain program focus on a small number of activities, and to phase in additional interventions gradually. Given their reliance on community workers, and a delivery model which often precludes continuous supervision or a sophisticated referral network, most CBD projects are not designed to provide comprehensive health care. Planners need to focus their attention on selected health and family planning priorities to ensure that these receive the necessary coverage. When activities requiring intensive client participation are instituted (ORT, contraception), it may be desirable to implement only one of these services during any one phase of the project.

The gradual phasing of activities grants a project flexibility, and may serve to maintain worker and community interest. Most importantly, it permits both workers and clients to master the intervention, and allows program managers to ensure that the logistical and supervisory systems are functioning adequately before new interventions are added.

The Workshop on Health and Family Planning Components in Community-Based Distribution Projects permitted valuable interchanges among field personnel, donor agencies, and the academic community. The papers, discussions, and conclusions arising from the meeting are the result of many years of experience and research. It is hoped they may serve to guide plans for future CBD programs, and encourage more agencies and institutions around the world to explore the potentials of the community-based approach to service delivery. In addition, future activities in CBD Operations Research are needed to further define optimal outreach, training, supervision, and logistical, record-keeping, and evaluation strategies. Given the numerous advantages of the CBD approach, particularly in rural areas of less developed countries, current and future efforts to improve this method of service delivery will play an important role in increasing access to health and family planning throughout the world.

Part One

Issues in Integration of Community-Based Distribution Programs

1
The Nature of Community-Based Distribution: Some Field Results and Problems

R. W. Osborn

An objective of this workshop is to examine the health and family planning activities employed in experimental and demonstration field projects in less developed countries. But before proceeding in depth into the complexities of these interventions (program activities), it is important that we have a shared understanding of the type of field structure implied in the phrase, Community-Based Distribution (CBD).

Family planning intervention projects have been previously reviewed by Cuca and Pierce (1977) and a more circumscribed appraisal of community-based and commercial contraceptive distribution has been made available by Foreit, Gorosh, Gillespie, and Merritt (1978). The present statement, based on three major surveys (Cuca and Pierce, 1977; Foreit et al., 1978; Osborn and Reinke, 1981), focuses on CBD projects rather than broader family planning and health projects in less developed countries. Incompleteness of data and rapidity of change make an exhaustive review well-nigh impossible. The goal of these few remarks is to provide an introduction to the setting in which activities -- that is, interventions -- are delivered.

CBD systems are non-clinical family planning delivery systems. Whereas there was general agreement as to the structure and function of clinic-based services, there is no similar agreement as to the nature of non-clinical family planning systems. CBD systems cannot be easily classified (Foreit et al., 1978; Korten, 1978), as shown by the following examples of so-called CBD systems:

- Outreach or mini-clinics located in villages or neighborhoods.
- A village depot managed by a resident.
- Village provider of services who visits households where he or she lives.
- Periodic sweeps of households by trained workers from the surrounding area.

There are, however, some shared characteristics among these approaches. As discussed by Foreit, et al. (1978), CBD systems can embrace the following structures:

- Provision of services in a non-clinical setting;
- Use of non-health or paramedical personnel to provide services; and
- Minimal use of screening and recording procedures.

The necessity for these structures became apparent in the early 1970s, when it was clear that traditional clinic-based approaches were reaching only segments of the population in need (Burkhart, 1981). Obstacles to the equitable provision of clinic-based services include lack of funds and shortages and maldistribution of trained health personnel.

Non-clinical delivery systems are designed to minimize costs and remove barriers to use for the rural and urban poor, who compose a high proportion of the population of most of the less developed countries. It is hoped that CBD systems, employing less expensive facilities and workers with lower levels of education, facilitate the extension of outreach among this population.

Behind the decision to establish CBD programs are the assumptions that family planning services are wanted; that minimally educated lay personnel can be trained to deliver them, either door-to-door or from a village-based supply depot; and that the use of contraceptives is constrained by a lack of service capacity.

Receptivity, or pre-existing community demand, will vary, and service capacity may be too limited or too great for that demand, as shown in Figure 1.1:

Figure 1:1. Service Capacity and Demand in CBD Projects

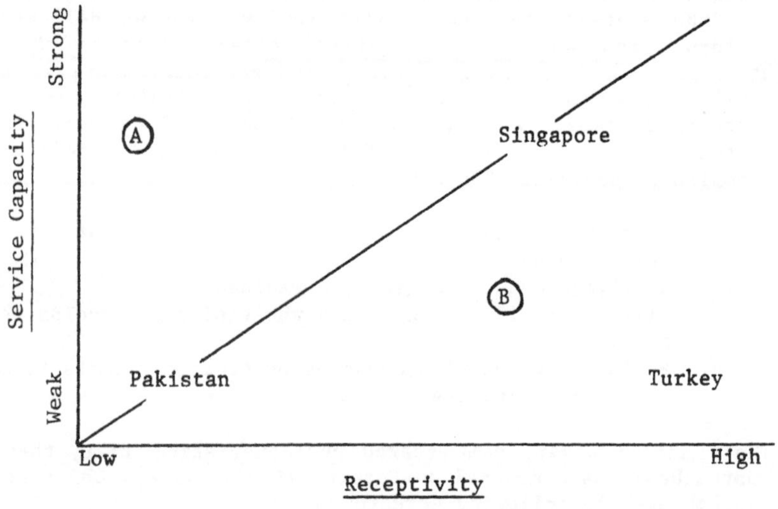

SOURCE: Korten, 1978.

Where capacity is limited, village workers can be trained to deliver services. Projects facing a situation illustrated by (A) would need to strengthen outreach or adopt information, education and communication (IE&C) interventions to increase demand. Most Asian and Latin American countries are at point (B), where demand is greater than services but a strengthened service would quickly meet pre-existing needs. At that point, contraceptive prevalence will cease to increase, and new efforts will be needed to improve both receptivity and service capacity.

The strong emphasis given to the supply-side approach is due in large measure to the efforts of the U. S. Agency for International Development (AID). Although other groups, including the International Planned Parenthood Federation (IPPF), also sponsored CBD programs, it was largely through AID efforts that systematic demonstration and research projects to document and evaluate the CBD approach were undertaken. Under the rubric of Operations Research, different interventions were introduced in delivery systems and results recorded. Among the findings from the 28 projects reviewed in the <u>Community-Based Distribution of Contraceptives Review</u> (Osborn and Reinke, 1981) are the following:

1. A trend toward increased range of contraceptives offered to village residents is seen throughout the 1970s. A broader mix is associated with higher use of contraceptives.
2. Increasingly, health services were added to non-clinical family planning delivery systems. In many countries, health delivery systems are inadequate or non-existent. As family planning delivery systems were developed, there was considerable pressure to add health interventions to these systems.
3. These non-clinical family planning delivery systems are affordable, culturally acceptable and effective in raising contraceptive prevalence to the 30 to 35 percent level.

As non-clinical delivery systems increase the number of contraceptives and health interventions they offer, problems arise concerning both receivers and providers of the service. These include:

1. Limits in the ability of poorly educated villagers to effectively deliver a multiplicity of interventions. When numerous or incompatible tasks are assigned to an individual, some tasks will suffer. Compatible tasks involve similar skills, are directed to similar target groups, and involve similar styles of work (Korten, 1978).
2. Possible side-effects of some interventions in some recipients, necessitating the provision of high-level medical backup to deal with them.
3. Questions about how to select the most appropriate intervention for a given community, and ways of introducing these into the population.

4. Pressures on CBD systems to deliver more and more -- now may not be the time for increasing this load.
5. Emphasis has been on distribution of contraceptives or primary health care, but there are frequent calls for an added concentration on the community and community development (Anonymous, 1979; Korten, 1978). As the data from the Shanawan-Egypt project show, mobilizing the community differs significantly from providing health care; and increased acceptance of contraception follows from increased attention to the community, its leaders and major groups.

These are some of the concerns that prompted the design of the present workshop. We anticipate that the papers and discussion over the next three days will answer some of these concerns. But as in all complex human undertakings, we also await the presentation of even more vexing problems throughout these proceedings.

REFERENCES

Anonymous. "Community Emphasis." People 6 (1979).

Burkhart, M.C. "Issues in Community-Based Distribution of Contraceptives." Pathpapers 8 (1981).

Cuca, R. and C.S. Pierce. Experiments in Family Planning. Baltimore, MD: Johns Hopkins University, 1977.

Foreit, J.R. et al. "Community-Based and Commercial Contraceptive Distribution: An Inventory and Appraisal." Population Reports Series J, (1978).

Huber, S.C. et al. "Contraceptive Distribution: Taking Supplies to Villages and Households." Population Reports Series J., 5 (1975).

Korten, D.C. "Managing Community Based Population Programmes: Insights from the 1978 ICOMP Annual Conference." Kuala Lampur, Malaysia, July 17-19, 1978.

Osborn, R.W. and W. Reinke, eds. Community-Based Distribution of Contraception: Review of Field Experience. Baltimore,MD: The Johns Hopkins University, Population Center, 1981.

Ravenholt, R.T. and D.G. Gillespie. "Striking Results of Household Distribution." People 14 (1977): 4-5.

Trainer, E.S. "Community-Based Integrated Family Planning Programs." Studies in Family Planning 10 (1979).

2
Issues in Integrated Family Planning and Health Programs

Duff G. Gillespie

The organized family planning program is a fairly recent phenomenon in the developing world. Much has happened since India declared the first official population policy in 1952. This paper focuses on one aspect of the evaluation of family planning programs - integration issues associated with community-based family planning delivery systems, which go beyond the respective countries' existing clinic-based health infrastructure.

One of the most dramatic changes that has occurred in family planning is in the number and types of delivery systems that have evolved. Initially, family planning programs mimicked the delivery systems of the developed world. As a result, family planning services were clinic-based with medical professionals as service providers. The clinic facility and staff primarily provided health services and, in a sense, family planning could be considered as being integrated with health. Free-standing, unipurpose, family planning clinics also existed but, as is the case now, they were not as common as multipurpose clinics and were usually associated with private family planning associations. These clinic-based delivery systems worked fairly well for urban populations. However, with the realization that a clinic-based system could never adequately serve the largely rural population of the developing world, modifications began to be made. Outreach workers traveled into communities to recruit new and follow up old acceptors. Mobile clinics were in fashion for a time, taking the clinic to the people. This metamorphic trend continued and became quite intense and innovative in the 1960s and 1970s. Delivery systems were developed that were no longer tied to a stationary clinic or a physician. The system that evolved has been generally termed community-based distribution.

In most community-based systems, family planning services are provided by specially trained lay persons from the community. Having nonphysicians provide such services as oral contraceptives was unthinkable in most countries a decade ago. Now, there is little exceptional about it (Huber et al., 1975; Foreit et al., 1978; Rosenfield et al., 1980). The first social marketing program was launched in India in 1969. These programs provide subsidized contraceptives through retail outlets; in ten years, 35 social marketing programs have been started throughout the world (Altman and Piotrow, 1980). From tentative efforts with household visitations in the Subcontinent (Osborn, 1974; Population Council, 1964) many programs have developed which systematically canvass households, providing a wide variety of family planning services. Household distribution projects are found in such diverse sociocultural settings as Korea, Mexico, Zaire, Egypt, and Bangladesh. Here again, a delivery system considered radical less than a decade ago is now, if not commonplace, certainly lacking singularity.

INTEGRATION

Calls for the integration of family planning services with other development activities have been long and persistent. Initially, this call was confined to family planning and health, especially maternal and child health (MCH) (Taylor, 1965); now, they encompass a wide variety of socioeconomic actions (Family Planning in the 80's: Challenges and opportunitues, 1981). Two international events did much to strengthen the trend towards integration. The Bucharest Conference produced a Plan of Action that emphasized the interdependence of population and socioeconomic variables. From this consideration, family planning was viewed as something that should be encompassed in a larger, comprehensive development effort (World Population Plan of Action, 1974). Even more influential was the Alma Alta Conference. The Alma Alta Declaration clearly states that family planning should be part of a broader primary health program (World Health Organization, 1978). A third meeting in Copenhagen, which concerned women in development issues, was too recent to assess its effect, but its conclusions are clearly akin to Bucharest and Alma Alta, especially the latter (World Conference of the United Nations Decade for Women, 1980). It is difficult to disagree philosophically with the general thrust of these gatherings. They call for some very desirable things: health, peace, equality, and development. Politically and ethically, integration is compelling. But, does it make sense programmatically?

DEFINITION OF INTEGRATION

There are many definitions of integration, but very few operational definitions. Not infrequently, statements, articles, and plans of action leave the term undefined. The vagaries of defining integration are understandable - it will unavoidably mean different things in different programs. In a sense, integration is defined by what particular programs do in the name of integration. Nevertheless, for discussion purposes, one needs a reference point.

Integration entails the combining of various functions or tasks. Implicitly, integration means that the elements to be integrated are distinct entities which, for whatever reasons, did not previously exist together. Otherwise, of course, there would be no reason to integrate. Any discussion of the pros and cons of integration must explore the reasons why these elements existed separately, for the rationales for their separate state may be more compelling than the rationales for combining them. Also, although this paper focuses on family planning and health, the concept of integration encompasses much more than these two rather broad fields. Indeed, just as important an issue in the present international climate concerns the integration of various health interventions into a holistic health effort. As a result, this paper will not only deal with the integration of health and family planning, but also discuss combinations of various health interventions.

Two important considerations to keep in mind when discussing integration are the locus of the integrative process and its purpose. Ness makes a useful functional distinction between administrative and service integration.

> Administrative integration proposes structural changes and speaks to issues of administrative authority, responsibility, jurisdiction and accountability. Service integration concerns linkages at the point of service delivery and speaks to issues of work flows, referrals and individual contacts. (Ness, 1979, p. 18).

Ness goes on to point out that one can have administrative integration and not service integration, and, somewhat paradoxically, that services can be integrated while the administrative infrastructure is unintegrated. Ness observes that there are temporal and spatial aspects to integration; for example, an immunization campaign can entail other developmental sectors for a short period and be confined to a specific geographic region.

RATIONALES FOR INTEGRATION

The reasons why organizations and development experts advocate the integration of family planning with other development efforts are often philosophical and lack any empirical basis or logical consistency. An example of faulty reasoning is found in the product of one recent working group that considered the integration of family planning with rural development.

> There has been increasing interest on the part of policymakers and administrators in the integration of family planning services with other socio-economic development activities, especially those designed for rural development. This is partly due to a realization of the limitations of unifunctional family planning programs in dealing with the multi-faceted nature of fertility regulation. It is also due to a growing awareness, as exemplified in the World Population Plan of Action, that effec-

> tive fertility regulation must be accompanied by the improvement of socio-economic conditions for the rural population (UNFPA, 1979, p. 1).

Two points are made above. First, the statement correctly notes that family planning programs typically do not address all the factors that influence fertility. Second, it implies that without an improvement in socioeconomic conditions, fertility regulation will be ineffective. The debate about the relative importance of development versus family planning is a long one (Davis, 1967). It is still not clear what type or what level of socioeconomic development gains must be realized before the demographic transition begins, or, for that matter, if such an improvement is critical for a demographic transition (van de Walle and Knodel, 1980). The debate will continue and is somewhat removed from the concerns of this paper. A preferred position is that socioeconomic conditions and family planning <u>both</u> influence fertility (Birdsdall, 1977; Maulden and Berelson, 1978; McGreevey and Birdsall, 1974; Rich, 1973). For this discussion, assume that there must be an improvement in socioeconomic conditions, as the above rationale states.

Given that contemporary family planning programs do not concern themselves with all development sectors and that improvement of the socioeconomic environment negatively influences fertility, it does not necessarily follow that family planning should be integrated with other development sectors. Countries can make and have made major improvements in health, the status of women, income, income distribution, housing, education, and a wide range of other variables without integrated family planning programs. Very desirable goals, such as female education and reductions in child mortality, can be attained with interventions quite separate from family planning efforts. Stating that these goals are desirable and that, if reached, they will reduce fertility, is not sufficient reason for advocating the integration of family planning programs. Integration of family planning with these efforts must be shown to make it easier, quicker, or cheaper to achieve these goals.

Scores of rationales have been given for integration, but all are encompassed within the following six categories:

1. <u>Political acceptability</u>: A growing number of countries require that family planning be integrated with other development projects. Therefore, to have a family planning program, it must be integrated. While this is not a justification for integration <u>per se</u>, it makes moot any discussion of the pros and cons of integration.
2. <u>Expediency</u>: Some situations allow no programmatic or fiscal alternative to an integrated approach. Like the first rationale, this is no justification of an integrated approach, but is in fact the reason for many integrated projects.
3. <u>Community acceptability</u>: This common rationale basically states that communities will not accept family

planning unless it is integrated with other development activities.

4. Community needs and desires: Since the community desires other development services, the family planning program should provide them. While this rationale is seldom stated so bluntly, it is frequently given for an integrated community-based program.
5. Synergistic effect: A powerful rationale is that combined development efforts will have a greater effect than if they were implemented separately.
6. Cost-effectiveness: Integrated approaches provide not only the desired effect, but cost less to attain it.

How well are these rationales supported empirically? Despite pleas for such efforts (ESCAP, 1977; Population Development Studies, 1979; Wolfson, 1978), there have been few large-scale attempts to initiate family planning integration with nonhealth activities. Two notable exceptions to this dearth of programs, both in Egypt (Social Research Center, 1980; Population and Development Project, 1980), integrate family planning with a wide range of development actions; neither has been functioning sufficiently long to determine its effectiveness. Additionally, the projects are not designed to determine the relative effectiveness of a family-planning-only versus an integrated family planning system. As a result, neither is likely to throw much light on the relative merits of the integrated versus the nonintegrated approach.

The situation regarding integration of family planning and health programs is markedly different from the case of nonhealth development sectors. Here, there have been scores of special programs and national programs. However, even such well-known efforts as the Taylor-Berelson maternity care and family program (Taylor and Berelson, 1968) were not designed to examine the various rationales for integration. Although the program has many commendable elements, there is nothing to indicate that it is a superior alternative to a unipurpose family planning effort (Castadot et al., 1975).

Two major projects have addressed the merits of a unipurpose family planning effort versus an integrated health delivery system. The Narangwal and Danfa projects represent the most sophisticated attempts to demonstrate whether an integrated approach actually does increase community acceptance of the program, respond to community health needs, have a synergistic effect, and produce superior cost-effectiveness ratios (Rural Health Research Center and The Johns Hopkins University; University of Ghana Medical School and UCLA School of Public Health, 1979). While these complex projects are discussed elsewhere, the results of both are sufficiently inconclusive to allow the individual's philosophy concerning integration more influence in interpreting the results than the projects' data. This "eye of the beholder" dilemma indicates that any superiority of one system over another is minor. Other experimental efforts as rigorous as Danfa and Narangwal, explicitly designed to prove the superiority of alternative delivery systems, are unlikely, yet the methodological problems in both studies were serious. They covered only small populations, together less than 150,000. They had major and intensive research components, raising the issue of the "Hawthorne effect" - which postulates that research activities can influence the factor being observed. And, perhaps most importantly, they cost millions of dollars.

Even without clear documentation of their superiority, integrated family planning and health delivery systems have become the rule rather than the exception throughout the developing world. Although it is unclear why this trend has occurred, several reasons are probable. First, the pronouncements of such organizations as the World Health Organization (WHO) supporting an integrative approach have most likely influenced policymakers. It should be noted that such events as Alma Alta did not happen in a vacuum, but reflected strong beliefs of the international health field, including teaching institutions.

Second, the organizational home for a national family planning effort can be created anew or placed within an existing unit. In Asia, the dominant pattern of the late 1950s and 1960s was to create a discrete organization for the government's family planning effort. For other regions of the world, the typical pattern has been to place family planning in an existing organizational unit, usually the ministry of health. Thus, the family planning effort became administratively part of the health program often organized as a distinct subunit of the ministry.

Third, in some countries, the population problem is not viewed as a demographic or development issue. Instead, the emphasis is on the maternal and child health consequences of birth spacing and timing. Any demographic effects resulting from a change in fertility behavior are considered to be of secondary importance, if that. This assessment is especially evident in Africa.

Fourth, some policymakers believe that family planning would not be politically or socially acceptable unless seen as part of a broader health program. Fifth, in well-established family planning programs, health interventions have been added to the family planning delivery system. In this case, the family planning infrastructure was more extensive than the health system and it was considered programmatically expedient to use the existing system for a health intervention. This is happening in Indonesia, where, in the rural areas, the family planning program is much stronger than the health program (U.S. Agency for International Development, 1979).

For whatever reasons, it is a fact that for the vast majority of countries, family planning is now considered a health intervention. It is imperative, therefore, to consider how family planning can best be integrated with health programs.

INTEGRATED DELIVERY SYSTEMS

Family planning services are difficult to deliver effectively, especially to isolated rural populations. It is equally if not more difficult to deliver primary health care services. And finally, it is difficult to increase female employment, agricultural productivity, literacy, and so on. To assume that the integration of several different and difficult development actions will result in an aggregated action which is less difficult is counter-intuitive. Indeed, there is every reason to assume that the integrative process results in a potentiating effect, with the combined difficulties of the separate development components being greater than their sum. If this is true, then parts of the integrated effort may be less effective than if they were implemented separately, or the entire integrated effort may perform more poorly than its components would if implemented separately. Although this discussion focuses on integrated health and family planning programs, most conclusions also pertain to integration with other development sectors.

The Alma Alta Declaration establishes a target of health for all by the year 2000. This is a worthy target, and no one would consider it inappropriate. But is it attainable? The debate has been joined by health experts. Some are quite confident.

> Primary Health Care is the outcome of collective human conscience, a recent awareness that there has been inequality in the distribution of health which is a human right. There has been a concentration of health in cities and amongst the wealthy with the result that disease, disability and premature death have flourished unchecked at the social periphery. Primary Health Care programmes aim at changing this situation, and the achievement of Health for All by the Year 2000 has now become a feasible proposition. Because PHC involves people rather than merely technology, the place of social scientists in medicine has become more essential and central than ever before (Bennett, 1979, p. 515).

> For those inclined to dismiss this as a hollow slogan [Health for All by the Year 2000], one need only look at the revolutionary impact that other idealistic statements have had: the American Revolution was predicated on the assertions that "All men are created equal," the French Revolution on "Liberte, egalite, fraternite," and Marxism on "Workers of the world unite, you have nothing to lose but your chains."
>
> To ask how close we have come to any of these noble ideals misses their central point, which is their capacity to inspire mankind to work towards achieving them.
>
> So too with "Health for all by the year 2000."
>
> Can this revolutionary idea be translated into simple, easy-to-understand language?
>
> Yes (Manuila, 1980, p. 3).

Others are not so sanguine about the health situation in the year 2000. One cannot help but believe that the cautious critics are, in part, reacting to the auspiciousness and ethereal quality found in such statements as those above.

Those who question the primary health approach do not question the goal, but doubt that it can be reached. Some state that the primary health strategy concentrates too much on health care delivery, ignoring more basic socioeconomic conditions that can lead to better health. Others believe that comprehensive primary health care is unattainable and not really necessary; they advocate selective health interventions that address specific, treatable diseases which are the major causes of mortality. Others think that it may be possible to successfully implement a global primary health system, but the probability of accomplishing this is not particularly high unless major changes are made in the way health is approached in the developing world, especially in the use of health technologies (Parker, 1978; Piachaud, 1979; Habicht, 1981).

It should be noted that the debate between those advocating primary health care and those proposing other alternatives is not academic and is not peripheral to family planning. Decisions are being made every day in ministries of health which revolve around primary health care and the role, if any, family planning will play in the system. Problems associated with the integration of family planning into a primary health system are outlined below.

Administrative Compartmentalization

Governments are not organized to maximize integrative efforts. As a result of specialization and the rise of special interest groups, governments are organized in functional units that have discrete mandates which they not only try to carry out, but protect and (not infrequently) expand. This compartmentalization not only occurs at high levels of government (for instance, ministries of health, education, and agriculture), but also at such lower levels of government as departments of maternal and child health, sanitation, and immunization. There are many policy and programmatic implications resulting from compartmentalization:

Budgetary. Typically, each functional unit has its own budget. An integrated effort often involves the commingling of funds and joint fiscal planning. After personnel, nothing is more jealously guarded than a budget. Administrators hate to lose control of their budgets, although they are quite willing to take over the responsibility of other budgets. Integration, then, poses budgetary threats for some and budgetary opportunities for others.

Personnel. An integrative process almost invariably entails changes in the roles of personnel. Some are given new and different tasks, while others are called upon to share responsibilities that were once totally in their domain. New job descriptions must be produced, formally or informally. Supervisory relationships are altered. Promotions and other work incentives often become confused. In short, personnel must reorient themselves in many ways, and the directions this orientation takes are often confused.

Logistical. Functional units often have their own logistical and transportation systems. Even where a larger system is shared, there are allocations of resources and space for respective units. An immunization program will, for instance, have control of cold-chain equipment and relevant drugs. The same can be said for malaria, rural sanitation, and other programs and units. An integrated approach assumes that there will be a sharing and combining of resources. However, once the integration approach begins, questions concerning who is responsible for and controls commodities become critical. Vehicles often appear to be the most vigorously defended resource.

Political. The lines of authority become confused when programs are integrated. Who takes credit for success or blame for failure? If a unit's budget and staff are not considered as components of a primary health effort, what are the implications for future funding and personnel levels? Administratively and organizationally, integration can result in uncertainties.

The forces for integration are powerful, but so are the forces for compartmentalization, the latter being evident for a much longer period - say, since the beginning of the Industrial Revolution. Administrative integration is flowing against the tide. Specialization is still the hallmark of governments and organizations; problems are addressed by breaking them down and assigning their various parts to specialists.

A recent example of this tendency is WHO's creation of the special Diarrhoeal Disease Control Program. The program is successfully encouraging the formation of special programs to combat diarrheal disease in member countries. So far, such programs exist or are in the planning stage in about 70 countries. But although WHO states that these programs should become part of a national primary health program, it does not address the problem of how a special program becomes incorporated into the overall health system. If the control of diarrhea is integral to a primary health program, why create a separate program? On the other hand, special programs highlight the problem and make it easier to quickly amass the expertise and resources required to attack the problem now.

The fact that governments are compartmentalized does not mean that they cannot successfully mount an integrated program. It does mean that there are barriers to integration that must be surmounted and that this process will take time and energy. The more functional areas involved, the more units and personnel that must be brought together in a coordinated effort. The long-term prognosis for any integrated program depends on an integrated administration. Although one can envision a relatively short-term integrated project, without an integrated administration, it is difficult to imagine a long-term program being successful without an integrated infrastructure at all levels. It should be noted that international organizations and donors that are encouraging integration are not themselves organized to enhance integration and, in general, have organizational units that are the functional equivalents of those found in governments.

Selecting Integrated Services

Primary health care subsumes norms that optimize the number and types of services. The preface to the Alma Alta Declaration highlights this comprehensive approach to health.

> Primary Health Care is essential health care made universally accessible to individuals and families in the community by means acceptable to them, through their full participation and at a cost that the community and country can afford. It forms an integral part both of the country's health system of which it is the nucleus and of the overall social and economic development of the community.
>
> Primary Health Care addresses the main health problems in the community, providing promotive, preventive, curative and rehabilitative services accordingly. Since these services reflect and evolve from the economic conditions and social values of the country and its communities, they will vary by country and community, but will include at least: promotion of proper nutrition and an adequate supply of safe water; basic sanitation; maternal and child care, including family planning; immunization against the major infectious disease; prevention and control of locally endemic disease; education concerning prevailing health problems and the methods of preventing and controlling them; and appropriate treatment for common disease and injuries [World Health Organization, 1978, p. 2 (emphasis added)].

In the developing world today, very few health systems can include all the services implicit in the above statement. Indeed, in many rural areas, the health infrastructures are grossly inadequate or nonexistent. To insist that a primary health care program must be comprehensive will mean that for vast areas and large populations, it will be years before a delivery system can be put in place. It is questionable that such a sophisticated system will be possible for some countries even by the year 2000. Appreciating the fact that a delivery system addressing a small number of health conditions can be put in place more quickly and cover a much larger population than a comprehensive delivery system, a number of experts have advocated community-based delivery systems that are restricted in scope. Walsh and Warren have termed this "interim strategy" as "selective primary health care" (Walsh and Warren, 1979).

Basically, the selective approach to primary health care entails the identification of the major causes of mortality and morbidity in a population. Then effectivness of existing health technology in treating or preventing the various diseases is assessed. Lastly, the relative ease and cost of introducing the various technologies are compared. From this process, the service components of the delivery system are constructed. The process is neither as mechanical (Hirschhorn, 1980) or as simple as it sounds.

The number of health services is very difficult to restrict. The exclusion of a particular service tends to be viewed as depriving the population. Since the health needs in the developing world are so great, some desired and needed services will be excluded; difficult compromises must be made.

Foremost in considering what should and should not be included in a delivery system is safety. Community-based delivery systems rely heavily on lay personnel. Thus, some interventions are excluded because they have the potential for misuse or because the therapy has potentially serious and negative side effects if not properly administered. Others are excluded because they are too complex and difficult to implement.

Many preventive health measures are not included because they entail major and sustained behavior modifications. Diarrheal diseases will not be prevented until communities implement environmental health measures. These measures, however, require altering basic behaviors in terms of food storage and consumption, waste disposal, and personal hygiene. While these objectives should be pursued, they will take a very long time to achieve and may be impossible without parallel changes in the socioeconomic environment. Health programs should not ignore such difficult health measures, but the immediate priority should be the reduction of deaths due to diarrhea. The technology exists for accomplishing this through oral rehydration (Hirschhorn, 1980; Parker et al., 1980). While the changes in behavior necessary for an effective oral rehydration program should not be underestimated, they are clearly less complex and extensive than the changes necessary to prevent diarrhea.

Effective health measures that can be acted upon now should be implemented. They should not be deferred until the country establishes the requisite critical mass of trained personnel, commodities, buildings, funds, and logistical systems to attack major health problems. The effect of a selective approach to primary health care is not insignificant. With a few select interventions widely and effectively employed, significant health improvements can be realized. For instance, in examining the cause of death among children in rural Bangladesh, Chen and coworkers concluded: "The delivery of a few selected basic immunizations and oral therapy for watery diarrhoea could eliminate about 40 percent of deaths among children under five (Chen et al., 1980).

Considerations of the prevalence of a disease, the existing technology for addressing the disease, and the cost, safety, and complexity of effectively delivering this technology, are critical in determining the acceptance or rejection of a particular intervention. Equally important is an appreciation of the political and sociocultural setting where the delivery system will be implemented. Any delivery system should be sensitive to nontechnological or system-specific variables that may influence the performance of the delivery system. Knowledge of a community's life style and political structure contributes to the successful planning and implementation of a delivery system. Such slogans as "Health for and by the people" have appeal. Nevertheless, they are difficult to operationalize, much less achieve.

One should not assume that villagers know what is best for them, or that they can intuit what will or will not work. If this were the case, many of their endemic problems would not exist, or could be solved simply by making resources available to them. At the same time, there is no guarantee that a country's health professionals will understand village life and its problems. And certainly one should never assume that international health experts from prestigious organizations possess a touchstone for predicting the best course of action. Still, while the last category of persons is seldom essential to the design of a delivery system, the participation of the first two is very important indeed. Villagers, like international health experts, may not be able to predict all outcomes. But they can recognize obviously stupid, inappropriate actions which to urban medical personnel appear both appropriate and brilliant. For example, village leaders can prove very valuable in identifying individuals or classes of individuals who would be inappropriate as community health workers because of caste, religion, politics, or class. Local advice should not be followed blindly, however: villagers who can identify poor choices may not be able to select appropriate ones. Community-based health programs represent a new event and, if successful, a radical happening for most rural communities. No one can predict with certainty what services and organizational strategies a delivery system should emphasize. Health experts can address technical issues, and community members can help avoid gross blunders that quickly doom the system to failure. Still, the only way to be sure a particular system will work is to try it. Abstract pronouncements and feasibility studies do little more than delay implementation (Huber et al., 1975).

Implementing Integrated Services

The health community does not agree on how the health problems of the developing world can be alleviated. Yet, something approaching unanimity is found on two points: First, delivery systems must use community workers to deliver at least some health services. Second, in order to have a meaningful effect, the delivery system must have wide coverage. Most countries do not have an adequate number of health personnel to provide this wide coverage. Although some interventions can be accomplished with a one-time, short-term approach (for example, immunizations), other interventions require that services be easily accessible to the community more or less continuously. Examples of the latter are family planning, oral rehydration therapy, pregnancy management, and obstetrical services. It is these services that are most often found in community-based distribution systems. Implicitly, the community-based approach will mean that service delivery points will consist of far-flung lay personnel residing in a village with often precarious links to professional health service units and medical supply depots. The delivery system is a vulnerable one.

The vulnerability of the system increases with an increase of its parts. Developing a training program for community workers who have limited health experience and education is difficult with a very limited number of services. Yet Heiby, for instance, reports one effort in which illiterate traditional birth attendants were expected to master 300 discrete skills and areas of knowledge (Heiby, 1981). A logistical system that must maintain a steady supply of, say, 10 drugs, may be taxed in isolated rural areas and collapse if it must handle twice that amount. Likewise, supervisors who concern themselves with the performance of workers in 10 functional areas may find it impossible to oversee 20 services. And, most importantly, the provision of multiservices in the field becomes more difficult with the greater number of services. Community health workers can easily become overextended if they are asked to do too much. Instead of providing good coverage for all services, they may concentrate on selected services - most likely those that are easiest to provide and require minimal sustained motivation on the part of the user. In some cases, the quantity and quality of services may decrease across the board.

The implications for the effective implementation of a primary health care program as advocated by WHO and others should not have to be belabored. Still, while it seems obvious that inherent problems in community-based delivery systems will be exacerbated as the services become more extensive, there are strong advocates for complex integrated programs, including, as noted earlier, integration with obviously different development sectors. A call for caution is emphatically not a condemnation of integration - it is a call for a sober realization that wanting something to happen is not good enough. We must aim for realistic, attainable objectives.

INTEGRATION AND FAMILY PLANNING

By itself, family planning is easier to deliver than is a complex integrated family planning and health system. This is true even if the overall system is a "lean" one, affecting only a few health services. The concern here is that health programs reflecting the philosophy of Alma Alta will overburden fragile delivery systems or so encumber them that they will never penetrate large regions of the world. In short, without care, integration could hold back the family planning effort and, for that matter, other health interventions.

Family planning can get lost in an integrated health system or even be excluded. It is mentioned almost in passing in the Alma Alta Declaration. Walsh and Warren, in their influential article on selective primary health care (Walsh and Warren, 1979), do not bother to mention family planning, even if only to reject its inclusion. One does not have to look far to find health programs that are devoid of any family planning.

Lastly, there is the question of money. Integrated health programs are unavoidably more expensive than family planning programs. Almost without exception, family planning is integrated into health systems; it is seldom vice versa. Through placement in the health system, family planning may not only lose its identity, but also its earmarked funds. This is a one-way street, and the dangers it poses are even more serious when considering integration with nonhealth sectors. Berelson and Haveman recently addressed this point and concluded:

> . . . [T]he debate over the proper policies for fertility reduction must take into account effectiveness per unit of investment along with other considerations. It is not helpful, often it is less than helpful, simply to assert as a policy recommendation that increased popular education or improved health or higher standard of living or more women's liberation would reduce fertility without appreciating the relative effectiveness per dollar of expenditure on such efforts, not to mention the programmatic means to effect them (Berelson and Haveman, 1980, p. 230).

This concern about the use of "population funds" is not a simple, mean manifestation of territoriality, but a deeper concern that sufficient funds be allotted to maintain and develop strong family planning efforts throughout the developing world. Moreover, it is important not to fall into a simplistic "family planning versus health" or "family planning versus development" debate. That is not the salient issue.

The paramount concern is that limited resources and talents will be diffused over so broad a range of problems that the resulting efforts will be ineffectual. The answer lies in the concentration of efforts - it is much better to do a few things very well than to do many things very badly. Deciding where the effort will be concentrated will always lead to disagreement among many and disappointment for some. It is to be hoped that family planning will always be included among the services offered.

NOTES

1. Evaluation and monitoring systems are beyond the scope of this paper. However, in the initial stages of implementation, it is wise to have a feedback system in place so that administrators can quickly detect problems. Equally important, the de-

livery system should be flexible so that corrective actions can be quickly made, as is usually required in such new ventures.

REFERENCES

Altman, D.L. and P.T. Piotrow. "Social Marketing: Does it Work?" Population Reports J,21 (1980): 393-434.

Bennett, F. "Primary Health Care and Developing Countries." Social Science and Medicine 13,5 (August 1979): 505-514.

Berelson, B. and R.H. Haveman. "On Allocating Resources for Fertility Reduction in Developing Countries." Population Studies 13,2 (1980): 227-237.

Birdsall, N. "Analytical Approaches to the Relationship of Population Growth and Development." Population and Development Review 3,1 and 2 (1977): 63-103.

Castadot, R.G., I. Sivin, P. Reyes, J.O. Alers, M. Chapple, and J. Russell. "The International Postpartum Family Planning Program: Eight Years of Experience." Reports on Population/Family Planning 18 (1975): 56.

Chen, L.C., M. Rahman, and A.M. Sarder. "Epidemiology and Causes of Death among Children in a Rural Area of Bangladesh." International Journal of Epidemiology 9,1 (1980): 25-34.

Davis, K. "Population Policy: Will Current Programs Succeed?" Science 158 (1967): 730-739.

ESCAP. "Report and Selected Papers on the Expert Group Meeting on Organizational Aspects of Integrated Family Planning with Development Programmes." Asian Population Studies Series 36, Bangkok, 1977.

Family Planning in the 1980's: Challenges and Opportunities. Background document for International Conference on Family Planning in the 1980's, Jakarta, Indonesia, April 26-30, 1981.

Foreit, J.R., M.E. Gorosh, D.G. Gillespie, and C.G. Merritt. "Community-based and Commercial Contraceptive Distribution: An Inventory and Appraisal." Population Reports J,19 (1978): 1-29.

Habicht, J.P. "Health for All by the Year 2000." American Journal of Public Health 71,5 (1981): 459-461.

Heiby, J.R. "Low-cost Delivery Systems: Lessons from Nicaragua." American Journal of Public Health 71,5 (1981): 514-519.

Hirschhorn, N. "The Treatment of Acute Diarrhea in Children: An Historical and Physiological Perspective." American Journal of Clinical Nutrition 33 (1980): 637-663.

Huber, S.C., P.T. Piotrow, M. Potts, S.L. Isaacs, and R.T. Ravenholt. "Contraceptive Distribution: Taking Supplies to Villages and Households." Population Reports J,5 (1975): 69-88.

Manuila, A. "Introducing World Health Forum." World Health Forum 1,1 and 2 (1980): 3-4.

Mauldin, W.P. and B. Berelson. "Conditions of Fertility Decline in Developing Countries, 1965-75." Studies in Family Planning 9,5 (1978): 89-148.

McGreevey, W.P. and N. Birdsall. The Policy Relevance of Recent Research on Fertility. Washington, DC: The Smithsonian Institution, 1974.

Ness. G.D. "On Integration in Family Planning Programming." In Report on UNFPA/EWPI Technical Working Group Meeting on Integration of Family Planning with Rural Development. Population Development Studies (1). New York: United Nations Fund for Population Activities (1979).

Osborn, R. W. "The Silakot Experience." Studies in Family Planning 5,4 (1974): 123-129.

Parker, A. "Health Technology and Primary Health Care." Social Science and Medicine 12 (1978): 29-41.

Parker, R.L., W. Rinehart, P.T. Piotrow. "Oral Rehydration Therapy (ORT) for Childhood Diarrhea." Population Reports L,2 (1980): 41-75.

Piachaud, D. "The Diffusion of Medical Techniques to Less Developed Countries." International Journal of Health 9,4 (1979): 629-643.

Population Council. "Pakistan: The Medical Social Research Project at Lulliani." Studies in Family Planning 4 (1964): 5-9.

Population and Development Project, 1980.

"Resolutions and Decisions." World Conference of the United Nations Decade for Women. Copenhagen, July 14-30, 1980, A/Conf, 94/34/ADD. 1, August 14, 1980, pp. 1-56.

Rich, W. Smaller Families Through Social and Economic Progress. Washington, DC: Overseas Development Council, 1973.

Rosenfield, A., D. Maine, and M. Gorosh. "Nonclinical Distribution of the Pill in the Developing World." International Family Planning Perspectives 6,4 (1980): 130-136.

Rural Health Research Center and Johns Hopkins University. Narangwal Population Study: Integrated Health and Family Planning Services. Punjab, India and Baltimore, MD.

Social Research Center. Integrated Social Services Delivery System: Menoufia, Progress Report. Cairo: The American University in Cairo (December 1980).

Taylor, C.E. "Health and Population." Foreign Affairs (1965): 475-486.

Taylor, H.C. and B. Berelson. "Maternity Care and Family Planning as a world Program." American Journal of Obstetrics and Gynecology 100,7 (1968): 885-893.

United Nations Fund for Population Activities (UNFPA). Report on UNFPA/EWPI Technical Working Group Meeting on Integration of Family Planning with Rural Development. Population Development Studies (1): New York: UNFPA, 1979.

U. S. Agency for International Development. Project Paper: Indonesia Village Family Planning/Mother-Child Welfare. Jakarta: USAID (October 1979): 138.

University of Ghana Medical School and UCLA School of Public Health. Danfa Comprehensive Rural Health and Family Planning Project: Ghana, Final Report. Accra and Los Angeles: September 1979.

van de Walle, E. and J. Knodel. "Europe's Fertility Transition." Population Bulletin 34,6 (1980): 44.

Walsh, J.A. and K.S. Warren. "Selective Primary Health Care." New England Journal of Medicine 301,18 (1979): 967-974.

Wolfson, M. Changing Approaches to Population Problems. Paris, Development Centre of the Organization for Economic Cooperation and Development, 1978.

World Health Organization. Primary Health Care Report on the International Conference on Primary Health Care. Alma Alta, USSR, September 6-12, 1978. Geneva: World Health Organization (1978): 49.

"World population plan of action." Reprinted in: Studies in Family Planning 5,12 (1974): 381-392.

3
The Danfa, Lampang and Narangwal Projects: A Comparative Review

William A. Reinke

Concern continues to mount for the nearly universal inadequacy of health services coverage in the rural areas of less developed countries where the majority of the world's most impoverished families reside. These also tend to be areas of high fertility. A variety of projects have been launched, therefore, to improve the combined coverage of health, nutrition, and family planning services to women and children in a manner that is locally appropriate, effective, and generally affordable to the populations served and their governments.

The three USAID projects reported here have been followed with special interest because of their size, scope, duration, and the exceptional attention devoted in each to data gathering and evaluation. Services in all of the projects extended over a period of approximately five years, the projects have been completed, and extensive analysis of both inputs and results has been conducted. Project designs contained many similarities; yet distinct differences were present, thereby making comparative analysis especially rewarding.

The Narangwal (India) Research Project carried out its experimental service activities in a population of approximately 30,000 during the period 1969-1974. The Danfa (Ghana) project was also research-oriented and served an area in excess of 60,000 population from 1970-1978. The Lampang (Thailand) project was a development effort that extended to an entire province of 650,000 people from 1974-1979. Thus, while the projects were separate enterprises in three different countries, in retrospect they offer together some useful insights into the sequencing of research, demonstration, and general implementation.

It is neither appropriate nor feasible in this brief paper to discuss each of the projects exhaustively. Rather, a comparative review of project experience will be conducted under five headings:

1. Project Aims and Design
2. Project Organization and Management
3. Services Provided
4. Personnel Selection, Training, and Utilization
5. Data Acquisition, Processing, and Analysis

After citing major similarities, differences, and findings in these separate respects, the paper concludes with certain composite impressions and recommendations.

PROJECT AIMS AND DESIGN

The underlying research question at Narangwal concerned determination of the most effective means of combining health and family planning services. Specifically, the question was whether contraceptive use increased significantly when family planning services were combined with health services to childbearing women and/or their children, rather than being provided separately. If, indeed, the hypothesized synergism were found to exist, a corollary question was anticipated: could the incremental benefits of integration be achieved at reasonable cost? In fact, the study showed that consideration of the latter question provided the more compelling evidence for advantages of integration. Provision of health services to women and children required less family planning input per se to produce family planning benefits similar to those obtained through family planning alone, and substantial health benefits were achieved as well.

Effective integration of services was likewise a fundamental research issue at Danfa, but the approach there differed in two important respects from that of Narangwal. First, the service components under investigation were different. Whereas health services for women and children were examined separately and together at Narangwal, only their combination was studied at Danfa. The latter project, however, added health education as an explicit component to be assessed separately and in combination with health services.

The second notable distinction between project designs was in the incrementalization of service inputs. The Narangwal design provided for quantitatively similar but qualitatively different resource allocation to each of the experimental groups. Additional services to certain experimental groups in Danfa, on the other hand, were accompanied by corresponding increases in inputs in those cells.

Each of the approaches has advantages and disadvantages for marginal analysis of costs and benefits. In practice, however, only the comprehensive services group in Danfa received discernible benefits during the early project years. The large (relative to Narangwal) number of persons included in other experimental groups, coupled with the limited inputs provided, left many families effectively uncovered by services and caused personnel to be underutilized. Modifications in service delivery and outreach were accordingly made in the course of project implementation. This experience has confirmed the desirability and feasibility of combining health services with family planning. Such services must be chosen selectively, however, both in terms of service category and target population. This point is elaborated further under the heading of Services Provided.

Accepting the value of integrated services, the Lampang project sought to demonstrate the feasibility of successful large-scale implementation throughout an entire province of 650,000 population. Thus, in Lampang a single pattern of interventions was introduced to provide women and children with comprehensive coverage of health, nutrition, and family planning services. The purpose of the project was to increase services utilization at a cost that would convince policy makers of the desirability of wider replication.

PROJECT ORGANIZATION AND MANAGEMENT

All three projects were sponsored by the U. S. Agency for International Development (USAID) through U. S. universities. The Narangwal project was carried out by Johns Hopkins University under a blanket cooperative agreement between Hopkins and the Government of India. The University of California at Los Angeles (UCLA) and the University of Hawaii provided technical back-up to the Danfa and Lampang projects respectively.

The roles of the universities and, especially, of the governments differed, however. Service personnel in Narangwal were project employees, and feedback of results to the routine government services was relatively informal through the Indian Council of Medical Research and through periodic conferences involving senior officials of the Ministry of Health.

The Danfa project was carried out through the University of Ghana Medical School. Thus, the project had a decided medical education thrust. As a result, project success was measured as much in terms of strengthening the medical school Department of Community Health as in improvements in the Danfa health services. Moreover, the representativeness of attained service improvements can be considered suspect in view of the project's location and the unique involvement of medical school personnel.

The Lampang project was the most fully integrated with normal government services. The Project Director was also a senior officer in the National Ministry of Health, and the Project Field Director was simultaneously Lampang Provincial Chief Medical Officer.

Given the variability in size of the study populations and in project control over interventions, it is not surprising that the Narangwal project yielded the greatest measurable quantitative improvement in health, while Lampang produced the least definitive results. On the other hand, Lampang has produced the most tangible evidence of post-project maintenance and expansion of project interventions. Even so, assimilation of Lampang experience into routine government services has been incomplete at best. For example, the project was intended to produce an improved, streamlined management information system for routine adoption by government health services. This intention remains largely unfulfilled, even though project information was compiled within the framework of existing provincial health services. Constraints in the control over and evaluation of Lampang interventions has introduced the serious risk that hidden mistakes and inefficiencies will be replicated on a much broader and more costly scale.

Comparison of the organization of the three projects highlights the continuing difficulty of balancing the achievement of research objectives against the goal of routine application of research findings.

SERVICES PROVIDED

The fundamental concern in all three projects was to bring a broad range of preventive and curative health services, along with family planning, closer to the community. At Narangwal this was accomplished by placing a trained family health worker in each village. The worker was thus readily accessible for patient-initiated care, and in addition she was able to undertake a systematic visiting program in individual homes for the identification and treatment of diarrhea, respiratory problems, and other illnesses and malnutrition, as well as the promotion of health and family planning. The proximity and frequency of contact proved to be extremely effective in combatting malnutrition and respiratory illness, including pneumonia, but was inadequate for the treatment of dehydration from diarrhea. As a result, mothers were instructed in its recognition and treatment and in the preparation of oral rehydration solution.

The wide range of family planning methods offered (pill, condom, IUD, injectables, and sterilization), along with health services, yielded an acceptance rate in excess of 50 percent. At the end of the project in 1974, about one-third of the eligible couples were currently practicing family planning. The condom proved to be a valuable method, in part because it was the most popular method of initial acceptance, and in part because experience with the condom stimulated switching to other, more effective methods. By the end of the project, about one-fourth of the users were using highly-effective injectables, and one-fifth were sterilized.

The Lampang project also relied on village-level workers, but these were unsalaried community volunteers with no prior experience and minimal training. In addition to training and utilizing Village Health Volunteers (VHVs), therefore, the project aimed at the strengthening of health center, district-level, and provincial health services. The intent was to increase the overall utilization of government health services, to provide simple preventive and curative care at the village level, and to encourage more appropriate clinic facilities for referral services.

Probably because the VHVs were compensated solely through commissions on the sale of drugs and contraceptives, primarily pills, their activities were largely limited to provision of simple curative care and promotion of family planning. Contraceptive prevalence at the start of the project was already at the 50 percent level. The VHVs, therefore, served largely as a more convenient source of contraceptive supplies than the formerly used health centers. The project did succeed in raising contraceptive prevalence above 60 percent, however.

The provincial hospital Department of Community Health was strengthened and more effectively integrated into the overall provincial health care delivery system. In particular, outreach was provided through mobile units that provided medical care and conducted vasectomy camps in selected villages on a rotating weekly basis. In view of the high pre-existing prevalence of oral contraception, the stimulus to switch from a temporary to a permanent method was probably at least as effective as the recruitment of new acceptors.

Health center midwives and sanitarians were given one year of training as medical assistants. Upon their return to their health centers after training, they were qualified to provide comprehensive primary care and to supervise the VHVs in their areas. Their enhanced clinical skills, which were in demand from the community, dominated their attention with the result that outreach supervision activities were often neglected.

The baseline community survey showed malnutrition to be a common and serious problem. Problems in data gathering and analysis delayed identification of the severity of the problem, and even after it was recognized, little was effectively done about it. Child Nutrition Centers were organized, but these failed to reach many of the most needy younger children. The difficult task of mounting an effective nutrition surveillance system for identification and treatment of high-risk cases was never accomplished. The widespread presence of VHVs made accomplishment possible, but they were not adequately trained, motivated, or supervised in this regard.

The original intent of the Danfa project was to improve the capability of the family health center to provide comprehensive care and to augment health service delivery with health promotion and family planning activities. Of the four experimental areas, the only one providing direct care through the project was the area that already contained the medical school teaching health center. It was soon discovered that, regardless of health center capability, it failed to attract clients at the periphery of the area to be covered. Moreover, the activities in areas not receiving direct care were clearly inadequate to make a measurable impact on health or fertility. The project thrust was accordingly modified to enhance the services provided and to extend them to the periphery. Child Welfare Centers were reorganized into Morley-type "under-fives" clinics, satellite clinics were formed, and worker outreach, along with community participation, were stressed. A three-phase program of progressive involvement of the community was developed. Phase I gave attention to: health education; nutrition education, demonstration, and supplementation; environmental sanitation; and the training of traditional birth attendants. Phase II was marked by the introduction of community based malaria prophylaxis and immunization. In Phase III a Village Health Worker (VHW) program was introduced.

Project-related reductions in morbidity and malnutrition were largely unconfirmed. Pre-school mortality reduction was obtained only in the area receiving health care. Family planning acceptance levels reached 30 percent and above only where health care and/or education was provided. Twelve-month continuation rates averaged 36 percent. They were higher for IUD acceptors, who were most often in the area receiving health care. This was the only area in which measurable reduction in fertility was discerned. Family planning results tended to be most favorable when VHWs were employed under the supervision of mobile health teams.

PERSONNEL SELECTION, TRAINING, AND UTILIZATION

The primary providers in the Narangwal project were hospital-trained auxiliary nurse midwives who were retrained by the project as family health workers (FHWs). Initially, a four to six month period of retraining was envisioned before assignment as an FHW. Early experience led to a substantially reduced period of in-service training, followed by field placement with an experienced FHW and regularly scheduled in-service training based upon actual problems encountered in the field.

The Lampang project relied mainly on two new types of fieldworkers, one less trained and one more trained than the Narangwal FHWs. The most peripheral worker was a community volunteer who was given a few days of training and returned to the community as a Village Health Volunteer. The second type of worker was a previously trained midwife or sanitarian recruited from the Lampang government health services, given extensive additional training for twelve months and returned to government service, usually at the same service base as before, as a medical assistant. In spite of the heterogeneity of previous training and experience and future roles, the medical assistant training was uniform. The difference in knowledge and skills of these two types of workers was considerable. The VHVs were probably inadequately trained to carry out the range of activities included in the project. On the other hand, the medical assistant may have been in some respects inappropriate, inefficient, and excessive. Unfortunately, the relationship between content of training and field practice has not been evaluated systematically. It is quite clear, however, that the tremendous difference in length of VHV and medical assistant training, coupled with lack of synchrony in the timing of the training, meant that VHVs were in the field for many months during their critical period of early service without adequate supervision, motivation, or in-service instruction.

The Danfa project converted existing uni-purpose workers, e.g., sanitation assistants, into Health Education Assistants (HEAs). As already indicated, Village Health Workers were also added late in the project. Otherwise, considerable reliance was placed upon existing cadres of workers with revised job descriptions and more carefully specified operating procedures. All three projects retrained traditional birth attendants with generally satisfactory results.

All three projects conducted functional analyses of health needs in relation to worker service activities. In fact, personnel responsible for these studies in each case had been associated with the original development of functional analysis methodology in Narangwal in the 1960s. While the analyses were useful in assessing changing patterns of utilization of service personnel over the course of the projects, they were not employed to examine the congruence between field performance and training curricula.

DATA ACQUISITION, PROCESSING, AND ANALYSIS

All three projects placed heavy emphasis on data gathering and evaluation. Most notably, exceptional attention was given to the analysis of resource utilization and costs. Distribution of personnel time among project functions was carefully measured, both for purposes of assessing the balance of effort and for allocating personnel costs by service component over time.

Community health surveys were conducted in all three cases. Survey information was generally of reasonable quality except for the usual under-reporting of vital events in Danfa.

A relatively sophisticated service statistics system was employed in Narangwal. Because the project itself provided a large proportion of the services received in a limited number of study villages, the service statistics system worked effectively and provided invaluable evaluative data. In contrast, the Lampang project relied heavily upon routine government service reports. Many of the service indicators needed for study purposes were not contained or inaccurately reported in the government data. Little or no project effort was devoted to quality control or supplementation of government reports.

An IBM 1130 computer was made an integral part of the Danfa project. Otherwise, the projects were strikingly weak in the prompt processing of field data for management feedback purposes. The isolated location and inadequate staffing of data processing personnel in Narangwal meant that the monumental data gathering efforts far outstripped data processing capabilities. The Lampang project relied upon a Bangkok facility for data processing. The Bangkok computer was inadequate for the job to be done, and adequate coordination with this outside group was never achieved.

OVERALL CONCLUSIONS

The Narangwal, Lampang, and Danfa projects together demonstrated the validity of the intuitively appealing notion that a comprehensive package of health and family planning services are mutually reinforcing in effectiveness, and provide service efficiencies. In fact, in reviewing these projects, one is left with the distinct impression that if analytical capabilities had been as fully developed as the service delivery systems under study, the case for comprehensive care would have been made even more dramatically.

To be feasible for general coverage, comprehensive care must be carefully selective both in specific service components included and in high-risk populations targeted. An improved management information system providing rapid feedback of project experience for fine-tuning of service activities is therefore an essential element that was generally weak in the projects reviewed. Refinement and streamlining of data gathering and analysis for primary care is as important as simplification of the delivery system; yet it has received much less attention to date.

Although these projects fell short in providing definitive answers with respect to optimal service components, they did add impressively to our knowledge about these matters. The possibility of producing significant impact on diarrheal and respiratory diseases was demonstrated. Locally important diseases, e.g., malaria in Danfa, can be tackled effectively. Malnutrition, on the other hand, is a common problem that is difficult to handle through traditional health interventions. Only in Narangwal was significant progress made; and then through intensive, relatively costly effort in a limited population. The case of malnutrition highlights the difficulty of transferring the experience of a limited trial to a larger population served under routine conditions.

These projects also provide insights into the selection, training, and management of service personnel. The projects clearly indicate the importance of providing multiple services close to the people. This requires reasonably skilled personnel widely distributed. The minimally trained VHV of Lampang is inadequate to the task, especially in the absence of adequate in-service training and supervision. On the other hand, vastly expanded training of medical assistants is neither feasible nor appropriate. Much more objective assessment is needed in matching service components, consequent skills needed, resulting training requirements, and pre-requisites of trainees.

REFERENCES

Government of Thailand, Ministry of Public Health. Summary Final Report of the Lampang Health Development Project, Vol. I. Development Project Documentary Series. Bangkok: 1981.

Rural Health Research Center. The Narangwal Population Study: Integrated Health and Family Planning. Narangwal, India: 1976.

University of Ghana Medical School and UCLA School of Public Health. Danfa Project Final Report. Accra, Ghana or Los Angeles, CA: 1979.

4
Selection of Family Planning and Health Interventions for Community-Based Distribution Projects

Maria J. Wawer

The number of community-based distribution (CBD) projects that include both family planning and other health components has steadily increased in many countries. This paper will not enter into a broad discussion of the philosophy and advisability of integrating family planning and health in CBD projects. Given the political reality in many countries, as well as a genuine need for health interventions in underserviced communities, the combination of family planning and health services is frequently inevitable. It is thus useful to consider ways of improving mechanisms of intervention selection to ensure an effective mix of program services. Such a mix should not strain existing CBD manpower and technical resources, but provide a coherent and adequately varied service to optimize worker and recipient satisfaction.

ASPECTS OF INTERVENTION SELECTION UNIQUE TO CBD PROGRAMS

The selection of interventions for CBD projects should reflect the fact that such projects differ from clinic-based family planning or primary health care services in a number of significant ways. After receiving training, CBD workers return to their own villages or travel between villages, frequently distributing services house-to-house. Their work is usually fairly autonomous. Although medical backup is available for some projects, in most cases one must choose interventions that do not require elaborate follow-up, medical examination, or laboratory tests and in which the potential for significant side effects is small.

The timing and frequency of contact between CBD workers and their clients, and thus the continuity of care, vary enormously among projects. In some, workers make several sweeps through an area in order to promote and deliver family planning and health supplies but do not remain in close contact with recipients, as is the case in the service model being tested in the Zaire PRODEF CBD Project. Individuals may then be expected to get further provisions from local clinics, which are sometimes situated far from the client's home. In other projects, the worker is permanently based in the village, a model being used in the Moroccan VDMS expansion and in the Sudan Community-Based Health and Family Planning Projects. Still other programs use a combination of the two approaches: sweeps and permanent village workers.

The interventions selected must be tailored to the given context. In the case of periodic sweeps, it may be preferable that the intervention offer long-term effects from a single administration (such as may be provided by Depo-provera or antiparasitics), or be directed at an acute condition that can be treated simply with one or two doses of medication (malaria in semi-immune subjects). Another possibility is that the medication schedule be sufficiently simple and have few enough side effects that the client can continue to take it safely for long periods of time without ongoing supervision (for example, oral contraceptives). Programs in which the trained CBD worker remains in the village may be better candidates for the introduction of medication or procedures requiring repeated administration or follow-up.

The education level of selected CBD workers and their subsequent training will be important in determining the complexity of the chosen interventions. CBD workers often work alone and may be expected to remember and apply various medical principles over long periods of time without the benefit of ongoing clinical supervision and recourse to higher medical opinion. If, in a given project, CBD workers can only be given limited training regarding simple concepts, they cannot be expected to deliver services requiring frequent, complex diagnostic decisions.

In order to enhance the project's effect, conditions with high initial prevalence, which permit frequent worker-community contacts, can be included in CBD programs. Also, the condition being treated must be sufficiently common so that workers can practice the associated technical skill frequently enough to maintain proper techniques.

A clinic-based health system can accommodate the use of bulky supplies and equipment - the patients do the walking. In the case of many CBD programs, supplies must be mobile and fit onto a truck or horse or into a worker's kit. The worker's own travel must be organized. Thus logistics, transportation, physical maintenance of supplies and scheduling of treatment administration can become complex. The simpler these requirements and the more they dovetail, the greater the likelihood of success.

As has been suggested, each of these considerations becomes appreciably more complex if multiple interventions are to be implemented - creating the component "mix." Dosage schedules, physical support systems, worker training - all require extra planning.

In addition, interventions must be chosen in a way that ensures some equitable balance between the time and energy spent on each one in the field. Since day-to-day supervision of CBD fieldworkers is not always available, workers may tend to spend more time on an intervention perceived as being in greater demand, on one that is easier to implement, or conversely, on one that consumes disproportionately more time due to its complexity. Such imbalances can occur to the detriment of other equally important activities. The sale of antibiotics proved so successful among clients in the Nicaraguan partera program that the emphasis placed on this service was considered to be among the factors leading to inadequate promotion of the project's family planning components (Heiby, 1981).

Finally, when CBD projects do experience significant difficulties in field implementation of selected services, it is often due to having attempted too much, given the support level and resources available to the projects, rather than too little. Indeed, conflicting tendencies have appeared in CBD projects: workers, planners, and villagers have on occasion asked for broader project services (Heiby, 1981; Bertrand, 1981), while program evaluations have generally not revealed positive effects of service expansion on the acceptance of the project's chief services. Concerns have been expressed that expansion of the CBD mandate to include more services, including health, might dilute efforts in reproduction regulation, strain resources or logistics, and lead to villagers' decreased comprehension of program goals (Heiby, 1979; Center for Family and Population Studies, 1978; McCord, 1980). Projects face difficulties in setting realistic CBD goals suited to each program's logistics, time, and training capacity (McGuire, 1981; Walsh and Warren, 1980).

GUIDELINES FOR CBD INTERVENTION SELECTION

The short duration of many programs makes it difficult to analyze and rectify problems during the project's life span. This renders the task of setting basic guidelines for service selection and implementation (with respect to such points as the number of interventions, and training) very important. Such guidelines can themselves be tested and modified.

Prior Analytic Process

This paper presents an overview of the type of analysis needed in choosing a health intervention for a given project, and elements to be considered in selecting a mix of family planning and health services. Ideas are drawn not only from experience accrued in projects sponsored by the Research Division of the USAID Office of Population, but also from other agencies with CBD or similar projects: International Planned Parenthood Federation, the Population Council, Family Planning International Assistance, and others.

The selection of program interventions for CBD family planning projects can be considered to be a three-step process. To maximize project impact on the community's well-being, the first consideration must be local health and family planning needs. The seriousness of a health problem in terms of mortality and disability, its extent as measured by incidence or prevalence, and the target group by age and sex are all important in setting priorities. Numerous models and analyses proposed for this task are available in the literature (Walsh and Warren, 1980; Sai, 1977; Taylor and Berelson, 1974; Taylor et al., 1980) and will not be reviewed here. Conditions associated with malnutrition and infectious diseases, including diarrheal diseases and measles, are among accepted priority targets.

Secondly, it is important to explore whether evidence exists supporting the idea that specific health or development activities promote the acceptance of family planning. A number of authors and agencies have suggested different types of components for integration with family planning. These have included the provision of post-partum services, maternal and child health services, the use of antiparasitics, and, increasingly, social development activities. The basis for such suggestions has included the child survival hypothesis (couples are less likely to accept family planning unless they are assured that existing children will survive) (Taylor et al., 1980), and the observation that early post-partum contraception has specific advantages: it delays subsequent pregnancy. Information about contraception may be more easily imparted to a group of post-partum women already in contact with health personnel and more open to the family planning message because of the psychological setting (Taylor, 1979).

In a more general sense, any intervention that increases client contact with the family planning promoter, and simultaneously promotes community respect, has been considered a good partner in an integrated project. Such "partners" have included parasite control efforts, gynecological services, "social development," and income-generating activities (Japanese Organization for International Cooperation in Family Planning, 1980; Curlin, 1981; Kols and Wawer, 1982), as well as CBD interventions aimed at men.

Despite the various theories and hypotheses, there is currently no conclusive evidence that any <u>one</u> specific type of intervention encourages the use of family planning. Although this lack of a "magic bullet" may be seen as a drawback, it nonetheless has the advantage of permitting component selection based both on community health priorities and the realities of local constraints. It is at this point that the final step in component selection is undertaken. This involves an analysis of local health priorities to determine which of the desired activities are actually feasible in a given project. The issue becomes one of selecting a realistic number of interventions from the priority categories, simplifying the delivery process of those selected, and perhaps choosing some that may not have the greatest potential public health impact but that are prized by the community and may encourage use of the CBD program as a whole.

Selection Factors

The following factors must be considered in intervention selection:

- What is the extent of the health problem in this particular area? Is it perceived as an important issue by people in the region?
- What are current practices related to the condition as performed both by clients and by the health establishment?
- What will the ambient reactions be? Will local or national legal and professional groups react favorably? Will regulations permit treatment by different levels of workers? Will the intervention compete with local dispensing patterns of "high cost drugs;" and if so, what are potential consequences?
- What should strategy decisions be regarding the medication to be used, potential simplifications of treatment schedules, and alternate approaches in dealing with a given condition?
- Is adequate manpower available to deliver the intervention being considered? Can community agents be trained to do any necessary diagnosis, recognize complications of the disease or its treatment, follow standing orders, teach related concepts to clients?
- How complex is the necessary client education?
- Will adequate project support in the form of supervision, ongoing in-service training, referral, and backup be available to ensure that the health aspects and client education are dealt with appropriately?
- Will equipment and supplies be regularly available? In the case of an intervention such as oral rehydration, will necessary local supplies be available: utensils and ingredients, the latter in the case of home preparation of sugar-salt solutions?
- Should an intervention of limited benefit to public health but with high community acceptance be included in the project and will it increase the sustained acceptance of the CBD project as a whole?
- Is the intervention popular: that is, do the community and workers accept it, or is the intervention one with low immediate acceptance due to lack of information, skepticism, incongruence with community values or beliefs? Conversely, is it highly popular, potentially increasing acceptance of the whole program or perhaps threatening to monopolize all the workers' time?

Only if the availability of the resources and conditions above can be ensured should one proceed with full-scale field implementation of an intervention. The experience of previous CBD projects, as well as small pilot studies, can assist in determining whether a project's manpower and other resources are adequate and whether local conditions, including clients' attitudes, will prove problematic.

Factors in Selecting a Service Mix

Program planning becomes more complex once a decision is made to deliver multiple family planning and health interventions. There are no specific models or formulae to help determine the number and types of interventions that will provide the greatest health effects without overwhelming workers, clients, and logistics. With enough inputs (manpower, training, supervision, time, referral backup), one can incorporate almost anything into a CBD, or any alternative health setting for that matter. Certainly Matlab, Narangwal, and the Guatemala INCAP CBD projects illustrate the broad scope of potential activities.

In most cases, resources are much more limited. Limits to the intervention mix possible will depend on five major constraints:

- Manpower (both worker and supervisory);
- Client population, including their interest in the services offered and the amount of information they can absorb in a given time frame (time referring to both the length of the home visit and to the length of the program);
- Duration of the project, which will influence the phasing of activities, the number of client contacts possible, and the time allotted per contact; and
- Other resources (including financial) which will determine the ability to procure stock, and organize logistics and transportation.

The fifth constraint, which will not be considered in this paper, involves the difficulties inherent in developing administrative and managerial structures for CBD projects and coordinating the project's work within the local and national health and family planning matrix.

Finally (although not strictly a constraint), the question of replicability must be considered in selecting a mix of project services. If the project is to provide useful information for future planning, the mix selection should encompass the number and types of services to be included in future programs, to test the possibility of their implementation.

Classification of Interventions by Resource Requirements

A CBD project may be rich in certain resource areas, be it manpower, training staff, storage, or transportation. It is also possible that a CBD will serve a fairly sophisticated client group with some previous exposure to the given interventions and an ability to learn, accept, and assimilate a wide range of services. However, not all projects will have equal resources in all areas, making it important that the chosen mix be congruent with project strengths and not over-extend limited resource sectors.

It is useful to consider each intervention in terms of the major resources and backup required for successful operationalization. The following classification is based on degrees of input needed for implementation, as determined by field observations and discussions with individuals in the family planning and health fields. Interventions are classified according to required: client learning and cooperation, training and technical proficiency from workers, supervision necessary, and schedule adherence.

- Clients must learn relatively complex information or tasks: Oral contraceptives (clients must remember to follow the drug schedule, what to do if they forget a pill, etc.) and oral rehydration (ORT requires the learning and retention of fairly precise information and technical skills). Other interventions which are relatively complex from the client's viewpoint, but less so than oral contraceptives or ORT, include other contraceptives (clients are required to know techniques of use - foam, condom); and information and education about nutrition, breastfeeding, and sanitation (IE&C efforts require that the client learn multiple facts, though the technical skills discussed are often less specific and a "mistake" or misunderstanding is unlikely to lead to immediate negative consequences, unlike contraceptive failure or misuse of ORT).
- Large technical input by the worker: Immunization; injections such as penicillin and tetanus toxoid; first aid; obstetrical and gynecological interventions. Such interventions require relatively complex scheduling, diagnostic activities, equipment maintenance, etc.
- Greater than average supervisory and retraining for workers: ORT, antibiotics, immunization, oral contraceptives, obstetrical procedures, and tetanus toxoid are either technically complex, or require that the worker be capable of communicating a substantial amount of information to the client. Worker skills in these domains need monitoring.
- Careful supervision and retraining of clients: ORT, antibiotics, oral contraceptives. (The demands on the client in the case of these three interventions are relatively great. In the case of antibiotics, for instance, clients need to be monitored for drug compliance.)
- Careful scheduling (transportation, worker displacement): Immunization, antihelminthics, tetanus toxoid, obstetrical procedures. Travel schedules are predicated on suggested treatment schedules or natural events such as pregnancy, and thus require worker travel at specific

times. Resupply of contraceptives, especially pills, also has to be carefully scheduled.

A number of other interventions may not require as large or highly scheduled an input of resources. These include use of vitamins, folate and iron, nutritional supplements, skin ointments such as scabicides, and palliatives (aspirin, cough syrup, etc.). Antihelminthics also allow some flexibility: treatment every three to four months may be optimal, but administration is simple and a delay of several months between doses is unlikely to engender serious health problems.

To complicate the decision-making process, one should consider that specific interventions may be resource intensive for one aspect but relatively simple for another. ORT tends to be labor and supervision intensive and requires a high degree of client comprehension and participation, but technical backup, such as storage and transportation, is not complex. The use of chloroquine for treatment of malaria puts fewer clinical, technical, and teaching demands on workers, and requires almost no client participation after they have received their dose of medication from the worker. Ongoing worker contact with the client community is important, however, since cases of malaria are to be treated as they arise. Antihelminthics represent a relatively easy intervention requiring no complex tasks for the worker and little in the way of sophisticated instructions for patients. In addition, antihelminthics have few potentially serious side effects if the client misunderstands directions and does not take a full course of treatment. (As discussed by Keusch in this volume, the use of antihelminthics raises a different set of questions regarding their potential effect and usefulness.)

Most CBD family planning projects offer oral contraceptives and other family planning methods, including referral for IUD insertion or sterilization. The family planning portion of a CBD home visit does not contain elements the worker would find technically difficult to perform. However, the CBD worker must be able to remember, explain and teach a fairly large number of points and stand ready to fully answer client questions. Once a method is selected, explanation of its use has to be clear and detailed since the recipient cannot afford to make a mistake. Contraception is thus a labor and time intensive intervention and requires a relatively high degree of learning on the part of the client.

In planning the content of a CBD visit, it may be preferable to choose the mix from a number of resource categories described previously, rather than from within a single category. This may enhance complementarity and avoid competition among activities in the field. For example, during home visits in which the worker explains contraception, it may be advisable <u>not</u> to routinely include a second intervention requiring a large teaching and learning component, such as ORT. If the two are combined, the visit is likely to be long, increasing worker and client fatigue, and the opportunity to effectively influence the client may be decreased. In addition, unless the client can clearly remember all the information, the chance for subsequent error in the usage of one or the other intervention is increased.

In the same way, it may be useful not to simultaneously institute two interventions requiring different follow-up or treatment schedules (for example, immunization and antihelminthics) unless adequate transportation permitting multiple trips is assured and the worker's schedule can be arranged to accommodate travel demands.

A sample sequence of activities which avoids stress on resources at any given moment includes the following: On the first visit, contraceptives plus one or two interventions from among the less complex group can be offered. This group includes chloroquine, simple first aid, nutritional supplements, and possibly antihelminthics or palliatives such as aspirin. Subsequent visits can offer a resupply of contraceptives in addition to phasing in one of the more complex activities, such as ORT or antibiotics.

RESEARCH NEEDS

The categories above can serve as a basis for organizing the selection of components. There is clearly a need for research to determine the usefulness of such categories and the effect of combining elements from among similar or different categories of activities. For example, what is the effect on client and worker performance of offering both oral contraceptives and oral rehydration during a single home visit? How does the inclusion of a number of technically complex tasks increase the extent of necessary supervisory activities for a given level of worker?

Research of this nature will provide general guidelines that can be adapted and further tested in different situations. Obviously, individual projects will have to test the appropriateness of a specific course of action within their own context, adapting the guidelines to their needs. A number of measures can be taken to ensure that selected interventions are congruent with the resources of a given project. Such strategies, some of which appear self-evident, are discussed in the following section.

SUGGESTED STRATEGIES FOR THE IMPLEMENTATION OF INTERVENTIONS

1) The number of interventions to be used in each project, especially during its early phases, should be kept small. If the project design calls for a limited number of sweeps through target communities, it is particularly important that the focus of the visits be simple and clear, to avoid confusion among both clients and workers and to ensure that interventions of highest priority are adequately covered. A project designed with permanent CBD workers in the village can offer a larger number of services since workers can introduce each one gradually into the community or stand ready as the need arises. Careful supervi-

sion is important in order to ensure that workers remember the skills necessary, perform multiple tasks appropriately, and set priorities in their work in accordance with project goals (Heiby, 1979).

2) Phasing provides an important and frequently underused mechanism by which project services can be expanded. It permits both clients and workers to comprehend and incorporate a small number of new concepts or activities at a time and can increase worker motivation through the perception that their role is expanding and becoming more interesting. Furthermore, phasing allows a project to work out the managerial and logistic problems caused by each new intervention separately. Field supervision and worker and client satisfaction in early stages of the Sudan Community Based Health and Family Planning Project suggest positive results in the phased delivery model (Wessley, 1981).

3) Each intervention can be simplified for field use. For example, wherever possible, the medication with the simplest dosage schedule or the least complex technical approach should be used. Worker training should deal with as many field situations as possible to decrease the possibility of unexpected decision-making being necessary in the field.

4) Instead of attempting to provide complex technical services, such as immunization, CBD projects may explore the possibility of cooperating with programs already offering the service. Cross-referral between a CBD project and, for example, a local Expanded Project for Immunization or public health team, with mutual information and education efforts and, where possible, shared transportation, can improve the visibility and the effort provided by each. The Zaire PRODEF and family planning CBD project has been exploring the possibility of combining transportation and joint public meetings with the local public health team (Mangani, 1981).

5) Ongoing monitoring and evaluation of the CBD project is crucial to detect problems of "fit" among the interventions offered and project resources. As previously mentioned, field testing of services prior to full-scale implementation is very important. Service statistics, supervisory records, observation of home visits, and post-visit interviews with clients to test their comprehension, retention, and practice are all important.

Project managers should be in a position to react to data from these sources by decreasing the number of interventions or phasing them in gradually where necessary; or by increasing services where demand is high and the necessary financial and logistic supports are available. The effect that the addition of new services has on the provision of existing interventions should be examined at all times.

6) Finally, what does the term "CBD project" actually imply? Do a few sweeps through an area, without the provision of local depots manned by permanent staff, really constitute a community-based effort? The number of services that can be delivered in such a setting is small, and the result of each, including the family planning interventions, will probably be limited.

Placing workers in a village but providing little supervisory contact or retraining should also be avoided. Programs that demonstrate this problem have fortunately been rare, but where they have occurred, they have not fulfilled the hopes of a community based effort (Heiby, 1981).

In summary, the autonomous role of CBD workers in the delivery of preventive and curative services to individuals who have not necessarily expressed prior interest is both difficult and complex, but it is also potentially very valuable. Programs are obligated to meet local needs, but interventions should be selected and adapted in a realistic way vis-a-vis local manpower and resources. Where such constraints are not sufficiently considered, not only worker and client motivation suffers, but the activity itself is unlikely to fulfill its potential benefits.

REFERENCES

Bertrand, J.T. "Factors Relating to the Effectiveness of Distribution in CBD Programs." Paper presented at PAA Annual Meeting, Washington, DC, April 10, 1981.

Center for Family and Population Studies (CFPS). Annual Report. New York: Columbia University, May 1978.

Curlin, C. Centre for Family Planning Activities, personal communication, June, 1981.

Heiby, J.R. "Nicaragua Trip Report." Washington, DC: U.S. Agency for International Development (USAID), 1979.

Heiby, J.R. Research Division, Office of Population, USAID, personal communication, February, 1981.

Japanese Organization for International Cooperation in Family Planning (JOICEFP). "A Brief Guideline in Designing an Integrated Family Planning and Parasite Control Project (first draft)." Oct. 1980.

Kols, A. and M.J. Wawer. "Community-Based Health and Family Planning," Population Reports Series L,3 (November/December 1982).

Mangani, N., Director, PRODEF FP CBD Project, Nsona Mpangu, Bas Zaire, personal communication, August, 1981.

McCord, C. "Evaluation of Menoufia, Egypt OR Project." Washington, DC: American Public Health Association, May 1980.

McGuire, E., Population Advisor, Research Division, Office of Population, U.S. Agency for International Development, personal communication, March, 1981.

The Population Council. "Household Distribution Project, Boyaca, Colombia." AID Contract Pha-C-1199, August 1, 1980.

Sai, F.T. "Defining Family Health Needs - Standard of Care and Priorities." Planned Parenthood Federation Occasional Essay #4 (May 1977).

Taylor, C.E. et al. Benefits of Integration of Family Planning and Health Services: The Narangwal Experience. Washington, DC: World Bank, 1981.

Taylor, H.C. "Maternal and Child Health Family Planning Program, Introductory Remarks." Technical Workshop Proceedings, Oct. 3 - Nov. 2, 1979, New York.

Taylor, H.C. and B. Berelson. "Comprehensive Family Planning Based Maternal Child Care Services. A Feasibility Study for a World Program." Studies in Family Planning 11,2 (1974): 21-25.

Walsh, J.A. and K.S. Warren. "Selective Primary Health Care: An Interim Strategy for Disease Control in Developing Countries." Social Services and Medicine. Part C: Medical Economics 14C,2 (June, 1980): 145.

Wessley, S., Sudan Community Based Health and Family Planning Project, Khartoum, personal communication, March 26, 1981.

Part Two

Contraceptive Services in CBD Programs

5
Family Planning Components in Community-Based Distribution Projects: Risk/Benefit Considerations in the Choice of Methods

Ronald H. Gray and
Miriam H. Labbok

Modern contraceptive technologies such as combined oral contraceptives and IUDs were developed in the late 1950s and introduced on a large scale in industrialized countries more than two decades ago. A concern with the safety of the new drugs and devices led health authorities to assume that physicians were necessary to minimize potential health hazards. However, evidence suggests that the complex diagnostic skills of physicians are not necessary for the safe provision of clinical family planning (Huber and Huber, 1975).

When family planning services evolved in developing countries during the 1960s, a Western physician-oriented model was frequently adopted. It soon became apparent that programs depending upon physician services could not reach the majority of the population in need of family planning because of the shortage of doctors, their concentration in urban areas of predominantly rural countries, as well as the cost of such services. Furthermore, the perceived role of the physician and the social distance between the physician and the client may impede the information, education and counseling necessary for family planning. As a consequence, responsibility for family planning was often delegated to nonphysicians within the health system, such as midwives, auxiliary and nurse midwives, or specially trained paramedical personnel. Such programs were still based on a health service model, frequently using clinics as the service delivery point and adopting a passive approach to client recruitment and follow-up; often the user and the service provider were socially or geographically removed from each other. Nevertheless, studies in several countries showed that nonphysicians could provide modern family planning methods such as oral and injectable contraceptives, IUDs, and sterilization as safely and effectively as physicians (Atkin et al., 1980; Kennedy and Rodriguez, 1981).

The inability of a health-service-based program to provide adequate family planning care demonstrated a need for family planning workers drawn from the community. This led to the development of Community Based Delivery (CBD) programs in which lay workers from the community use simplified procedures and provide family planning in a nonclinic setting. Such programs have evolved in a variety of ways, adapting to local circumstances and adopting a number of experimental approaches including direct use of the commercial sector. The programs have in common a nonclinic focus which implies that trained lay workers, often with minimal direct supervision or referral back-up, and without the prestige or support of the medical system, make family planning widely available, frequently in circumstances where clients have no other source of services (Gillespie and Merrit, 1977; Foreit et al., 1978; Rahman et al., 1980; Altman and Piotrow, 1980).

The present paper examines the health-related aspects of contraceptives used in CBD programs, especially with regard to the nature of the methods, safety considerations, simplified procedures needed to counsel and screen new clients, monitoring and support of users, and the requirements for supervision and referral. Having defined the characteristics and constraints of the methods, consideration will be given to the requirements for training, mix of methods, and logistics.

PROBLEMS IN THE ASSESSMENT OF CONTRACEPTIVE RISK

The consequences of family planning on health depend largely on the balance between contraceptive risks and benefits and the risks of childbearing. However, inadequate data on morbidity or mortality, and the absence of data on contraceptive safety from developing countries makes it impossible to quantify the contraceptive-related risks in a CBD setting, and the final assessment must be based on indirect evidence. Moreover, the risks vary with the individual, depending on age, parity, prior obstetric history and the presence of concomitant illness or other risk factors. The pregnancy-related risks vary from society to society depending on the levels of maternal mortality, the hazards of induced abortion and the availability of maternity services.

The interpretation of studies of contraceptive-related health risks is complex. As general background, it is important to note that the strength of an association between contraceptive use and a particular illness as commonly measured by the relative risk, is of less public health relevance than the actual increase in morbidity or mortality attributable to contraceptive exposure. For example, a small increase in the relative risk of a common disease will present a greater public health problem than will a large increase in the relative risk of a rare disease. It is this potential excess of morbidity and mortality, called attributable risk, that is most difficult to quantify and most likely to vary from one population to another, due to variation in disease prevalence. From a practical point of view, the objective is not merely to identify a possible risk factor, but more importantly to identify subgroups in the population who are at particular risk, since this provides the rationale for screening potential users who may have contraindications to the method.

RISKS ASSOCIATED WITH PREGNANCY IN DEVELOPING COUNTRIES

Studies in both developed and developing countries have shown that births to very young or older women, short birth intervals, and high parity are jointly associated with a high risk of ill health for both mothers and their children. Family planning is a positive health measure if it reduces the number of births to women under 20 or over 30 years of age, reduces the number of births of parity four or more, and allows two to three years between births (Omran et al., 1976; Maine, 1981).

Maternal mortality, excluding deaths from abortion, is frequently excessive in developing countries. Surveys of national data by Tietze (1979) suggest a range of maternal mortality rates between 40 and 180 per 100,000 births in the developing countries compared with rates under 20 per 100,000 in industrialized countries. Rates are highest among women under the age of 20 or over 30, and increase with higher parity. These statistics underestimate the burden of pregnancy-related mortality, because of underreporting and the selective inclusion of countries with national data. Survey data from Bangladesh suggest maternal mortality rates of approximately 450 to 800 per 100,000 births depending upon age (Table 5:1) (Chen et al., 1975), and data from the Gambia suggest that maternal mortality may be as high as 1,000 per 100,000 (Billewicz and McGregor, 1981).

Table 5:1. Estimated Maternal Mortality Rates by Age: Matlab, Bangladesh

AGE	MATERNAL DEATHS PER 100,000 BIRTHS
10 - 19	860
20 - 29	450
30 - 39	580
40 - 49	670

SOURCE: Chen et al., 1975.

It is difficult to obtain reliable statistics on abortion-related deaths, but estimates vary from around 50 to more than 100 per 100,000 in developing countries, as compared with less than 2 per 100,000 in most developed countries (Liskin et al., 1980). A study in Bangladesh suggests that approximately 25 percent of all pregnancy-related deaths are attributable to induced abortion (Rochat et al., 1981). In summary, deaths due to childbearing are excessive in developing countries, and the prevention of pregnancy afforded by family planning is a major public health benefit.

COMBINED ORAL CONTRACEPTIVES

The majority of CBD programs have provided oral contraceptives because they are highly effective, relatively simple to administer, and require minimal "clinical" skills. Also, they have a high margin of safety (Foreit et al., 1978; Rosenfield et al., 1980; Osborn and Reinke, 1981).

Drugs and Mode of Use

Most programs employ preparations containing 50 μg or less of estrogen and 1 mg or less of progestin. At these dosages ovulation is inhibited in the majority of cycles, with increased cervical mucus viscosity and endometrial changes providing additional protection should breakthrough ovulation occur. Placebo or iron and vitamin tablets are included in some packaging to allow for uninterrupted pill-taking which simplifies use and may provide some nutritional benefit.

Policy with regard to the initiation of postpartum contraception is complex. If women are not lactating they should commence contraception immediately postpartum or within four weeks. However, for the woman who is breastfeeding, considerations of safety (discussed below) suggest that treatment should be delayed for at least six weeks until lactation is fully established and any possible effect of steroid transfer through the milk on the health of the suckling infant is likely to be negligible. Since the risk of conception in a fully breastfeeding, amenorrheic woman is minimal (Van Ginneken, 1977), and it is desirable to avoid unnecessary contraception or the possible adverse effects of estrogen on lactation, the initiation of oral contraceptive use can be delayed until the resumption of menses, which maybe in the vicinity of six months among women with prolonged lactational amenorrhea.

Efficacy of Oral Contraceptives

The use-effectiveness of oral contraceptives depends upon the pregnancy and continuation rates. Low dose combined contraceptives have high theoretical effectiveness, but appreciable pregnancy rates are frequently observed in family planning programs and clinical trials largely because women fail to comply with the strict pill-taking regimen. Pregnancy rates are higher among women wishing to space their births than women wishing to limit future reproduction (Vaughan et al,, 1977; Hatcher et al., 1980). Better patient counseling and supervision would probably minimize the problem of poor pill-taking; this could be an advantage of the more intimate provider/user relationship afforded by the CBD setting.

The risk of a breakthrough ovulation due to missed pills is greater with lower dose preparations, especially those containing 30 μg of estrogen. Thus, the margin of safety with respect to pregnancy is reduced with these preparations, and it may be advisable to avoid using the very low dose drugs in CBD programs. Preparations containing more than 50 μg of estrogen are also inadvisable, since higher doses are unnecessary (Mishell, 1979; Hatcher et al., 1980).

Continuation rates vary depending on the motivation of the user, the counseling and support of the provider, and the cultural setting, especially as this relates to the perception of common side effects, such as nausea or bleeding disturbances. Nausea and vomiting are more frequently reported with higher-estrogen doses, and amenorrhea or bleeding problems tend to be associated with the higher-progestagen doses (Hatcher et al., 1980). Some evidence suggests that women of lower body weight may experience more drug-related side effects (Talawar and Berger, 1977). However, these pharmacological relationships are not clear-cut, and the frequency of side effects may be less important than the user's subjective perception of them (Briggs, 1976). Thus, proper counseling and support is of critical importance, and CBD programs may have advantages in this regard.

Combined oral contraceptives containing 50 μg of estrogen and around 0.15 mg of norgestrel or 1 mg of norethisterone provide satisfactory contraceptive protection without excessive drug-related side effects. Little evidence from clinical trials suggests the substantial advantage of one regimen over another within this dose range (WHO Task Force, 1981). Although the availability of more than one pill regimen may be of benefit to some women who experience side effects, probably no major advantage is to be gained from the provision of multiple pill formulations within a CBD program. The confusion that might arise from different preparations, the additional complexity of the provider's task, and the possible increase in side effects caused by switching dosages, make multiple dosage schedules inadvisable.

One-year pill continuation rates in selected CBD programs vary from 33 to 82 percent per 100 women (Foreit et al., 1978), but the absence of data on continuation rates for many CBD programs limits generalization of these findings. Also, information on method continuation may be incomplete or unreliable as some programs estimate continuation from the number of cycles dispensed and not on the actual number of cycles used.

Effect of Oral Contraceptives on Health

Studies in industrialized countries, largely the United States, the United Kingdom, and Scandinavia, have shown an association between combined oral contraceptives and an increased risk of morbidity and mortality from cardiovascular disease (Dalen et al., 1981; Stadel, 1981; Royal College of General Practitioners, 1981). Additional concerns have been raised about the risks of neoplasia (WHO, 1978) and the possible adverse effects of these drugs on the fetus due to inadvertent exposure during pregnancy, or on the health of the breastfed child exposed to steroids through milk (WHO, 1981; Wilson and Brent, 1981). In addition, oral contraceptives affect carbohydrate and lipid metabolism, liver function, vitamin and mineral metabolism and possibly immunological mechanisms (WHO, 1975; Mishell, 1979; Wynn et al., 1979). The literature is massive and the technical interpretation of the results often difficult. Moreover, the paucity of data from developing countries limits the generalization of these findings to CBD settings.

The following review will concentrate only on the more serious reported hazards. The objective is to assess their relevance to CBD programs and the implications for client screening and diagnosis of complications.

Cardiovascular Disease

Oral contraceptives have been implicated as risk factors in venous thromboembolism, arterial thrombosis, subarachnoid hemorrhage, and hypertension. The risks are related to the dose of the estrogen and progestagen components and to the duration of drug use. In all studies, the oral contraceptive-related risk increases with age and is potentiated by the presence of other known cardiovascular risk factors such as smoking, obesity, surgery and immobilization, or a history of cardiovascular disease (Dalen et al., 1981; Stadel, 1981; Royal College of General Practitioners, 1981). Estimates of the excess morbidity or mortality attributable to pill use depend upon the prevalence of the disease under consideration, the prevalence of other known cardiovascular risk factors, and the interaction among these risk factors and pill use (Stadel, 1981). Table 5:2 shows an estimate of excess mortality attributed to the pill in developed countries. The excess deaths are mainly due to myocardial infarction or stroke among women over the age of 35 who smoke cigarettes.

Clinical evidence suggests that venous thromboembolism and myocardial infarction are uncommon in developing country populations, and the prevalence of risk factors such as smoking or obesity are generally low in these societies as compared with industrialized countries, although smoking is not uncommon in some developing countries (Miall and Bras, 1972; Chumnijarakij and Poshyachina, 1977; Heiby, 1978; Chow and Nair, 1980). Thus, the low frequency of the disease and of the concomitant risk factors in developing countries would place women at minimal risk of venous and arterial thrombosis.

Estimates of mortality associated with different reversible methods of contraception suggest that contraceptive-related deaths are lower than deaths from pregnancy and childbirth in industrialized countries, with the exception of pill use over the age of 40 (Tietze et al., 1976; Vessey, 1978; Beral, 1979). Less precise estimates from developing countries suggest that pill mortality is much less than maternal mortality at all ages (Rochat et al., 1978; Potts et al., 1978).

A particular problem arises with the provision of the pill for older women in CBD programs. Should there be an arbitrary age, say 35 or 40 and above, beyond which the pill is contraindicated? UK studies do not show a significant excess cardiovascular mortality among non-smoking pill users aged 30 to 35

Table 5:2. Excess Mortality From Cardiovascular Disease Associated with Oral Contraception and Smoking in Older Women

DISEASE, AGE GROUP AND SMOKING STATUS	EXCESS DEATH PER 100,000 USERS PER YEAR ATTRIBUTABLE TO ORAL CONTRACEPTIVES
ALL CARDIOVASCULAR DISEASE[1]	
35 - 44 YEARS	
Non-smokers	15
Smokers	48*
45+ YEARS	
Non-smokers	41
Smokers	179*
MYOCARDIAL INFARCTION[2]	
30 - 39 YEARS	
0 - 14 Cig./day	4
15+ Cig./day	19
40 - 44 YEARS	
0 - 14 Cig./day	35
15+ Cig./day	185

* Statistically significant excess

SOURCES: 1. Royal College of General Practitioners, 1980.
2. Stadel, 1981.

(Royal College of General Practitioners, 1980), whereas studies of pregnancy-related deaths show a marked rise of mortality among such older women in developing countries (Chen et al., 1975; Nortman, 1974; Maine, 1981). In developing countries the risk of childbearing probably exceeds the risks associated with the pill in these older age groups, and age could be considered as an indication for contraceptive need rather than a contraindication to pill use per se. However, the pill should not be given to older women who smoke, are obese, or have a history of cardiovascular disease. In CBD programs, every reasonable effort should be made to identify women at risk of thromboembolic cardiovascular disease. Despite the lack of direct evidence for pill-related cardiovascular mortality in developing countries, evidence does show that the prevalence of thromboembolic disease is low, and maternal and abortion-related mortality is often very high. A checklist of symptoms of ischemic heart disease and cerebrovascular disease is given in Table 5:3.

Table 5:3. Possible Questions that Could be Used for Screening for Contraindications to Oral Contraceptives

CONTRAINDICATION	POSSIBLE QUESTIONS*
1. PREGNANCY & LACTATION	
A. Pregnancy in New Interval Acceptor	Was your last menstrual period more than five days ago?
Risk of Pregnancy	Is there any possibility that you might be pregnant now?
B. Early Lactation	Have you breastfed your baby for less than six weeks?
2. CARDIOVASCULAR DISEASE RISK FACTORS	
A. Venous Thrombosis	Have you ever had severe swelling and pain in your calf or leg?
B. Coronary Heart Disease	Have you had severe pain in the center of your chest?
Congestive Cardiac Failure	Have you felt breathless after moderate exertion or when lying down?

* If the response to any of these questions is YES: Do not prescribe the pill for a new acceptor, and stop use in a current user; refer if cardiovascular disease, neoplasia or liver disease are suspected.

Table 5:3 (Cont.). Possible Questions that Could be Used for Screening for Contraindications to Oral Contraceptives

CONTRAINDICATION	POSSIBLE QUESTIONS*
C. Hypertension	Have you ever been told that you have high blood pressure?
D. Cerebrovascular Disease	Have you had severe headache, fits, fainting, paralysis, or sudden blurring of vision?
E. General	Have you been told that you have had heart disease?
3. NEOPLASIA	
A. Genital	Over the past six months, have you had abnormally heavy menstrual bleeding, bleeding between periods or after intercourse?
B. Breast	Have you noticed a lump growning in your breast, or abnormal discharge or bleeding from your nipple?
4. LIVER DISEASE (JAUNDICE)	Over the past six months, have you had any illness which caused your skin and eyes to turn yellow and your urine to become brown?

* If the response to any of these questions is YES: Do not prescribe the pill for a new acceptor, and stop use in a current user; refer if cardiovascular disease, neoplasia or liver disease are suspected.

The evidence concerning the underlying risk of hypertension and other non-atherosclerotic forms of cardiovascular disease is less clear. Hypertension does occur in some developing country populations, although high blood pressure appears, in general, to be less prevalent, than in comparable age groups among industrialized-country populations (Shaper, 1972; Grimley-Evans and Rose, 1971). Two large cohort studies have shown that between 4 and 5 percent of normotensive women using oral contraceptives develop frank hypertension, whereas this was observed in less than 2 percent of non-users or ex-users of the pill. The risk of hypertension is increased with prolonged pill use in older women and women with a history of high blood pressure and with prolonged duration of pill use (Dalen, 1981; Stadel, 1981). However, a recent study of black women in the United States failed to observe a pill-related increase in blood pressure (Blumenstein et al., 1981). In the absence of adequate data from developing countries, the relevance of these observations for pill users in CBD programs is unclear. However, the excess frequency of hypertension associated with the pill is probably 2 to 3 percent, and the most relevant finding is that 95 to 96 percent of women have normal blood pressure while using oral contraceptives (Dalen, 1981).

It is not feasible to screen women for high blood pressure or to monitor blood pressure changes in a CBD program. The cost of sphygmomanometers, equipment maintenance problems, and the difficulties of training personnel are prohibitive. The best compromise is to screen women by taking an adequate but simplified history of cardiac disease (Table 5:3).

Cardiovascular diseases of infectious origin such as rheumatic heart disease (Agarwal, 1981) occur more frequently in the developing world, and cardiac pathology due to Chagas disease may reach a high prevalence in areas of Latin America (Arean, 1976). The effect of oral contraceptives on these diseases has not yet been evaluated. In both rheumatic heart disease and Chagas disease, congestive cardiac failure is a major complication and cause of death, and with rheumatic heart disease there is a risk of arterial embolism arising from thrombi formed on damaged heart valves. Theoretically, the increase in blood pressure or the increased risk of thrombosis with steroids could affect these conditions. Table 5:3 also includes a checklist of symptoms suggestive of congestive failure or embolism.

Neoplasia

Numerous studies, largely confined to industrialized countries, have examined the risk of genital, breast, pituitary, skin and liver neoplasia in relation to pill use. Early studies suggested that the pill is associated with an increased risk of cervical carcinoma *in situ* or an accelerated progression from dysplasia to carcinoma *in situ* (Stern, 1977; Peritz et al., 1977; WHO, 1978). However, these findings have not been confirmed by more recent investigations which controlled for other known cervical cancer risk factors, such as age at first intercourse or multiple sexual partners (Swan and Brown, 1981). Cervical cancer is a common genital tumor in developing countries because of the early commencement of intercourse (Waterhouse et al., 1976). The disease is relatively frequent during the reproductive years, and the early detection of preinvasive lesions is hampered by the lack of cytological screening services.

Endometrial carcinoma is predominantly a disease of the postmenopausal woman, and its incidence in developing countries appears to be much lower than in the West (Waterhouse et al., 1976). Several studies suggest that combined estrogen/progestagen pills provide a protective effect against this disease (Weiss and Sayvetz, 1980; Kaufman et al., 1980). There is no evidence that the pill affects the risk of benign endometrial tumors such as fibroids (WHO, 1978). Choriocarcinoma is thought to be more common in some developing countries of South Asia, but there is no clear evidence for an effect of pill use on this disease (Stone et al., 1976; WHO, 1978; Berkowitz et al., 1980).

Ovarian carcinoma is less frequent in developing countries than in developed countries, and the pill may protect against malignant neoplasms, possibly because of the prevention of ovulation (Newhouse et al., 1977). Also, the pill reduces the incidence of benign ovarian tumors such as luteal cysts (WHO, 1980).

Extensive studies have not demonstrated an increased risk of breast cancer in relation to oral contraceptives (WHO, 1978; Vessey et al., 1981; Royal College of General Practitioners, 1981), and breast cancer is a relatively uncommon disease in developing countries as compared with industrialized countries (Waterhouse et al., 1976). Evidence suggests that more intensive screening of pill users may facilitate the earlier detection of smaller growths (Matthews et al., 1981). Numerous studies show that oral contraceptives reduce the risk of benign breast tumors such as fibrocystic disease and fibroadenoma (WHO, 1978; Brinton et al., 1981).

The pill does not appear to affect the risk of benign pituitary adenomas, including prolactin-secreting tumors responsible for the amenorrhea galactorrhea syndrome, despite earlier reports suggesting such a relationship (WHO, 1978). There is no evidence that the pill affects the risk of melanoma (Adam et al., 1981).

Studies in the United States suggest that the pill increases the risk of rare hepatocellular adenomas, particularly among older women with prolonged pill use. These tumors, although benign, may cause fatal hemorrhage (WHO, 1978). No epidemiological evidence suggests an effect of the pill on hepatocellular carcinoma, although case reports of such an association have appeared. Hepatic cancers are thought to occur more frequently in some developing countries, especially in Africa (Waterhouse et al., 1976), and further study of this disease in specific locations may be needed.

In summary, the only proven effect of the pill on neoplasia is that it is protective against endometrial and ovarian cancers and benign breast diseases, and that it increases the risk of benign liver tumors. Nevertheless, it is advisable to exclude the possibility of genital and breast malignancy before giving steroids since these growths can be hormonally dependent. Since the incidence of most cancers is low during the reproductive years, malignant neoplasms should not present a problem in CBD programs. However, benign breast disease is relatively frequent among younger women, and it is important to ensure that such women are not incorrectly prevented from using the pill, since they need of contraceptive protection, and oral contraceptives reduce the risk of these benign lesions.

Effects on Progeny

No consistent evidence shows any substantial increased risk of congenital abnormalities, chromosomal anomalies or spontaneous abortion associated with pill exposure in utero (WHO, 1981a; Wilson and Brent, 1981). There may be a small increase in the risk of some specific abnormalities such as those of the cardiovascular system, but this would be of little public health significance, considering the reduction in the number of congenitally abnormal births that would result from the reduced number of conceptions due to pill use. However, it is important to avoid unnecessary exposure and women should be screened for pregnancy prior to initiation of pill treatment. In cases of accidental conception, pill use should be stopped as soon as pregnancy is diagnosed.

Pill use by lactating women may affect the health and development of the breastfed infant. Early studies of high dose preparations suggested that the estrogen content of the pill might reduce milk volume and perhaps affect the duration of lactation (Buchanan, 1975; Hull, 1981; WHO, 1981a). As yet, no evidence exhibits a clinically important effect with pills containing 50 μg or less of estrogen, but it is advisable to delay the initiation of pill use for six weeks post partum when lactation should be fully established and any suppressant effects of the steroids would be minimal.

The steroids contained in the pill are transferred via the milk to the breastfeeding infant in quantities of approximately 0.05 to 0.1 percent of the maternal dose (Nilssen and Nygren, 1979; Hull, 1981; WHO, 1981a). This has not been shown to have any adverse effect on the infant, but animal studies of higher doses suggest the possibility of functional abnormalities. In the neonate, hepatic and renal metabolic and excretory functions are immature, and there is more free steroid because serum hormone binding is low. Also, the hypothalamus is still undergoing differentiation (Nilsson and Nygren, 1979). Therefore, it would be inadvisable to give steroids to mothers of very young breastfed infants, particularly during the neonatal period.

It has been suggested that pill use by amenorrheic women may lead to the premature resumption of menses after discontinuation of oral contraception and this could place women at higher risk of pregnancy (Mosley, 1976; Bhatia et al., 1981). Data from Bangladesh suggest that the birth interval is shorter among pill users than non-users of contraception, but it is not clear to what extent these findings reflect a pill effect per se, or the self-selection of contraceptive users who may start the pill because they intend to reduce the duration or intensity of breastfeeding. It is advisable to avoid unnecessary use of the pill during lactational amenorrhea, especially since added contraception may not be necessary, and estimates from a theoretical reproductive model suggest that the adoption of contraception after the resumption of menses is the most efficient strategy for prolonging the birth interval in societies with long periods of postpartum amenorrhea (Potter et al., 1979). Also, the risk of conception in lactating amenorrheic women is negligible during the first six weeks postpartum and minimal within the first six months in the presence of intense breastfeeding and amenorrhea (Van Ginneken, 1977). Therefore, pill use could safely be delayed until six weeks postpartum, and in societies with long lactational amenorrhea, pill use could be deferred for 6 months or more without excessive risk of conception. If there is concern over the effects of combined oral contraceptives on milk volume, the progestagen-only "minipill" could be used during the postpartum phase (see below). However, this would increase the complexity of the CBD worker's tasks and add logistic problems which might have considerable programmatic implications.

Drug Interaction and Steroid Metabolism

Several drugs can accelerate steroid metabolism by inducing hepatic enzymes. As a consequence, blood levels of contraceptive steroids can fall below effective levels causing breakthrough ovulation and accidental pregnancy, or loss of cycle control. The most important drugs in this regard are rifampicine (an antibiotic used in tuberculosis therapy), other antibiotics such as ampicillin or neomycin, and anticonvulsants such as phenobarbitone or phenytoin (British Medical Journal, 1980). Widespread use of rifampicin could theoretically present a problem in populations with a high prevalence of tuberculosis, especially in CBD programs that dispense antibiotics.

Since steroids are metabolized in the liver, it is generally considered unwise to give oral contraceptives to women with active liver disease. Also, there may be an increased risk of acute hepatitis associated with pill use (Morrison et al., 1977).

Direct Health Benefits

Combined oral contraceptives appear to reduce the risk of several diseases. Such a protective effect has been observed with benign breast tumors and cancer of the ovary or endometrium. The pill may also reduce the risk of pelvic inflammatory disease (PID) by increasing the viscosity of cervical mucus, prevent the loss of iron by reducing menstrual flow, and diminish the frequency and severity of menstrual disorders. In addition, oral contraceptives appear to reduce the risk of rheumatoid arthritis and possibly other autoimmune conditions (Rinehart and Piotrow, 1979). CBD workers should be made aware of these advantages to help promote acceptance.

Screening Procedures in CBD Projects

Screening procedures are necessary to identify women with contraindications to pill use and to help identify complications as they arise. Such screening should be comprehensible to the provider and the client, short enough to be memorized by a non-literate provider, and carefully phrased so as not to deter potential acceptors. Moreover, the questions must be sufficiently specific so that women are not incorrectly excluded. The simplest approach is to elicit key symptoms, and a number of checklists have been developed to facilitate the screening process (Rosenfield, 1977; Gray, 1978). Table 5:3 is one possible checklist of questions. The list is intended to be more extensive than would be practical or necessary in a CBD setting, so as to provide a framework from which CBD planners can select questions which are appropriate, feasible, and comprehensible in their local cultural setting. CBD workers should be trained in the use of such a checklist, and in the management of clients with suspected contraindications or complications (e.g., the referral of patients with symptoms of cardiovascular, neoplastic, or liver disease). As a part of routine training and supervision, workers should also be taught the common side effects such as nausea, vomiting, headache, or breakthrough bleeding, and the management of these conditions through reassurance and support.

PROGESTAGEN-ONLY MINIPILL

The progestagen-only minipills have not been used in CBD programs. These drugs contain low doses of progestagen, usually norgestrel 50 to 70 μg or norethisterone 300 to 500 μg, and are taken daily without interruption. Pregnancy rates vary, but are generally around 2 per 100 women years. Many women experience irregular, generally shorter cycles, and breakthrough bleeding is common. Continuation rates are generally lower than with combined oral contraceptives. (Vessey et al., 1972; Eckstein et al., 1972; Rinehart, 1975; Gray, 1979).

The progestagen-only minipills do not reduce milk volume in lactating women and may even enhance milk production (Rinehart, 1975; Hull, 1981). Thus, the main potential advantage of these drugs in a CBD program would be as a postpartum contraceptive for women who are breastfeeding if there is concern about the effects of combined estrogen/progestagen pills on lactation.

The minipill could be prescribed for breastfeeding mothers until it is deemed "safe" to give the combined oral contraceptives at around six months postpartum. However, this would add to the complexity of CBD workers tasks because they would need to manage two pill regimens, and remember when it was appropriate to change from the minipill to the combined preparation. Also, this would entail additional logistic and supply problems. The screening procedures for minipill acceptors would be similar to those for the combined pill.

Unless low-dose, estrogen-containing, combined preparations are shown to have a clinically significant deleterious effect on lactation, it is doubtful whether there would be significant advantages to introducing minipills into a CBD program. On present evidence, there is probably not a rationale for adding minipills.

INJECTABLE CONTRACEPTIVES

Injectable contraceptives are not provided by USAID, but supplies may be made available to CBD projects through other sources. The drugs in most frequent use are Depo-Provera (150 mg of Depot medroxyprogesterone acetate every three months) and Norigest or Noristerat (200 mg of Norethisterone enanthate intramuscularly every two months for the first six months, then at two to three month intervals thereafter). Following this regimen the pregnancy rates for both drugs are less than 1 per 100 women over one year (WHO, 1977; WHO, 1981b). The continuation rates are generally better than with the pill, but lower than with the IUD (Fraser and Weisberg, 1981).

Both drugs are potent progestagens and disrupt the menstrual cycle, which may make them less acceptable in some cultural settings. Amenorrhea is more frequent and protracted with Depo-Provera than with Norigest, but the frequency of prolonged, heavy or irregular bleeding is roughly comparable with the two drugs (Gray, 1979; Gray et al., 1981). Amenorrhea is not a health hazard per se; however, the possibility of pregnancy must be excluded. Since pregnancy tests or physical examinations are impractical in most CBD settings, the worker would have to depend upon symptoms of pregnancy which tend to occur in the late first trimester. Prolonged or heavy bleeding may require treatment with a cycle of oral contraceptives or oral estradiol, and if this does not control the bleeding, oily depot estradiol injection or even occasionally dilatation and currettage may be needed (Koetswang, 1979).

Weight gain, headache and abdominal discomfort are reported by more than 5 percent of users (WHO, 1977). Following discontinuation of Depo-Provera, the return of fertility is delayed by approximately nine months after the last injection, but there is no evidence of a permanent impairment of fertility (Pardthaisong and Gray, 1979). The return of fertility after Norigest is more rapid (Fraser and Weisberg, 1981).

Other side effects or potential complications are theoretically similar to those due to the progestagenic component of oral contraceptives, but no studies have adequately evaluated the cardiovascular risk of injectable methods. Theoretically women using injectable methods should be screened in a manner similar to pill users to exclude an increased risk of arterial disease due to HDL cholesterol changes and increased blood pressure (Fraser and Weisberg, 1981). Toxicological studies in animals have demonstrated carcinogenic effects in some species at high doses and prolonged exposures. However, the relevance of these findings to human use is questionable (WHO, 1981).

This brief review highlights some of the problems associated with the use of injectables in CBD programs. There is a need to train workers to give injections while maintaining sterile techniques, to manage amenorrhea by excluding pregnancy, to treat excessive bleeding by supplementary estrogen, to cope with common side effects such as weight gain or headache, and to counsel clients on potential delays in the return of fertility. These are more complex tasks than those associated with oral contraception. Nevertheless, injectable contraceptives are often perceived as advantageous by potential users because they are convenient and injection is an acceptable mode of drug administration in many cultures. A CBD study in Bangladesh showed that the addition of Depo-Provera to a pill program significantly increased the prevalence of contraceptive use. (Bhatia et al., 1980; Rahman et al., 1980).

IUD

Referral for IUD insertion is available in several operations research projects, but complete provision of IUD services by CBD workers is not generally attempted because of the complexity of the clinical tasks. Notwithstanding, several studies have shown that many categories of health workers can be trained to provide IUD services, and training manuals and procedures have been developed for this purpose (Akin et al., 1980; Gray et al., 1980).

The IUD is particularly suited for women who want to delay the next birth for a considerable time, or who want no more children (WHO, 1980). Program continuation rates with IUDs are frequently higher than with other methods, but the prevalence of IUD use is substantially lower than pill use in most countries (Piotrow et al., 1979).

Inert IUDs such as the Lippes Loop are most frequently used, but there has been increasing use of copper devices (Copper 7 and Copper T) over the past decade. Pregnancy rates, expulsions rates and rates of removals for bleeding and pain are significantly higher with the Lippes Loop than the copper devices during the first two years of use (Table 5:4). The copper devices in current use require replacement after three to five years, but new IUDs with a higher copper content are likely to have a longer duration of effectiveness. Most IUDs lead to increased menstrual blood loss which is more pronounced with the inert devices than the copper IUDs and may lead to iron deficiency anemia in predisposed subjects (Piotrow et al., 1979). Where cost of the device is not a major consideration, it would be preferable to use the copper IUDs rather than the Lippes Loop.

There is a two to nine fold increased risk of pelvic inflammatory disease (PID) associated with IUD use, and the risk is generally higher among women who are younger, are exposed to sexually transmitted diseases, or have a prior history of PID. (Sennanyake and Kramer, 1980; Westrom, 1980; Gray and Silkey, 1981). Ectopic pregnancy is observed more frequently among accidental conceptions occurring among IUD users than among other contraceptive users (Vessey et al., 1979). Also, conceptions with an IUD _in situ_ are likely to result in spontaneous

Table 5:4. Medical Discontinuation Rates After Two Years with the Lippes Loop D and Copper T 220C

	CUMULATIVE NET DISCONTINUATION RATES AFTER 2 YEARS PER 100 WOMEN (± SE)	
	Lippes Loop D	Copper T 220C
Pregnancy	3.3 (± 0.7)*	1.2 (± 0.4)
Expulsion	10.0 (± 1.1)*	6.6 (± 1.0)
Removal for Bleeding and Pain	12.9 (± 1.5)*	8.8 (± 1.2)
All Reasons	33.4 (± 1.8)	29.8 (± 1.7)
Women Months of Observation	14,822	16,576
Number of Insertions	894	889

* Significant difference

SOURCE: World Health Organization, 1979.

abortion which may be complicated by sepsis (Vessey et al., 1979; Foreman et al., 1981).

It is unlikely that CBD workers would be required to insert IUDs or perform pelvic examinations. However, workers should be trained to counsel women on the value of the IUD as a reliable and convenient contraceptive, the need for insertion by a trained person, and the likelihood of some short-term post-insertion pain and bleeding. Workers should be aware of the risk of expulsion, PID and pregnancy including ectopic gestation or spontaneous abortion, and the need for referral of clients with these complications. A checklist to facilitate management is shown in Table 5:5.

STERILIZATION

Sterilization is increasing in popularity in the Third World and is provided as a referral method in several CBD programs. It is highly effective and appropriate for the couples who have completed their desired family. The greatest single health benefit stems from the reduction of multiparous births among older women, with a reduction in morbidity and mortality of both mother and infant. Sterilization itself entails surgical risks in addition to the risk of failure and of ectopic pregnancy (McCann, 1978; Memford et al., 1980; Peterson et al.,

Table 5:5. Checklist for Follow-up of IUD Users

QUESTIONS	RESPONSE		INSTRUCTIONS
SINCE I LAST SAW YOU:	YES	NO	IF THE RESPONSES FALL IN "YES" BOX, BE SURE TO FOLLOW THE INSTRUCTIONS BELOW
1. Have you had intermenstrual bleeding or heavy or prolonged bleeding?	☐	☐	If during the first 3 months after insertion, reassure the woman that this is likely to decrease with time. Provide iron supplements Refer the woman if these symptoms are intolerable.
2. Have you had pain severe enough to limit your normal life?	☐	☐	If this occurs during the first 3 months after insertion, reassure and provide analgesics. If the woman finds this intolerable, refer her.
3. Was your last period late or have you missed a recent period?	☐	☐	This may indicate pregnancy. Refer.
4. Have you had fever or or chills, and pains in the lower abdomen?	☐	☐	This may indicate pelvic inflammatory disease. Refer.
5. Has the IUD been expelled?	☐	☐	Refer for insertion or provide other contraception.

SOURCE: Gray et al., 1980.

1981; McCausland, 1980). However the preventive health benefits outweigh these risks if standards of surgical skill and operative facilities are adequate.

In a CBD setting, the worker should be trained to advise sterilization if a client desires no more children and if she is multiparous, or has suffered illness due to pregnancy or deliveries. It must be made clear that this method cannot be considered reversible.

Sterilization procedures generally include minilaparotomy, laparoscopy, and vasectomy. The actual tubal ligation is performed by banding, fulguration, or surgical ligation. With minilaparotomy a 2 to 3 cm incision is made 3 cm above the pubis under local anesthesia. The tube is visualized by uterine elevation. Each tube is then ligated and the abdomen closed with absorbable sutures. The major complications are wound infection, hematoma, medication reaction, and bladder injury. The incidence of side effects varies with different clinics and operators.

With laparoscopy, the patient is sedated, a small periumbilical incision is made usually under local anesthesia, the abdomen is usually inflated with CO_2 or room air, and the laparoscope is inserted. The tubes are ligated by cautery or application of a band. The risks of this procedure are bowel damage on entering the abdomen, misapplication of the band, or burns secondary to cautery (Peterson et al., 1981).

Table 5:6 highlights methods that lend themselves to field settings due to low morbidity, relative simplicity and high efficacy. Two other procedures, colpotomy and culdoscopy, are no longer recommended as the incidence of complications is about twice that of other procedures.

The CBD worker must have sufficient information to counsel the client concerning the procedure, the place where it is provided, and time required to undergo the procedure. The worker must also be able to recognize postsurgical problems including wound infection, septicemia, and hemorrhage and must have access to clinical backup.

Recently, there has been much concern with postoperative and long-term side effects of sterilization procedures. Although some studies have shown otherwise (Lawson et al., 1979), postoperative pain may be increased with methods that provoke ischemic changes (e.g., bands) as compared with cautery, but if

Table 5:6. Sterilization Procedures for CBD Programs

OCCULUSIVE TECHNIQUE	ABDOMINAL APPROACH	RANGE OF REPORTED FAILURE RATES	EQUIPMENT COSTS
Pomeroy - Ligation and Resection	Minilap	0 - 0.4	Low
Madlener - Ligation and Resection	Minilap	0.3 - 2.0	Low
Bipolar or Low Thermal Current Fulguration	Laparoscopy	0.1 - 2.0	High
Spring Loaded Clip Application	Laparoscopy	0.2 - 0.6	High
Band or Fallope Ring Application	Laparoscopy	0 - 2.1	High

this does occur it is a short-term phenomenon which may be partially alleviated by infusion of a local anesthetic on the target area. There have been many attempts to study long-term changes that may occur. A major area of research has been menstrual function following tubal sterilization. This concern arose from early recall studies with inadequate control groups which seemed to show increased menorrhagia postoperatively (Williams, 1951; Sacks and Lacroix, 1962; Neil et al., 1975). However, subsequent extensive research has failed to reconfirm this. Chamberlain and Foulkes (1975) attributed symptomatic changes to discontinuation of a previous contraceptive method (i.e., oral contraceptives) and others found similar associations (Lieberman et al., 1978; Rubenstein et al., 1979; Lawson et al., 1979). Kwak and coworkers (1980) and Sapire and Davey (1980) compared postoperative menstrual flow before operation and at six-month intervals for two years in women who underwent electrocoagulation, and band procedures and found no significant change with either technique. In summary, CBD workers should be informed of possible symptomatic changes, due to the switch in contraceptive method, and possible ischemic pain, so that they may better advise tubal sterilization clients postoperatively.

The risk of pregnancy following sterilization varies with the surgical procedure and the skill of the operation (Nortman, 1976a; I-Cheng Chi et al., 1980). Moreover, the risk of ectopic gestation among accidental pregnancies following sterilization is high (Honore and O'Hara, 1978; McCausland, 1980). CBD workers should be informed both of the risk of failure and of the life-threatening nature of ectopic pregnancy.

Since vasectomy is a frequent form of sterilization in some developing countries, CBD supervisors should be informed of recent controversies to allay rumors. Perhaps the most important concern stems from Alexander's work (1978; 1980) showing increased atherosclerotic plaquing in vasectomized rhesus monkeys related to increased antibody formation. However, epidemiological studies on humans (Walker et al., 1981) have not related vasectomy to an increased rate of nonfatal myocardial infarction. In the future, as more men have vasectomies, there will be larger cohorts to observe for longer periods of time; but human data to date are encouraging.

BARRIER METHODS

Barrier methods of contraception are those that provide a temporary physical or chemical barrier between the sperm and the ovum. The most commonly used barriers are condoms, diaphragms, and spermicides in cream, gel, or foam. All of these methods necessitate planning and use immediately prior to coitus.

Barrier methods are especially useful in nonclinical situations, because they entail virtually no contradindications or side effects except for occasional allergic reactions. The major drawback of these methods in nonclinical situations include the need for frequent resupply and storage and, in the case of the diaphragm, initial fitting and refitting postpartum.

The condom is the only male method supplied in a CBD setting. Instructions should include the principles of how barriers work, one-time use, usage before penetration, removal without leakage, and the necessity of use with each act of intercourse. Because the condom is frequently associated with illicit sex, it may be necessary for the CBD workers to explain that it is an acceptable and respectable method. Disposal may also pose a problem in certain settings. While the theoretical failure of this method is 1 to 3 percent, the actual failure rate is frequently 4 to 10 percent or even higher (Tatum and Connell-Tatum, 1981).

The diaphragm, used in conjunction with a spermicide, forms a physical and chemical barrier. Its use in CBD settings is limited by the need for fittings and refittings after each birth. In populations where radical forms of female circumcision are common insertion may be difficult. The CBD workers should understand the principle of the method, the need for proper insertion and proper fit, the necessity for spermicide before each act of coitus, the necessity of leaving the diaphragm in place for many hours, and the desirability of careful inspection, washing, and storage of the diaphragm. Each of these presents difficulties in many developing country settings. Although the theoretical failure rate of this combined method is as low as 2 to 3 percent, actual failure rates range from 2 to over 17 percent (Wortman, 1976b). With the difficulties of spermicide resupply, diaphragm insertion, and fitting and storage, the failure rates could be even higher in a CBD context.

Spermicides containing the spermicidal detergents nonoxynol-9 and octoxynol, are the most commonly utilized formulations, but mercurial and other compounds are also on the worldwide market, as is the new detergent menfegol. The mechanism of action is immobilization of sperm by destruction of cellular integrity. The most important factors in determining effective use are proper placement of the spermicide in sufficient quantity and in a timely fashion before coitus. New vehicles, such as foaming tablets, simplify storage in warm climates where glycerine-based suppositories melt and aerosol cans may be too expensive. These tablets, however, must be used well before coitus to allow time for the foaming action. The theoretical failure rate of spermicide alone is low, but pregnancy rates are generally around 15 per 100 women years or more (Coleman and Piotrow, 1979).

These barrier methods all necessitate manipulation of the genitalia which may be culturally unacceptable or, in areas of radical female circumcision, very difficult. The special advantage of these methods is their lack of major side effects and their possible antibacterial effect. They have been shown to be associated with decreased rates of venereal disease, and there are indications that they may decrease the spread of herpes (Coleman and Piotrow, 1979; Cole et al., 1980). The diaphragm and cervical cap may however be linked to toxic shock syndrome (Dan, 1981), and a recent study, although it had major methodological shortcomings, suggests that spermicides may be associated with an increased risk of congenital abnormalities (Jick et al., 1981).

Resupply and logistics are major considerations with these methods in CBD projects. Assuming coitus three times weekly, a couple would need 156 units annually. Once the acceptor is instructed as to proper usage, there is little need for continuing contact with the CBD worker except as a resupply source or to switch to a more efficacious method. Since barriers such as condoms and spermicide pills lend themselves to marketing situations, subsidized sales through the commercial sector may serve as an additional source of resupply.

ABORTION

While abortion is not a part of CBD programs. CBD workers should understand the risk of an unwanted pregnancy and be familiar with the availability of abortion whether legal or illegal. The worker should be acquainted with the safe facilities if available. The CBD worker should also be informed of: the type of termination procedures available, the need for referral early in pregnancy to minimize risk, and the postoperative signs of complications such as hemorrhage or infection which need immediate clinic referral.

PERIODIC ABSTINENCE

Periodic abstinence, natural family planning, and rhythm are all terms to describe avoidance of intercourse during the fertile period of each month. This method of contraception has undergone many changes since the 1930s, when Ogino and Knaus independently identified the timing of ovulation in relation to subsequent menses. This finding allowed a reasonable guess as to the period when ovulation would occur each month based on the experience of previous cycles. Commonly called the Calendar Method, since it depends on the use of an individualized "calendar", its efficacy is limited by the natural irregularities that occur from month to month.

In recent decades, two new methods have been proposed which are based on the recognition of the signs and symptoms of ovulation. The cervical mucus or ovulation method is based on abstinence during the period when mucus secretion is profuse. Most women who experience this change can identify it when alerted to its significance. Hence it may be used to give women a better understanding of their own fertility and serve as an aid to couples trying to conceive. However, vaginal infections, douching, and recent coitus can cause confusion and misinterpretation.

It has long been known that the basal body temperature rises following ovulation, and this is the basis of the "temperature method" of natural family planning. The more recently developed sympto-thermal method (STM) combines recognition of symptoms, such as mucus changes and mittelschmertz in women who experience it, with tracking of the basal body temperature. The temperature is taken daily before rising with a special thermometer which allows a more exact reading. This temperature is then charted and observed for the rise that is generally registered around the time of ovulation. With proper training, experience, and ongoing counseling most women can master these techniques (Liskin, 1981).

Recently, the efficacy of the ovulation and sympto-thermal methods have been evaluated in two clinical trials (Wade et al., 1979; WHO, 1981c). In training participants, it was found that a high level of motivation was necessary for a couple to stay with the program beyond the training period. There were considerable pregnancies and withdrawals during training. In those women who remained in the posttraining study, pregnancy rates with the ovulation method range from 19.6 to 24.8 percent, as compared with 9.4 percent for the sympto-thermal method.

In CBD projects, the use of these techniques has certain advantages and disadvantages. The major advantage is that once the method is taught, monitored, and shown to be completely understood, the only resupply necessary will be charting materials and replacement thermometers if necessary. This method is approved by most religious groups and may promote communication between partners. The main disadvantages are the increased risk of unwanted pregnancy, the extended period of initial instruction, the ongoing counseling and the necessary, intimate supervision needed. In areas where CBD is introduced, the population frequently is not skilled in charting numbers, temperature monitoring, or communicating on the subject of sexual activity with their spouses. Furthermore, this method is not acceptable to a large number of couples who find genital manipulation, abstinence, or daily charting distasteful. In addition a certain percentage of women have irregular cycles limiting predictability, while others are unable to properly interpret their body signs. Due to the absence of regular cyclical variations in basal body temperatures and mucus lactating women are another group who cannot use this method.

The CBD worker training must be sufficient to allow for nearly perfect abilities to interpret and teach the charting technique. With this method the worker must plan substantial time at each contact. Contact with the client must be frequent and continual. There is no simple set of questions to be asked at each visit. Rather, the worker must carefully review charting, behavioral decisions based on these charts, and problems or lack of adherence to the abstinence periods. This entails a considerable workload and sophistication for the worker, especially if some couples have difficulties with abstinence, problems of menstrual irregularity, infections or misinterpretation. In view of the low efficacy and worker demands, this method is probably not appropriate in most CBD programs.

Other methods that rely on cooperation between partners include prolonged abstinence and withdrawal. While not acceptable to all couples, these methods should be included in reproductive health training. The problems with these methods are that with prolonged abstinence unplanned coitus may occur; and withdrawal cannot be performed properly or consistently by all couples. Furthermore, the efficacy is low. The CBD workers should be aware of these methods as a fallback for specific situations of risk such as periods when commodity delivery is disrupted, when an IUD is expelled, or pills forgotten.

METHOD MIX

The appropriate mix of family planning methods for a given CBD program depends upon the resources available in terms of personnel skills and tasks, training facilities, clinical back-up, program design, and cost. These programmatic factors will be modified by health considerations and sociocultural factors influencing method acceptability. Although it is recognized that adding additional methods will increase the level of acceptance of family planning, this implies opportunity costs in terms of the complexity of worker tasks or dilution of effort. Hence, method mix should be as flexible and comprehensive as possible given these constraints. These tables are meant as teaching tools or aids for program decisions based solely on resources or sociocultural considerations. They do not include any measure of output for a particular method and are not meant to be the sole criteria for method choice.

From the above it is clear that decisions on method mix are complex, and to simplify selection the following matrices in Tables 5:7 and 5:8 have been devised as checklists to assist program managers. The matrices are based on the preceding discussion of method-specific characteristics and constraints. These tables are meant as models for teaching tools or aids for program decisions. They do not include any measure of output for a particular method and are not meant to be the sole criterion for method choice. Table 5:7 demonstrates possible health and sociocultural considerations, and Table 5:8 summarizes the resource factors which may have an influence on choice of methods.

Obviously the impact and implications of the different resources are not strictly comparable, and in neither chart are the pluses or minuses quantitative or additive. They are merely intended as a checklist or guide for formulating a relevant list. To demonstrate proper usage of these charts, consider a situation where CBD workers are relatively sophisticated and will have limited time for training or client contact, but do have good clinical backup. Using Table 5:8 the program manager may consider sterilization, oral contraceptives, injectables, spermicides, and condoms. If CBD workers are unsophisticated with a limited amount of time and poor clinic backup, but with reasonable resupply prospects, oral contraceptives would be a first choice with condoms and spermicides. However, if lactation is widespread and many acceptors are recently postpartum, considerations noted in Table 5:7 may indicate special considerations regarding oral contraceptive use, and initiation of the use of other methods. Similarly, if regular menstruation is important, injectables might be inadvisable.

These are not the only factors that influence method selection. Past studies have indicated that single-method programs do not achieve the same level of acceptance as those that offer

Table 5:7. Health and Cultural Factors Influencing Choice of Methods to be Considered in Program Planning

	STERILI-ZATION	ORAL CONTRA-CEPTIVES	INJECT-ABLES	IUD
HEALTH				
High Levels of STD or PID	NI	I	I	C
High Levels of Smoking	NI	C	C	NI
High Prevalence of Vascular Disease	NI	C	C	NI
Lactation	I	NI/C	NI	NI
High Prevalence of Iron Deficiency and Inadequate Dietary Iron	NI	I	I	C
Frequent Use of Rifampicin for TB Therapy	NI	C	C	NI
Severe Forms of Female Circumcision	NI	NI	NI	C
CULTURAL				
Regular Menses of High Importance	NI	I	C	NI
Injections Preferred	NI	NI	I	NI
Restrictions on Genital Contact	I	I	I	C
No Storage Place	I	C	I	I

Chart may be read as follows: If factor exists, stated method is indicated, has no impact, or is contradicted (e.g., if there are high levels of STD or PID, sterilization has no impact on it; if there are high levels of smoking OCs are contraindicated).

KEY: I = Indicated

NI = No Impact

C = Contraindicated

Table 5:7 (Cont.). Health and Cultural Factors Influencing Choice of Methods to be Considered in Program Planning

	DIAPHRAGM	CONDOM	SPERMI-CIDE	RHYTHM/ WITHDRAWAL
HEALTH				
High Levels of STD or PID	I	I	I	NI
High Levels of Smoking	NI	NI	NI	NI
High Prevalence of Vascular Disease	NI	NI	NI	NI
Lactation	NI	NI	NI	NI
High Prevalence of Iron Deficiency and Inadequate Dietary Iron	NI	NI	NI	NI
Frequent Use of Rifampicin for TB Therapy	NI	NI	NI	NI
Severe Forms of Female Circumcision	C	NI	NI	NI
CULTURAL				
Regular Menses of High Importance	NI	NI	NI	I
Injections Preferred	NI	NI	NI	NI
Restrictions on Genital Contact	C	C	C	C
No Storage Place	C	C	C	I

Table 5:8. Resource Factors Influencing Choice of Methods to be Considered for Inclusion in a Specific Program

	STERILIZATION	ORAL CONTRACEPTIVES	INJECTABLE	IUD	DIAPHRAGM/ SPERMICIDE	CONDOM	SPERMICIDE	RHYTHM/ WITHDRAWAL
CBD Worker Sophistication	++	+	++	++	++	+	+	+++
Length of Training:								
Clinic Worker	+++	+	+	++	++	+	+	++
CBD Worker	+	+	++	++	++	+	+	+++
Clinics for Referral and Backup	+++	+	++	+++	++	-	-	-
Total Time per Visit to Household	++	+	+	+	++	+	+	+++
Ongoing Worker Availability to Client	+	+	+	++	++	+	+	+++
Logistics/ Resupply	-	++	++	+	+++	+++	+++	-
Commodity Cost	+++	+	+	+	++	+	++	-

The +'s indicate the level of the resource necessary to consider including the method. This chart does not include any output considerations, but is simply a tool to aid in the decision as to which methods may be considered for inclusion in a program. (See footnote on next page for key.)

a mix of methods. With the addition of each new method, follows a concomitant increase in prevalence. Therefore, the program planner must not only choose a single method that is appropriate, but rather a "cafeteria" or mix of methods that is appropriate.

In summary, no contraceptive method meets all requirements, but an appropriate mix of methods can provide couples with a sufficient range of alternatives to meet their needs without imposing an unreasonable burden on the CBD program or worker.

CONCLUSIONS

The considerations of risks and benefits governing the mix of methods used in CBD programs are numerous and complex, but in general, it is clear that the risks associated with childbearing in developing countries far exceed any health risks that might be associated with contraceptive use.

Oral contraceptives are appropriate for the CBD setting because they are highly effective, relatively easy to deliver and use, and have a high margin of safety. Most studies on pill safety have been conducted in developed countries and it is likely that pill related risks such as cardiovascular disease, are much less in developing countries. It is desirable to use simple screening procedures such as a checklist of questions to identify contraindications to pill use, but it is essential to restrict such questions to a small number of appropriate, feasible and locally comprehensible items. Moreover, women should not be deterred from adopting the pill by overemphasizing hypothetical risks, and attention should be given to the benefits of oral contraceptive efficacy and ease of use, and in terms of potential health benefits. CBD workers should also be trained to manage side effects and to refer suspected complications.

It is inadvisable and probably unnecessary for breastfeeding amenorrheic women to use oral contraceptives for up to six months in traditional societies. The progestagen-only "minipill" might be more appropriate for lactating women, but the additional complexity of the CBD workers' tasks and the logistic problems associated with a second pill regimen would probably offset any theoretical advantage. On present evidence there is probably no rationale for adding minipills to CBD programs.

KEY TO TABLE 5:8:

+++ = high level of the resource is necessary to consider including the method

++ = medium level of the resource is necessary to consider including the method

\+ = lower level of the resource is necessary to consider including the method

\- = resource is not a necessary element in considering including the method

Similarly, although individual women might benefit from having a choice of combined oral contraceptive dose/drug regimens, the problems of multiple pill regimens probably make this alternative impractical in most CBD settings. In balance, combined pills containing 50 μg of estrogen and around 0.15 m g of norgestrel or 1 mg of norethisterone provide satisfactory protection without excessive side effects. In programs which utilize antibiotics, workers should be informed that the use of antibiotics can reduce the efficacy of the pill leading to breakthrough bleeding or even pregnancy.

Injectable contraceptives have been used successfully in some CBD programs and appear to be acceptable and to contribute to increased contraceptive prevalence. However, CBD workers must be trained to give injections while maintaining sterile techniques, to manage menstrual problems such as amenorrhea or excessive bleeding, to cope with common side effects and to counsel clients on potential delays in the return of fertility. These tasks are more complex than those associated with the pill.

The IUD is a useful adjunct to CBD programs but workers cannot be expected to provide insertion or perform pelvic examinations. However, the workers should be trained to counsel clients and to manage complications such as bleeding, pain, expulsion, PID and pregnancy by referral. Checklists could facilitate these tasks. Sterilization is also useful as a referral method, and workers should be able to inform women of the advantages of sterilization and to recognize postoperative problems such as infection or hemorrhage. Both the IUD and sterilization require accessible clinical backup facilities.

Barrier methods are an advantage in the CBD setting due to the simplicity of use and lack of major side effects. The exception is the diaphragm which requires skilled fitting procedures. Provision of adequate and continuing supplies of other barrier methods may present problems, since such clients need an average of 150 units annually. Commercial channels lend themselves to the distribution of condoms or spermicides. The negative correlation of barrier method use with the spread of sexually transmitted diseases is an important potential benefit of those methods.

Abortion is not appropriate to a CBD program, but where abortion facilities are available, CBD workers should be trained to counsel clients.

Natural family planning methods may have a role is some CBD contexts, especially in predominantly Catholic populations. However, these methods require considerable counseling skills and time which may place a heavy demand on CBD workers and necessitate careful and lengthy training. Also, pregnancy rates may be high with these methods. These considerations limit the potential for natural family planning in most CBD settings.

In summary, method mix must depend on a risk-benefit analysis specific to the conditions of each CBD program. Programatic concerns, especially resources in terms of personnel, logistics and finance, as well as cultural parameters must be carefully considered in deciding which mix of methods is appropriate to a CBD setting. Consideration must be given to the complexity of workers' tasks and to the competing demands of different methods on workers' time and skills.

REFERENCES

Adam, S.A. et al. "A Case Control Study of the Possible Association between Oral Contraceptives and Malignant Melanoma." Br. J. Cancer 44 (1981): 45.

Agarwal, B.L. "Rheumatic Heart Disease Unabated in Developing Countries." Lancet (Oct. 24 1981): 910.

Alexander, N.J. and D.J. Anderson. "Vasectomy: Consequences of Autoimmunity to Sperm Antigens." Fertility and Sterility 32,2 (1979): 253.

Alexander, N.J. and T.B. Clarkson. "Vasectomy Increase in the Severity of Diet-induced Atherosclerosis in Macaca Fascicularis." Science 201 (1978): 538.

Altman, D.L. and P.T. Piotrow. "Social Marketing: Does it Work?" Population Reports Series J,21 (1980): J-422.

Arean, V.M. "American Trypanosomiasis." In Tropical Medicine, edited by G.W. Hunter, J.C. Schwartzwelder, and D.E. Clyde. 5th Edition. W.B. Sanders Co. (1976): 440-450.

Atkin, A., R.H. Gray, and R. Ramos. "Training Auxiliary Nurse-Midwives to Provide IUD Services in Turkey and the Philippines." Studies in Family Planning 11,5 (May 1980).

Beral, V. "Reproductive Mortality." Brit. Med. J. (Sept. 15, 1979).

Berkowitz, R.S. et al. "Oral Contraceptives and Post-Molar Trophoblastic Tumours." Lancet (October 1980): 752.

Bhatia, S., W.H. Mosley et al. "The Matlab Family Planning Health Services Project." Studies in Family Planning 11,6 (1980).

Bhatia, S., S. Becker, and Y.J. Kim. "The Effect on Fecundity of Pill Acceptance in the Postpartum Amenorrhea in Rural Bangladesh." Studies in Family Planning 13,6 and 7 (1982): 200-207.

Bialy, G. et al. "Periodic Abstinence: How Well Do New Approaches Work?" Population Reports Series I,3 (September 1981).

Billewicz, W.Z. and I.A. McGregor. "The Demography of Two West African (Gambian) Villages 1951-75." Journal of Biosocial Science 13,2 (April 1981): 219.

Blumenstein, B.A., M.B. Douglas, and W.D. Hall. "Blood Pressure "Changes and Oral Contraceptive Use: A Study of 2,676 Black Women in the Southern United States." Am. J. Epid. 112 (1980): 539.

Briggs, M.H. "Combined Oral Contraceptives." In Regulation of Human Fertility, edited by E. Diczfalusy. Proceedings of a WHO Symposium on Advances in Fertility Regulation. Copenhagen: Scriptor (1977): 253-282.

Briggs, M.H. "Steroid Contraception: Metabolic and Endocrine Effects." In Risks, Benefits and Controversies in Fertility Control, edited by J.J. Sciarra, G.I. Zatuchni, and J.J. Speidel. New York: Harper & Row (1978): 214-229.

Brinton, L.A. et al. "Risk Factors for Benign Breast Disease." Am. J. of Epid. 113,3 (March 1981): 203.

British Medical Journal Editorial. "Drug Interaction with Oral Contraceptive Steroids." Brit. Med. J,2 (1980): 93-94.

Buchanan, R. "Breastfeeding - Aid to Infant Health and Fertility Control." Population Reports Series J,4 (July 1975).

Chamberlain, G. and J. Foulkes. "Late Complications of Sterilization by Laparoscopy." Lancet 2 (1975): 878.

Chen, L.C. et al. "Maternal Mortality in Rural Bangladesh." Studies in Family Planning 5 (1975): 334.

Chi, I-C. et al. "An Epidemiologic Study of Risk Factors Associated with Pregnancy following Female Sterilization." Am. J. Obstet. Gynecol. 136 (1980): 768.

Chow, L.P. and N.K. Nair. "Oral Contraceptive Use and Diseases of the Circulatory System in Taiwan: An Analysis of Mortality Statistics." Int. J. Gynaecol. Obstet. 18 (1980): 420.

Chumnijarakij, T. and V. Poshyachinda. "Postoperative Thrombosis in Thai Women." Lancet (June 21, 1975): 1357.

Coleman, S. and P.T. Piotrow. "Spermicides - Simplicity and Safety are Major Assets." Population Reports Series H,5 (Sept. 1979).

Cole, C.H. et al. "Vaginal Chemoprophylaxis in the Reduction of Reinfection in Women with Gonorrhoea." Br. J. Vener. Dis. 56 (1980): 314-8.

Connell, E. et al. "Tubal Sterilization - Review of Methods." Population Reports Series C,7 (May 1976).

Dalen, J.E. et al. "Oral Contraceptives and Cardiovascular Disease." Amer. Heart J. 101 (1981): 629-39.

Dan, B. Epidemiology Branch, Center for Disease Control. Personal Communication, September 1981.

Eckstein, P. et al. "Clinical and Laboratory Findings in a Trial of Norgestrel, A Low-dose Progestagen-only Contraceptive." Brit. Med. Journal (July 1972): 195-199.

Foreit, J.R. et al. "Community-Based and Commercial Contraceptive Distribution: An Inventory and Appraisal." Population Reports Series J,19 (March 1978): J-1.

Foreman, H. et al. "Intrauterine Device Usage and Fetal Loss." J. Am. Coll. of Obstet. & Gyn. 58,6 (December 1981): 669.

Fraser, I.S. and E. Weisberg. "A Comprehensive Review of Injectable Contraception with Special Emphasis on Depot Medroxyprogesterone Acetate." Med. J. of Aust. 1,1 Special Suppl. (January 1981): 19.

Gillespie, D.G. and C.G. Merrit. "Operations Research on Household and Village Contraceptive Distribution Systems." In Village and Household Availability of Contraceptives: Africa/West Asia, edited by T.S. Gardner, et al. Seattle, Washington: Battele Memorial Institute (1977): 113-114.

Gray, R.H. "Checklists for Screening Subjects on Admission to Clinical Trials." Geneva: WHO, Unpublished Documents, 1978.

Gray, R.H. "U.K.: Patterns of Bleeding Associated with the Use of Steroidal Contraceptives." In Endometrial Bleeding and Steroidal Contraception, WHO Symposium, Geneva (1979): 14-49.

Gray, R.H. Manual for the Provision of Intrauterine Devices IUDs. Geneva: World Health Organization, 1980.

Gray, R.H., R.A. Parker et al. "Vaginal Bleeding Disturbances Associated with Discontinuation of Long-acting Injectable Contraceptives." Brit. J. of Obstet. and Gyn. 88,3 (March 1981): 317.

Gray, R.H. and B. Silkey, "Pelvic Inflammatory Disease: Causes and Consequences." Paper presented at the Symposium on Changing Health Risks of Women, The Johns Hopkins University School of Hygiene and Public Health, Baltimore, MD, 1981.

Grimley-Evans, J. and R. Geoffrey. "Hypertension." Brit. Med. Bull. 27,1 (1971): 37.

Hatcher, R.A. et al. Contraceptive Technology 1980-1981, 10th Edition. New York: Irvington Publishers, 1980.

Heiby, J.R. "The Association of Oral Contraceptives and Myocardial Infarction in Less Developed Countries." In Risks, Benefits and Controversies in Fertility Control, edited by J.J. Sciarra, G.I. Zatuchni, and J.J. Speidel. New York: Harper & Row (1978): 162-170 .

Honore, L.H. and K.E. O'Hara. "Failed Tubal Sterilization as an Etiologic Factor in Ectopic Tubal Pregnancy." Fertility and Sterility 29,5 (1978): 509.

Huber, D.H. and S.C. Huber. "Screening Oral Contraceptives Candidates and Inconsequential Pelvic Examinations." Studies in Family Planning 6,2 (1975): 49-51.

Hull, V.J. "The Effect of Hormonal Contraceptives on Lactation: (Lument Findings, Methodological Considerations and Future Prospects." Studies of Family Planning 12,4 (1981): 134-155.

Jick, H. et al. "Vaginal Spermicides and Congenital Disorder." JAMA 245,13 (April 1981).

Kaufman, D.W., S. Shapiro et al. "Decreased Risk of Endometrial Cancer among Oral-Contraceptive Users." Medical Intelligence 303,18 (1980): 1045.

Kay, C. "Breast Cancer and Oral Contraceptives: Findings in Royal College of General Practitioners' Study (papers & short reports)." Brit. Med. J. 282 (June 1981): 2089.

Kennedy, B.L. and R. Rodriquez. "The Delivery of Family Planning Services in Developing Countries by Paramedical Personnel: A Review of 40 Countries." Paper presented at the APHA Annual Meeting, Los Angeles, 1981.

Koetswang, S. "A Randomized, Double-Blind Study of Six Combined Oral Contraceptives." Report by the Task Force on Oral Contraceptives, WHO Special Programme of Research Development and Research Training in Human Reproduction. Contraception 25,3 (1981): 231-241.

Koetswang, S. "Present Management of Abnormal Bleeding Associated with Steroidal Contraceptives." In Endometrial Bleeding and Steroidal Contraception. WHO Symposium, Geneva (1979): 50-65.

Kwak, H. et al. "Menstrual Pattern Changes in Laparoscopic Sterilization Patients Whose Last Pregnancy was Terminated by Therapeutic Abortion: A Two-Year Follow-Up Study." Journal Reprod. Med. 25 (1980): 67.

Lawson, S., R. Cole, and A. Templeton. "The Effect of Laparoscopic Sterilization by Diathermy or Silastic Bands, or Post-operative Pain, Menstrual Symptoms and Sexuality." Brit. J. Ob. Gyn. 86 (1979): 659.

Layde, P.M. and V. Beral. "Further Analysis of Mortality in Oral Contraceptive Users." Lancet (March 1981): 541.

Lieberman, B., E. Belsey, A. Gordon, C. Wright, A. Letchworth, and P. Niven. "Menstrual Patterns after Laparoscopic Sterilization Using the Spring-loaded Clip." Brit. J. Ob. Gyn. 85 (1978): 376.

Liskin, L.S. et al. "Complications of Abortion in Developing Countries," Population Reports Series F,7 (1980): F107.

Liskin, L.S. "Periodic abstinence: How well do new approaches work?" Population Reports Series I,3 (1981).

Maine, D. Family Planning: Its Impact on the Health of Women and Children. New York: The Center for Population and Family Health, College of Physicians and Surgeons, Columbia Univ. (1981): 56.

Matthews, P.N., R.R. Millis et al. "Breast Cancer in Women Who Have taken Contraceptive Steroids." Brit. Med. J. 282 (March 1981).

McCann, M.F. "Laparoscopy Versus Minilaparotomy." In Risks, Benefits and Controversies in Fertility Control, edited by J.J. Sciarra, G.I. Zatuchni, and J.J. Speidel. New York: Harper & Row (1978): 68-80.

McCausland, A. "High Rate of Ectopic Pregnancy following Laparoscopic Tubal Coagulation Failures." Am. J. Obstet. Gynecol. 136,1 (1980): 97.

Metcalf, M., and J. MacKenzie. "Incidence of Ovulation in Young Women." J. Bio. Soc. Sci. 12 (1980): 345.

Miall, W.E. and G. Bras. "Heart Disease in the Tropics." Brit. Med. Bull. 28,1 (1972).

Mishell, D.R., Jr. "Oral Steroids." In Reproductive Endocrinology, Infertility and Contraception, edited by D.R. Mishell and V. Davajan. Philadelphia: F.A. Davis Company (1979): 487-523.

Morrison, A.S., H. Jick, and H.W. Ory. "Oral Contraceptives and Hepatitis. A Report From the Boston Collaborative Drug Surveillance Program." Lancet 1 (1977): 1142-1143.

Mosley, W.H. et al. "Interactions of Contraception and Breast-feeding in Developing Countries." Journal of Biosocial Science suppl. #4. Proceeding of Six Biomedical Workshops of the International Planned Parenthood Federation (1976): 93-112.

Mumford, I.S.D., P.P. Bhiwandiwala, and I.C. Chi. "Laparoscopic and Minilaparotomy: Female Sterilization Compared in 15,167 Cases." Lancet II (1980): 1066.

Neil, J., A. Noble, G. Hammond, and L. Rushton, "Late Complications of Sterilization by Laparoscopy and Tubal Ligation." Lancet 2 (1978): 699.

Newhouse, M.L., R.M. Pearson et al. "A Case Control Study of Carcinoma of the Ovary." Br. J. Prevent. Soc. Med. 31 (1977): 148.

Nilsson, S. and K. Nygren. "Transfer of Contraceptive Steroids to Human Milk." Research in Reproduction 11,1 (January 1979).

Nortman, D. "Parental Age as a Factor in Pregnancy Outcome and Child Development." Reports on Population/Family Planning 16 (August 1974): 1-49.

Omran, A.R. et al. "An Overview of the Study." In Family Formation Patterns and Health. Geneva: World Health Organization (1976): 507-535.

Osborn, R.W. and W.A. Reinke. Community Based Distribution of Contraceptives. Baltimore: The Johns Hopkins Population Center, January, 1981.

Pardthaisong, T., R.H. Gray, and E.B. McDaniel. "Return of Fertility after Discontinuation of Depot Medroxyprogesterone Acetate and Intrauterine Devices in Northern Thailand." Lancet (March 1980): 509.

Peritz, E. and S. Ramcharan. "The Incidence of Cervical Cancer and Duration of Oral Contraceptive Use." Am. J. of Epid. 106,6 (1977): 462.

Peterson, H.B., H.W. Ory et al. "Deaths Associated with Laparoscopic Sterilization by Unipolar Electrocoagulating Devices, 1978 and 1979." Am. J. Obstet. Gynecol. 139,2 (January 1981): 142.

Piotrow, P.T. et al. "IUDs - Update on Safety, Effectiveness, and Research." Population Reports Series B,3 (May 1979): B-50.

Potter, R.G., F.E. Korbin, and R.L. Langsten. "Evaluating Acceptance Strategies for Timing of Postpartum Contraception." Studies in Family Planning 10 (1979): 151-163.

Potts, M., J.J. Speidel et al. "Relative Risks of Various Means of Fertility Control when used in Less-Developed Countries." In Risks, Benefits and Controversies in Fertility Control, edited by J.J. Sciarra, G.I. Zatuchni and J.J. Speidel. New York: Harper and Row (1978): 28-51.

Rahman, M., W.H. Mosley et al. "Contraceptive Distribution in Bangladesh: Some Lessons Learned." Studies in Family Planning 11,6 (1980).

Rinehart, W. "Minipill - A Limited Alternative for Certain Women." Population Reports Series A,3 (September 1975).

Rinehart, W. and P.T. Piotrow. "OCs - Update on Usage, Safety, and Side Effects." Population Reports Series A,5 (January 1979): A-133.

Rochat, R.W., D. Kramer, P. Sennanayke, and C. Howell. "Induced Abortion and Health Problems in Developing Countries." Lancet 2 (1980): 484.

Rochat, R.W., H.W. Ory, and K.F. Schulz. "Methods for Measuring Safety and Health Hazards of Presently Available Fertility Regulation Agents in the Developing World." Singapore J. Obstet. and Gyn. 9,1 (1978): 14.

Rochat, R.W., S. Tabeen et al. "Maternal and Abortion Related Deaths in Bangladesh, 1978-1979." Int. J. Gynaecol. and Obstet. 19 (1981): 155.

Rosenfield, A. et al. "Nonclinical Distribution of the Pill in the Developing World." Int. Family Planning Perspectives 6,4 (December 1980): 130-136.

Rosenfield, A. "Medical Supervision for Contraception: Too Little or Too Much." Int. J. Gynaecol. & Obstet. 15 (1977): 105-110.

Royal College of General Practitioners. "Further Analyses of Mortality in Oral Contraceptive Users." Lancet (March 1981): 541.

Rubenstein, L., L. Benjamin, and V. Kleinkopf. "Menstrual Patterns and Women's Attitudes following Sterilization by Fallope Rings." Fertility and Sterility 31 (1979): 641.

Sacks, S. and G. LaCroix. "Gynecologic Sequelae of Post-Partum Tubal Ligation." Ob. Gyn. 19 (1962): 122.

Sapire, K. and D. Davey. "The Effect of Sterilization by Bipolar Cautery and Fallope Ring on Menstrual Bleeding Patterns." South African Medical Journal 58,22 (1980): 889.

Senanayake, P. and D.G. Kramer. "Contraception and the Etiology of Pelvic Inflammatory Disease: New Perspectives." Am. J. Obstet. & Gynecol. (December 1980): 852-860.

Shaper, A. "Cardiovascular Disease in the Tropics. Blood Pressure and Hypertension." Br. Med. J. 3 (1972): 805-807.

Stadel, B.V. "Oral Contraceptives and Cardiovascular Disease (first of two parts)." NE J. of Medicine 305,11 (1981): 612-618. And "Oral Contraceptives and Cardiovascular Disease (second of two parts)." NE J. of Medicine 305,12 (1981): 672-677.

Stern, E., A.B. Forsythe et al. "Steroids Contraceptive Use and Cervical Dysplasia: Increased Risk of Progression." Science 196 (June 1977): 1460.

Stone, M., J. Dent, A. Kardna, and R.D. Bagshawe. "Relationship of Oral Contraception to Development of Trophoblastic Tumour after Evaluation of Hydatidiform Mole." Brit. J. Obstet. & Gyn. 82 (1976): 913.

Strauss, L.T., M. Speckhard et al. "Oral Contraception During Lactation: A Global Survey of Physician Practice." In. J. Gynaecol. Obstet. 19 (1981): 169.

Swan, S.H. and W.L. Brown. "Oral Contraceptive Use, Sexual Activity, and Cervical Carcinoma." Am. J. Obstet. Gynecol. (January 1981): 52.

Talwar, P.P. and Berger, G.S. "Side Effects of Drugs: The Relation of Body Weight to Side Effects Associated with Oral Contraceptives." Brit. Med. Journal (June 1977): 1637-1638.

Tatum, H.J. and Connell-Tatum, E.B. "Barrier Contraception: A Comprehensive Overview." Fertility & Sterility 36,1 (July 1981).

Tietze, C. "Maternal Mortality Excluding Abortion Mortality." World Health Statistics Report 30 (1979): 312.

Tietze, C. and J. Bongaarts. "Mortality Associated with the Control of Fertility." Family Planning Perspectives 8,1, (Jan/Feb. 1976).

Van Ginneken, J.K. "The Chance of Conception During Lactation." J. Biosocial Science suppl. #4 (1977): 41.

Vaughan, B., T. Trussell et al. "Contraceptive Failure among Married Women in United States, 1970-73." Family Planning Perspectives 9,6 (Nov/Dec. 1977).

Vessey, M.P. "Contraceptive Methods: Risks and Benefits." Brit. Med. J. 9 (September 1978).

Vessey, M.P. and E. Mears. "Randomized Double-Blind Trial of Four Oral Progestagen-Only Contraceptives." Lancet (April 1972): 915-921.

Vessey, M., L. Meisler et al. "Outcome of Pregnancy in Women using Different Methods of Contraception." Brit. J. Obstet. & Gyn. 86 (July 1979): 548.

Wade, M.E. "A Randomized Prospective Study of the Use-Effectiveness of Two Methods of Natural Family Planning: An Interim Report." Am. J. Obstet. Gynecol. 134 (1979): 628.

Walker, A. et al. "Vasectomy and Non-fatal Myocardial Infarction." Lancet 8210 (1981): 13.

Waterhouse, J. et al. Cancer Incidence in Five Continents, Vol. III. Scientific Publications No. 15. Lyon: International Agency for Research on Cancer (IARC), 1976.

Weiss, N.S. and T.A. Sayvetz. "Incidence of Endometrial Cancer in Relation to the Use of Oral Contraceptives." N. Eng. J. Med. 302 (1980): 551-554.

Westrom, L. "Incidence, Prevalence, and Trends of Acute Pelvic Inflammatory Disease and its Consequences in Industrialized Countries." Am. J. Obstet. & Gynecol. 138,7: 880-891.

William, E., H. Jones, and R. Merrill. "The Subsequent Course of Patients Sterilized by Tubal Ligation." Am. J. Ob. Gyn. 61 (1981): 423.

Wilson, J.G. and R.L. Brent. "Are Female Sex Hormones Teratogenic?" Am. J. Obstet. Gynecol. 141,5 (November 1981).

Wortman, J. "Tubal Sterilization; Review of Methods." Population Reports Series C,7 (1976a): 1-95.

Wortman, J. "The Diaphragm and Other Intravaginal Barriers - A Review." Population Reports Series H,4 (January 1976b).

Wynn, V. et al. "Comparison of Effects of Different Combined Oral-Contraceptive Formulations on Carbohydrate and Lipid Metabolism." Lancet (May 1979): 1046.

World Health Organization (WHO). "Advances in Methods of Fertility Regulation." Report of a WHO Scientific Group, Technical Report Series No. 575. Geneva: (1975).

______ . (Expanded Programme of Research). "Multinational Comparative Clinical Evaluation of Two Long-Acting Injectable Contraceptive Steroids: Norethisterone Oenanthate & Medroxyprogesterone Acetate." Contraception 15,5 (May 1977).

______ . "Steroid Contraception and the Risk of Neoplasia, Report of a WHO Scientific Group." Technical Report Series No. 619, Geneva: (1978).

______ . "Special Program of Research: Development and Research Training in Human Reproduction. An Assessment of the Lippes Loop D and the Copper T 220C." (HRP/79.1 Rev.1) Geneva: WHO (1979): 1-4.

______ . "A Prospective Multicentre Trial of the Ovulation Method of Natural Family Planning. II. The Effectiveness Phase." Fertility and Sterility 36,5 (1981): 591.

______ . "The Effect of Female Sex Hormones on Fetal Development and Infant Health, Report of a WHO Scientific Group." Technical Report Series No. 657. Geneva: (1981a).

______ . "Multinational Comparative Clinical Trial of Long-acting Injectable Contraceptives: Norethisterone Enanthate Given in Two Dosage Regimens and Depot-medroxyprogesterone Acetate. A Preliminary Report." Contraception 25 (1982).

6
Family Planning and Health in Rural Bangladesh

Shushum Bhatia

BACKGROUND

In October 1977, the International Centre for Diarrheal Disease Research, Bangladesh (ICDDR,B) restructured a nonclinical, village-based family planning project into an integrated, community maternal child health and family planning program in 70 villages of the Matlab field surveillance area. The present paper concentrates on the family planning component of the program and discusses aspects of integrating family planning with other health services. Selected health services of the Family Planning Health Service Project (FPHSP) are described in greater detail elsewhere (Bhatia, this volume; Oral Rehydration Therapy discussion, this volume).

The population covered by project services was approximately 80,000. The remaining 79 villages, with a similar population served as the comparison area. The results of an earlier contraceptive distribution program begun in 1975 confirmed a substantial unmet need for family planning in rural areas of Bangladesh. A gradual decline in contraceptive use over the two-year period of the earlier project indicated, however, that this need was not being adequately met by the simple household delivery of limited contraceptive supplies (oral contraceptives and condoms). Although contraceptive prevalence increased from a baseline of 1% to 17.8% within three months, followup surveys indicated that continuation rates for new acceptors were just over 25% at two years. In addition, many recipients were found to be using the pills incorrectly. (Rahman, 1980). A detailed study of the program strategy indicated that a major deficiency was the poor training and lack of supervision among the village workers who were responsible for maintaining supplies and counseling clients. The majority of clients did not return to the lady village workers (LVWs) when experiencing side effects, and community rumors resulted, in part, in limited recruitment of new acceptors (Rahman, 1980). Also, the limited range of methods available left little alternative for those women experiencing side effects, resulting in discontinuation of use.

To overcome the deficiencies of this project, major modifications in field structure and program activities were introduced in October of 1977. The new Family Planning Health Services Project (FPHSP) offered a full range of contraceptive methods to better meet the needs of individual women. This "cafeteria" approach, in turn, required the availability of well-trained fieldworkers who could offer individualized services and counseling to women. To facilitate the program, close supervision and good medical support were necessary as well.

It was hypothesized that the provision of a fuller range of technologies, if delivered with personal concern and support, even though alien to traditional and rural societies, would better meet the fertility control needs of individual women. This should become evident through higher contraceptive acceptance and use rates.

In societies with limited access to and availability of health services, particularly for women and children, the provision of family planning services alone fails to place family planning into its appropriate context as one of many measures to promote health for the family. By providing an integrated program and introducing selected health services for women and children, the FPHSP aimed to both legitimize and reinforce the concept and principles of family planning. Furthermore, by adopting an integrated program strategy, the FPHSP aimed to reach those couples who saw no rationale for accepting fertility control in isolation. This paper examines the effects of the integrated approach on contraceptive use and fertility rates in the area.

Since the family planning services were the first to be provided, the health interventions were gradually introduced; it is not possible to draw definite conclusions regarding the impact of the health interventions on contraceptive acceptance and use rates. However, when evaluating the results of the project, it is useful to note that even before the health components could be introduced, the supervisors had to constantly reassure the communities and the workers regarding the early provision of such services due to continuous pressure from both workers and village women. This constant interaction among the field supervisors, workers, and the communtiy may have affected the family planning results of the project, although the effect cannot be quantified directly.

CLINICAL FACILITIES AND FIELD ORGANIZATION

Central facilities for delivering the full range of family planning services and selected maternity services were developed in the family planning clinic at Matlab Bazaar. The facility, staffed by a physician, two female family planning visitors and other support staff, provided oral pills, condoms, foam tablets, depo-provera injections, and male and female sterilization. Treatment for severe side effects or complications associated with contraception and management of selected childbirth-related emergiencies, were also available at the clinic. Severe and complicated cases of diarrhea, referred from the program area, were treated at the Matlab Diarrhea Treatment facility.

Four subcenter clinics were established in the FPHSP area. Each clinic served a population of 20,000, and was housed in the village community center. The activities at the subcenters ranged from management of side effects and complications associated with various contraceptive methods to menstrual regulation services, IUD insertions and removals, and treatment of minor ailments. The facilities served as storage sites for the oral rehydration packets or the salts and molasses used for treating diarrhea. The subcenters were also used as training sites for the village workers. Each subcenter was staffed by a resident lady family planning visitor (LFPV) and a male support worker.

At the village household level, family planning and selected MCH services were provided by 80 female village workers (FVW). Each FVW covered a population of approximately 1,000 or about 200 families. Each worker visited about 20 families per day, thereby contacting each family bimonthly. Since the new FVWs were recruited from among village housewives, they were provided with an intensive two-week program at one of the subcenters, followed by two weeks of closely-supervised field training. Training covered basic information regarding reproduction; a general introduction to family planning and its relationship to personal and family health and welfare; fairly detailed information regarding specific methods; methods of motivating potential recipients and recordkeeping. FVWs were also trained to give intramuscular injections. FVWs were divided into eight groups of 10 women each for training. Didactic lectures were avoided, and active discussion was encouraged. Following the preservice training, weekly in-service training sessions were conducted in the subcenters (Bhatia et al., 1980).

Within each of the four subcenter areas, 20 FVWs were supported and supervised by one male senior field assistant and one female family planning visitor. Two senior supervisors each supervised and facilitated the work at two subcenters. The overall management and supervision of the clinical aspects of the field operation was the responsibility of the physician, while one senior-level supervisor was made responsible for the overall logistics, administration, and nonclinical field activities.

HEALTH INTERVENTIONS IN THE FPHSP PROJECT

Initially the FPHSP project provided modern contraceptive methods and related family planning services exclusively. During this period, through training provided at weekly sessions, the FVWs gradually gained increasing knowledge about MCH care. Over time they were able to transmit information about nutrition and hygienic practices during pregnancy, delivery, and breastfeeding. By June 1978, FVWs began to deliver tetanus immunization and iron and folate tablets to pregnant women. By the beginning of the second year, they had trained about 1,500 mothers to provide oral rehydration for diarrhea.

The criteria for selection of the health interventions, and the sequence in which they were introduced, were based on results of social surveys and epidemiologic studies which facilitated the identification of priority areas. New topics were introduced gradually to enable FVWs to absorb and assimilate the additional knowledge, and to test its relevance and appropriateness in the field on a gradual basis.

IMPACT OF THE FPHSP

The impact of the FPHSP could be examined in two ways. One way would be to consider each component of the program separately and evaluate each intervention by analyzing the indicators directly related to it, such as, contraceptive use rates and/or fertility rates to evaluate the family planning component, changes in neonatal mortality for the tetanus immunization program, reduction in childhood diarrheal deaths for oral rehydration, etc. A second method would be to examine the effect of one intervention on the results of another: e.g., the impact on contraceptive acceptance of reduction in neonatal mortality brought about by tetanus immunization of pregnant women. As has been stated earlier, the latter would be quite problematic because of the manner in which the FPHSP was implemented. In the following section, some preliminary results of the family planning are examined separately, as are those for tetanus toxoid and oral rehydration in the other sections of this volume noted above.

Family Planning

The results of the family planning component of the program have appeared in several articles (Bhatia et al., 1980; Phillips et al., 1981; Bhatia, 1983), and will be summarized briefly. The present report will concentrate on some preliminary results from an analysis of trends in the contraceptive acceptance and use rates, along with changes over time in the characteristics of contraceptive users. A few findings from an analysis of the demographic impact of the program will also be mentioned.

Acceptors

A total of 5,929 women (46 percent of married women of reproductive age) used contraception during the first 18 months of the program. In order to detect differences in the demographic characteristics of women who accepted contraception in the first few months of the program versus those who accepted later, the first 18-month period was divided into six trimesters, the first beginning in October 1977 and the sixth in January 1979. Figure 6:1 gives the distribution of the new acceptors during each trimester by selected demographic characteristics. Of these, 20 percent accepted during the first trimester; 42 percent in the second trimester; approximately 10 percent each in the third and fourth trimesters, respectively; 8% in the fifth trimester, and the remainder in the last trimester.

It is apparent that women who accepted in the first few trimesters of the program were predominantly those who were

Figure 6:1. Percent Distribution of New Acceptors Over Six Trimesters, Beginning October 1977, By Selected Characteristics

DESIRE MORE CHILDREN

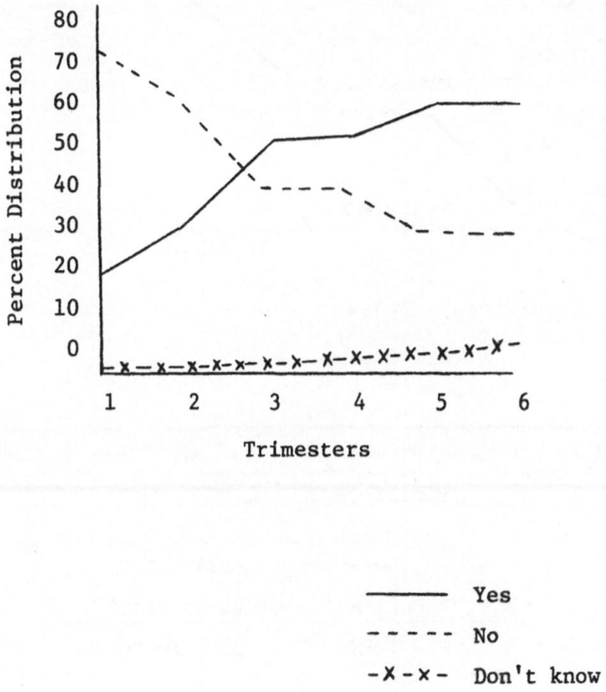

Figure 6:1 (Cont.) Percent Distribution of New Acceptors Over Six Trimesters, Beginning October 1977, By Selected Characteristics

AGE OF WOMEN

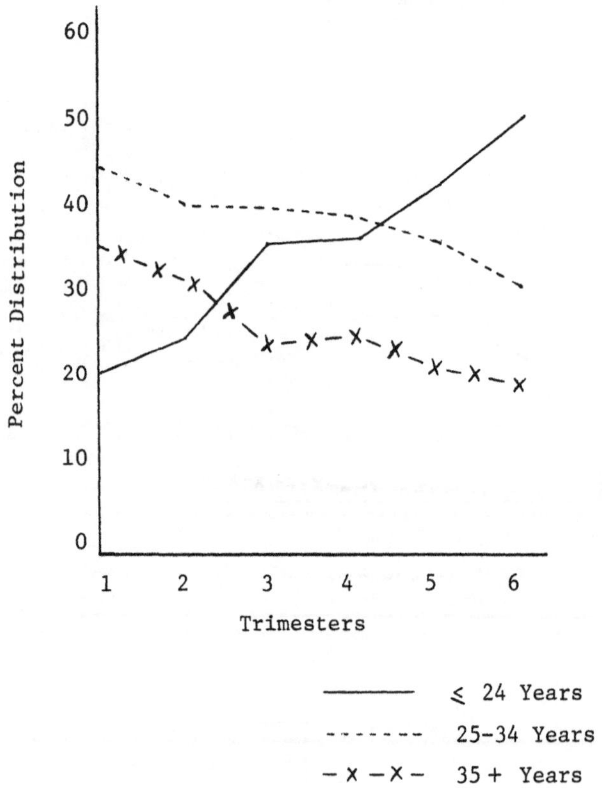

Figure 6:1 (Cont.) Percent Distribution of New Acceptors Over Six Trimesters, Beginning October 1977, By Selected Characteristics

NUMBER OF LIVING CHILDREN

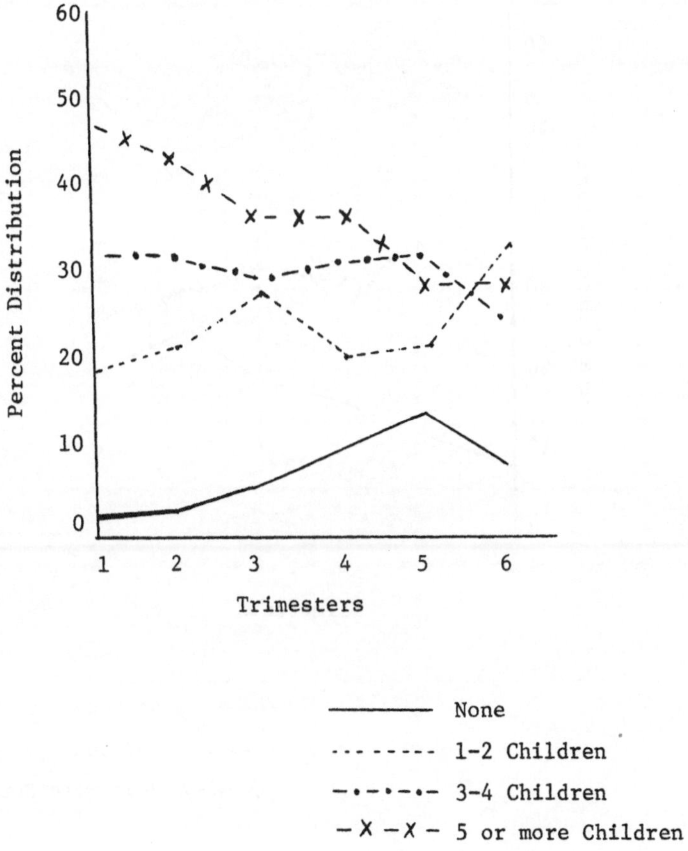

Figure 6:1 (Cont.) Percent Distribution of New Acceptors Over Six Trimesters, Beginning October 1977, By Selected Characteristics

NUMBER OF SONS

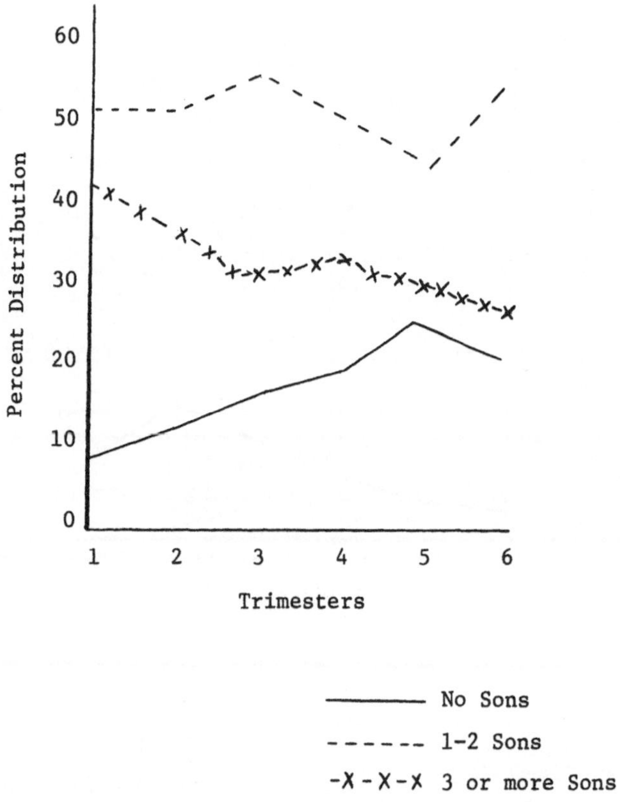

older, had more children (particularly sons), and those who did not desire more children. The mean age and the mean number of living children of women who accepted in the first trimester were 31.2 years and 4.4 children, respectively. By the sixth trimester, the mean age and the mean number of living children of the acceptors had declined to 26.2 years and 3.3 children, respectively.

At the start of the program, the acceptance level was made up by women 25 and older. As the program continued, older women represented a diminishing contribution to overall acceptance level. With increasing duration of the program, the proportion of acceptors who were younger women, under 20 and 20-24 years of age, gradually improved - from 0.3 and 0.7 in the first trimester to 0.9 and 1.1 in the sixth trimester, respectively. A similar trend was noted with respect to acceptance rates by the number of living children.

Contraceptive Use Pattern: The contraceptive use rates for nonpregnant married women of reproductive ages increased from 10.8 percent at the end of the first trimester to 35.7 percent at the end of the sixth trimester. The largest increments in prevalence rates until July 1978 occurred among women who were over 30 years, but between July 1978 and April 1979, of all age categories, the 25-29 year age group experienced the largest increase in prevalence of use.

Contraceptive Mix: The contraceptive mix offered by the program was expanded substantially in the new FPHSP, the entire range (pills, IUD, DMPA (depo-provera), foam tablets, condoms, tubal ligation, vasectomy) not being fully available until January 1978. At that time, depo-provera was the method of choice for 75 percent of users, and pills were used by over half of the remaining contraceptors. During the first months of the expanded program, women changed methods frequently: on the average, each contraceptor accepted 1.3 methods. Such experimentation, prior to selection of a final method, was made possible by the availability of choice. By April of 1979, tubal ligation and vasectomy were the most prevalent modern methods among older women, whereas younger and lower parity women were using foam tablets, condoms or pills. IUDs were also increasing in popularity in the latter groups (Bhatia, 1983).

Fertility Rates

Fertility rates were calculated from the longitudinal demographic surveillance system data, which collected data independently for both the FPHSP and the comparison areas, showed that at the end of the first year, overall fertility in the experimental area was 25 percent lower than that in the comparison area (Phillips, 1981). Figures 6:2 and 6:3 show the fertility rates among women aged 15-29 years and 30-34 years, respectively. It is apparent that the FPHSP had a sustained effect on fertility among women under age 30 and a pronounced impact upon

Figure 6:2. Quarterly Fertility Rates Among Women Aged 15-29 in Treatment and Comparison Areas of the FPHSP, 1974-1980

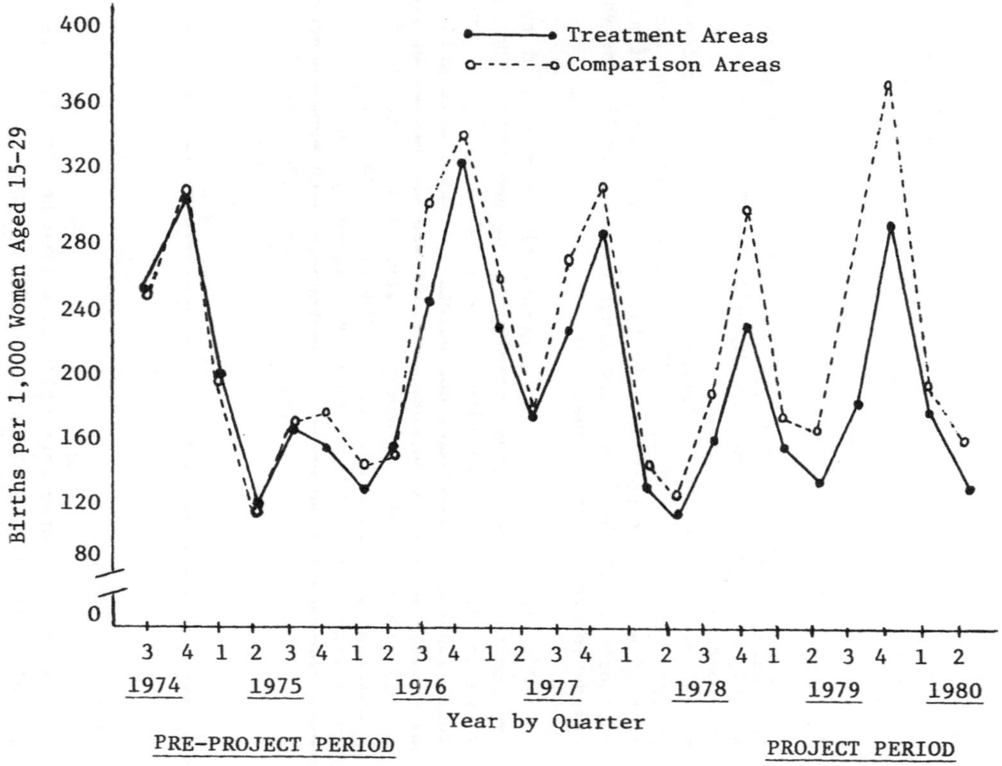

Figure 6:3. Age-Specific Fertility Rates Among Women Aged 30-44 in FPHSP Treatment and Comparison Areas

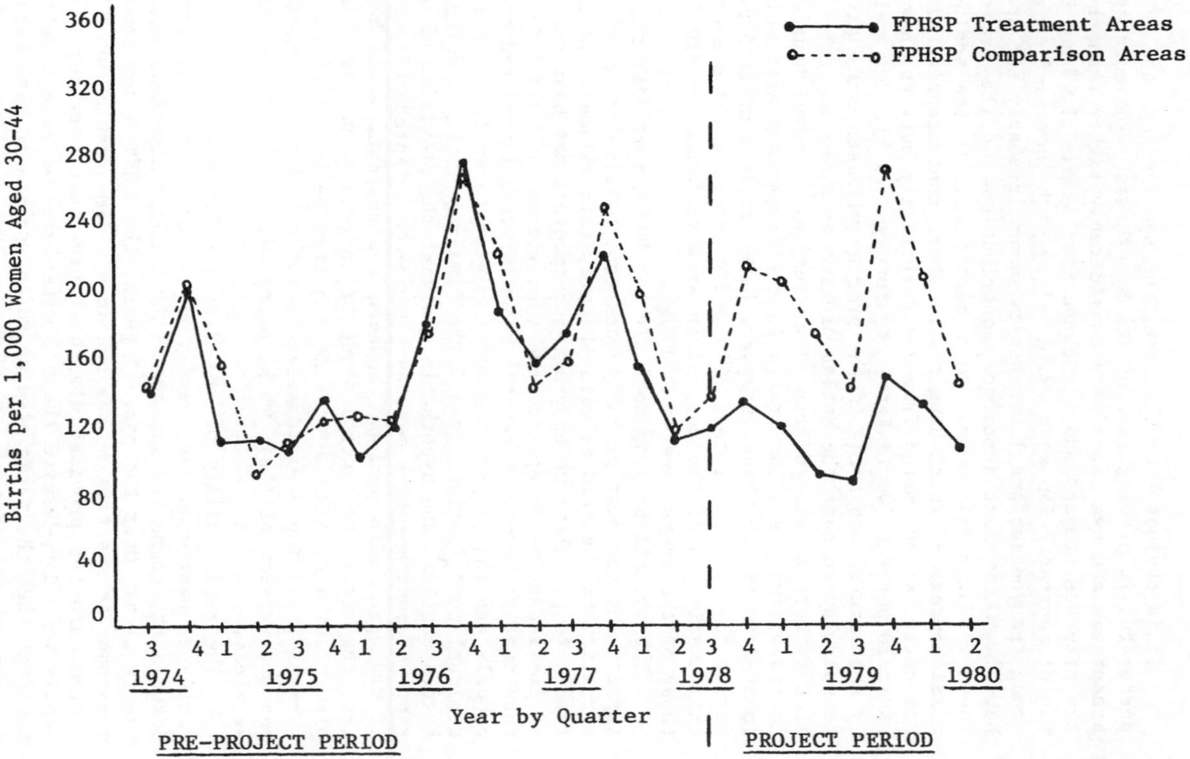

women 30 and over, and that these effects were not restricted to the peak fertility season.

CONCLUSIONS

It is obvious from the foregoing section that the FPHSP was successful in proving some of its hypotheses. The contraceptive acceptance and use rates were considerably higher than those of the previous project and the comparison area. The rise in the use of contraception as a whole, along with increased acceptance among the younger and lower parity women, probably for spacing, have been the most important contributions of the program. These findings are particularly significant in the socio-cultural context of rural Bangladesh, where contraceptive prevalence rates, as estimated from World Fertility surveys, have been under 10 percent (World Fertility Surveys, 1978). The relatively high prevalence rates in the program villages could give rise to speculation that the Matlab program area may be socio-economically more developed than other regions of rural Bangladesh. Contraceptive prevalence rates in the comparison area which is located in Matlab Thana, however, have remained under 5 percent during the program period. The socio-economic and demographic characteristics of the comparison area villages are similar to those of the areas covered by FPHSP.

The overall program not only has had a fertility reduction impact, but has most probably been responsible for reduction in mortality in the area as well (Bhatia, this volume). It is difficult to postulate which program components may have facilitated contraceptive acceptance and use, either qualitatively or in quantitative terms, as several measures were introduced simultaneously and the project was not designed to evaluate their individual contributions toward the family planning results. As stated earlier, the hypothesis was that the provision of a full range of contraceptive methods along with selected MCH services, if delivered with personal concern and support, would better meet the fertility control needs of individual women. The implementation of such a program required well-trained village workers providing individualized services, strong support for and supervision of their work, along with good medical back-up services.

The replicability of the Matlab FPHSP project, however, could be questioned for these very reasons. The good rapport between the community and the ICDDR,B could also have affected the results. Over the past 17 years, the ICDDR,B has conducted numerous vaccine trials, has operated a demographic surveillance system, and has provided diarrheal treatment services to the population. But despite these limitations, we cannot overlook the fact that the integrated approach appears to have been considerably more successful than the earlier contraceptive distribution project in the area, which had also been carried out by ICDDR,B (Rahman et al., 1980). However, the generalization of this on a national scale still needs to be determined.

REFERENCES

Bhatia, S. "Contraceptive Users in Rural Bangladesh: A Time Trend Analysis." Studies in Family Planning 14,1 (1983): 20-29.

Bhatia, S., W.H. Mosley, A.S.G. Faruque, and J. Chakraborty. "The Matlab Family Planning Health Services Project." Studies in Family Planning 11,6 (1980).

Phillips, J.F., W. Stinson, S. Bhatia, M. Rahman, and J. Chakraborty. "The Demographic Impact of 2 Contraceptive Service Projects in Matlab Thana of Bagladesh: A Compendium of Findings for the 1975-1980 Period." Working paper No. 23. Dacca: International Centre for Diarrhoeal Disease Research, Bangladesh, 1981.

Rahman, M., W.H. Mosley, A.R. Khan, A.I. Chowdhury, and J. Chakraborty. "Contraceptive Distribution in Bangladesh: Some Lessons Learned." Studies in Family Planning 11,6 (1980).

Rahman, M., L.C. Chen et al. "Reduction of Neonatal Mortality by Immunization of Nonpregnant Women and Women during Pregnancy with Aluminum Adsorbed Tetanus Toxoid." Scientific Report No. 41. Dacca: International Centre for Diarrhoeal Disease Research, Bangladesh, 1981.

Snyder, J.D., M. Yunus, M.A. Wahed, and J. Chakraborty. "Home Administered Oral Therapy: A Measure of Safety and Efficacy." (mimeo).

World Fertility Survey (WFS). "WFS Bangladesh Fertility Survey 1975." First Report, Ministry of Health and Population Control, Government of the People's Republic of Bangladesh, December 1978.

Yunus, M., S. Zimicki, and J. Chakraborty. "Oral Rehydration Project. Research Plan and Implementation." Presented at Inter-Regional Course on Health Services Research Evaluation, Dacca, September 7-18, 1981.

Zimicki, S. and J. Phillips. Personal communication, September, 1981.

Part Three

Adapting Oral Rehydration Therapy to CBD Programs

7

Oral Rehydration for the Treatment of Diarrhea: Its Value as a Health Component in Community-Based Family Planning Distribution Programs

Richard A. Cash

Diarrheal disease is a major killer of children in the developing world just as it was in developed countries less than 75 years ago. In recent years interest in the treatment of diarrhea has greatly increased, especially methods of treatment based on the use of oral rehydration therapy (ORT). This interest was stimulated in part by the world-wide commitment to primary health care as expressed in the Alma Alta Declaration of 1978. ORT represents an inexpensive way to treat all types of diarrhea and, when properly taught, therapy can be put directly in the hands of the population: care is then truly primary.

With continuing reports of the effectiveness of ORT programs, the natural tendency is to integrate it with other programs, among them family planning. Rationales for combining ORT and family planning have included the concept that a low-cost, effective, acceptable treatment such as rehydration therapy can act as an entry point for community motivation regarding the latter service. Proponents of the child survival hypothesis have postulated that since ORT can reduce childhood mortality, this provides yet another convincing argument to combine services. (The child survival hypothesis is based on the theory that couples are more inclined to adopt family planning if they have reasonable assurance that their existing children will survive to reach maturity.) As the number of programs where contraceptives are distributed at the community level increases, so does the trend to add the distribution of ORT packets to the task of community-based family planning workers. Whether such integration will increase the effectiveness of either program is not clear, however. Will the programs act synergistically, or detract from each other's effectiveness?

The effectiveness of community-based ORT programs is still being evaluated. Unresolved controversies include the proper formula to be used, the form in which ORT should be delivered, and optimal methods of linking ORT to other community-based programs.

The purposes of this paper are then threefold:

1) To examine the treatment of diarrheal disease with oral therapy;

2) To explore the issues involved in the implementation of diarrhea treatment programs at the community level; and
3) To determine whether adding ORT to other community-based programs is an effective way of delivering services.

CLINICAL EFFECTS OF DIARRHEAL DISEASE

Acute watery diarrhea leads to deficits in water and electrolytes. Acidosis, potassium, and sodium deficiencies result from the loss of bicarbonate, potassium, and sodium in the stool. Extracellular fluid diminishes with increasing stool loss and clinical signs of dehydration become manifest.

Dehydration is primarily isotonic and very few infants, especially in less developed countries develop serious hypertonic dehydration (serum sodium levels above 160 mEq/liter). That hypernatremia is so uncommon in developing countries may be due to most children's being breastfed: Breast milk has a much lower solute load than cow's milk and feeding volumes tend to be smaller (Hirschhorn, 1980). In addition to the loss of water and electrolytes, diarrhea affects the nutritional status of the child. Several mechanisms may contribute to the nutritional depletion: these include loss of appetite; the withholding of food and the inappropriate use of certain foods in treating the case; the catabolic effect; direct loss of nutrients in the stool; vomiting; and intestinal malabsorption.

TREATMENT

Guidelines for treating diarrhea have been well established and there are a number of reviews on the subject (World Health Organization, 1980; Cash, 1979). Replacement of initial fluid and electrolyte deficits, continued maintenance to ensure a normal state of hydration by the replacement of ongoing fluid and electrolyte losses, and the proper feeding of the child during the acute and convalescent phases of diarrhea are the principles of therapy. The effective use of intravenous (IV) therapy for the treatment of diarrhea goes back to the turn of the century. During ensuing years treatment was refined to the point where in the 1960s, the proper use of IV fluids was able to reduce mortality from cholera to less than 1 percent. However, there are limitations to the use of IV fluid. The correct fluid and the equipment needed (IV tubing and needles) are often not available; the cost of IV fluid may be prohibitive; IV fluid must be administered by a well-trained health provider (inserting such a needle and monitoring fluid volume requires skill and patience); and lastly, children treated with IV replacement are totally dependent on the health workers -- over- or under-hydration occur all too commonly.

Because of the limitations of IV fluid therapy, the search for an effective means of oral hydration has continued. The use of oral fluids found some role in the treatment of mild dehydration in the late 1940s and early 1950s, although routine use of an oral solution, particularly in moderately and sometimes seriously dehydrated patients with severe diarrhea, was not begun until the late 1960s. At that time oral therapy was shown to be clinically effective in treating cholera (Nalin et al.,1968). Even in the most severely ill cholera patient, up to 80 percent of IV fluid can be saved if oral therapy is used effectively (Nalin et al., 1968; Pierce et al., 1968). A series of studies followed, including field trials of oral therapy (Cash et al.) and its use in children (Nalin and Cash, 1971) and the testing of substrates other than glucose, such as glycine (Nalin et al., 1970) and sucrose (Sack et al., 1978) after recognition that glucose is necessary to aid sodium transport across the intestinal lumen (Curran, 1965). The applicability of oral therapy to diarrhea of varying etiologies has been clearly shown (Sack et al., 1978). Furthermore, it was demonstrated that patients who were moderately (and sometimes severely) dehydrated could be treated with oral therapy alone (Cash et al., 1970). Within the adverse conditions of a crowded refugee camp, the treatment proved very effective (Mahalanabis, 1973).

The World Health Organization currently recommends a formula having the following composition: sodium chloride (table salt) - 3.5 gm, sodium bicarbonate - 2.5 gm, potassium chloride - 1.5 gm, glucose - 20 gm, and water - 1.0 liter. This gives an electrolyte composition of 90 mEq/liter of sodium, 20 mEq/liter of potassium, 80 mEq/liter of chloride, 30/mEq liter of bicarbonate, and 111 mmoles/liter of glucose.

Advantages and Disadvantages

Oral therapy solution requires no special equipment and is made from inexpensive ingredients and available drinking water; it is, therefore, a low-cost intervention. It is also more likely to be readily available than IV treatment in areas far from health centers. Technical skills required for the administration of oral therapy are minimal and it is safer to use than IV fluids. However, there are certain limitations. Patients in shock or in altered states of consciousness cannot be rehydrated with oral therapy and initially require IV fluids, while some patients with moderate to severe dehydration may not be able to maintain normal hydration with ORT alone. Severe vomiting and less commonly, very high fever can compound the difficulties of oral rehydration in such patients. A few patients may have a transient glucose malabsorption that will limit absorption of the oral solution. Lastly, the actual preparation and delivery of the solution in remote areas may prove problematic.

ORT and Feeding

An integral part of any diarrhea treatment program, particularly an oral therapy program, is proper instruction on the feeding of children. Infants and children who are being breastfed should continue uninterrupted nursing. Children taking cow's milk formula should not interrupt feeding for more than six hours and thereafter may receive full strength milk (Rees and Brook, 1979), although some field programs advocate diluting such milk to half strength for the first 24 hours. Cows milk should be mixed or combined with other food and given in smaller, more frequent, individual amounts. If the child has a negative reaction to half-strength formula, milk can be withdrawn and substituted by cereals or non-milk formula, where available; such milk intolerance is uncommon. Recent studies have demonstrated that when normal levels of lactose were given to lactase-deficient children, absorption was normal and no significant diarrhea resulted (Brown et al., 1979). Milk can be well tolerated and well utilized by young lactose malabsorbers if provided in relatively low individual doses and in conjunction with additional food (Brown et al., 1980). Feeding of other foods such as cereals should continue uninterrupted and feeding should be increased during convalescence to make up for reduced nutritional intake during the course of the illness (Rohde, 1978). Whereas the appetite of the child may be reduced during diarrhea (Hoyle et al., 1980), the intestinal absorption of nutrients is only partially affected (Molla et al., 1981). These ideas may contradict long-standing folk beliefs or the beliefs of Western-oriented health practitioners.

Antibiotics are generally not recommended for the treatment of diarrhea except when the patient has clinical symptoms of an illness known to be responsive, such as shigellosis or cholera. It should be noted that even in these illnesses, fundamental principles of treatment still include replacing lost fluids and appropriate feeding.

ADDITION, SUBSTITUTION, OR ELIMINATION OF COMPONENTS OF THE ORAL THERAPY MIX

Early use of oral therapy, especially in the home, may arrest or reverse progress to the severe dehydration that leads to hospitalization or death. Some alteration of the oral rehydration solution (ORS) may be required if the program goal is to extend oral therapy beyond the hospital or clinic into the community. The following section examines the effects of several important variables to be considered in planning community-based oral rehydration activities - the amount of salt to be used, the type of sugar, and the volume of water in which these substances are dissolved.

Glucose, Sucrose, or Other Substrates

In most cases of diarrhea, ORS containing either glucose or sucrose is equivalent. However use of glucose solutions may lead to more rapid improvement and less vomiting (Nalin et al., 1978), and for more severe cases, glucose may be preferable: some evidence suggests that glucose is better absorbed and that sucrose may occasionally lead to the production of greater stool volume. (Molnginah, 1975).

In deciding on the approach to be taken in a program, a number of factors must be considered. Sucrose may be easier to obtain than glucose, especially in communities far from central production and distribution units. It would be incorrect to assume, however, that sucrose is always available. A number of countries have experienced sugar shortages which are almost certain to recur. The quantity of sucrose by weight needed to prepare ORS is twice that of glucose, since only half the sucrose molecule (the glucose fraction, and not the fructose) assists in the intraluminal absorption of sodium and water. In areas with recurrent sucrose shortages, centralized production of the mixture becomes essential. If the situation offers a choice between sucrose and glucose for such centrally produced ORS, glucose should be selected.

It should also be noted that glucose is more hydroscopic than sucrose, and must be packaged in foil. Such packaging may represent a substantial expenditure for a project. In many developing countries, however, this relative economic advantage of sucrose is diminished, since water absorption by both sugars is high in warm, humid climates. Foil packaging becomes needed to produce ORS containing sucrose if the relative humidity is greater than 85 percent (National Academy of Sciences, 1981).

Another substrate has been prepared by powdering rice and dissolving it in water. When the other electrolytes were added, the resulting solution proved effective (Molla et al., 1981), and early reports indicate that absorption may be better than that achieved with glucose alone. Amino acids, such as glycine, have also been used in place of glucose and found to be effective (Nalin et al.,). Though the addition of amino acids will add to the cost, an inexpensive protein mix might have use in an appropriate situation.

Sodium

With the exception of severe cholera in adults, the WHO recommended level of sodium is suitable for all age groups, although concern has been raised that 90 mEq/liter of sodium may be too high for infants with immature kidneys (Bart and Finberg, 1976). The concern results from reports of hypernatremia in the 1950s, when children in the United States suffering with diarrhea were given concentrated cow's milk in conjunction with ORT. Concentrated cow's milk has a high sodium content and can also produce an osmotic water loss in the large bowel. The feeding of cow's milk is uncommon in most developing countries where breastfeeding is the general practice. The sodium concentration of breast milk (2 to 3 mEq/liter) is substantially lower than that of cow's milk. If water or breast milk is given ad lib between feedings of ORS (not added to the oral therapy), the resulting amount of sodium ingested will approximate that which an infant would receive in ORS with 50 mEq of sodium per liter. Another approach, advocated to ensure the administration of sufficient free water, is a two-for-one regime: that is, two parts of ORS are given to one part of plain water. Such a formulation complicates treatment and giving breast milk or ad lib water in between ORS intake seems much more consistent with a simplified treatment regimen.

In a study comparing ORS with either 50 or 90 mEq/liter of sodium, a number of infants in the low-sodium group developed asymptomatic hyponatremia; conversely a small number in the high sodium group experienced mild asymptomatic hypernatremia (Nalin et al., 1980). In an earlier study in India, ORS administration with both normal (90 mEq/liter) and low (50 mEq/liter) sodium concentrations proved to be effective (Chatterjee, 1978) and in a field trial in Bangladesh involving more than 5,000 patients, no clinical cases of hypernatremia could be attributed to oral therapy containing 90 mEq/liter of sodium (Snyder, 1981). It appears to be an uncommon occurrence, having little effect on large-scale programs.

From a programmatic point of view, it is much easier to recommend one formula rather than multiple formulas. The difficulties inherent in producing and distributing even one type of packet and in training clients to use the formulation correctly can only increase with the introduction of different packets designed for particular age-groups. The need for program simplicity dictates the need for a single approach.

Potassium

Diarrhea leads to substantial potassium losses. As diarrhea increases in volume, the concentration of potassium per milliliter of fecal matter diminishes but the overall deficit increases. When potassium is not included in the ORS, hypokalemia may occur. In a recent study in Honduras, a simple sugar-salt solution corrected dehydration, but hypokalemia persisted in a number of cases, albeit without clinical symptoms (Clements et al., 1980). Such hypokalemia appears to be particularly problematic in more severe cases of diarrhea (Islam et al., 1980). Dietary sources of potassium include bananas, coconut water, and citrus fruit juice. While bananas are among the richest sources, containing 100 mEq/Kg of potassium (U.S. Department of Agriculture, 1975), a large number would nonetheless have to be consumed to correct potassium deficits. Breast milk also contains potassium but at the relatively low concentration of 13 mEq/liter. The loss of potassium in large amounts can lead to the recognizable signs of hypokalemia, such as muscle flaccidity, decreased bowel tone, and possible cardiac arrhythmias, although clinical signs of acute potassium deficiency have not been noted in the field among children with diarrhea receiving sugar and salt solution. In fact the effects of a chronic subclinical hypokalemia are unknown.

Given current gaps in knowledge regarding the importance of potassium replacement in diarrhea, projects with ready access to packets of complete ORT formula should elect to use them. The feeding of potassium-rich foods and potassium-containing indigenous sugar should be urged in other cases.

Bicarbonate

Bicarbonate replacement may not be necessary in mild to moderate cases of diarrhea. In recent studies in Bangladesh, however, it was shown that when fluid loss exceeded 50 ml/kg, acidosis was only slowly corrected by renal or respiratory mechanisms (Islam et al., 1980). The consequences of prolonged acidosis are not well defined. Acidosis may mask hypokalemia, and true potassium deficiency may not be noted in patients deficient in bicarbonate who are treated with ORT.

Water

It has been suggested that water used in the preparation of oral therapy be pathogen-free, implying that the water should be boiled or collected from an uncontaminated source. The approach may cause difficulties in the field, since in many areas the additional fuel needed to heat water for ORS is not readily available. In addition, the cultural context of food preparation and the boiling of water may have different significance depending on where the project is being implemented. Concepts such as "hot" and "cold" applied to food must be understood and adapted to the local teaching of ORS preparation (Wellin, 1955). Potable water, such as that from a tube well, is often not available, or its taste or quality may be unacceptable.

In designing an oral rehydration program, one must examine the evidence concerning the use of unboiled or mildly contaminated water. Current data regarding the effect of glucose or sucrose on the multiplication of organisms in contaminated water are contradictory. Laboratory studies have suggested that significant growth of fecal coliform organisms occurs in oral therapy solution prepared from naturally contaminated water (Shields et al., 1981), but this has not been a universal finding (World Health Organization, 1980). These studies, however, may not duplicate all field conditions. In the Gambia, patients with diarrhea had no increase in duration of illness if ORS was made with contaminated rather than sterile water (Watkinson et al., 1980). It was estimated that excess *Escherichia coli* in the solution represented no more than 5 percent of the *E. coli* commonly ingested in food. Data are lacking as to the effect of enteric pathogens ingested by an individual already experiencing diarrhea caused by another pathogen.

The overall recommendation by WHO is that ORS be made with ordinary drinking water, and that prepared solution not be kept more than 24 hours. Given the lack of data to the contrary and difficulties inherent in attempting to boil water, there is no reason to alter the WHO recommendation at this time.

Containers and Volumes

The volume of ORS prepared may determine use patterns and product safety. The smaller the volume prepared, the more likely it will be used within a short period of time with less chance for bacterial growth. However, making up smaller packets will increase project expense, since packaging constitutes a significant cost of production. Smaller packets may also create the impression that only a small volume is required to treat diarrhea.

In order to produce a safe electrolyte concentration, a standardized ORT packet requires a standardized volume of water in which it will be dissolved. In much of the world a standardized measure is not available, but if there is such a measure (for example, a beer bottle), packets should be adapted to it. A standardized container can also be produced and sold commercially, though this would increase the initial cost of the oral rehydration program. The salt and sugar crystals can be put into a plastic container that expands to the appropriate volume, or premixed and sold as the fluid. Where such approaches are not feasible technically or economically, house-to-house visits to mark local containers at a set volume can also achieve standardization. A method to achieve a standard measurement of water is essential if the program is to be extended beyond health centers and into the community.

FORM IN WHICH SALTS ARE DELIVERED

Table 7:1 summarizes the advantages and disadvantages of different methods of delivering ORT.

Packets

Production of packets at some central facility has the major advantage of providing a complete standardized formula. The use of glucose as substrate is more feasible in this situation than in programs that stress home preparation from market ingredients. A packet can be designed so that it is easily recognized by the community; advertising campaigns can use the recognition factor to sensitize the community to the use of ORS. When the commercial sector is part of a country-wide program, packet recognition becomes essential. The disadvantages inherent in using prepared packets are equally clear. Prepackaging increases the cost of ORS and packets subsequently need to be distributed. The primary care systems in many countries may experience difficulties in the distribution of commodities. If packets are prepared at the periphery, such as in the clinic, some of the distribution problems may be decreased, although the need for quality control in the weighing and mixing of ingredients will remain paramount.

Table 7:1. Advantages and Disadvantages of the Different Methods of Delivering ORT Ingredients to the Community[1]

PLAN	ADVANTAGES	DISADVANTAGES[2]	SITUATION
Prepackaged ORT using formula recommended by WHO	- Standardized - Highly visible and identifiable. - Effective for severe, moderate, and mild diarrhea.	- More expensive. - Ingredients (pre-mixed packets) may not be available at the central depot.	Effective for a health delivery system that can reach the bulk of the population, and can provide training in mixing and usage for each client.
Prepackaged ORT using formula recommended by WHO but substituting sucrose for glucose	- Sucrose may be more readily available	- Less effective for severe diarrhea. - May be more vomiting. - Ineffective if sucrose intolerance develops.	Effective for a health system that can reach the bulk of the population.
WHO formula mixed at local clinic or depot (spoon set).	- No dependence on central facilities. - No packaging costs.	- Increased risk of error. - Storage of ingredients may be a problem.	Effective for a system of urban and rural clinics with outreach to patients

[1] Adapted from Management of the Diarrheal Diseases at the Community Level. Committee on International Nutrition Programs, National Academy of Sciences, Washington, 1981.

[2] For home-based use all methods require a standard container or standardization of a container in the home, individual instruction, and frequent follow-up. In all methods requiring the client to mix the solution at home, individual instruction in measurement is necessary.

Table 7:1. (Cont.): Advantages and Disadvantages of the Different Methods of Delivering ORT Ingredients to the Community

PLAN	ADVANTAGES	DISADVANTAGES	SITUATION
Home mixing using salt/sugar formula; double-spoon method	- Reduced costs. - Direct participation of community and family. - Less dependence on health system. - May permit earlier institution of treatment at home.	- May or may not be as effective as WHO formula. - Measurement of ingredients varies. - Requires individual instruction of users.	Can be effective where majority has no access to an organized health service but where there is strong community involvement in health.
Home mixing using salt/sugar formula; pinch and scoop method.	- Requires no packets, spoons, or devices. - Minimum investment. - Encourages self-reliance.	- May not be as effective as WHO formula. - Requires individual instruction of users. - Measurement of ingredients is more variable.	Can be effective where provision of measuring spoon is not practical.
Any distribution scheme using formula with lower sodium content (e.g., 60 mEq/liter).	- Decreases risk of hypernatremia.	- Risk of hyponatremia. - Less effective in severe diarrhea caused by V cholerae or E coli.	Can be effective where supervision and surveillance is impossible.

Spoons

Plastic spoons have been developed to measure an exact quantity of each of the ingredients needed to prepare a fixed volume of ORT. Most projects that supply spoons for use in home preparation of ORT do so only for the sugar and salt. A program based on production of ORS in health posts can provide four spoons to mix a complete formula. If multiple spoons are used, all ingredients must be available in the health post and spoons should be color-coded to correspond to the color of the particular salt or sugar container. The cost of packaging is thus eliminated, but the population remains dependent upon distribution of preweighed salts through the health centers.

A simpler modification is based upon use of a spoon that measures only sucrose and salt. Such spoons have been calibrated for mixing with 200 or 1000 ml of water and have been used extensively in Indonesia. Advantages of the spoon method include the fact that spoons can be designed to be identified with the use of ORS, require only a one-time distribution, and do away with the need for prepackaging ingredients. Limitations are that the spoons may be lost, that spoons designed for home use produce an incomplete formula lacking bicarbonate and potassium, and that the volume of salt and sugar varies depending on the degree to which the spoon is filled. As in all programs, clients must still be taught methods of measuring the required water correctly.

Pinch and Scoop

An individual can be taught how to prepare the ORS using her hand to measure the correct amount of salt and sugar (sucrose). A four-finger scoop of sugar and a two-finger pinch of salt are added to 200 ml of water. This method obviates the use of implements, and once taught, an individual is far less dependent on the health delivery system. Disadvantages are similar to those of the spoon, in that the amounts of ingredients used often vary, the salt and sugar formula prepared is incomplete, and a method of measuring a standardized volume of water must be available to the population. As indicated, reports on the use of this method and other village-based measuring techniques have indicated wide variability in the electrolyte composition. Solutions have been prepared containing high sodium levels above 120 mEq/liter. (Levine et al., 1980; Harland et al., 1981). Recent studies from Bangladesh demonstrate that the variability of sodium levels in the pinch-and-scoop method (Cutting and Ellerbrook, 1981; Bangladesh Rural Advancement Committee, 1979) or other home-based preparations (Chen et al., 1980) can be minimized with well-designed intensive personal instruction. (Bangladesh Rural Advancement Committee, 1979). In addition, if the method is designed to produce a sodium concentration of 60 mEq/liter, the chance that a client may prepare a mixture having a sodium concentration above 120 mEq/liter are considerably lowered, as shown in one pinch-and-scoop program (Bangladesh Rural Advancement Committee, 1979).

FACTORS TO CONSIDER IN DEVELOPING A DIARRHEA CONTROL PROGRAM

Keys to the reduction of mortality and morbidity from diarrhea are accessibility to an effective ORS program and its appropriate use in the home. Studies in Bangladesh (Rahaman et al., 1979), India (Kielman and McCord, 1977), and Egypt (Ministry of Health, Egypt, 1981) have suggested that a reduction in diarrhea-related mortality of up to 50 percent may be achievable when the public has complete access and makes full use of ORT. Whether the effect can be sustained, or achieved in other programs, will await further observations. Early use of ORS may also lead to a reduction in malnutrition (Republic of the Philippines et al., 1977) if coupled with education regarding appropriate feeding both during and after the diarrheal episode.

Increasing the accessibility of ORS will require the selection of a method of preparing ORS, and result in some of the trade-offs discussed earlier. Selection of an oral rehydration program design will also depend on health sector and nonhealth sector variables. Health sector factors might include the location and accessibility of clinics and the availability, training, and attitudes of health personnel. The attitudes and practices of private physicians, pharmacists, and traditional healers should be considered in addition to those of government health workers. If the population has limited access to official health providers, a community-based program might be developed using volunteer workers to distribute packets or to teach mothers the pinch-and-scoop method.

Factors outside the health system that might influence both access to health services and the selection of a distribution strategy include:

- the role of women in society;
- the educational level of different groups in the population;
- the physical infrastructure of a country, including roads;
- the methods of communication and the degree to which mass media reach the population; and
- the income distribution and purchasing power of the urban and rural poor.

Lessons learned elsewhere can be adopted; experiences from a number of diarrhea programs emphasizing ORS have recently been reviewed (ORT for childhood diarrhea, 1980).

As health sector limitations are frequently raised, the following section will concentrate on examining those factors outside the health system that might shape an oral rehydration program.

Physical Infrastructure and Population Density

Distribution of the population and the physical infrastructure of roads, railroads, and waterways will determine the accessibility of both clinics and supplies. Denser, urban populations are easier to serve than those in rural areas. In some areas of the world, especially those countries in Saharan and sub-Saharan Africa, populations are widely dispersed and roads are few and often impassible for part of the year. Providing health services to these populations, supervising community-based workers, and distributing supplies is difficult and costly. More than 50 percent of the cost of providing primary health care in these rural settings may be spent on transport. If for no other reason than the isolation, keeping health personnel in these environments is difficult. In such a setting, two conflicting pressures must be considered prior to service implementation. Difficulties in transportation and the lack of storage sites for packages may encourage a pinch-and-scoop oral rehydration program. On the other hand, the use of pinch-and-scoop techniques requires more intensive client training than does the use of packets, consequently requiring greater input from training personnel.

In contrast, in a country such as Egypt, 99 percent of the population lives on 3.5 percent of the land, and over 90 percent of the population is within 4 km of some type of government health facility. Providing supplies and personnel is potentially easier in this environment, and the continuous provision of prepared packets presents less of a problem.

Mass Communication

Availability of mass media will enhance a society's ability to disseminate information regarding proper therapy. Statistics on the number of radios and televisions, and circulation rates of newspapers may nonetheless be misleading. Whereas mass media may stimulate the population to seek oral therapy, direct instruction of the mother by a trained worker is necessary to teach appropriate preparation and use. To the extent that programs such as those in Bangladesh (Bangladesh Rural Advancement Committee, 1979; Chen et al., 1980; Rahaman et al., 1979) or Egypt (Ministry of Health, Egypt, 1981) are successful, credit must be given to the quality of individual instruction - not to mass media campaigns which may only serve to sensitize the population.

Income Levels

Background knowledge regarding clients' ability to pay for services is of critical importance in setting up an oral rehydration program. Health providers may need to be subsidized if they are to distribute ORS free of charge, or a new cadre of workers may need to be developed. In some countries, the client population may be able to afford a small fee and thus help to pay for the program.

In some countries, ORT supplies may be available via private pharmacies and small shops, where fees will be solicited. The degree to which clients can be encouraged to avail themselves of such sources will also depend on their ability to pay.

Women's Role

Consideration of the role of women is crucial in implementing a diarrhea control program. Their role includes responsibility for feeding practices and the provision of treatment, as well as the decision to seek health care. If women are confined to their home or compound, it may be difficult to educate them about diarrhea treatment or encourage the early transport of children to a health facility. A program has been developed by the Bangladesh Rural Advancement Committee (BRAC), which deals with a female population that is largely illiterate and not very mobile (Bangladesh Rural Advancement Committee, 1979). Oral replacement workers (ORWs), women 20 to 50 years of age who can read and write Bengali, go house to house in their program area, teaching one woman in each household how to prepare and use oral therapy. The ORW gives the woman 10 points to remember (Appendix A) and shows the woman how to measure sugar and salt using the pinch-and-scoop method. The worker also accurately marks a home container to indicate the correct water volume. Visits last 20 to 30 minutes. Follow-up visits three to four weeks later have indicated that 98 percent of village women remember seven or more points. Samples of 996 ORS mixes from 1,079 randomly selected households showed a mean sodium concentration of 47 mEq/liter with only 0.4 percent above 120 mEq/liter (expected sodium concentration was 66 mEq/liter).

Women who participate in the marketplace as they do in Indonesia are more accessible (Rohde et al., 1979). As many Indonesian women are involved in the commercial sector, they have a greater awareness of weights and measures - important skills in preparing ORS at home.

The worth assigned to women in a given society may determine the level of illness necessary for the family to seek outside assistance for a female child. There is evidence that in societies where male children are more highly valued, males are brought to health facilities more frequently than females (Chen et al., 1981). This is further reflected in differential mortality rates. A home-based program, by decreasing the need for clinic visits, may help reduce the mortality differentials.

Education

The educational level of the population, particularly women, will determine the type of training and the sophistication of health messages which can be delivered by the program. In addition, literacy levels generally reflect the degree of development of a society as a whole. Schoolchildren may serve as a good entry point for the introduction of health ideas to the family; for example, introducing ideas of oral rehydration therapy into primary school curriculum has been used effectively in Indonesia (Rohde and Sadjimin, 1980) and Bangladesh (Abed, 1981).

Political Commitment

The support of governmental and professional groups is needed for community-based programs, especially if the ORT technology is to be placed in the hands of nonhealth professionals. Political commitment to primary care is an important first step in the process, but governments must also recognize the need to extend training and awareness beyond the medical profession to pharmacists, community workers, and the general population. It is often physicians who represent the major resistance to the extension of services to the community.

COMMUNITY-BASED PROGRAMS -- THE RATIONALE

The previous sections have reviewed the rationale for oral therapy, the value of each of the components of the formula, and the various ways that ORS can be delivered to the population. Additionally, some of the factors outside the health sector that bear on the implementation of oral therapy programs were examined. The rationale for providing ORS via community-based programs merits further comment.

Diarrhea therapy is most effective when it is begun early in the course of illness. Communities or individuals having limited access to medical care providers may benefit the most from community-based programs. In many countries of the developing world, clinics are passive in their response to illness in the community: that is, they wait for patients to come to them. As already discussed, problems of transportation, cost and the limited social mobility of women inhibit clinic use. Even if the patient arrives, however, clinic workers cannot be assumed to have the training and technology to deal effectively with the problem. Clearly, any program that delivers services to the community will provide greater access to care. Such a program, moreover, need not depend on a system of packet distribution. A community-based oral rehydration therapy program might rely on the distribution of spoons, or home-based instruction regarding the pinch-and-scoop method. It must be stressed, however, that repeated surveillance and client follow-up are essential in any home-based program.

In order to ensure the success of a community-based diarrhea control program, there is no substitute for direct and prolonged contact between the teacher/provider and the student/recipient. Instructions on how to prepare and use ORS and how to feed the child with diarrhea, cannot be given through indirect messages or large group discussions. The family planning commodity distributor must understand that ORS packets are not just a commodity that is put in the recipients' hands, but rather that a direct and frequent involvement of worker and consumer is essential. The distribution of products may be relatively easy compared to the repetition of instructions on a house-to-house basis necessary to ensure proper usage. The path of least resistance may lead to distribution without instruction, rendering the program meaningless and potentially harmful. Direct contact is also needed to provide the community worker with knowledge of why a particular program succeeded or failed. The message of oral rehydration therapy - or any other health intervention - must be consistent with the reality of the situation in which care will be provided. The extent of the problem, availability of resources, and educational and cultural factors and beliefs must all be considered (Hendrata and Rohde, 1981).

If ORS is to be tied to a family planning program, the population must understand why such a tie exists. It must be made clear to the recipients what one activity has to do with another. If ORS is misunderstood by the consumer as being another form of birth control, deleterious consequences can result. Careful client education is essential if the role of each intervention is to be understood.

SUMMARY AND CONCLUSIONS

Oral rehydration therapy is an effective means of treating dehydration associated with diarrhea. It is inexpensive, easy to prepare and use, accessible, and relatively safe. If combined with correct dietary practices such as continued feeding (especially breastfeeding) during diarrhea and a compensatory increase in nutritional intake following recovery, the child's nutritional state will be relatively unaffected by diarrhea. The ORS formula recommended by WHO is the best single formula currently available for all age-groups. Various components can be changed (sucrose for glucose) or eliminated (bicarbonate or potassium), but this may lead to diminished effectiveness.

ORS can be packaged or delivered to the health sector or community in a number of ways. The method of delivery will be determined by two major factors: (1) the health sector, including such variables as the availability and knowledge of health personnel, the cost of treatment, and the degree of health service integration; and (2) the nonhealth sector where crucial factors include the role of women, the educational level of the society, the physical infrastructure and population distribution, levels of income and purchasing power, and political commitment to community-based programs. Each society has a different combination of the above and will have to adapt an oral rehydration program to its own resources. There will always be trade-offs among safety, effectiveness, and the accessibility of ORS. It is crucial that lessons gained from hospital, clinic, and field experiences be examined for those elements that are useable in other programs.

Successful delivery of ORS in community-based distribution family planning programs will depend upon a healthy recipient perception of the linkage between the different services, and the provision of quality training and supervision of the community worker to ensure correct instruction of others in the use of the product.

Appendix 7:A. Message Given to Mothers by Oral Therapy Workers of BRAC[1]

TEN POINTS TO REMEMBER

1. DIARRHEA - more than one watery stool in a day.

2. TRANSMISSION - occurs when the feces of an infected person or carrier enters someone else's mouth.

3. TREATMENT - of diarrhea is oral replacement mixture, fluid, and food.

4. ORAL REPLACEMENT MIXTURE _ is a mixture of sugar and salt in water. Lobon-gur[2] mixture is one kind of oral replacement mixture.

5. LOBON-GUR MIXTURE - is made by mixing a three-finger pinch of salt (up to first crease of index finger) to 2 four-finger scoops of gur in one-half seer[3] of tube-well or boiled water and stirring.

6. BEGIN giving lobon-gur mixture after the first watery stool.

7. AMOUNT of lobon-gur mixture for children should equal the amount of water in the stools. If the mother does not know, let the child have as much as desired.
   For adults, give one-half seer for each stool.

8. DANGER of lobon-gur mixture when:
   1. TOO MUCH SALT is added to mixture.
   2. SMALL, FREQUENT FEEDINGS are not given to infants and small children.

9. A DOCTOR should be consulted when:
   1. Diarrhea lasts more than two days.
   2. The patient cannot take fluid by mouth.
   3. The patient has severe diarrhea and cannot replace the water lost in his or her stools with lobon-gur mixture.

10. NUTRITIONAL ADVICE for patients with diarrhea includes the following:
    1. DURING diarrhea the patient should continue to take food and fluid.
    2. AFTER diarrhea the patient should take more than normal amount of food and fluid for seven days.

---

[1] Adapted from Bangladesh Rural Advancement Committee (BRAC) Oral Therapy Program, Dacca, Bangladesh. September 1979.

[2] Lobon is salt and gur is unrefined sugar.

[3] One-half seer is equivalent to 500 cc.

REFERENCES

Abed, F. H., 1981, personal communication.

Bangladesh Rural Advancement Committee (BRAC), Oral Therapy Program. Mohakhali C/A, Dacca, Bangladesh. September 1979.

Bart, K. J. and Finberg, L. "Single solution for oral therapy of diarrhea." (Letter) Lancet (7986):633-634, 1976.

Brown, K. H., Parry, L., Khatum, M. D., and Ahmed, G. "Lactose malabsorption in Bangladeshi village children: relation with age, history of recent diarrhea, nutritional status and breast feeding." American Journal of Clinical Nutrition 32:648, 1979.

Brown, K.H., Khatun, M., Parry, L., Ahmed, M.G. "Nutritional consequences of low-dose milk supplements consumed by lactose-malabsorbing children." The American Journal of Clinical Nutrition, 33: May 1980, pp. 1054-1063.

Cash, R. A. "Oral therapy for diarrhoea." Tropical Doctor 9: 25-30 1979.

Cash, R. A., Nalin, D. R., Rochat, R., Reller, L. B., Hague, Z. A., and Rahman, A. S. M. M. "A clinical trial of oral therapy in a rural cholera-treatment clinic." American Journal of Tropical Medicine and Hygiene 19 (4):653-656, 1970.

Cash, R. A., Nalin, D. R., Forrest, J. N., and Abrutyn, E. "Rapid corrections of acidosis and dehydration of cholera with oral glucose and electrolyte solution." Lancet 2 (7672): 549:550, 1970.

Chatterjee, A., Mahalanabis, D., Jalan, K. N., Matra, T. K., Agarwal, S. K., Dutta, B., Khatua, S. P., and Bagclu, D. K. "Oral rehydration in infantile diarrhea: controlled trial of a low sodium glucose electrolyte solution." Archives of Diseases in Childhood 53 (4):284-289, 1978.

Chen, L. C., Black, R. E., Sarder, A. M., Merson, M. H., Bhatia, S., Yunus, M., and Chakraborty, J. "Village-based distribution of oral rehydration therapy in Bangladesh." American Journal of Tropical Medicine and Hygiene 29 (2):285-290, 1980.

Chen, L. C., Huq, E., and D'Souza, S. "Sex bias in the family allocation of food and health care in rural Bangladesh." Population and Development Review 7 (1):55-70, 1981.

Clements, M. L., Levine, M. M., Black, R. E., Hughes, T. P., Rust, J. and Tome, F. C. "Potassium supplements for oral diarrhoea regimens." (Letter) Lancet 2 (8199):854, 1980.

Curran, P. F. "Ion transport in the intestine and its coupling to other transport processes." Federation Proceedings 24 (4) Part 1:993-999, 1965.

Cutting, W. A. M., and Ellerbrook, T. V. "Homemade oral solutions for diarrhea (Letter)." Lancet (1), 998, 1981.

Harland, P. S. E. G., Cox, D. L., Lyew, M., and Luido, F. "Composition of oral solutions prepared by Jamaican mothers for treatment of diarrhea." Lancet 600:601. March 14, 1981.

Hendrata, L. and Rohde, J. "Oral Rehydration: Where do we go from here?" Advances in International Maternal Child Health, D. B. Jelliffe, ed., Oxford University Press, London, 1981.

Hirschhorn, N. "The treatment of acute diarrhea in children: an historical perspective." American Journal of Clinical Nutrition 33 (3):637-663, 1980.

Hoyle, B., Yunus, M., and Chen, L. C. "Breast feeding and food intake among children with acute diarrheal disease. American Journal of Clinical Nutrition 33:2365-2371, 1980.

Islam, M. R., Greenough, W. B. 3rd, Rahaman, M. M., Choudhury, A. K. A., and Sack, D. A. "Lobon-gur (common salt and brown sugar) oral rehydration solution in the diarrhoea of adults." Dacca, Bangladesh, International Centre for Diarrhoeal Disease Research, Bangladesh (ICCDR,B). Scientific Report No. 36:17, 1980.

Kielmann, A. A., and McCord, C. "Home treatment of childhood diarrhea in Punjab villages." Environmental Child Health 23 (4):197-201, 1977.

Levine, M. M., Hughes, T. P., Black, R. E., Clements, M. L., Matheny, S., Siegel, A., Cleaves, F., Gutierrez, C., Foote, D. P., and Smith, W. A. "Variability of sodium and sucrose levels of simple sugar/salt oral rehydration solutions prepared under optimal and field conditions." Journal of Pediatrics 97 (2):324-327, 1980.

Mahalanabis, D., Choudhuri, A. B., Bagchi, N. G., Bhattacharya, A. K., and Simpson, T. W. "Oral fluid therapy for cholera among Bangladesh refugees." Johns Hopkins Medical Journal 32 (4):197-205, 1973.

Ministry of Health, Arab Republic of Egypt, "Diarrheal Disease Control Study, Final Report on Phase 1, SRHD Project," Rural Health Department to USAID and WHO (EMRO), April 1981.

Molla, M., Molla, A. M., Rahim, A., Sarker, S. A., Khatoon, M., and Rahman, M. "Effects of diarrhea on absorption of macronutrients during acute stage and after recovery." Workshop on interactions of Diarrhea and Malnutrition: Pathophysiology, Epidemiology, and Interventions. Bellagio, Italy, May 11-15, 1981.

Molnginah, Suprapto, P.A., Soenarto, J., Bachtin, M., Sutrisno Sutaryo, D., Rohde, J.E. Letter, Lancet, August 1975, p. 323.

Nalin, D. R., Cash, R. A., Islam, R., Molla, M. and Phillips, R. A. "Oral maintenance therapy for cholera in adults." Lancet 2 (7564):370-373, 1968.

Nalin, D. R., and Cash, R. A. "Oral or nasogastric maintenance therapy in pediatric cholera patients." Journal of Pediatrics 78 (2):355-358, 1971.

Nalin, D. R., Cash, R. A., Rahman, M., and Yunus, M. "Effect of glycine and glucose on sodium and water absorption in patients with cholera." Gut 11:768-772, 1970.

Nalin, D.R., Mata, L., Vargos, W. Lorie, A.R., Levine, M.M., De Lespedes, C., Lizano, L., Simson, A. "Comparison of Sucrose and Glucose in Oral Therapy of Infant Diarrhea." The Lancet, 8084:277-279, 1978.

Nalin, D. R., Harland, E., Ramlal, A., Swaby, D., McDonald, J., Gangarosa, R., Levine, M., Akierman, A., Antoine, M., MacKenzie, K., and Johnson, B. "Comparison of low and high sodium and potassium content in oral rehydration solutions." Journal of Pediatrics 97 (5):848-853, 1980.

National Academy of Sciences, Management of the Diarrheal Diseases at the Community Level. Committee on International Nutrition Programs, Washington, 1981.

"Oral rehydration therapy (ORT) for childhood diarrhea." Population Reports, Series L(2), November-December, 1980.

Pierce, N. F., Barwell, J. G., Mitra, R. C., Caranasos, G. J., Keirnowitz, R. I., Mondal, A., and Maryi, P. M. "Effect of intragastric glucose-electrolyte perfusion upon water and electrolyte balance in Asiatic cholera." Gastroenterology 55 (3):333-343, 1968.

Rahaman, M. M., Aziz, K. M. S., Patwai, Y., and Munshi, M. H. "Diarrhoeal mortality in two Bangladeshi villages with and without community-based oral rehydration therapy." Lancet 2 (8147):809-812, 1979.

Rees, L., Brook, C. G. D. "Gradual reintroduction of full-strength milk after acute gastroenteritis in children." Lancet:770-771, 1979.

Republic of the Philippines, World Health Organization, John Snow Public Health Group, and International Study Group. "A positive effect on the nutrition of Philippine children of an oral glucose-electrolyte solution given at home for the treatment of diarrhoea: report of a field trial." Bulletin of the World Health Organization 55 (1):87-94, 1977.

Rohde, J.E. "Preparing for the next round: convalescent care after acute infection." American Journal of Clinical Nutrition, 31(12):2258-2268, December, 1978.

Rohde, J. E., Ismail, D., Sadjimin, T., Suyadi, A., and Tugerin. "Training course for village nutrition programs." Tropical Pediatrics and Environmental Child Health 25 (4):83-96, 1979.

Rohde, J. E., and Sadjimin, T. "Elementary school pupils as health educators: role of school health programmes in primary health care." Lancet 7 (8182):1350-1352, 1980.

Sack, D. A., Islam, S., Brown, K. H., Islam, A., Kabir, A. K. M. I., Chowdhury, A. M. A. K., and Ali, M. A. "Oral therapy in children with cholera: a comparison of sucrose and glucose electrolyte solutions." Journal of Pediatrics 96 (1):20-25, 1980.

Sack, D. A., Chowdhury, A. M. A. K., Eusof, A., Ali, M. A., Merson, M. H., Islam, S., Black, R. E., and Brown, K. H. "Oral hydration in rotavirus diarrhoea: a double blind comparison of sucrose with glucose electrolyte solution." Lancet 2 (8084):280-283, 1978.

Shields, D. S., Shields, M. N., Guerrant, R. L., Araiyo, J. G., Brown, S. E., de Sousa, M. A., and Hook, E. W. "Electrolyte/glucose concentration and bacterial contamination in home-prepared oral rehydration: a field experience in Northeastern Brazil." Journal of Pediatrics, 1981 (in press).

Snyder, J., 1981, personal communication.

U.S. Department of Agriculture, Nutritive Values of American Food in Common Units, Agriculture Handbook No. 456, Washington, D.C., 1975, p. 16.

Watkinson, M. Lloyd-Evans, N., Watkinson, A. "The use of oral glucose electrolyte solution prepared with untreated well water in acute non- specific childhood diarrhea." Transactions of the Royal Society of Tropical Medicine and Hygiene 74:657-662, 1980.

Wellin, E. "Water boiling in a Peruvian town." In: Health, Culture and Community. Benjamin Paul (ed.) Russell Sage Foundation, New York, 1955.

World Health Organization (WHO). Diarrheal Disease Control Program: "A Manual for the Treatment of Acute Diarrhea." Geneva. 1980.

World Health Organization. "Clinical Management of Acute Diarrhea." Report of a Scientific Working Group New Delhi: WHO, (DDC/79.3), October-November 1980.

8
Oral Rehydration Therapy: Implementation Issues in Community-Based Distribution Programs

Maria J. Wawer

Diarrhea, interacting with malnutrition, represents one of the most important causes of death in children in less developed countries. As many as 10 percent of all children may die before age five from the effects of this condition, including acute dehydration (Parker, 1980). Oral rehydration therapy (ORT) has been documented to be a useful intervention for cases of diarrheal dehydration of viral, choleral and other bacterial etiology (Kielmann, 1977; Nalin and Hirschhorn, 1979; Nalin et al., 1979). Literature reviewing the physiological actions of ORT and the results of clinical and field trials is abundant (Cash, 1979; Bradley et al., 1978; Pierce and Hirschhorn, 1977; Finberg et al., 1979).

ORT fulfills at least two important criteria for selection in community-based distribution (CBD) projects: the condition it addresses is potentially serious, and the intervention is effective. There are a number of important steps in the planning and implementation of the intervention, in order to ensure that it is successful in decreasing childhood morbidity and mortality, and in acquiring community acceptance. Care must also be exercised to ensure that the service does not overextend project manpower.

PROGRAM PLANNING

Information is needed about the extent of the diarrheal problem in the project area, particularly its socioeconomic distribution and seasonal variation. Such data can assist in selecting the appropriate target group in order to maximize the effect of worker efforts. The information need not necessarily be gathered *de novo*, since incidence and prevalence can be based on existing national or regional data. Seasonal variations are of particular importance for two reasons: stocks have to be adequate to meet peak demands, and both workers and mothers should be taught ORT preparation at a time when they have a chance to practice their roles repeatedly. If several months elapse between the time mothers are taught ORT preparation and the beginning of the diarrhea season, they may forget important points and may require retraining.

The target group's perception of diarrhea as a problem, and cultural practices related to its treatment (including dietary practices), must be determined. For example, the seriousness of diarrhea might not be fully comprehended by the community. It has been estimated that children in less developed countries (LDCs) may average three to five or more episodes of diarrhea per year, but that as few as 1 percent of episodes lead to severe life-threatening dehydration (Parker, 1980; Black et al., 1979). Since a mother may see anywhere from 15 to 25 cases of diarrhea in each of her children before the age of five, will she make the connection between the death of a child with diarrhea and the frequent episodes of diarrhea, most of which appear fairly benign? It is also important to know the measures mothers take when confronted with a case of diarrhea in their children. This information is necessary prior to formulating the ORT training segment for CBD workers, since workers will need to know how to deal with local customs and beliefs.

Along with client perceptions, it is important to determine the local dispensing patterns of diarrhea medication by pharmacies, private doctors, and other health personnel. Negative rumors associated with ORT in the Egyptian Menoufia project arose partly out of efforts by pharmacists to discredit the treatment; they feared a loss in income with the diminished sale of antibiotics for diarrheal illness (McCord, 1980). Ideally, health personnel should be included in the program to lend support to the ORT activities.

Selecting an appropriate type of manpower to implement ORT does not appear to present a problem, in that most CBD workers, including illiterate or semi-illiterate individuals, can be trained to make ORT solution and to teach its preparation to other mothers (Wessley, 1981; Vella, 1981; Bangladesh Rural Advancement Committee, 1979). Problems can arise, however, if the field personnel selected are not acceptable to the community. It has been suggested that one of the difficulties experienced in the Menoufia project resulted from the use of high school graduates as distributors: they were perceived as young and inexperienced by married village women (Tekce, this volume).

Teaching the preparation of ORT often requires lengthy, intensive one-to-one training, first for the worker, and later for the client. The Sudan Community-Based Health Project devotes approximately one week to train both literate and illiterate midwives home preparation and distribution of prepackaged UNICEF rehydration salts (Oralyte). Training is intensive, including field practice in the preparation and administration of the solution to dehydrated infants (El Tom, this volume). Two or three months after training, the midwives have been found to prepare the mixture appropriately. Indirect supervision has indicated that village women taught by the midwives, over a span of several visits, also measure a liter and mix the solution correctly (Wessley, 1981).

The length of time necessary for adequate worker training has to be tailored to the workers' needs and their educational level. There are currently no concrete data on an optimal length of training. Training should be competency based and continue until workers prepare, explain, and supervise client preparation of ORT adequately and have demonstrated these abilities in field tests.

As indicated by Cash (this volume) training for clients has to be accomplished on a one-to-one basis, with careful observation to determine whether the woman understands, and is able to repeat, key points.

Repeat visits are important to ensure that clients have learned and remember correct preparation and usage. Clements reports that four months after instruction, four of five Sudanese women incorrectly prepared the solution because they could not remember the six-tea-cup technique for measuring water (Clements, 1980). The Egyptian SRHD project found that after three home visits, 74 percent of women selected the correct size of spoon for sugar/salt solution preparation. Ninety-six percent selected spoon size correctly after nine visits. In early visits in the SRHD program, women receiving prepackaged Oralyte tended to prepare concentrations exceeding the WHO recommended level of 90 mEq/liter of sodium, although the levels were generally not dangerously high. An opposite trend was seen in the preparation of sugar-salt solution, with the production of hypotonic solutions, (between 20 and 60 mEq/liter) in approximately 70 percent of households (Mobarak, 1981). The need for multiple contacts with clients to minimize variations in ORT preparation has also been noted in the Dacca Concerned Women's Project (Curlin, 1981).

In planning adequate supervision for an ORT program, planners and trainers are advised to consider both direct and indirect supervision. In the first supervisory model, the supervisor observes the activity performed by the CBD fieldworker: does he or she prepare the mixture correctly, explain it to the client, and have her repeat the process and instructions regarding its use? If ORT training is carried out in groups, does the CBD worker check each woman's knowledge and ability?

Indirect supervision implies visits to the client's home after the CBD worker has completed his or her visit, in order to ensure that the worker's message was adequately transmitted and remembered by the client. Can women duplicate correct preparation and usage several weeks or months later, as well as immediately following the CBD contact? Although data to determine an optimal frequency for indirect supervision are unavailable, a project can begin routine indirect supervision at one to two weeks after the passage of the CBD worker (to determine whether the message was delivered adequately in the first place), and then one or two months later to check the client's memory. The number of repeat visits to be made by the worker will depend on the results of the supervisory visits. If knowledge and ability to prepare the solution correctly are inadequate at the time of the first supervision, repeat home visits by workers should be scheduled. Workers may also need retraining to improve their teaching techniques. Retraining and motivation of clients can be carried out in a group setting in order to maximize project resources. Flexibility in the scheduling of worker activities is important to permit repeat home visits or additional group meetings, should these become necessary.

Higher level referral and medical backup may be needed if the underlying diarrheal condition warrants it - if the child is very ill or shows no improvement. Side effects due to ORT itself are rare, if the solution is prepared correctly. Regarding possible hazards of ORT, much has been written about the potential of hypernatremia in infants receiving high solute loads including (in some estimates) the 90 mEq/liter of sodium recommended by WHO and found in Oralyte, packaged by UNICEF (Finberg et al., 1979; Skinner and Moll, 1956; Colle et al., 1958). Thus far, field and clinical observations have not noted significant clinical problems associated with hypernatremia using the WHO standard solution (Nalin, 1979; Chatterjee et al., 1978; Center for Vaccine Development, 1979). The advantage of the WHO solution is that the concentration is considered effective for all causes of diarrhea, including cholera, which produces high fecal sodium losses. Distinguishing cholera from other diarrheas may be difficult in the field, and the selected solution should be efficacious for children with this potentially serious condition (World Health Organization, 1978). Parker has suggested that alternating plain water with ORT solution will safeguard even young infants from hypernatremia, with thirst acting to ensure the consumption of adequate free water between administrations of ORT (Parker, 1980). Thus, it appears unlikely that hypernatremia will be a cause for referral in a well-supervised ORT program.

Hypokalemia represents another potential side effect in projects using home sugar/salt mixture without added potassium. Clements found that of 29 infants given simple sugar/salt solution, 13 developed hypokalemic laboratory values, as compared with only six of 32 children receiving "complete" glucose electrolyte solution. Not one in either group of children had clinical symptoms associated with low potassium values (Clements et al., 1980). The usefulness of bananas or other relatively high potassium foods as an adjunct to sugar-salt solution remains unproven. Clements has estimated that a child would have to ingest the equivalent of two or three bananas per day to balance stool potassium losses (Clements et al., 1980), although smaller amounts may still be useful.

Referral may be necessary in cases where a child is already severely dehydrated before ORT is begun, or in a small percentage of cases with severe diarrhea and vomiting who do not respond adequately to the treatment and who may require temporary intravenous rehydration. Although ORT is valuable in cases of cholera and severe dysentery, additional medication may be warranted for certain diarrheas of specific etiology (tetracycline in cases of shigella and cholera, and metronidazole for amebiasis). Mothers in an ORT program can be taught to go to a health post in the case of bloody or mucoid stools, signs of severe or worsening dehydration, or severe vomiting. ORT should be started before going to the health center and continued en route, especially if the trip is of more than 15 to 20 minutes' duration.

Health center personnel should be taught correct methods of dealing with dehydration (oral rehydration, rehydration via nasogastric tube or IV when warranted), and appropriate use of antibiotics. One can ethically institute an ORT program in areas with no medical backup: although some children will die in spite of ORT, the therapy itself, if properly prepared and administered, will not cause serious side effects and many children can be saved through its use. However, one does risk losing community acceptance if ORT is perceived to "fail"; community education efforts must take this into account.

A major preprogram decision involves the selection of supplies: the choice between prepared Oralyte packets versus locally packaged formulations or home preparation of sugar-salt mixture. Important issues in this regard have been reviewed by Cash (this volume).

A program that chooses to use both packets and sugar-salt solution must be prepared to increase training and supervisory activities to ensure that recipients understand the preparation of each method, and that confusion between two methods of preparation does not lead to error. Generally programs are not encouraged to attempt the simultaneous implementation of both methods because of the potential to overextend personnel and the scope for client error.

SPECIFIC PROGRAM STRATEGY DECISIONS

Preparation of ORT

Measuring Water

As has been extensively reviewed by Cash (this volume), one of the most important aspects of correct preparation of ORT is the accurate measurement of water. A variety of methods has been tested to assist village women in measuring a liter. In the Sudan, a six standard teacup method was found to have two drawbacks: there is no guarantee that a cup of standard proportions was available in most households, and the "recipe" itself proved difficult to remember (Clements, 1980). The provision of plastic liter containers in Egypt became quite expensive, and problems of logistics particular to each country can make this approach impractical. The use of a local household container, marked at the liter level with indelible paint or a clear scratch, has several advantages: the client does not have to remember complicated numbers, and there is no extra cost associated with the use of the container. One does have to be certain, however, that the pot is one that will always be available for the preparation of ORT, that the mark is indeed clear and permanent, and that the pot is placed on a flat surface at the time the liter mark is made. Some variation would have to be adapted in areas where not all households have a vessel of sufficient size to hold a liter.

Water Source

Cash (this volume) has reviewed decisions to be made regarding acceptable water supplies, whether water should be boiled, and how long ORT solution should be allowed to stand before a fresh batch is prepared.

A suggestion to boil and cool the water used for ORT may be ideal, but is often impractical and can significantly delay the inception of therapy (it may take up to two or three hours to cool water in the hot ambient temperatures found in many developing countries) (Parker, 1980; McCord, 1980). It is preferable to advise clients to use the cleanest available source of water, clean utensils prior to preparation, and follow preparation techniques that avoid extra contamination. The solution should be discarded after 24 hours.

The addition of a chemical disinfectant such as iodine to ORT packets has been discussed in the literature. Iodine is relatively inert and is unlikely to cause chemical deterioration of ORT components (Cash and Chen, 1980), but no ORT field tests with added iodine have been reported. Exposing ORT solution to the ultraviolet rays of the sun can decrease bacterial counts, without negatively affecting the chemical constituents of the solution (Cash and Chen, 1980). This strategy may be worth testing in areas where water supplies are known to be contaminated.

Administration of ORT

When should ORT be started?

Should mothers be advised to wait until the child has two or three diarrheal stools - definite "diagnosis" of diarrhea - or should she begin ORT immediately after the first loose stool, on the assumption that a rapid attack of diarrhea can dehydrate the child quickly? Although its ability to rehydrate is not in dispute, ORT has not yet been proven to be better at preventing dehydration than other fluids (Parker, 1980).

The use of an ORT packet after every episode of one loose stool may add to client and program costs. However, there is a rationale for beginning ORT after the first watery stool recognized by the mother as being different in consistency from her child's regular bowel movements: more copious, more watery, explosive, foul smelling, different in color. It is usually impossible to judge the severity of the diarrhea to follow from the appearance of the first diarrheal stool. Asymptomatic dehydration, equivalent to 3 or 4 percent of body weight, can occur within a few hours after the start of diarrhea; ORT helps to compensate for this undetected loss as it takes place (Population Reports, 1980). Second, ORT minimizes the symptoms associated with increasing water and electrolyte loss, such as vomiting, lack of appetite, and lethargy. Third, teaching a family to start treatment as soon as diarrhea begins is easier than trying to explain the difference between diarrhea with and without dehydration, and avoids the potential problems of delay caused when mothers wait to count stools. Prompt replacement with ORT also ensures that treatment is simpler because it is given when two important homeostatic mechanisms (thirst and renal function) are still intact (Bradley et al., 1978). Finally, encouraging mothers to give ORT early in the course of illness may help to emphasize the importance of prompt treatment. If mothers are instructed to wait until they have seen two or three stools, there may be a tendency to delay treatment even longer.

How much ORT should mothers be taught to administer?

A number of different protocols have been suggested (Bradley et al., 1978; Bhatia, no date; Black et al. 1980; Cutting, 1979), and they advocate approximately 600 ml of fluid in the first four to six hours and another 800 to 1400 ml per 24 hours for maintenance of mild diarrhea, with double or triple this amount for moderate to severe diarrhea. These quantities would apply to infants of up to one year of age, with more being given to older children.

In field situations, one may suggest that ORT, upon being started, be given ad libitum for about four hours until thirst is abated. If reluctant to drink, the child can be encouraged to take two or three 200-ml glasses during this period. If vomiting occurs, this amount should be given slowly and in frequent small quantities. In mild to moderate diarrhea (five stools per day), the child can then be given between 100 and 200 ml (average 150) after each bowel movement, bringing the total per day to approximately a liter to a liter and a half. In a child with "very much" diarrhea, with "many" stools - six or more per day - the mother should be encouraged to use ORT more frequently, both after and between bowel movements. If the child is thirsty, more ORT can be given on each administration: thirst can be used as a gauge of amounts needed in cases where diarrhea may be more severe than the mother suspects, or if the child is older and bigger, and needs more fluid. In all cases, children should be allowed water and breast milk ad libitum between administrations of ORT, both to ensure maximal fluid intakes and as a safety factor if the ORT solution is too concentrated (Parker, 1980).

Field instructions to mothers can be made quite simple: "Slowly give your child two or three glasses of this fluid (as much as he or she will drink) during the few hours after you first see diarrhea, then one glass after each loose stool, or more if the child is thirsty and wants more. Give the child as much water, tea, breast milk, and other food as he or she will take in between the ORT." (An appropriately sized glass or cup will have to be identified for each mother.) "In all cases, if your child begins to look more weak, tired, or dried out (sunken eyes, dry mouth, decreased skin turgor), try to give more ORT and do it more frequently; do it slowly so that the child doesn't vomit. Be sure you give ordinary water and breast milk in between."

Should Feeding Be Continued During Diarrhea?

North American clinical practice has generally advocated "resting the gut" during diarrhea. The rationale for this practice is based on the possibility that nonhuman milk and solid foods may exacerbate diarrhea, and that cow's milk and some foods contain sufficient sodium concentrations to increase the risk of hypernatremia. The high solute concentration of these foods may place an excessive load on the excretory capacity of the infant's kidneys. However, the trend in developing countries is currently away from food restriction in field situations. In a recent summary of 14 field projects using ORT and providing additional information on feeding practices, all advocated continued feeding during diarrhea. Three did specify the discontinuation or dilution of cow's milk for up to 24 hours (Parker, 1980). Although feeding during diarrhea does tend to increase stool volume and frequency, increased absorption and a net positive retention of nutrients have been reported (Chung, 1948), regardless of whether the etiologic agent was rotavirus or cholera (Molla et al., 1980).

Another concern regarding continued feeding is the occurrence of lactase deficiency in diarrhea. Since lactase, necessary for the digestion of milk lactose, is produced in the brush cell border of the intestinal mucosa, it is among the first enzymes whose activity is decreased in diarrhea. Theoretically, ingested milk is then poorly digested and absorbed and can lead to increased fermentation in the gut, with further exacerbation of diarrhea. A WHO Scientific Working Group has concluded that lactase deficiency is generally not of clinical significance, and only where it is specifically suspected should cow's milk be stopped for 8 to 10 hours and then given in dilute forms (World Health Organization, 1978). Breast milk, although it contains lactose, should be continued in order to prevent the cessation of lactation, and to reduce the cumulative malnutrition that might result from withholding food for 20 to 30 "diarrhea" days per year (World Health Organization, 1978).

When Should Community Workers Refer Children to a Health Facility?

A list of symptoms requiring referral may include:

*- frank blood in diarrhea (amoebic or bacillary dysentery).
*- very heavy vomiting in spite of slow administration of ORT using a cup and spoon, severe enough to impair the intake of fluid.
*- signs of initial severe dehydration or of worsening dehydration despite ORT administration (loss of skin turgor, sunken fontanelle and eyes, inability to drink, dry mouth, decreasing urination, marked lethargy, shock indicated by pallor or coldness, coma).
*- high fever.

- signs of acidosis: deep breathing, lassitude, apathy.
- weight loss (if weight was known before and can be accurately checked again).
- hypernatremia (difficult to diagnose clinically): irritability, "doughy" consistency of the skin, periorbital edema, as well as signs of dehydration.

Starred points represent priority areas for referral. The other areas are more difficult to diagnose and are likely to overlap with symptoms of dehydration.

Program Implementation Steps

Steps for ORT program implementation, a number of which have been discussed above, should follow an organized sequence. These include:

a) seeking the agreement of the health system to diffuse potential opposition;
b) selecting a method of ORT preparation, (as delineated by Cash);
c) identifying specific personnel needed and available (workers, supervisors and managers), and preparing a task analysis to describe their activities in the proposed setting;
d) preparing training manuals and standing orders;
e) developing the supply system, transportation, storage, and identifying a well-defined backup approach if the main supply system breaks down;
f) identifying the referral and medical backup system;
g) finalizing training programs for all levels of staff;
h) elaborating an ongoing supervisory routine for both direct and indirect supervision;
i) testing trial implementation with extensive monitoring to test manpower readiness, client reactions, the supply system, and other supports;
j) scheduling reinforcement training: retraining, particularly before the onset of the peak diarrhea season, should be part of the ongoing program.
k) monitoring and evaluating mechanisms should be defined and established in advance.

Although all the points above are important, special attention should be paid to the elaboration of a training course for CBD workers, and to ensuring adequate stock distribution and teaching of ORT in the home.

The training of workers to prepare, implement, and teach ORT in the field is time-consuming and requires adequate field practice. This implies the existence of a person in charge of training. The trainer's role should include the coordination of information and education for local health personnel who will serve as backup to the project. If necessary, the individual in charge of training can fulfill other program functions, but training should not be shared, in an uncoordinated way, among program staff who happen to be "available" at a given moment.

The logistics and supplies necessary to ensure adequate distribution of ORT to homes must be organized. Since rehydration should begin as early as possible after the onset of diarrhea, Oralyte must be readily available in the home. Plans for this redistribution (via depots, home delivery, etc.) must be finalized, and simple procedures for estimating the required number of Oralyte packages developed. Estimates can calculate the number of children under five, the average number of diarrhea episodes per year in the given region, and the average duration of each episode. An average of one packet is needed per diarrheal day.

EVALUATION

Evaluation requires that specific program goals be established from the beginning of ORT implementation.

Process Evaluation

Process evaluation focuses on whether the program is accomplishing the activities necessary to reach program goals, and whether these activities are being satisfactorily performed, in accordance with predetermined levels.

Points to be examined include:

- number of patients seen with diarrhea
- number of mothers taught ORT
- number of ORT packets distributed and levels of stock available in the home
- number of packets requested by women after original distribution (or bought from all potential sources)
- percentage of local women using ORT after the CBD home visit
- percentage of women using ORT correctly (emphasis should be placed on defining the type of errors - major or minor), and
- adequacy of local supplies.

Workers' daily logs, supervisory data, dispensary statistics, community questionnaires and surveys, and spot surveys directed at clients can provide necessary data.

If any of the above points appear to present problems, further analysis of the factors leading to these problems should be undertaken. For example, if women mix inappropriate ORT concentrations, is it because workers explain poorly, the supply of containers is inadequate, or are supplies so scarce or expensive that women attempt to dilute the packets? Process evaluation needs to concentrate on early feedback of use for supervision, retraining and management.

Outcome Evaluation

Outcome evaluation is long-term, and concentrates on the overall effect desired by the program: a reduction in infant mortality and morbidity from diarrhea. This evaluation is not easily accomplished: the time frame must be sufficient. Two or more years are frequently required, since results over a shorter period may be due to temporary changes in the severity of diarrhea in the area. Requirements for assessing outcome include:

(a) Baseline information on preprogram morbidity and mortality from diarrhea, acquired via:
  - surveys,
  - verbal autopsies (cause of death derived from interviews with mothers) carried out immediately prior to the inception of the program,
  - local health records,

(b) A second survey at one year or near the end of the program to determine whether ORT is used in the homes and the current level of diarrhea-related morbidity and mortality. Survey results can be supplemented by examination of CBD and local health records.

Although pre- and post-program height and weight data theoretically represent another indication of program outcome, accurate data are difficult to obtain, and represent too subtle an index to be evident within the short time frame of many CBD projects. The use of such indices requires more data collection than can be carried out in most service programs.

SUMMARY

From the viewpoint of a CBD program, ORT has certain specific advantages: it is useful from a health perspective, and the technology required is simple. Since experience indicates that an ORT program requires multiple worker-client contacts, use of the intervention can increase program visibility. The cost of the product itself is relatively low: under 7¢ a package for UNICEF-issued packets (usually substantially less for those prepared locally), and transportation and storage do not demand sophisticated facilities.

It must be considered, however, that in order to ensure effective implementation and monitoring, the time expenditure of CBD manpower may be substantial. The CBD worker's ability to explain and demonstrate ORT clearly, and to supervise the client's "trial run," is crucial and must be field tested. Of all interventions, this is perhaps the one in which the worker has to teach the client the most complex composite task: error can have immediate and potentially serious consequences. A number of projects have demonstrated that implementation can be successful and worthwhile, but the time demanded of field personnel and supervisors should not be underestimated.

REFERENCES

Bangladesh Rural Advancement Committee (BRAC), Oral Therapy Program. Mohakhali CA, and Dacca, Bangladesh: September 1979.

Bhatia, S. Project Files, Matlab Family Planning, Bangladesh.

Black, R.E. et al. "Epidemiologic Studies of Acute Gastro-Enteritis in Bangladesh." Presented at the 13th Joint U.S. - Japan Cooperative Medical Science Program, 13th Joint Conference on Viral Diseases, Atlanta, Georgia, October 1979.

Black, R.E. et al. "Glucose versus Sucrose in Oral Rehydration Solutions for Infants and Young Children with Rotavirus-associated Diarrhea." Pediatrics 1980.

Bradley, R.S. et al. "The Current Status of Oral Therapy in the Treatment of Acute Diarrheal Illness." Am. J. Clin. Nutr. (1978): 2251-2257.

Cash, R.A. "Oral Therapy for Diarrhea." Trop. Doctor 9 (January 1979): 25-30.

Cash, R. and L. Chen. Possible Disinfection of Oral Rehydration Solutions. Washington, DC: Water and Sanitation for Health Project, Coordination and Information Center, U.S. Agency for International Development, 1980.

Center for Vaccine Development, University of Maryland; Bustamante Hospital for Children; and University Hospital of the West Indies. Comparison of 'High' and 'Low' Sodium and Potassium Content in Oral Glucose - Electrolyte Therapy of Infant Diarrheas. Kingston and Baltimore: 1979 (unpublished).

Chatterjee, A. et al. "Oral Rehydration in Infant Diarrhea: Controlled Trial of a Low Sodium Glucose Electrolyte Solution." Arch Dis Child 53,4 (1978): 204-209.

Chung, A.W. "The Effect or Oral Feeding at Different Levels on the Absorption of Foodstuffs in Infantile Diarrhea." J Pediatrics 33,1 (1948): 14-42.

Clements, M.L. "Trip Report, Sudan Community Based Family Health Project, August to September, 1980."

Clements, M.L. et al. "Comparison of Simple Sugar/Salt versus Glucose/Electrolyte Oral Rehydration Solutions in Infant Diarrheas." 1980 (unpublished).

Colle, E. et al. "Hypertonic Dehydration (Hypernatremia): The Role of Feedings High in Solutes." Pediatrics (1958): 2-12.

Curlin, P., Center for Development and Population Activities, personal communication, 1981.

Cutting, W. "Management of Diarrhea in Children at the Primary Care or Peripheral Level." Ann Soc Belge Med Trop 59 (1979): 221-235.

Finberg, L. et al. Oral Therapy for Dehydration in Acute Diarrheal Diseases with Special Reference to the Global Diarrheal Diseases Control Program. (BAC/DDC/79.1), Geneva: World Health Organization, Diarrhoeal Disease Control Programme, 1979 (unpublished).

Kielmann, A.A. and C. McCord. "Home Treatment of Childhood Diarrhea in Punjab Villages." Environ. Child Health 23,4 (August 1977): 197-201.

McCord, C. Evaluation of Menoufia, Egypt OR Project. Washington, DC: American Public Health Association, 1980.

Mobarak, A.B. "Diarrheal Disease Control Study, Final Report, Phase I." Egypt: SHRD Project, Rural Health Department, MOH, Arab Republic of Egypt, April 1981.

Molla, A. et al. Intake and Absorption of Nutrients in Children with Cholera and Rotavirus Infection during Acute Diarrhea and After Recovery. Dacca, Bangladesh: International Center for Diarrheal Disease Research, 1980.

Nalin, D.R. et al. "Oral Rehydration and Maintenance of Children with Rotavirus and Bacterial Diarrheas." Bull WHO 57,3 (1979): 453-459.

Nalin, D.R. and N. Hirschhorn. Research on Oral Rehydration Therapy for Diarrheal Dehydration. (WPR/BVD (DDC)/79.6), Regional Planning Meeting on Diarrheal Disease Control, 1979.

Parker, R.L. Oral Fluid Therapy in Diarrhea and Dehydration: Current Concepts and Practical Considerations. Baltimore, MD: Johns Hopkins School of Hygiene and Public Health, July 1980 (unpublished).

Pierce, N.F. and N. Hirschhorn. "Oral Fluid -- A Simple Weapon Against Dehydration in Diarrhea." WHO Chronicle 31 (1977): 87-93.

Population Reports. "ORT for Childhood Diarrhea" Series L,2 (1980).

Skinner, A. and F. Moll. "Hypernatremia Accompanying Infant Diarrhea." Am J Dis Child 92 (1956): 538.

Sunoto. "Diarrheal Disease of Children in Southeast Asia." Paediatr. Indonesia 19 (1979): 231-242.

Vella, V.K., Centers for Disease Control, personal communication, 1981.

Wessley, S., Sudan Community-Based Health Project, 1981, personal communication.

World Health Organization (WHO). Clinical Management of Acute Diarrhea. (WHO/DDC/79.3), Report of a scientific working group, New Delhi, 1978.

________ . Clinical Management of Acute Diarrhea. (WHO/DDC/79.3), Report of a Scientific Working Group, New Delhi, 1978.

9
Oral Fluid Therapy and Diarrheal Mortality Among Children in Egyptian Villages

Belgin Tekce

INTERVENTION AND STUDY DESIGN

In 1979, a project was undertaken in the delta region of Egypt to promote family planning, health, and social welfare services in an integrated manner. The population serviced by the project consisted of 1.4 million rural inhabitants of the Menoufia governorate. The implementation of the services was phased over a three-year period, adding one-third of the population to the project each year through 1981. The action component was accompanied by an extensive research program designed to evaluate the impact of the broad range of services provided to the rural population.

This paper evaluates the introduction into the rural areas of the governorate of a set of measures to promote oral rehydration therapy (ORT) among children with diarrheal disease - a prevalent condition and a major cause of death among young children in Egypt. According to official statistics, diarrheal disease is the single most important cause of death in the first year of life, accounting for around 50 percent of all recorded infant deaths. The understanding and management of diarrheal disease also has implications beyond morbidity and mortality directly attributable to this condition. Evidence regarding the synergism between infection and nutritional deficiency suggests that reducing diarrheal morbidity, in addition to saving lives, has lasting effects on the growth and development of survivors, and therefore has major public health implications[1]. Nevertheless, identification of priorities in diarrheal management are not always clear; the range includes community-level activities such as providing clean water and sanitation, improving nutrition, and treatment of the individual. In the Menoufia project priority was given to intervention at the patient-care level.

Most deaths from diarrheal disease result from loss of fluids and electrolytes, and early, rapid rehydration forms the basis for good treatment. During recent years, treatment of dehydration in acute diarrheal disease has become greatly simplified due in large part to advances in oral rehydration techniques[2]. Patients with severe dehydration will continue to need other techniques of rehydration, but the number of such cases can be reduced if oral therapy is used in early stages of diarrhea. ORT has been instituted and used to advantage in a variety of settings as an effective and practical method of preventing deaths due to diarrhea and its accompanying dehydration[3]. It is a simple technique particularly suited to early home management of diarrhea.

The fluids used in ORT can be prepared in several ways. In the Menoufia project, the prepackaged oral rehydrant Oralyte (UNICEF oral rehydration salt packets containing the composition suggested by the World Health Organization) was used.

The impact a specific therapy has on mortality depends in part on the effectiveness with which this knowledge is transferred to those who care for the sick. In settings characterized by high diarrheal morbidity and mortality, mothers and health professionals have established ways of treating the disease. The task of an ORT program is to find ways of altering their behavior such that oral rehydration becomes a standard component of diarrheal management both at home and in the clinic.

Intervention

The particular thrust of the Menoufia project's approach was to build a capacity for home management of childhood diarrhea by making ORT widely known and used among rural mothers. There were modifications made in the mechanisms used to promote ORT over time, but the emphasis on the importance of the role of the mother in management of diarrhea remained unaltered throughout the project. This study concerns the effects of the first year of implementation; the modifications of procedures are described in detail elsewhere[4].

During the initial year, the project sought to increase maternal knowledge and use of ORT through a program of household visits to reach all women with children under five years of age. Each household was visited once, and the visit was designed to accomplish several objectives. Mothers were taught the importance of early management of diarrhea through oral therapy, instructed in the preparation and administration of Oralyte solution, and advised about proper feeding during and after diarrheal episodes. Mothers were also instructed on danger signs requiring prompt referral to a medical facility. They were offered two packets of Oralyte and advised to obtain one-liter plastic bottles for preparing the solution and further supplies of packets from health units or village depots.

A printed pamphlet of instructions concerning ORT was left with the mother at the end of the home visit. These instructions were to be conveyed orally and the actual preparation of the mixture was demonstrated during the household contact. A summary of the instructions given to mothers can be found in Appendix I.

The household-level education and distribution program was carried out by specially trained female high school graduates recruited from each village. The program in the first three counties started in May and lasted through July 1979. During this period approximately 45,000 mothers living in 105 villages were reached. According to the distribution records, 98 percent of the mothers who were contacted accepted the packages offered. A utilization survey conducted about four months after the distribution among a sample of 500 mothers showed that 80 percent of the mothers had obtained the plastic bottles.

Medical backup for the project was provided by Menoufia's extensive network of rural health facilities and nine hospitals, each of which has had been equipped with an intravenous (IV) rehydration center since mid-1979. Health service doctors from the three counties were offered a short training session by the project in the use of ORT and instructed to encourage mothers in its use. Health units and depots in villages without such units were stocked with the packets and instructed to resupply mothers as necessary.

The design of the intervention with its emphasis on educating mothers, combined with the extensive public health services in the countryside, contributed to the expectation that a substantial reduction in diarrheal deaths would occur among children within a relatively short period of time. The measurable effect of the program was expected to be within the range of a one-third to a one-half reduction in childhood deaths due to diarrhea (McCord, 1979).

Study Design

In order to assess program impact, a study was designed to test the effect of the household-based promotion of ORT (the treatment) on early childhood death rates and on the distribution of death between diarrhea and other causes in 12 of the villages. Two sets of villages were selected from the Menoufia Governorate, one from districts which were to receive treatment in the first year and the other, to serve as a control, from those districts programmed for the third year. Each set included two villages selected by a random procedure from three strata: (a) villages with health and social service units; (b) villages with health units only; (c) villages without any units. The total number of villages selected was thus twelve, of which six were treatment villages and six served as controls.

The usual sources of information for studies on childhood deaths and on causes of death have been official death certificates. However, the public reporting system has recognized shortcomings both in terms of coverage of child deaths, particularly during infancy, and accuracy of diagnostic statements about the causes of death (Rashad, 1981; Fergany, 1976; Omran, 1973). This study incorporated special surveys to identify child deaths during the study period and to investigate their causes.

Data were collected via multiround socio-demographic surveys conducted at yearly intervals to monitor a broad range of project activities in the two groups of villages. The information from the first round of surveys was used in this study to obtain a list of the population by household in the 12 villages. It was also used to identify selected characteristics of the households to gain an understanding of the physical and social environment of child care.

The second round of the survey was used to obtain vital events that had occurred during the year. An important technique was the assessment of changes in the composition of household members. When the intersurvey period is of a one year duration, the household change technique, while a powerful tool for obtaining vital events, cannot by itself reveal one particular type of event, namely the deaths of infants born between survey rounds. To obtain better coverage of these events two additional probes were used.

Pregnancy outcome was asked of all women who were recorded as being pregnant in the first round: Outcomes for women who were no longer residing in the study area were obtained from remaining household members, relatives or neighbors. In addition, direct questions were asked about the occurrence of any other births or deaths in the household using a locally important reference date from the time of the first survey. (These dates referred to harvests and to religious holidays.) When events of interest were identified, additional questions were then asked to specify a date more closely.

Although each group of villages was surveyed twice, the intersurvey periods did not completely coincide. The midpoint of the approximately one-year intersurvey period for treatment villages was on average six months earlier than the corresponding period for control villages. In the treatment villages the initial survey was followed by household distribution of Oralyte with an average time lag of around one month. Data was collected for the entire intersurvey period of both village sets, but we also examined them in terms of matched months in the post-distribution period to remove any effect the time lag might have had on mortality outcome in the treatment villages.

All deaths of children under five reported through the multiround survey were investigated by a specially trained team of doctors. The doctors were interns at different hospitals in the governorate. Medical interviews were conducted with the person who took care of the child prior to death, usually the mother, to obtain information on the course of the terminal illness and circumstances of these deaths. The purpose of the interview was to determine the most probable primary cause of death and whenever possible to also identify any associated cause. A relatively full history was obtained for each case including background information on parents, an account of the fatal episode, a review of the condition of body systems by a series of fixed questions, feeding practices prior to and during the terminal illness, treatment information and, if diarrhea was present, specific practices used to treat the child prior to death. A cause of death was assigned using all the information obtained in the medical interview.

Conferences were held periodically with the investigating doctors to review forms and discuss the plausibility of the cause assignments. A group of doctors from outside attended as well. Final cause assignments were made only after each form had been reviewed by a medical consultant to the investigation.

Our evaluation of the quality of basic information on causes of death is that both in terms of coverage of child deaths and disease identification, it constitutes a definite improvement relative to the information available from the death certificate system. For example, our procedures produced distributions of deaths between the first month and higher ages that are more plausible than those of the registration system which shows very few deaths below one month. In addition, we noted rather high rates of death due to tetanus neonatorum which is not found at all in the cause-of-death certificates.

ENVIRONMENT AND CHILD MORTALITY

The project did not attempt to alter the incidence of diarrheal disease by trying to change the conditions that generate it. The aim was to reduce fatality by intervening at the therapy stage to prevent dehydration and thereby reduce diarrheal and overall child mortality. The project therefore closely monitored child deaths and their causes in the post-treatment period. However, in order to understand the environment (familial and medical) within which these deaths occurred, it is useful to bring together information from the survey and other studies. Assessment of this environmental context is important in interpreting the outcome of the health intervention.

Project Setting

Menoufia governorate, located north of Cairo, comprises one of the most heavily inhabited areas of the country, with a population density of approximately 1,100 persons per square kilometer. The 12 villages studied are all situated within a 25 kilometer radius from Shebin-El-Kom, the capital of the governorate. They are directly linked to the nearest towns by taxis and, in most cases, by public buses.

As is typical of the delta, the villages form tightly nucleated settlements amidst cultivated fields. The density of village settlement, the inadequacy of water supply and waste disposal, as well as the generally low level of household amenities, make it difficult for mothers to control routes of transmission for infectious diseases. The physical aspects of the home environments in treatment and control villages were practically the same.

In the homes of married women in these villages, the predominant source of drinking water was pumps (59 percent), followed by piped water (39 percent). Only 15 percent of women have access to taps or piped water within their home. Previous reports and current observations indicate that many villagers prefer "Nile water" for a variety of purposes. Whatever health education may have accomplished in changing habits related to the source of drinking water, observation suggests that irrigation canals are still widely used for washing kitchen utensils and laundry, bathing people and animals, and for waste disposal. From the viewpoint of the village women, this eliminates the chores involved in carrying water over a distance, storing it, and disposing of it several times daily.

The manner of disposal of human feces was conducive to fecal contamination of the environment. Over one-fourth of the women lived in households where there was no fixed latrine, whether private or shared with another household. Instead, variable locations were used for defecation, such as the roof, barn, or the fields. As importantly, where there were fixed latrines, a negligible proportion (5 percent) had water within the facility.

Handling, storage and preparation of food was carried out under difficult conditions. As can be expected, it was rare for women to have a special place allotted only for cooking (12 percent). The use of bottled gas was negligible (7 percent). Education regarding general hygiene and the preparation and storage of ORT needs to take these characteristics of home environments into account.

Education was seriously lacking among rural couples and particularly among women. The data indicate that about 40 percent of husbands and 80 percent of wives were illiterate. Only 22 percent of husbands and 5 percent of married women had completed primary school. There were no differences between the two groups of villages with respect to educational levels. Health education of mothers clearly has and will continue to have an important potential role in this setting.

One aspect of life in rural Menoufia which is quite exceptional is the availability of health facilities and personnel. As of 1979, the governorate has 44 health centers and 111 health units serving a population of 1.4 million persons[5]. There are also several general and specialized hospitals in towns, as well as a large training hospital in the capital. In 1979, 221 doctors were listed as working in the rural health facilities, exceeding the number required to serve. In addition, there are a substantial number of private practitioners, some resident in the villages. Time and money constraints still impose some limits on rural accessibility to health care; but the supply, in terms of quantity and proximity, is quite exceptional for such an area in a less developed country.

Population Characteristics

The 12 study villages have a total population of 50 thousand equally divided between the treatment and control groups. Project data indicate that, as expected, the population is young: 40 percent of the population is less than 15 years of age. The birth rate for the 12 villages combined is high (39 per thousand) while the death rate is moderate at 12 per thousand. The levels of these vital rates were almost identical for the two groups of villages (Table 9:1).

Table 9:1. Vital Rates for Two Groups of Study Villages, Menoufia Governorate, 1979-1980.

VILLAGES	POPULATION (thousand)	RATES PER THOUSAND	
		Births	Deaths
Treatment group	24.6	39.3	12.3
Control group	25.5	39.1	11.8
All villages	50.2	39.2	12.0

Children under the age of five constituted 15 percent of the population but contributed 54 percent of all deaths in the 12 villages combined during the 1979 to 1980 period. The age pattern of mortality during the first five years of life is shown in Table 9:2. The death rates are quite similar between the two groups of villages.

There are two distinctive features for the age pattern of childhood deaths in these villages. First, although the risk of dying in the first month of life is quite high, it is even higher in the remainder of infancy. The ratio of neonatal to postneonatal deaths was found to be 1:2, in contrast to the infant mortality situation in developed countries where the ratio is typically around 1:0.5. Deaths in the initial month of life in rural Menoufia are largely attributable to neonatal infections (primarily tetanus followed by septicemia) and to immaturity.

Table 9:2. Mortality Rates Among Children Under Age Five in Study Villages, Menoufia Governorate, 1979 to 1980.

AGE GROUP	RATES PER 1,000		
	Treatment Villages	Control Villages	All Villages
Under 1 year[a]	117.1	113.4	115.2
neonatal[a]	40.4	36.6	38.4
postneonatal[a]	76.7	76.9	76.8
1 to 4[b]	17.8	17.0	17.4
Number of deaths	169	174	343

[a]per 1,000 live births.

[b]per 1,000 population.

This hard core of infant mortality is partially amenable to improvements through better maternal care. It is in the post-neonatal period, however, that infectious diseases, mostly diarrheal and respiratory, begin to dominate early life.

The relatively high mortality of children from one to four years is due largely to deaths which occur in the second year of life. The level of mortality in the second year of life is 66.9 per thousand, which is even more striking than the level of infant mortality when compared to levels in developed countries. The indication is that the factors which make the postneonatal period so hazardous to child health continue to operate through the second year of life. The timing and manner of weaning is a critical factor in this period.

DIARRHEAL DISEASE MORTALITY

Treatment Effect

The basic task of this study was to assess whether the therapeutic intervention significantly lowered deaths due to diarrhea among children under age five living in treatment villages, as compared to children under age five in control villages. The discussion focuses on diarrheal deaths as the primary cause of death. Since the effect of the intervention on deaths may vary by age, it is useful to examine cause-specific death rates by age.

Age-specific death rates due to diarrhea and to all other causes combined are given in Table 9:3. Deaths due to causes other than diarrhea provide a good test of the comparability of the two groups of villages, and indeed mortality from non-diarrheal causes is similar between them. Comparison of the age-specific diarrheal death rates between the treatment and control villages clearly shows no difference in mortality due to diarrhea[6]. The conclusion which emerges is that the program was not effective in lowering diarrheal mortality among children in the treatment villages.

The epidemiological distribution of diarrheal deaths over time may be a source of bias. More than half of all diarrheal deaths occurred during the four-month period from June through September. These are the months of heavy crop activities, which may result in relative neglect of children, and are also the hottest months when fluid loss is accelerated by climatic conditions. As was noted, the introduction of oral therapy in the treatment villages occurred on average a little over a month after the initiation of mortality data collection. The lag is relatively short but occurred in the peak diarrhea season. It is necessary to explore whether a difference between treatment and control was being masked by attributing deaths to ineffective treatment when treatment had not yet started.

A ten-month period of observation (August through May) can be demarcated to compare deaths belonging only to the calendar months during which all 12 villages were under observation and after intervention had been completed in the treatment villages.

Table 9:3. Death Rates Due to Diarrheal Disease Compared with All Other Combined Causes Among Children Under the Age of Five, in Treatment and Control Villages, 1979-1980.

AGE	POPULATION[a]	DIARRHEAL DEATHS		NON-DIARRHEAL DEATHS	
(Years)		Cases	Rate/1,000	Cases	Rate/1,000
		Treatment Villages			
Under 1	768	54	70.3	62	80.8
1 to 4	2,977	34	11.4	19	6.4
Under 5	3,745	88	23.5	81	21.6
		Control Villages			
Under 1	820	59	71.9	62	75.6
1 to 4	3,115	24	7.7	29	9.3
Under 5	3,935	83	21.1	91	23.1

[a]Person-years; midperiod population multiplied by the length of the observation period in years which is 1.002 for the treatment and 1.068 for the control group.

Note: None of the differences is statistically significant at a 0.05 probability level (one-tail test).

Death rates due to diarrheal disease and to other causes combined for the two groups of villages during the 10 matching calendar months are shown in Table 9:4. The difference in diarrheal death rates between the two groups remains insignificant in magnitude and is in the opposite direction from that expected.

Table 9:4. Death Rates Among Children Under Age Five in Treatment and Control Villages during Ten Matched Months, 1979-1980.

VILLAGES	PERSON YEARS	DIARRHEAL DEATHS		NON-DIARRHEAL DEATHS	
		Cases	Rate/1,000	Cases	Rate/1,000
Treatment	3,053	60	19.7	69	22.6
Control	3,069	49	15.0	63	20.5

The important issue at this point is the programmatic implications of the negative finding. One must ask why the introduction of oral rehydration therapy did not have an effect on diarrheal deaths in the rural Menoufia setting. It is important to examine process variables in order to determine how the project may have been improved.

One can dispense quickly with the question of whether oral therapy is an effective method of preventing deaths due to diarrhea. The efficacy of oral fluid therapy to rehydrate patients and to maintain hydration is well established. Early institution of oral rehydration also prevents development of fatal dehydration and has been observed to shorten the duration of diarrheal attacks[7]. It is important, therefore, to examine closely what has been learned about diarrheal disease and the behavior of mothers and health professionals to determine how a demonstratively effective therapy can be learned and adopted in the rural Egyptian setting.

Characteristics of Diarrheal Disease

The history of the onset and progress of the terminal diarrheal episode as recounted by the mothers offers general information on the characteristics of diarrheal disease and its management among young children in Menoufia villages. The onset of clinical disease was acute and progressed rapidly with liquid or semi-liquid stools varying from 3 to 20 or more bowel movements per day. In over 90 percent of cases, diarrhea was accompanied by repeated vomiting. Fever was also usual along with malaise and tenesmus. Presence of blood or pus in the stools was rare. The average clinical course of the terminal diarrheal episode was four days. A history of recurrent acute attacks was usually reported. In such cases one or more attacks had happened relatively recently, or the final episode was associated with a past history of a progressively depleted condition (malaise, wasting) with recurrent acute episodes of diarrhea and vomiting.

Physical signs of dehydration were commonly recognized and reported by the mothers in terms of sunken eyes, dry skin (diminished skin turgor) and general lethargy. In certain extreme cases of dehydration, diarrhea and vomiting decreased considerably prior to death which was mistakenly interpreted as improvement in the child's condition. It is important to note that the mothers were usually familiar with the kinds of changes that accompany dehydration, so education could be built upon that knowledge. The presence of vomiting, often reported to be severe among the fatal cases, may have made mothers reluctant to administer oral fluids, and this hesitation would need to be addressed.

Feeding Patterns

A typical feature of the fatal diarrheal episodes was a history of improper nourishment both prior to and during the fatal attack. Prolonged breastfeeding without timely addition of food supplements, or weaning on starchy diets were practices repeatedly found in diarrheal disease. Among deaths due to diarrhea, nutritional deficiency was identified as an associated cause in 38 percent of the cases.

The relationship between feeding practices and mortality is too complex to be investigated properly in a study of this type. One basic reason is that the feeding patterns of all the children at risk of dying are not known from the study: information about feeding is available only for those who died. Nevertheless the information given by the mothers on feeding practices prior to as well as during the course of the terminal disease was evaluated to gain an impression of the extent to which these practices may have played a role in diarrheal mortality and may have presented a general health problem.

Among the children who died from all causes in infancy, breastmilk alone (73 percent) or supplementation with external milk (16 percent) was the predominant feeding regimen. External milk was likely to be fresh animal milk (52 percent), commonly buffalo or cow milk, but powdered milk had begun to rival fresh milk even in these rural communities.

Since breastfeeding is almost universal in Egypt, it was expected that the proportion breastfeeding would be high among all infants and among the infants who died. The interesting point was the distribution of diarrheal deaths among infants on different milk diets. As can be seen in Table 9:5, diarrheal deaths contributed considerably less to deaths from all causes among infants who were wholly breastfed. External feeding was not only likely to be prepared under highly unsanitary conditions but is also usually heavily diluted.

Table 9:5. Diarrheal Deaths as Proportion of All Deaths in Infancy According to Milk Regimens Prior to Onset of Fatal Episode (in percents).

AGE (months)	BREAST MILK ONLY	EXTERNAL MILK & BREAST MILK	EXTERNAL MILK ONLY	
0 to 5	28	63	60	
6 to 11	76	71	86	
Under 1 year	41	67	79	
				Total
Number of diarrheal deaths	62	22	15	99
Number of deaths from all causes	150	33	19	202

Note: The table excludes children who were receiving food supplements and refers only to those exclusively on milk diets.

Provision of foods to supplement breastfeeding can begin earlier, but is essential for healthy development of the infant beyond the sixth month. Among the children who died during the ages of 6-11 months, 85 percent had not yet received any food supplementation. This proportion was still considerable for those who died in the second year of life: 38 percent between the ages of 12-17 months, and 16 percent between 18-23 months, had not yet received any supplementary food in their diet. The delayed introduction of food supplements may be one of the reasons underlying high postneonatal and second year death rates in these villages.

Home Management of Diarrhea

Home management of diarrhea among fatal cases consisted virtually entirely of dietary restrictions. During diarrheal episodes mothers commonly restricted diet to herbal infusions made from caraway, anise, and fenugreek (helba) as well as rice water and tea. It should be noted that, although such food restriction is considerable, the emphasis on giving fluids can be used to advantage in promoting oral therapy. The over-restriction of diet is seen clearly in Table 9:6. The restriction of diet aggravates the child's situation, so that even if the diar-

Table 9:6. Feeding Practices During Fatal Diarrheal Episode in Twelve Study Villages.

FOOD ITEM	TOTAL RECEIVING BEFORE ILLNESS	STOPPED DURING ILLNESS	
		Number	Percent
Breast feeding	132	96	73
External milk	63	53	84
Solid or semi-solid food	51	46	90

Note: Categories of feeding are not mutually exclusive; the child may be receiving one or both of the others in addition.

rheal episode is not fatal, nutritional deficiency is a frequent aftermath of repeated episodes.

The practice of curtailing the child's diet during diarrheal attacks was equally prevalent among mothers in both groups of villages. Household visits to introduce ORT were intended to provide a point of entry for advising mothers on proper feeding during the illness. Future efforts for management of diarrhea would benefit greatly by placing special emphasis on instructing the mothers to maintain adequate diets during and after attacks. This advice should be an important component of treatment by health personnel in general. In the study population, mothers rarely received advice regarding feeding during the course of visits to health personnel for treatment of diarrhea even in the face of starvation diets.

Treatment during Fatal Diarrheal Disease

Strikingly, mothers made extensive use of medical resources for diarrhea which is, after all, a common childhood disease. Despite heavy field and household work, mothers sought help, frequently more than once, for treatment. The background information on the availability of health services in the governorate discussed earlier may help put into perspective what is otherwise a very exceptional pattern for rural communities. Questions regarding sources of treatment were designed to permit a variety of answers, pertaining both to formal and informal sources of treatment. For diarrheal disease, sources were uniformly reported to be health unit doctors, private doctors, and hospitals.

Among cases of diarrheal death, the proportion of children receiving treatment from at least one source was over 90 percent (Table 9:7). The typical case involved more than one visit for treatment. Considering that the average duration of the terminal diarrheal episode was around four days, this means that con-

Table 9:7. Visits for Treatment During the Fatal Diarrheal Episode, 1979-1980.

VISITS	TREATMENT VILLAGES		CONTROL VILLAGES		ALL VILLAGES	
	Number	Percent	Number	Percent	Number	Percent
First	80	91	78	94	158	92
Second	52	59	46	55	98	57
Third	17	19	22	27	39	23
Diarrheal deaths (number)	88		83		171	

siderable effort was made to obtain multiple sources of therapy in a limited time. Treatment was sought two or more times in 57 percent, and three times in 23 percent, of the fatal cases. There were no significant differences in the proportions receiving treatment between the two groups of villages.

The presence of a health unit within the village did not make a significant difference in terms of seeking treatment. About 93 percent of the children were taken at least once for treatment to some practitioner (not necessarily a health unit) in villages with health units, as compared to 88 percent in villages without health units. The difference would probably have been greater if private alternatives to the public health system were not so readily available as in Menoufia.

Sources for treatment are shown in Table 9:8. Private doctors were the preferred source of treatment on first and second visits. Among the children who were treated a third time, 56 percent received hospital care. This pattern of increased hospital care for those treated two or more times is not unusual in the sense that when previous therapy fails to improve the condition, referral to a hospital becomes necessary for intravenous rehydration. Health centers are not equipped to provide IV therapy, although some private clinics make it available. What is remarkable is that viewed in terms of cases rather than visits, fully 35 percent of the children who died of diarrhea in these villages had been hospitalized at least once during the fatal episode (Table 9:9). There was no difference between the two groups of villages in terms of hospitalization of fatal cases.

The type of treatment provided for fatal diarrhea indicated heavy reliance on administration of a multiplicity of syrups, injections, and tablets. Among the children who received treatment, 84 percent received some form of syrup, 56 percent received injections, and 13 percent were given tablets. The medical management of childhood diarrhea appeared to be dominated by inappropriate measures: although medical opinion varies, use of

Table 9:8. Source of Treatment During the Fatal Diarrheal Episode, 1979-80.

SOURCE	VISITS					
	FIRST		SECOND		THIRD	
	Number	Percent	Number	Percent	Number	Percent
Health unit doctor	51	32	8	8	4	10
Private doctor	100	63	56	57	13	33
Hospital	7	4	34	35	22	56
Total	158	100	98	100	39	100

Table 9:9. Hospital Care During the Fatal Diarrheal Episode, 1979-1980.

VILLAGES	DIARRHEAL DEATHS	CHILDREN HOSPITALIZED	
		Number	Percent
Treatment	88	32	36
Control	83	28	34
All	171	60	35

drugs is seldom to be recommended since most drugs are ineffective for the majority of the common causes of childhood diarrhea.

ORT was used in treating 33 percent of the fatal diarrheal cases in both sets of villages combined (Table 9:10). The proportion receiving oral therapy was higher in treatment villages (35 percent) than in control (30 percent), but the difference was not statistically significant[8]. The difference in use is about the same when we take children who received treatment as the universe rather than all diarrheal deaths (Table 9:10). This information suggests that one important reason for the lack of difference in mortality outcomes due to diarrhea between the two groups of villages lies in the ineffectiveness of the intervention strategy to increase the utilization of ORT in treatment villages. It is also important to ask why ORT was not effective in the cases where it was used, and to examine how it was implemented.

Table 9:10. Utilization of Rehydration Therapy Among Cases of Diarrheal Death in the Two Groups of Villagers, 1979-80.

REHYDRATION THERAPY	TREATMENT VILLAGES		CONTROL VILLAGES		ALL VILLAGES	
	Number	Percent of Treated	Number	Percent of Treated	Number	Percent of Treated
Oral alone	23	29	20	26	43	27
Intravenous alone	15	19	20	26	35	22
Both	8	10	5	6	13	8
Received rehydration	46	58	45	58	91	58
Treated	80		78		158	
Diarrheal deaths	88		83		171	

Practically no families in the treatment villages reported initiating ORT at home prior to medical consultation. A careful review of the history of the fatal episode for the children who received oral rehydration salts, in both groups of villages, indicated that this therapy was used only upon medical advice in all cases except one. One mother in a treatment village reported trying to treat her child by giving two packages of oral rehydration salts prior to going to the health unit. It is possible that the several probes in the medical interview failed to pick up all the cases where ORT may have been initiated by the family, but these omissions could only be a negligible number[9]. Information from fatal cases suggests that the program objective of reaching directly into the household for the purpose of promoting early home use of ORT was not realized.

Apart from not initiating ORT at home, the manner of administering oral fluids once they had been advised by a medical practitioner indicated that project strategy had not been effective in communicating instructions about its proper use to either parents or practitioners. The value of oral therapy lies in preventing dehydration and in correcting it in its early stages. The timing of therapy and the quantities administered and their frequency are critical to the success of ORT. Oral fluids should be given as soon as diarrhea starts and be administered frequently in small amounts day and night until stools are no longer watery. On the whole, oral fluids were given too late and too little. Indications were that on average less than two packages had been consumed by each child. Considering that most of the diarrheas occurred when ambient temperatures were high, and that the fatal episodes averaged four days and were accompanied by vomiting, the quantities used were totally inadequate to replace fluid losses. Moreover, ORT was instituted on the first day of the diarrheal episode in only about 60 percent of the cases. Fluid loss is extremely rapid among young children and dehydration can become severe in a matter of hours.

The promotion of ORT might be expected to increase awareness of the importance of fluid therapy among physicians in management of diarrhea, but as Table 9:10 shows, there was no significant difference between the two groups of villages in the use of IV rehydration either alone or as backup for oral therapy. The proportions of children who died who had received IV rehydration were practically identical between treatment (29 percent) and control groups (32 percent).

It should be noted that project personnel encountered resistance to the household promotion of ORT in a few communities and particularly among some doctors. There seems to be several factors involved in this negative reaction. First, there had been no plan in the initial year of implementation to involve the communities or the health unit personnel in the organization of the household distribution. The program may have been viewed by the health unit doctors as interfering in their responsibility for health in the villages[10]. More importantly, the mortality findings suggest that there was a genuine lack of appreciation of the role of ORT in medical management of diarrhea. Again the strategy of the intervention in the first year fell short of providing an adequate training in oral therapy to the health unit personnel. A short training session was held, limited to physicians, and was attended by only one-half of those invited (Assaad et al., 1980). In view of the extensive contact this rural population maintains with health professionals, it is very important that they be thoroughly acquainted with the new therapy and support its home use by encouraging and advising mothers.

It is also possible that the use of ORT was curtailed somewhat by the fact that the home distributors were young women whose credibility may have been questioned by the mothers. In addition a more careful supervision of the home visits, especially concerning the actual time spent on ORT explanation in the home, and the content of the instructions given to mothers would have been useful. Credibility of the source and quality of the instruction are key elements in an intervention that seeks to make fairly substantial behavioral changes among mothers.

It is not possible to evaluate fully the quality of care available to all children with diarrhea in these villages on the basis of the information on dead children. The children who died represent the failures of medical as well as nonmedical systems of care. A full evaluation would need to take into account the children who recovered as well as those who died.

PROGRAMATIC IMPLICATIONS

Although data pertaining to the use of ORT in nonfatal cases of diarrhea are lacking, there is no evidence that the intervention lowered diarrheal mortality among children in treatment villages. An intervention program needs to alter the existing behavior of mothers and health professionals with respect to management of diarrhea in order to produce desired effects.

The role of dehydration in producing death did not appear to be appreciated by either mothers or medical practitioners. ORT when used was utilized too late and too little to serve as a means of replacing vital fluids. The use of IV rehydration was very limited in all villages. Had the importance of rehydration been appreciated, almost all the fatal cases would have received IV rehydration even if ORT were not fully accepted. Clearly, a good training program must be formulated to teach both mothers and health professionals that rehydration is the key to effective management of diarrhea.

The intervention effort also failed to instruct mothers about the importance of maintaining proper diets during diarrheal episodes. If mortality due to diarrhea is to be reduced, the overlap between rehydration and nutritional care needs to be underlined. Despite the traditional practice of restricting diets severely during diarrheal episodes, treatment rarely included advice to mothers on proper feeding. In view of the customary reluctance to feed, it is necessary to help mothers understand that whatever is taken by mouth is not all lost and that in spite of increased frequency of stools the child will improve more rapidly if fed properly.

The more important question raised by the study pertains to the appropriateness of the intervention strategy to the task of reducing diarrheal mortality among children. Given the prevalence of diarrheal disease and the rapidity with which dehydration develops, the concentration of health education on mothers and on home management of diarrhea was the appropriate approach. Single entry efforts, however, even as intensively targeted as the household distribution, are not likely to produce changes in sickness care practices without adequate community preparation and careful follow up. Household distribution may be used as a central event to introduce ORT into village communities but its acceptance and proper use require reinforcement over time. The reinforcement could come from community-level health education efforts organized at regular intervals and from the health professionals themselves. In view of the well-staffed and extensive network of health facilities, it should not be too difficult to schedule periodic home visits to check home supplies of oral rehydration solution as well as to give continued health education to mothers. Additional training and motivation for public sector doctors is likewise called for. The extensive contact with private sector physicians suggests that an effort to mobilize this sector to participate in promoting ORT could be very useful.

Clearly death rates may be high or low at given levels of morbidity depending upon the availability of effective sickness care. The scope for lowering death rates, however, is likely to remain limited as long as the processes that generate disease are not altered.

A strategy that addresses the issues of susceptibility and exposure to diarrheal disease, as well as its treatment, is more likely to produce a sustained decline in diarrheal mortality over the long term. Given the multiplicity of sources for infection in the Egyptian countryside a program for reducing diarrheal morbidity is admittedly difficult to formulate and to implement. Efforts must be multilayered encompassing a range of activities from community mobilization to alter the infrastructure of environmental hygiene and sanitation, to health education programs for changing health care as well as sickness care practices. Intervention strategies need to address multiple aspects of household behavior that have a bearing on diarrheal disease, including: water use, waste disposal, food preparation and storage, child feeding (particularly weaning habits) and proper home treatment.

The study indicated a number of factors that can assist in future efforts to educate mothers regarding the management of diarrhea in rural Egypt: they do recognize signs of dehydration, provide liquid for children with diarrhea, and seek medical care. It is the task of health educators to teach mothers the significance of the signs they see and to relate them to the necessary action. A good intervention would also provide instruction and follow up at the level of the health system so that effective therapy would gradually be taught and spread among mothers. Childhood diarrhea is a major health problem in rural Egypt and its control remains a high priority challenge.

ACKNOWLEDGEMENTS

The Menoufia Integrated Social Services Delivery System Project was a cooperative effort between the local administration of Menoufia Governorate, particularly its Departments of Health and Social Welfare, the Ministries of Health and Social Affairs, and the Social Research Center of the American University in Cairo. It was funded by a grant from the United States Agency for International Development. This study was conducted while the author was a Research Associate at the Social Research Center.

The support and encouragement of Dr. Saad Gadalla, the Director of the Center, is gratefully acknowledged. I am indebted to Dr. W. H. Mosley for incisive comments and discussions. The research benefited greatly from the assistance of Dr. Salah Saleh Abdelhadi as the medical consultant with contributions from medical doctors A. Rizkallah, F. A. Akabawy, and N. Nour. Azza Beshir and Denise Batani provided very able research assistance.

NOTES

1. There is an extensive literature on the synergism between acute diarrheal disease and nutritional deficiency in early childhood. An excellent review of the epidemiological, clinical and experimental evidence on the interrelationship between nutrition and infection with particular reference to weanling diarrhea is given in N. S. Scrimshaw, C. E. Taylor, and J. E. Gordon, Interaction of Nutrition and Infection (Geneva: WHO, 1968). See also Republic of Philippines, World Health Organization, John Snow Public Health Group, and International Study Group, "A positive effect on the nutrition of Philippine children of an oral glucose-electrolyte solution given at home for treatment of diarrhea: report of a field trial," Bulletin of the World Health Organization, 55,1 (1977): 87-94.

2. There are numerous studies on the development of oral therapy and on proper fluid composition. A useful overview of its development and documentation of its use in a variety of settings is given in "Oral rehydration therapy (ORT) for childhood diarrhea," Population Reports Series L, no. 2 (November-December 1980). For a good review of guidelines for treatment of diarrhea see World Health Organization, Diarrheal Disease Control Program: A Manual for Treatment of Acute Diarrhea (Geneva: WHO, 1980).

3. In addition to Population Reports, cited in note 2, see R. A. Cash, D. R. Nalin, R. Rochat, L. B. Reller, Z. A. Hague, and A.S.M.M. Rahman, "A clinical trial of oral therapy in a rural cholera-treatment center," American Journal of Tropical Medicine and Hygiene 19,4 (1970): 653-56; M. M. Rahaman, K.M.S. Aziz, Y. Patwari, and H. M. Munshi, "Diarrheal mortality in two Bangladeshi villages with and without community-based oral rehydration therapy," Lancet 2 (October 20, 1979): 809-812; A. A. Kielmann and C. McCord, "Home treatment of childhood diarrhea in Punjab villages," Environmental Child Health 23,4 (August 1977): 197-201.

4. The significant changes in approach were the formation of a central team of canvassers for conducting household visits, provision of more extensive specialized training in oral therapy to health facility physicians, and community preparation in the form of village meetings to discuss diarrheal disease management organized prior to the household visits. For a detailed discussion of the problems and modifications in approach see Muhamed Feteha, "The distribution of oral rehydration salts in Menoufia, Egypt: A process of developing approaches through implementation," paper presented at the 15th Annual Conference on Statistics, Computer Sciences and Operations Research, Institute of Statistical Studies and Research of Cairo University, Cairo, Egypt, 15-18 December 1980.

5. A detailed study of the rural health services in the governorate was undertaken as part of the research activities of the Menoufia Project. The information on public health services is from the report of this study. See M. El Nomrossy, "Survey and evaluation of health services in the villages of the Menoufia Governorate." Social Research Center, American University in Cairo, 1980.

6. For the first year of life, the statistical test of the effect of treatment can be carried out also by using the infant death rate due to diarrhea. This is deaths from diarrhea among children under age one divided by births in the population for the year. The rates are 54.5 per thousand in treatment and 55.3 per thousand in control villages and again indicate no difference.

7. A study carried out in rural Punjab found that the mean duration of diarrhea decreased significantly following an intensive program promoting early home use of oral rehydration solution. Kielmann and McCord, cited in note 3, p. 199.

8. The finding concerning use of oral therapy in the control villages should not be surprising since the Ministry of Health in Egypt had already introduced a national program for provision of oral rehydration therapy through its facilities in 1977. A powder with the same composition as Ora-

lyte, but manufactured in Egypt in packets of smaller size, was made available in rural health facilities.

9. This is supported by the findings of an anthropological study which included structured interviews on villagers' health practices and participation in health services. The study was conducted during the first half of 1980 in one of the villages where household distribution had been carried out. The study reports that when questioned about treatment for diarrhea for children, the respondents mentioned stopping breastfeeding, giving home remedies in the form of boiled herbs, and going to the doctor but none mentioned oral rehydration salts. M. Assaad and S. El Katsha, "Villagers' participation in formal and informal health services in an Egyptian delta village." Regional Papers, The Population Council, West Asia and North Africa Region, June 1981, p. 7.

10. This point of view emerged strongly during the course of interviews held with a number of doctors and is referred to in the report by Feteha, cited in note 4, pp. 5-6.

REFERENCES

Assaad, M., S. El Katsha, and S. Saleh. "Report on the General and Specialized Training Program, Menoufia Project." Cairo: Social Research Center, The American University in Cairo, 1980.

Fergany, N. "A Reconstruction of Some Aspects of the Demographic History of Egypt in the Twentieth Century." Technical Papers R31. Cairo: The American University in Cairo, January 1976.

McCord, C. "Oral Fluid Treatment for Diarrhea, Menoufia Governorate, Egypt." (AID/pha/C-1100) Washington, DC: American Public Health Association, 1979.

Omran, A. "The Mortality Profile." In Egypt: Population Problems and Prospects, edited by A.R. Omran. Chapel Hill, NC: University of North Carolina, 1973.

Rashad, H. "Evaluation of the Completeness of Mortality Registration in Egypt." Regional Papers. West Asia and North Africa Region, The Population Council, 1981.

APPENDIX I

Summary of ORT instructions given during household visits:

a) If a child has diarrhea (liquid stools), start giving ORT immediately.

b) Prepare the treatment by putting the contents of one packet into the designated bottle. Add clean water from a tap or pump up to the red sign and close tightly. Shake till salt is dissolved.

c) For children under one year of age, the amount to be given is 3/4 of a bottle over 24 hours. Start the treatment by feeding the mixture to the child by spoon until the child takes 10 spoonfuls. Increase the amount given over time as the child takes it. Give the prescribed amount over 24 hours, in small doses as described, and not all at once. If the child is being breastfed, this should continue.

d) For children one year and over, the dosage is 1½ bottles if under three years, and 2 bottles for children three to five years over 24 hours. Start by giving half in glass and repeat every half hour over 24 hours. Do not give the entire amount at once. If the child is being breastfed, this should continue. If the child is receiving food, give fat-free boiled food during the treatment. After diarrhea is cured, increase the amount of food or lactation to fortify and to help the child recover.

e) General instructions for all children under age five: If the prescribed amount is not all taken during 24 hours, throw away left over solution and wash the bottle. If the child continues to have diarrhea for more than 24 hours even though the prescribed amount is given, prepare a new bottle and continue to give treatment for another 24 hours. As soon as you have used a packet of the treatment, go to the health unit to take another packet.

f) Take the child to the health unit for examination if any one of the following occurs:

- the child continues to vomit and cannot take liquids.

- the diarrhea gets worse or is accompanied by blood.

- the diarrhea continues for more than 2 days.

- the child is very weak.

APPENDIX [illegible]

[illegible] of [illegible] given during [illegible]

1. [illegible]
[illegible]

2. [illegible] the [illegible] with [illegible] the [illegible] one [illegible] to [illegible] and [illegible]

3. [illegible] about the [illegible], the [illegible] the [illegible] should [illegible] that the [illegible] child [illegible] the [illegible] the [illegible] and [illegible] the [illegible]

4. [illegible] the [illegible] and [illegible] of [illegible] and [illegible] the [illegible] the [illegible] the [illegible] after [illegible]

5. [illegible] the [illegible] and [illegible] the [illegible] the [illegible] children [illegible] that [illegible] the [illegible] the [illegible]

6. [illegible] of the [illegible] the [illegible]

(1) [illegible] the [illegible] of the [illegible]

— the [illegible] the [illegible]

— [illegible] the [illegible]

— the [illegible] of the [illegible]

— the [illegible]

Part Four

Antihelminthics in CBD Programs

10
Antihelminthic Therapy in Community-Based Family Planning and Health Projects

Gerald T. Keusch

We are surrounded. All around us there are parasitic worms ready to infect the human species. The "unholy" trinity alone (the giant roundworm Ascaris lumbricoides, the whipworm Trichuris trichiura, and the hookworms Ancylostoma duodenale or Necator americanus) frequently coinfect the same host, and account for 3 billion infections. When other agents are added to this total, there are more helminth infections than people on the globe.

Given the prevalence of helminth infections, it is important to consider the advantages and disadvantages of antihelminthic interventions in community-based distribution (CBD) family planning programs. This paper will review elements of helminth biology and treatment which are important to consider in planning such projects. Since the effects of the parasites on nutritional status and development are unclear, the potentially limited role of antihelminthic interventions will be assessed.

HELMINTH BIOLOGY

Although many individuals are multiply infected by helminths, many remain uninfected. This epidemiology is accounted for by the biology of the worm and by the sociology of the host. In order to discuss the control of helminth infections within the context of CBD programs, it is reasonable to focus attention on the most widespread and prevalent agents, Ascaris, Trichuris, and hookworms. These infections may affect public health and can be dealt with through community-based projects.

The three share a similar life cycle, involving no intermediate host. A noninfectious egg is excreted into the soil, develops into infectious form, and is then transmitted to the human without passing through a vector. In a sense, the soil acts as the intermediate host in which essential biological transformations occur (Beaver, 1975). The involvement of soil is, therefore, not simply physical or mechanical. Indeed, the endemicity of these three infections depends not only on direct fecal contamination of soil, but also on conditions essential for the development of the worm and for protection of the infectious stage until a suitable host comes along. Probably the most important characteristic of soil in this regard is its capacity to absorb and hold water, which in turn depends on its texture, particle size and composition. When suspended in soil and water, helminth eggs settle near, but well below the surface, coated by a blanket of fine silt and clay (Beaver, 1975). In the ground this blanket protects the eggs from direct sunlight and drying.

In contrast to Ascaris and Trichuris, in which the infectious embryo develops within the egg, the infectious hookworm larva hatches in the soil. The larvae move up and down in the soil in opposition to the movement of water. Porous sandy soils are best suited to this migratory behavior (hydrotaxis) of hookworm, whereas Ascaris and Trichuris are of greatest threat in clay soils.

Rain also plays a role in the dissemination of eggs in the soil. Raindrops not only wet the ground, but also create a splattering effect that mixes and scatters the soil and contaminating feces. Heavy rain can dissipate a stool over several meters of flat surface, forming a zone of constant motion of soil, water, and feces (with its content of helminth eggs) up to a depth of 30 cm (Beaver, 1975). The potential for infection is thus spread over a considerable distance from the site of fecal soilage.

Soil-transmitted diseases can present intractable problems of control, since they have no vector which can be attacked in order to interrupt transmission (Stauden, 1976). Control of these infections requires a combination of improvements in sanitation, extensive behavioral modification (through health education) to stop indiscriminate defecation, and appropriate use of chemotherapy. Effective interventions must include each limb of this triad.

Life Cycles

A. lumbricoides appears to be highly host-adapted to the human (Pawlowski, 1982). An average number of six worms infect each host, suggesting that the global Ascaris population is roughly 7.8 billion. The sexes are distinct. Each female Ascaris is an extremely active reproductive factory, producing nearly a quarter million eggs per day. The environment receives the astounding number of 10^{13}-10^{14} eggs daily, many of which will develop to a potentially invasive stage. In a temperate climate eggs can remain viable in soil for more than six years, whereas both cold and extreme heat kill the embryo in a short while.

The life cycle is initiated by the oral ingestion of an infectious L_2 larva enclosed within the egg shell. Physical conditions in the gut, including the dissolved CO_2 content, reducing agents, and proper pH, result in hatching (Rogers and Sommerville, 1968). The released larva molts to an L_3 stage which invades the gut mucosa, enters the lymphatic system, and makes its way to the liver, through the heart, and into the lungs.

During this migration of 24 to 72 hours, two more molts occur to produce the young adult worms which break through the aveoli in the lung, ascend the bronchotracheal tree only to be swallowed and enter the gastrointestinal lumen. The worms finally settle in the small bowel, mature into the adult stage, and approximately two months after ingestion of the egg, the adults mate and egg production commences.

The life cycle of *T. trichiura* is quite similar except that larvae do not migrate systemically. First-stage *Trichuris* larvae emerging from ingested eggs penetrate the intestinal villi for a short period of about a week and then return to the lumen of the cecum and large bowel to continue development to maturity. This process takes around three months. *T. trichiura* females produce fewer eggs than *Ascaris*, on the order of 3,000 to 10,000 per day, but these are well protected and survive longer in the environment.

The life cycle of the hookworms *Necator* and *Ancylostoma* are quite different from the two nematodes just discussed in that a free-living larval stage develops in soil from the L_1 larva emerging from the egg. In well aerated, moist earth at an optimal temperature of 23 to 33°C, the process occurs in a day or two. The resulting rhabditiform larvae feed on bacteria and organic matter in the soil and store energy, largely in the form of lipids. The next molt, the infectious third-stage filariform larvae, use these energy stores to move within the soil. These worms may remain viable for several months under ideal conditions but in a tropical climate viability drops off sharply in the first 10 days and it is estimated that only 10 percent survive as long as three weeks (Schad et al., 1973). Upon contact with the definitive host, filariform larvae penetrate the skin and are carried in the circulation to the lung. There they molt in 24 hours and follow the *Ascaris* path through the alveoli, up the bronchi, down the esophagus to arrive in the small bowel. After a final molt, occurring within two weeks, the adult stage is achieved and within one to two months egg production will begin. *A. duodenale* infection can also be acquired via the oral route, as, for example, from larvae present on vegetables grown and fertilized with night soil.

Clinical Manifestations

Like most metazoans, the three organisms being considered do not multiply within the human body. Disease manifestations depend on the number of worms present (the worm burden), which is directly related to the frequency of infection of the host by eggs or larvae. The fact that these organisms do not multiply in the human host changes the entire consideration of the biology of the disease. Light infections are unequivocally inapparent and unimportant and remain so.

While the prevalence of *Ascaris*, *Trichuris*, or hookworm infection may be high, the distribution of the intensity of the infection is highly skewed. The majority of individuals are lightly infected and virtually asymptomatic and only a small minority of infections are heavy and clinically manifest. Thus, simple prevalence studies are insufficient to determine whether individuals are at risk of developing helminth-related symptoms. It is more important to know whether an individual has a light or heavy infection, as determined by the quantity of eggs per gram of stool. These features of helminth infection have been creatively likened to "guerrilla warfare as outlined by Chairman Mao, repeatedly infiltrating host defenses as individuals or in small groups and gradually building into large forces; warfare is usually by attrition and tends to be prolonged" (Warren, 1970).

The manifestations of ascariasis are caused by larvae migrating through the lung, or adults residing in the small bowel lumen (although in most individuals the infection is unnoticed unless adult worms are expelled from the mouth, nose, or anus). Larvae passing through the lungs - usually about two weeks after ingestion of ova - cause tracheobronchitis, rapidly changing pulmonary infiltrates, and marked eosinophilia, a constellation known as Loeffler's syndrome. This is usually self-limited in a week or two. The more serious complications are caused by adult worms. Ascaris have a propensity to crawl into small openings such as the ducts opening into the intestinal lumen. Blockage of the pancreatic or biliary duct is followed by acute pancreatitis or cholecystitis. It has been suggested that this aberrant migration of ascarids is more frequent in single-worm infections, or when all worms are of the same sex (Pawlowski, 1978). The more common complication caused by adult ascarids, intestinal obstruction by a bolus of tangled worms, occurs in heavy infection. Crowding also causes distal migration of worms, which may lead to acute appendicitis or intestinal perforation. It is difficult to estimate the incidence of these problems, since accurate numerators as well as denomina- tors for the number of infected individuals are generally unavailable and definitive diagnosis is frequently lacking. In one report from Cape Town, South Africa, intestinal obstruction secondary to A. lumbricoides accounted for about one sixth of all acute abdominal emergencies (Louw, 1974). While the estimated mortality rate from such complications is only six per 100,000 infected (World Health Organization, 1967), given the large number of infected individuals in the world this translates into a considerable number of avoidable deaths. This estimate could be very inaccurate, since most data regarding serious effects of ascaris are from hospital-based studies comprised of a non-representative population.

T. trichiura adults live primarily in the cecum and ascending colon, inserting their thin, whip-like anterior end into the mucosa. However, with crowding the infection proceeds distally. The only symptoms that can be definitely attributed to heavy infection with this worm are diarrhea, dysentery, and rectal prolapse. In the latter complication, a myriad of worms may be seen attached to the prolapsed mucosa. The cause of the intestinal symptoms is not clear; in many cases amebiasis is present concomitantly. As already noted, A. lumbricoides is often found together with Trichuris.

Hookworm infection is generally initiated by penetration of exposed skin, most frequently the soles of the feet as people walk barefoot through infected soil. Penetration of skin is usually without symptoms; however, a large number of invading larvae can cause intense pruritis, commonly termed "ground itch". Migration of larvae through the lungs can, as in the case of Ascaris, result in Loeffler's syndrome or an acute asthmatic attack. However, the principal disease is caused by adult worms in the intestinal tract. The worms have tooth like structures (Ancylostoma) or cutting plates (Necator) by which they attach to the gut mucosa, sucking a plug of tissue into their buccal cavity. This lacerates the mucosa, resulting in bleeding, which is intensified by strong sucking movements of the worm. Blood traverses the gut of the hookworm in a few minutes and the erythrocytes are expelled from the caudal end, the worm using the serum but not the cellular content (Ogilive et al., 1978).

Hookworms move from one site to another, perhaps three to four times per day, initiating new lesions that may continue to ooze blood for a considerable time, in part due to an anticoagulant produced by the worm (Roche and Layrisse, 1966). The major consequence of this activity is iron loss, even though a considerable proportion of the iron reaching the gut lumen may be reabsorbed (Farid et al., 1970). The extent of bleeding is greater with Ancylostoma infection (0.16 to 0.34 ml/worm/day) compared with Necator (0.005 to 0.13 ml/worm/day). The effect of hookworm infection on hematopoiesis is thus determined by the infecting species, the worm burden, and the underlying state of iron nutriture of the host. Severe anemia may frequently be seen in individuals infected with over 100 worms, especially when dietary intake is principally from vegetable iron of limited bioavailability. The role of iron loss in the pathogenesis of hookworm anemia is clearly shown by the ability to restore normal hemoglobin levels by iron supplementation alone.

Other hookworm-related symptoms include nausea, abdominal pain, and diarrhea; as a result, infected individuals may reduce food intake. The consequence of this is weight loss which may contribute to the development of malnutrition or the worsening of pre-existent nutritional deficiencies.

Volunteers infected on multiple occasions with N. americanus initially experience intestinal symptoms, but these disappear on subsequent reinfections concomitant with, and possibly related to, development of a systemic humoral immune response (Ogilive et al., 1978). Nutritional problems are thought to follow the loss of serum proteins through the bleeding lesions produced by the feeding habits of the worms. Using ^{131}I-albumin, Blackman and colleagues (1966) have shown losses of protein into the stool which correlate with the worm burden and amount to about 100 mg/day/100 N. americanus. It is unclear, however, how much of the labeled albumin entering the gut is metabolized, digested and reabsorbed and how much is actually lost. Blackman et al. observed no correlation between serum albumin level and worm burden, a finding confirmed in another study in South America (Villarejos et al., 1970) and in Bangladesh (Gilman).

CONTROL

Control of Soil-Transmitted Helminthiasis

The cycle for infections involves fecal excretion and deposition in soil of viable eggs. Cessation of indiscriminate defecation and of the use of night soil will interrupt transmission and ultimately eradicate the infection, inasmuch as the three agents discussed are largely restricted to human hosts. Basic sanitary measures to provide water for washing and facilities for safe disposal of feces are the cornerstone of such an effort. In the absence of continued contamination of soil, transmission will no longer be possible within a few years. The benefits of reduced prevalence and intensity of soil infection are direct and cumulative. In the case of hookworm, providing concrete floors around the house and wearing shoes can make significant inroads on the intensity of infection.

Treatment of soil to reduce viability of eggs or larvae is, at least theoretically, another strategy. However there are no candidate antihelminthic compounds for such use at this time.

The third strategy is chemotherapy of the infected subject. This may accomplish two things: reduction of worm burden and reduction in egg output. Two obvious benefits result from this option. First, because nearly all clinical manifestations are due to heavy infections, reduction in the number of worms present can be expected to alleviate or prevent symptoms. Indeed, from this perspective, it is not necessary to achieve cure to improve the health status of both individuals and populations but rather it is sufficient to simply reduce the worm burden. Second, a reduction in egg output, if prolonged, will lower the degree of soil contamination with infective forms and thus contribute to the efforts to interrupt the transmission cycle. In any serious attempt to control the infections, it seems clear that chemotherapy will be an essential component of the program, but insufficient as a single intervention.

Population at Risk

The distribution of helminth infection is influenced by age and sex, since these factors influence contact with soil. Preschool children have the highest Ascaris infection rates. Young children have lower hookworm prevalence and intensity, since infection results from multiple contacts over time with infected soil. By the same token, because of their greater participation in agricultural occupations, males have more hookworm than females. The intensity of intestinal worm infections tends to decrease in adults due to the host's immune mechanisms and the worms' life span being shorter than that of man's. Changes in behavior, such as reducing contact with infected soil, can lead to a difference in exposure and thus diminish worm loads.

It should also be apparent that a program does not have to be global to have effect. Efforts to control the impact of parasitic diseases can often be targeted at the members of the community most likely to become infected and clinically ill with each form of helminth.

Antihelminthics

Drug development has progressed remarkably in the past two decades, rendering many of the old drugs obsolete for reasons of both safety and efficacy. Nevertheless, the choice of an appropriate drug for mass chemotherapy must be made on the basis of the species distribution, intensity of infection, mode of transmission, and margin of safety for administration of the drug by minimally trained field people. "The use of broad spectrum antihelminthics as a substitute for knowledge has no sensible foundation beyond expediency" (Stauden, 1976). It is also important to point out that the treatment of individuals presenting to the hospital or outpatient health clinic will not affect the population as a whole, and that the treated and cured patient will become reinfected within a period of weeks or months of returning to the contaminated environment.

Of the four score drugs currently available to treat helminthic infections only a few are suitable for mass chemotherapy of humans (Table 10:1). These drugs are vastly different in structure, although many appear to act on the worm's neuromuscular junction resulting in its paralysis (Gilman). Because intestinal helminths depend on muscular activity to remain *in situ* in their favored habitat, paralysis leads to expulsion through peristalsis and excretion of intestinal contents. The ecological importance of motility of worms has dictated the use of assays of motility to screen possibly useful chemotherapeutic agents (Mansour, 1979). Worms treated *in vitro* remain viable and if the drug is washed away muscular activity is restored. Mebendazole differs in that a major action appears to be a selective and irreversible block of glucose uptake through an effect on cytoplasmic microtubules of the worm's absorptive cells (Mansour, 1979).. The consequence of this is depletion of glycogen and a marked decrease in ATP production leading to cellular death. The functional impairment this produces, in turn, is lethal to the worm.

The desirable characteristics for an ideal antihelminthic include: potency, activity against the worm but not the human host, freedom from side effects, efficacy when administered orally in a single dose, palatability, and, under special conditions, broad spectrum of activity. From the public health standpoint it must be: inexpensive, stable when stored at ambient conditions in tropical and nontropical environments, and safe to give without prior medical screening of the patient. It must also require minimal follow-up.

No drug meets all of these requirements although some appear to come reasonably close (Katz, 1982). Four of the drugs listed in Table 10:1 appear to be candidates for CBD chemotherapy programs: piperazine, levamisole, pyrantel/oxantel, and bephenium (Janssen, 1976; Miller, 1976; Botero, 1981; Keystone and Murdock, 1979). While multiple dose regimens extending over two

Table 10:1. Antihelminthics of Potential Utility in Community-Based Distribution Programs

CHEMICAL CLASS	DRUG	ADMINISTRATION	SINGLE DOSE[1] RECOMMENDED	COMMENTS
Diethylenediamine	Piperazine	Oral	Yes	Useful only for Ascaris
Benzimidazole	Levamisole	Oral	Yes	Interesting immunopotentiating effects
	Thaibendazole	Oral	No	Efficacy against susceptible worms requires multiple doses
	Mebendazole	Oral	No	In multiple doses also effective against Trichuris and hookworms. Not the drug of choice for tapeworms, but may be of use in in vasive larval tapeworm infection (cysticercosis, echinoiccosis)
Cyanine	Pyrvinum	Oral	Yes	Main use for Enterobius
Pyrimidine	Pyrantel	Oral	Yes	Multiple doses effective against hookworms
	Oxantel	Oral	Yes	Combination of pyrantel and oxantel, especially in multiple doses, very effective against Ascaris, Trichuris, and hookworms
Quaternary Amine	Bephenium	Oral	Yes	Bitter taste needs to be disguised

[1] For some agents, multiple dose regimens may be more effective.

Table 10:1 (Cont.). Antihelminthics of Potential Utility in Community-Based Distribution Programs

CHEMICAL CLASS	DRUG	SPECTRUM OF ACTIVITY OF SINGLE DOSE				FREQUENCY OF ADVERSE EFFECTS
		Ascaris	*Trichuris*	Hookworm	Other	
Diethylenediamine	Piperazine	+++	-	-		-
Benzimidazole	Levamisole	+++	+	++/+++[2]	*Enterobius*	±
	Thaibendazole	+	-	+	*Strongyloides*[3] *Trichinella*	+/++
	Mebendazole	++/+++	+	+	*Enterobius*[3] Tapeworms	-
					Capillaria[3] *philippinensis*	May result in expulsion of *Ascaris* from nose and mouth
Cyanine	Pyrvinum	-	-	-	*Enterobius*	-
Pyrimidine	Pyrantel	+++	-	-	*Enterobius*	-
	Oxantel	+++	+	+	-	-
Quaternary Amine	Bephenium	+++	+	+++	-	++ Nausea and vomiting

[2] *Ancylostoma* more susceptible than *Necator*.
[3] Drug of choice.

to three days are more effective in accomplishing cure, single dose regimens of these drugs will cure some individuals, reduce the worm burden in the remainder, and result in a significant reduction in egg output, suggesting that some damage has occurred to the surviving worms.

Antihelminthic therapy alone administered in the context of a CBD program is unlikely to have any significant health or nutrition benefit for the population treated (Keusch, 1982). While this does not preclude the use of antihelminthics in CBD programs, it does mandate a clear definition of the goals of their administration, and selection of the most appropriate agent, considering efficacy, cost and potential toxicity or side effects.

CHOICE OF DRUG

Goals of Antihelminthic Interventions

There are several goals to be considered: (1) demonstration of the impact of a CBD program by dramatically treating worms which are then expelled; (2) improvement in health or nutrition, (3) reduction of the worm burden in heavily infected subjects, (4) reduction of egg output to the environment, and (5) cure of infections. Goal 5 may not be appropriate for single dose CBD programs, because multiple doses are required to cure the majority of *Trichuris* and hookworm infections. Moreover, reinfection will occur in most cured patients within a few months unless transmission is also stopped. In contrast, worm expulsion, reduction of worm burden and decrease in egg output are all readily achieved in the context of CBD interventions. If maintained, the reduction in intensity of infections will reduce the likelihood of complications of *Ascaris* and *Trichuris*, and the prevalence of severe anemia due to hookworm. If the drugs are not given on a regular basis, the benefits are likely to rapidly dissipate and disappear.

Where *Ascaris* is the main problem, or when one wishes to demonstrate a dramatic effect, piperazine (a drug in use for over 30 years) is probably without equal from the standpoint of cost and safety. Some worms will be expelled in the stool in most, if not all, individuals who receive even a single dose. Piperazine has virtually no effect on the other helminths, since even the treatment of *Enterobius vermicularis* (the pinworm) requires multiple doses of piperazine.

Where hookworm is important, the agents to be considered are levamisole, pyrantil/oxantil and bephenium. Mebendazole is much less effective in its standard dose. The bitter taste of bephenium usually requires administration in a heavy sugar syrup and may cause nausea and vomiting - undesirable side effects in a CBD program.

Trichuris presents a problem since an effective regimen requires multiple doses inappropriate for a CBD program. When it is necessary to treat clinical symptoms due to *Trichuris*, mebendazole is probably the drug of choice (Keystone and Murdock,

1979). Some authors report a significant incidence of Ascaris expulsion from nose or mouth during treatment of poly-parasitized subjects (Chanco and Vidad, 1978; Pena Chavarria et al., 1973; Partono, 1974; Banzon, 1976; Chongsuphajaisiddhi et al., 1978; Seo et al., 1978), but complications due to ductal obstruction must be extremely rare under these circumstances. The literature is conflicting on the question of nasal expulsion after use of mebendazole. Reports are somewhat anecodotal, they are not designed as controlled comparative trials, and they do not consider other factors that may result in antegrade expulsion, such as fever. Nonetheless, in heavy mixed infections, some workers have suggested use of a paralysing agent, such as piperazine, in addition to mebendazole (Hauer, 1981). Prospective studies are needed to resolve these problems. In addition, use of mebendazole in CBD projects may be somewhat limited by potential teratogenicity, demonstrated in rodents though unproven in humans. Finally, there are insufficient data concerning safety in the child under two years of age.

At the same time, mebendazole is truly a broad-spectrum drug, substantially reducing Ascaris, Trichuris and hookworm burdens in full therapeutic doses with minimal toxicity (Keystone and Murdock, 1979). It is less active in a single standard 100 mg dose against hookworm than is pyrantel/oxantel, and no more active than piperazine against Ascaris. However, newer studies using mebendazole in single doses of 200 or 300 mg or in combination with a single dose of pyrantel/oxantel have reported substantial overall reduction in the intensity of hookworm and Ascaris, and even cures in the great majority of patients (Pena Chavarria et al., 1973; Partono et al., 1974; Seo, 1978; Hauer, 1981; Muttalib et al., 1981; Sinniah et al., 1980).

Hookworm and Trichuris should not be the chief targets for an antihelminthic chemotherapeutic attack in a CBD project, from either the public health viewpoint or in an effort to increase community acceptance of other CBD projects. If the desire is to demonstrate an effect for the latter purpose, the goal should be to treat Ascaris, as this will produce the most immediate and visible effect. Furthermore, the therapy can be targeted to young school-age children who will generally pass a larger number of worms. If piperazine is employed, the effect will be seen within 24 hours; mebendazole is slower acting and it may take several days before ascarids are passed. Such subtle issues should be considered in the choice of intervention, once the decision has been reached to implement an antihelminthic activity.

If the goal is to improve health, the pathogen of greatest significance is hookworm, and the target group will generally be young male adults with heavy infection. The treatment of choice for hookworm disease is iron by either supplementation or fortification (Keusch, 1982). The addition of antihelminthic therapy is of value, but is, strictly speaking, unnecessary to control the anemia. Levamisole is probably the most effective drug in a single dose regimen, but other choices include pyrantel/oxantel, bephenium and possibly the combination of pyrantel/oxantel and mebendazole (Sinniah et al., 1980).

Efficacy of the Intervention

Any mass chemotherapy program designed to have long-lasting impact on the transmission of soil-based helminthic infection in the individual or in the population must be periodic (at least several times per year) because of the frequency and rapidity of reinfection. Ideally, such a program should be combined with environmental sanitation and health education. Without this, the investments in the program will be wasted if mass drug distribution stops for any reason, for within a short while the prevalence and intensity of infection will be back to their original level (Borrows, 1975). If the intent of chemotherapy is not to achieve cure but primarily to reduce the intensity of infection in heavily parasitized segments of the population, then single dose therapy at considerably longer intervals may well suffice. Such a strategy will produce only secondary and slow reduction in helminth transmission from soil; it does so by decreasing daily soil contamination with eggs (a reduction, if you will, in the communicability of soil). Prospective, long-term surveillance of a population is required to determine the efficacy of such a program design and to measure the health benefits which might accrue from the effort.

It seems clear that any reduction in intensity of hookworm infection would reduce the incidence and severity of iron deficiency anemia, but the same effects could be achieved by iron supplementation or fortification of some suitable dietary staple. Several recent field studies have attempted to measure the more controversial nutritional benefits of periodic antihelminthic treatment to reduce A. lumbricoides infection in young children (Gupta et al., 1977; Willett and Kihamia, 1979; Stephenson et al., 1980). However, the results are inconclusive, in part because of flaws in the study design or the small magnitude of the improvements in anthropometric measures of nutritional status (Schultz, 1982). The best of these studies by Stephenson and co-workers (Stephenson et al., 1980) was of relatively short duration and it is unclear whether or not the small gains observed would be sustained or cumulative over a long period of time. Schultz (1982), who reviewed these and other studies on nutritional consequences of ascariasis, concluded that current data do not justify the institution of periodic mass chemotherapy to improve nutritional state and growth of children.

Since it is not yet possible to judge the immediate effects of mild or moderate Ascaris infections on individuals, nor to judge the cumulative effects on child development, the available data cannot be extrapolated to lend support to any large national or international program.

Cultural Responses

Many cultural aspects of health care delivery are not well defined. Dunn (1979) has recently pointed out the vast areas of ignorance that prevail concerning the behavioral aspects of controlling parasitic diseases. These include attitudes toward water and its use, defecation habits, trust in drug therapy, preferences for injectable medication, and concepts of the causality of disease. For example, in some Indian cultures in Mesoamerica, disease is thought to result from migration of worms from their normal habitat in the body to an abnormal site. Such concepts presuppose that worms may be important symbionts rather than commensals or pathogenic parasites. Drug-induced worm expulsion, especially via the oral or nasal route, may incite fear and thus detract from a CBD program. There is a critical need for good medical anthropologic studies to define such perceptions and to help in the design of health education efforts.

SAFETY AND MONITORING

CBD schemes for mass chemotherapy must assume the program will be targeted to infections of specific etiology, that single dose oral therapy will be chosen, that the drugs are extremely safe, that individual medical screening of patients is unnecessary, and that no specific training is required for non-medical personnel administering the drug. Individuals with obvious malnutrition or overt clinical symptoms such as pallor, weakness, breathlessness, asthma, or intestinal complaints of pain, tenderness, or diarrhea should be excluded from the routine drug regimen and referred to medical facilities for diagnosis and proper treatment. Recognition of such patients should not be difficult but it requires an effort to ensure that the channel of referral is open and that all CBD workers know how to use this option.

Monitoring over the long term has two objectives. First of all, cost-effectiveness and cost-benefit analyses cannot be ascertained without such data. Second, the development or selection of drug-resistant organisms is always a possibility in helminthic infections as it is in bacterial infections or in protozoal diseases such as malaria. Although this has not been a serious problem up to the present time, some resistance has been encountered in *N. americanus* and *Schistosoma mansoni* infections of humans and in veterinary infections due to *Haemonchus contortus* in sheep subjected to periodic antihelminthic therapy (Kelly, 1978).

Evaluation of efficacy will require periodic stool examinations by standard quantitative egg-counting methods (Beaver, 1975) in a representative sample of the population. Both prevalence and intensity of infection are important parameters since the most reasonable goal for chemotherapy is a reduction in both indices rather than eradication of infection in the treated population. Since the determinants of infection are rooted in the social, educational and economic aspects of the affected individuals, there is a need for projects to evolve and address broader aspects: the specific role of mass chemo-therapy may change with time (Mata, 1982). This underscores the need for parasitological surveillance to avoid the entrenchment of a program long after it has produced its maximum benefit and is no longer needed.

RESEARCH QUESTIONS

Helminthic infections have been around for a long time. The analysis of ancient feces preserved as coprolites reveals the presence of Enterobius as far back as 7800 BC, Schistosoma hematobium around 1250 to 1000 BC, and Ascaris and Trichuris from 800 to 350 BC (Durvel, 1975). Without a broadly conceived effort and diligent application of control measures, these infections are likely to continue to be around for a long time to come.

With the possible exception of Trichuris and Necator infection, the main research problem now does not seem to be development of better drugs, although this is still important (Stauden, 1976). Rather, the critical issues seem to be epidemiological and methodological, dealing with the institution and monitoring of control programs and evaluation of their consequences including side effects or drug resistance, and the cost-effectiveness and cost-benefit analysis necessary to assign priorities among programs. Such analyses must consider the possible effects of all aspects of the antihelminthics - for instance, the visual effect of antihelminthic therapy on worm expulsion - upon the credibility and acceptance of the other health and family planning components of a CBD program.

REFERENCES

Banzon, T.C., C.N. Singson, and J.H. Cross. "Mebendazole Treatment for Intestinal Nematodes in a Philippines Barrio. A Preliminary Report." J Philippine Med Assoc 52 (1976): 7-8.

Beaver, P.C. "Biology of Soil Transmitted Helminths: The Massive Infection." Health Lab Sci 12 (1975): 116-125.

Blackman, V., P.D. Marsden, J. Banwell, and C.M. Hall. "Albumin Metabolism in Hookworm Anemias." Trans Roy Soc Trop Med Hyg 59 (1966): 472-482.

Borrows, R.B. "Human and Veterinary Antihelminthics." Prog Drug Res 17 (1975): 108-209.

Botero, D. "Intestinal Parasitic Infections." Antibiotics Chemother 30 (1981): 1-9.

Chanco, P.P. and J.Y. Vidad. "A Review of Trichuriasis, Its Incidence, Pathogenicity and Treatment." Drugs 15, suppl. 1 (1978): 87-93.

Chongsuphajaisiddhi, T., A. Sabcharoen, P. Attanath, C. Panasoponkul, and P. Radomyos. "Treatment of Soil-Transmitted Nematode Infections in Children with Mebendazole." Ann Trop Med Parasit 72 (1978): 59-63.

Dunn, F.L. "Behavioral Aspects of the Control of Parasitic Diseases." Bull WHO 57 (1979): 499-572.

Durvel, D. "Laboratory Methods in the Screening of Antihelminthics." Proc Drug Res 17 (1975): 48-63.

Farid, Z., S. Bassily, and S. Lehman. "Iron Loss and Reabsorption in Ancylostoma duodenale Infection and Bilharzial Colonic Polyposis." Trans Roy Soc Trop Med Hyg 64 (1970): 881-884.

Gilman, R.H. Personal communication.

Gupta, M.C., S. Mithal, K.L. Arara, and B.N. Tandon. "Effects of Periodic Deworming on Nutritional Status of Ascaris -- Infected Pre-school Children Receiving Supplementary Food." Lancet 3 (1977): 108-110.

Hauer, F. "Experience with Mebendazole in Guatemala." Letter. Ann Int Med 94 (1981): 415.

Janssen, P.A.J. "The Levamisole Story." Prog Drug Res 20 (1976): 347-383.

Katz, M. "Adverse Metabolic Effects of Antiparasitic Drugs." Rev Infect Dis 4 (1982): 768-770.

Kelly, J.D. "Resistance of Animal Helminths to Antihelminthics." Adv Pharmacol Chemother 16 (1978): 89-128.

Keusch, G.T. "Workshop on Interactions of Nutrition and Parasitic Diseases. Summary and Recommendation." Rev Infect Dis 4 (1982): 901-907.

Keystone, J.S. and J.K. Murdock. "Mebendazole." Ann Intern Med 91 (1979): 582-586.

Louw, J.H. "Biliary Ascariasis in Childhood." S Afr J Surg 12 (1974): 219-225.

Mansour, T.E. "Chemotherapy of Parasitic Worms: New Biochemical Strategies." Science 205 (1979): 462-469.

Mata, L.J. "Sociocultural Factors in the Control and Prevention of Parasitic Infections." Rev Infect Dis 4,4 (1982): 871-879.

Miller, M.J. "Protozoan and Helminthic Parasites -- A Review of Current Treatment." Prog Drug Res 20 (1976): 433-464.

Muttalib, M.A., M.U. Khan, and J.A. Haq. "Single Dose Regimen of Mebendazole in the Treatment of Polyparastism in Children." J Trop Med Hyg 84 (1981): 159-160.

Ogilive, B.M., A. Bartless, R.C. Godfrey, J.A.Turton, M.J. Worms, and R.A. Yeates. "Antibody Responses in Self-infections with Necator Americanus." Trans Roy Soc Trop Med Hyg 72 (1978): 66-71.

Partono, F., Purnomo, A. Tangkilisan. "The Use of Mebendazole in the Treatment of Polyparasitism." Southeast Asian J Trop Med Pub Hlth 5 (1974): 258-264.

Pawlowski, Z. "Ascariasis. Host-pathogen Biology." Rev Infect Dis 4 (1982): 806:814.

Pawlowski, Z.S. "Ascariasis." Clin Gastroenterol 7 (1978): 157-178.

Pena Chavarria, A., J.C. Swartzwelder, V.M. Villarejos, and R. Zeledon. "Mebendazole, An Effective Broad Spectrum Antihelminthic." Am J Trop Med Hyg 22 (1973): 592-595.

Roche, M. and M. Layrisse. "The Nature and Causes of Hookworm Anemia." Am J Trop Med Hyg 31 (1966): 90-97.

Rogers, W.P. and R.I. Sommerville. "The Infectious Process and Its Relationship to the Development of Early Parasitic Stages of Nematodes." Adv Parasitol 6 (1968):327-348.

Schad, G.A., A.B. Chowdhury, C.G. Dean, V.K. Kochar, T.A. Nawalinski, J. Thomas, and J.A. Tonascia. "Arrested Development in Human Hookworm Infections: An Adaptation to a Seasonally Unfavorable External Environment." Science 180 (1973): 52-54.

Schultz, M.G. Ascariasis: Nutritional Implications." Rev Infect Dis 4,4 (1982): 815-819.

Seo, B-S., S-Y. Cho, and J-Y. Chai. "Reduced Single Dose of Mebendazole in Treatment of Ascaris lumbricoides Infection." Korean J Parasit 16 (1978): 21-25.

Sinniah, B., D. Sinniah, and A.S. Dissanaike. "Single Dose Treatment of Intestinal Nematodes with Oxantel-pyrantel Pamoate plus Mebendazole." Ann Trop Med Parasit 74 (1980): 619-623.

Stauden, O.D. "Chemotherapy of Intestinal Helminthiasis." Prog Drug Res 19 (1976): 158-165.

Stephenson, L.S., D.W.T. Crompton, M.C. Latham, T.W.J. Schulpen, M.C. Nesheim, and A.A.J. Jansen. "Relationships between Ascaris Infection and Growth of Malnourished Preschool Children in Kenya." Am J Clin Nutr 33 (1980): 1165-1172.

Villarejos, V.M., J. Bickers, S. Alvaro Rivers, A. Pena Chavarria, G.W. Hunter, III and E. Kotcher. "Pathogenesis of Anemia in Costa Rica. Epidemiologic Study of Hemoglobin and Serum Protein Levels and Hookworm Infection in Children." Am J Trop Med Hyg 19 (1970): 603-609.

Warren, K.S. "The Guerrilla Worm." New Engl J Med 282 (1970): 810-811.

Willett, W.C. and C.M. Kihamia. "Ascaris and Growth Rates: A Randomized Trial of Treatment." Am J Public Health 69 (1979): 987-991.

World Health Organization: Control of Ascariasis. Technical Report Series No. 379. Geneva: 1967.

11 Community-Based Distribution: The Case of Colombia

Fernando Gomez

This paper reports results of a three-year community-based distribution project carried out by the Maternal and Child Care (MCH) Division of the Colombian Ministry of Health and the Boyaca State Health Service. Financial and technical assistance were provided by the Population Council and the Agency for International Development.

The Boyaca CBD project constitutes the first of a series of pilot research efforts executed by the MCH Division of the Ministry of Health, designed to study models of delegating duties and expanding the roles of the 4,000 health promoters already working in rural areas. The project's aim was to train 100 local health promoters to deliver oral contraceptives and a broad-spectrum antihelminthic at the household level. Evaluation of the results of these activities represented a major component of the project, and provided data of potential use in planning future activities.

PRIMARY HEALTH CARE IN COLOMBIA

In Colombia, the public sector is the main supplier of health services, especially for low-income populations in both rural and urban areas. The activities of this sector are largely under the aegis of Institutions of the Ministry of Health. The provision of services is organized in a four-level pyramid. The two upper levels include university hospitals and regional hospitals, providing specialized medical care. The third level is formed by local hospitals and health centers which offer out-patient clinics, diagnostic facilities, and general and emergency hospitalizations. The fourth level includes the rural health posts: their staffing consists of an auxiliary nurse and a doctor, who attends the post once or twice weekly. Assigned to the health centers, and under the direct supervision of the auxiliary nurse, is the rural health promoter who plays a fundamental role in primary health care.

The first attempts to include members of the community in the provision of health services in Colombia were made in 1958. In 1968 and 1969, this pattern was strengthened with the establishment of a cadre of voluntary rural health promoters in the MCH programs. Promoters were appointed by the community and given a brief training course; they worked as volunteers for four hours a day, and received a small monetary compensation to pay for transportation.

In 1975, the Ministry of Health assessed the health situation in the country (Ministry of Health, Colombia, 1975). Major findings included:

1. Of the total population in the country, 36 percent still lacked health care.

2. Children below one year of age, who constitute 4 percent of the total population, were contributing 25 percent of the mortality. Much of this mortality was due to illnesses that respond to currently available therapy.

3. Nutritional deficiencies constituted one of the main health problems in children.

Based on this diagnosis, the Ministry of Health decided to strengthen its primary care programs. A move was taken to broaden the coverage of MCH services, improve access of the rural population to health services, increase preventive medicine programs, and enlarge the cadre of able paramedical and auxiliary personnel who would provide services under supervision.

To bring about these goals, the promoters' role was enlarged. In addition to health education, health promotion, and referral of patients, they were given seven basic activities that cover aspects of elementary health: medical care (first aid, pregnancy monitoring, normal delivery) and distribution of medication; nutritional education; vaccination; adequate water supply; development of sanitary sewage systems; hygienic trash disposal and zoonoses control; and housing improvement.

To assist them in carrying out these tasks, promoters were upgraded from their voluntary status and began to receive the legal minimum wage plus fringe benefits regularly given to the public sector. Workdays were increased from four to eight hours, and training was reinforced.

Each promoter now provides services to an average of 200 homes or approximately 1,000 people. In practice this number may be lower due to a provision under which every promoter services individuals no more than two hours' travel or 10 km from her home.

Since the expansion of their roles, promoters are theoretically authorized to distribute drugs and carry out some direct health activities. Generally, however, the promoters' actions have been oriented toward education and health promotion. Given these difficulties in determining the true potential of the promoters' role, the Ministry of Health decided to implement an experimental project using promoters to provide basic health care.

HOUSEHOLD DELIVERY OF CONTRACEPTIVES: THE BOYACA PROJECT

The experiment was begun in the state of Boyaca in 1978, using 100 health promoters. The goal of the project was to evaluate the feasibility of having such fieldworkers provide family planning methods and distribute an antiparasite drug without a preliminary medical checkup. The project set forth the following specific objectives:

1. To determine the effect of initial home delivery of contraceptives, without prescription, in increasing their use;
2. To determine the effect of home delivery of an antihelminthic in improving the nutritional status of rural children, aged 1 to 5, through a reduction in the severity and prevalence of intestinal parasitic infection in these children; and
3. To determine if an integrated health and family planning approach is more efficient in promoting contraceptive use.

Criteria for the Selection of Interventions

Contraceptives

Even though Colombia has undergone a dramatic decline in fertility, described in the literature, contraceptive use in urban areas differs significantly from that in rural areas. A 1978 use prevalence survey found that in urban areas 55.5 percent of the women in union were using contraceptives, of whom 45.8 percent were using modern methods (other than rhythm, withdrawal, or folk methods), while in the rural areas, only 19.8 percent of the women in union used contraceptives. Of these, only 23.8 percent used modern methods (Corporacion Centro Regional de Pobalcion et al., 1979). The unmet need in rural areas was documented in the 1976 Profamilia baseline survey conducted in the principal coffee-growing municipalities in Narino and Santanderes (Townsend, 1980). There, 71 percent of all women exposed to the risk of pregnancy and who did not want any more children were not using an efficient family planning method. Of the nonpregnant fecund women in union who had never used family planning methods, 23 percent stated that they intended to use contraceptives.

Thus, the design of the Boyaca project assumed a great potential demand for contraceptives in rural areas, and the possibility of satisfying demand through household distribution of family planning methods by promoters.

Antihelminthics

In Colombia, 88 percent of the population is estimated to suffer from mild infections of three different parasites (ascariasis, trichuriasis, and hookworm) (Ministry of Health, Colombia and Ascofame, 1969). Little action was being taken to treat this problem on a large-scale basis.

Design of the Project

Training

Normally, promoters receive a 12-week training course at the State School of Auxiliary Nurses, given by staff of the school and personnel from the State Health Department. The course covers topics such as environmental sanitation; medical care, including MCH and first aid (the largest single unit); information concerning the family and the community; delivery of drugs; and supervision. Training is carried out using lectures, movies, audiovisual aids, and practical experience.

For this project, an additional week of training was proposed to cover four important areas: family planning methods, their contraindications and side effects; parasite control; methods of weighing and measuring children; and motivational and administrative aspects of the study. All the promoters being currently trained at Boyaca are receiving this contraceptive and antiparasite training as part of their regular curriculum.

Experimental Design

Once the training phase was completed, promoters were randomly assigned into four experimental groups. The first group (Group I) distributed both antihelminthics and contraceptives. The second group (Group II) distributed only antihelminthics, and the third group (Group III) only contraceptives. The fourth group (Group IV) did not distribute drugs, and served as a control. Both the second and fourth groups referred individuals who desired to use family planning methods to Ministry of Health outlets.

Before starting the distribution of contraceptives, a list of contraindications was prepared and given to the promoters. Each time a user requested an oral contraceptive, the promoter reviewed this list with the person. If any doubts remained, users were referred for medical examination to a Ministry of Health outlet.

The promoter was to visit contraceptive users each month and provide them with another month's supply. During the first year, Noriday was the only oral contraceptive distributed. In the second year, the selection of methods was increased to include other brands of oral contraceptives, Neosampoon, and condoms.

Antihelminthics were originally distributed twice a year. However, due to the high reinfection rate in rural areas, where sanitary and environmental controls are lacking, it was decided to increase distribution to three times yearly.

Medical attention was readily available in case of side effects, or care needed for an unrelated condition. Since the project was part of the health system and was attached to a regional hospital, promoters were able to refer any individuals needing medical care to a nearby hospital or doctor.

Supervision

The study was organized so as not to produce changes in the structure of field activities, with the exception of the supervisory role. Field supervision of promoters was originally the responsibility of auxiliary nurses; in the project, the supervisory role was upgraded and given to registered nurses. Four nurses were put in charge of the 100 promoters. Supervisors are responsible for organizing the promoters' work schedules, setting targets, providing continuing education and on-the-job training, and evaluating the promoters' work. They also assist in preparing the promoters' monthly reports and ensure that adequate supplies are available to promoters in the field. Supervisors are expected to make a number of home visits with promoters to observe their activities. A monthly meeting is held by the supervisor and her promoters to review the work and to organize ongoing activities. The meetings also serve to discuss other administrative issues and to provide continuing education.

Evaluation and Results

Family Planning

Before initiating delivery of services, each promoter took a census of the population in her area. This census gathered data on women 15 to 45 years of age: age, number of living children, marital status, literacy, pregnancy status, desire to become pregnant, use of contraceptive methods, and source of contraceptive supplies. For children one to five years of age, weight, height and age were recorded. A final part of the survey gathered information on environmental sanitation in the household, the source of water, and sewage and garbage disposal. The censuses were repeated annually and constituted the main tool for evaluation. Each promoter reported her monthly activities on the same forms used to gather census information of women 15 to 45 and children one to five.

Family planning results were measured by changes in prevalence of contraceptive use. The study demonstrated that trained and supervised community agents can distribute oral contraceptives without the need for routine medical examination. Project results indicate that prevalence of use of effective methods increased during the study period, especially the use of oral contraceptives among users who received them directly from the promoter. The number of women referred to health centers for IUD insertion or female sterilization also increased in all four groups.

Table 11:1 shows the change in prevalence of use of efficient contraceptive methods between 1979 (before the initiation of promoter distribution of oral contraceptives) and 1981, 24

Table 11:1. Percentage of Women of Reproductive Age Currently Using Selected Family Planning Methods by Intervention Groups. Boyaca, 1979 to 1981.

METHOD	GROUP I Antihelminthics + Contraceptives			GROUP II Antihelminthics		
	1979	1981		1979	1981	
(Total number of women in group)	2,477	2,665		2,617	1,907	
	Percentage Use		Percentage Difference	Percentage Use		Percentage Difference
Oral	1.7	8.2	6.5	3.1	3.8	0.7
IUD	2.7	3.3	0.6	4.1	6.1	2.0
Sterilization	2.3	4.7	2.4	2.1	4.9	2.8
TOTAL	6.7	16.2	9.5	9.3	14.8	5.5

Group I distributed contraceptives and antihelminthics;
Group II distributed only antihelminthics;

Table 11:1 (Cont.). Percentage of Women of Reproductive Age Currently Using Selected Family Planning Methods by Intervention Groups. Boyaca, 1979 to 1981.

METHOD	GROUP III Contraceptives			GROUP IV No drugs distributed Control		
	1979	1981		1979	1981	
(Total number of women in group)	2,636	2,475		2,651	2,269	
	Percentage Use		Percentage Difference	Percentage Use		Percentage Difference
Oral	1.5	7.1	5.6	2.5	3.6	1.1
IUD	2.4	3.1	0.7	3.8	6.4	2.6
Sterilization	1.6	3.6	2.0	2.7	5.2	2.5
TOTAL	5.5	13.8	8.3	9.0	15.2	6.2

Group III distributed only contraceptives;
Group IV did not distribute project services.

months after the services were initiated. Groups I and III, where the promoters were distributing oral contraceptives to the household, showed the major increase in use of the three most effective contraceptive methods: increases of 9.5 and 8.3 percent, respectively, compared with an increase of 5.5 and 6.2 percent in Groups II and IV, respectively. Groups I and III also showed the larger increase in use of a single method. In Group I, use of oral contraceptives increased from 1.7 percent of users in 1979 to 8.2 percent in 1981. In Group III, use of orals increased from 1.5 percent of women in 1979 to 7.1 percent in 1981. The increase in female sterilization is slightly higher in Groups II and IV, and IUD insertion is higher in Groups II and IV.

Research results do not support the suggestion that delivery of family planning and an antihelminthics will have a substantial effect and lead to greater contraceptive acceptance: the difference in acceptance rates between Group I and III is not statistically significant.

Antihelminthics

It was decided to evaluate the effectiveness of the antihelminthic program in modifying the height and weight of children under five years of age. Efforts to measure these changes were unsuccessful and it was impossible to derive results to prove the hypothesis that the use of antihelminthics without the implementation of other environmental controls can curb helminth infections and contribute to children's health and growth.

Weight results were not very reliable, mainly because common bath scales were used. The instrument had been selected since it could be easily handled and the promoter could transport it on her rounds. However, the smallest unit of measure detectable was 500 gms, which is not sufficiently precise to yield useful longitudinal results in children between the ages of one and five. Furthermore, it was very difficult to teach the promoter to consistently weigh each child in a similar manner, and the scales constantly became uncalibrated and were less sturdy than expected.

The inconveniences and the unreliability of the data caused this phase of the project to be canceled during the second year. The results obtained during the initial 12 months show only a small improvement both in weight and height, but it is impossible to be sure that these improvements are due to the project intervention, particularly since data on a control group of children are unavailable.

General Observations

The community did not react against the distribution of contraceptives and no person or institution attacked it. An unfavorable reaction developed against antihelminthics in the second year, when the number of expelled parasites and their size declined: some sectors of the community rejected further treatment at this time. On the other hand, promoters preferred to distribute antiparasite drugs rather than oral contraceptives, and it was necessary to dismiss some promoters because of their refusal to distribute contraceptives.

An indirect result of the project was a statewide change in policy regarding the supervision of promoters. Based on the three years' experience in the project, Boyaca health authorities decided that registered nurses rather than auxiliary nurses would supervise promoters. The authorities' evaluation indicated that the promoters supervised by registered nurses were better trained and delivered more services (visited people more often, fulfilled targets and made fewer mistakes in reporting). They also found that supervision provided by registered nurses carried more authority and that community support was greater. The health authorities decided to appoint one registered nurse for each of the nine health regions in Boyaca; each would supervise the work of just over 30 promoters.

SUMMARY AND CONCLUSIONS

The Boyaca research project provided useful information for future planning. This three-year experience showed Ministry of Health authorities that:

1. A definite set of activities, different from those attempted before, can be delegated to the rural health promoter. The activities tested were very simple, and they helped to make better use of available manpower.
2. Household distribution of contraceptives by rural health agents is possible, and promoters can perform the task even in a conservative rural community such as Boyaca.
3. Prevalence of contraceptive use at the end of the project had increased compared with the baseline. However, the number of new users was low, and the cost per user was high due to the small population with which each promoter worked. Results did not support the theory that synergism between home delivery of family planning and antihelminthics could lead to a higher rate of contraceptive acceptance.
4. The effect of regular home distribution of antihelminthics on improvements in the growth of children, as measured by height and weight, could not be evaluated because measurements were not sufficiently precise and were discontinued after one year.
5. It was possible to replicate this experience in other places, as is actually being done in Meta State.
6. The project also demonstrated the need for more research of this type to look for a meaningful set of activities to be carried out by the promoters.

Currently the Ministry of Health is making arrangements to allow all the promoters in the country to distribute several contraceptives and antiparasite drugs. Nevertheless, the question remains whether this makes the best use of field personnel: in the current model, a small number of services are delivered at high cost. An evaluation of the health effect of Ministry of Health programs using community agents to deliver primary health care has never been undertaken by the Ministry. The promoter program is being extended more as a result of political reasons than for theoretical reasons or from an understanding of the program's potential. The promoters' time may still be highly underutilized. Because of the lack of research, changing realities (such as the increased availability of human resources in health and the urbanization process that the country is undergoing) are being ignored in planning promoters' activities and work sites. There is an ongoing need to explore and design comparative research projects that would fully evaluate the CBD delivery model and explore its full potential.

Based on the Boyaca experience, the following research ideas can be proposed:

1. What is the cost-effectiveness of using community agents vis-a-vis other types of personnel with more formal training?

2. Do voluntary or salaried personnel perform better, within the socioeconomic and political realities of countries such as Colombia?

3. What activities could potentially be delegated to community workers, considering their experience, the training that can be provided, and the health situation of the community?

4. What characteristics are desirable in a community health agent: level of education, sex, age, etc.?

5. What would be the best mix of services to be delivered by this personnel?

6. Should these workers be dedicated exclusively to health activities? If not, would it be more advantageous to orient their activities toward community development in which health would be only one among several actions?

REFERENCES

Corporacion Centro Regional de Pobalcion, et al. "Encuesta Nacional de Prevalencia de Uso de Anticonceptivos en Colombia, 1978. General Results." Bogota: CCRP, 1979.

Ministry of Health, Colombia and Ascofame. "Parasitismo Intestinal, Estudio de Recursos Humanos para la Salud y Educacion Medica en Colombia." (Study of Human Resources for Health and Medical Education in Colombia.) Investigacion Nacional de Morbilidad, Bogota, D.E., 1969.

Ministry of Health, Colombia. "Plan Nacional de Salud." Documents ISNS-II, 1975 (mimeograph).

Townsend, Marcia. "Baseline Post-test Report." 1980 (mimeograph).

12 Sociedade Civil Bem-Estar Familiar No Brasil (BEMFAM): Review of an Integrated Family Planning and Antihelminthic Therapy Project in Piaui State, Brazil

Walter Rodrigues and Claudia Valladao

In April 1979, BEMFAM launched a community-based (CBD) family planning project in the state of Piaui, in northeastern Brazil. This project has become a laboratory, testing various variables and program innovations for the rest of BEMFAM's community programs. The primary focus of these research activities has been on administrative issues and on the development and improvement of materials, techniques, and delivery systems. This paper describes BEMFAM's plans to integrate the delivery of family planning with a broad-spectrum antihelminthic program.

BEMFAM activities in Piaui are carried out under the auspices of the State Secretary of Health, who provides health post facilities and distributors for the program. (BEMFAM operates additional family planning posts in nonhealth facilities.) The Secretary of Health has a strong interest in integrating the many state health programs, an interest which complements BEMFAM's desire to explore the possibility of extending the CBD approach to the delivery of basic health services. This shared interest resulted in the family planning-antiparasite project begun in 1980.

PROJECT SETTING

Piaui is a large, sparsely populated state. Its 251,000 square kms make it approximately as large as Guatemala and Nicaragua combined. The 1980 census recorded a resident population of about 2.1 million inhabitants, yielding a density of 8.5 persons per square km. The only large city in Piaui is Teresina, the state capital, which has a population of 339,000. The rate of population increase is high, 2.4 percent per year, while the total fertility rate and the crude birth rate are estimated to be 5.9 and 40, respectively.

Socioeconomic indicators rank Piaui as the poorest, least developed state in Brazil. Despite the lack of development, however, a 1979 contraceptive prevalence survey found contraceptive use to be high (31 percent of married women of reproductive age), indicating a high level of acceptance for family planning even prior to the introduction of an educational and service program.

BEMFAM/JOICFP FAMILY PLANNING-ANTIPARASITE PROJECT

The major goals of this project, funded by the Japanese Organization for International Cooperation in Family Planning (JOICFP), were to develop an integrated service delivery model, and to reduce the prevalence of parasite infection in the target population. Research activity centered on the latter.

The project site is located in the county of Oeiras which has 47,300 inhabitants and a population density of 9.3 per square km. The population is 74 percent rural and 26 percent urban. Two family planning posts were opened in Oeiras (both located in the county seat) in early 1979 and antiparasite activities began in May 1980.

Antiparasite activities are located in 41 urban and rural schools. In rural areas, family planning services were gradually added to 15 of the rural schools during the eight-month period from September 1980 to April 1981. In the urban area, family planning activities were not located in the schools but remained in the health posts. Antiparasite workers included distribution of family planning information among their other activities. The combined antiparasite-family planning workers in the rural area were full-time schoolteachers. In the urban areas, they also included students aged 16 to 20.

In May 1980, antiparasite educational activities began, and fecal examinations were conducted from samples of 3,003 persons recruited through the schools on the basis of a quota sample designed to net entire families of four to six members. Overall, 44.9 percent of the examinations (Kato-Katz technique) were positive. The rural prevalence rate of intestinal helminths was 46.3 percent, and the urban rate 42.9 percent. Infection rates were fairly uniform for all ages greater than one year, ranging from 41 to 49 percent. The most common parasites were *Ancylostoma duodenale* (hookworm) found in 29.1 percent of the samples, *Ascaris* in 16 percent, and *Trichuris trichuris* (whipworm) in 3.2 percent. No other parasite of the several other species encountered attained an infection level higher than 1.4 percent.

A target of 30,976 acceptors for parasite treatment was set. In September 1980, the first blanket treatment was administered using pyrantel pamoate. In rural areas mothers came to the schools to collect the medication for the entire family, while in urban areas students distributed the medication to all households. At that time, family planning was available at four of the 31 rural schools participating in the project, being added to the other schools with integrated programs only after September. In the urban areas, the students offered family planning information (but not supplies) at each house they visited.

RESULTS

By the end of the September distribution, the antihelminthic had been distributed to 29,985 persons - 96.8 percent of the target and 63 percent of the total population. The antihelminthic recipients recruited in May were re-examined in November 1980. The results of 2,199 exams indicated that the proportion of positive cases had fallen to 14.6 percent. The prevalence of hookworm had declined to 10.7 percent and Ascaris to 2.8 percent.

A second blanket treatment was given in March 1981. The procedure was the same as in the first treatment distribution, except that the number of rural schools offering family planning with the worm medication had increased to 15. The medication was distributed to 21,408 persons. The 2,757 members of the sample who were examined in June 1981, revealed an infection rate of 9.5 percent including 5.9 percent prevalence rate for hookworm and 3.4 percent for Ascaris.

Evidence suggests an important short-term impact on parasite infection rates. Sixty-three percent of the population has received medication, and infection rates among a large segment of users declined from almost 45 percent to just under 10 percent. Hookworm infection was reduced from approximately 29 percent to 6 percent and Ascaris, from 16 percent to 3 percent.

Plans call for the continuation of the project for three more years, after which its administration will pass to the state Secretary of Health. The ultimate research objective is to see if minimal (3 percent) overall infection rates can be achieved through blanket treatments and thereafter maintained by education and latrine building. Treatment would then be provided only for individuals with symptoms or diagnosis of worms.

One assumption underlying integration of antiparasite activities with family planning is that the antiparasite activity will make the family planning component more acceptable to the local population. This suggests that an integrated family planning-antiparasite effort will have higher levels of contraceptive acceptance and use than a free-standing family planning project in the same area. Although the number of new acceptors of family planning increased after the introduction of antiparasite activities in Oeiras county, it is impossible to draw definite conclusions from this result: the addition of antiparasite treatment occurred concurrently with a large increase in the number of family planning posts in the county.

Moreover, the small amount of available evidence is not consistent with a positive impact on family planning acceptance by antiparasite treatment activities. During the 12 months prior to the launch of the antiparasite component, two BEMFAM family planning posts located in the county seat recruited 265 family planning acceptors, a number equivalent to 5 percent of all MWRA in the county. In contrast, the statewide acceptance rate for the same period was 11 percent. During the 12-month period following the introduction of the antiparasite component, 422 family planning acceptors, or 8 percent of MWRA, were recruited. During the same period, the statewide acceptance rate was 9 percent.

Four new posts were added in Oeiras county in September 1980, and this number grew steadily to 15 new posts by February 1981. The new rural posts accounted for 44 percent of county clients recruited after May 1980 and 56 percent of clients recruited after September 1980. No other county enjoyed an increase in posts. For example, the 10 other counties in the same supervisory region as Oeiras contained only 13 posts (1.3 per county) and had a combined acceptance rate of 7 percent, with a range of 5 to 27 percent. When all counties in the supervisory region are considered together, Oeiras ranks fourth among the 11 in acceptance rates.

In the 12 months preceding the antiparasite project, the two pre-existing family planning posts recruited 265 acceptors. In the 12 months after, they recruited 236. If the quarter in which the blanket treatment occurred is compared with the same quarter of the previous year, the two posts recruited 67 new acceptors from September to November 1979, and 64 from September to November 1980.

This result suggests that the addition of antiparasite medication to the project may have had little, if any, effect on the acceptance of family planning, other than that achieved through the opening of new posts.

It should be noted that integration of family planning and parasite control in Piaui revealed a set of service delivery problems which require resolution before the project can be duplicated on a large scale. The location of antiparasite activities in 31 rural schools, including 15 with family planning services, compelled the project to hire a special supervisor to serve Oeiras. In contrast, the family planning program in the rest of the state has one supervisor for approximately 10 counties. An expansion of the antiparasite project, as currently structured, to all of Piaui's 114 counties would involve prohibitive supervisory costs.

Schools have proven to be highly effective locations for the distribution of antiparasite drugs. However, other analyses have shown them to be among the least effective and least cost-effective locations for family planning posts. Family planning posts in nonhealth center locations in Piaui have been demonstrated to have costs per unit of output that are almost twice as high as those found in comparable health center locations (Foreit et al., 1983). Additionally, all nonhealth posts in the state have a median of nine new acceptors per quarter. An examination of school posts outside Oeiras reveals that only five of 23 attain or exceed the median, whereas, in Oeiras, only two of 14 school posts for which data are available reached or exceeded the statewide median. Much of the reason for this poor performance of school posts is due to the fact that many rural posts in Oeiras are located in very small villages (populations of less than 500).

In conclusion, BEMFAM is satisfied that community-based distribution of contraceptives can be adapted to the distribution of antiparasite medication and information. It is also recognized that many service delivery problems need to be resolved if integration is to be feasible on a large scale.

REFERENCES

Foreit, J. et al. "A Cost-Effectiveness Comparison of Service Delivery Systems and Geographic Areas in Piaui State, Brazil." In Evaluating Population Programs. International Experience with CEA/CBA, edited by I. Sirageldin et al. New York: St. Martins Press, and London: Croom-Helm, 1983.

Part Five

Nutrition Activities in CBD Programs

13
Nutrition Activities in Community-Based Projects

Sandra L. Huffman

Malnutrition among children and pregnant women is a significant problem affecting millions in developing countries, but treatment through hospital or clinic activities is expensive and difficult due to scarcity of trained clinical staff, resources, and logistic support. Preventive activities are the only practical solution to malnutrition. Family planning programs have extended beyond clinic-based activities to deliver contraceptives using minimally trained workers in urban and rural communities. Such community-based distribution (CBD) programs also offer the potential to promote child health by incorporating nutrition interventions.

The limitations of CBD projects in upgrading nutrition need to be understood. Any program that proposes to include nutrition activities must be able to monitor the target population at risk continuously and visit families in their homes. CBD programs that involve only a one-time visit (for example, to deliver pills or condoms) are not appropriate vehicles for nutrition activities. The frequency of visits may differ according to the nutritional problem addressed and the organizational structure of the CBD program, but repeated visits are essential since the conditions resulting from malnutrition are likely to recur. To be most effective, nutrition interventions must be reinforced through repetition.

The first priority for all approaches to prevent malnutrition is mapping the population and listing family members by age, sex, and reproductive status of the women (nonpregnant, pregnant, lactating). These lists enable the worker to concentrate on those most likely to need nutrition services. Registering subsequent births is an important ongoing activity which identifies children for inclusion in nutrition programs and permits accurate growth monitoring.

After taking a census, activities will vary according to the type of nutrition program to be conducted. Since most activities necessitate continued participation by the mother or her children, an important element to continued participation is mother's confidence in the CBD worker. Indeed the worker's rapport with the community assumes special significance in nutrition activities since the effects of the program are often not immediately evident (unlike curative activities), and are thus less likely to bring about consumer satisfaction as easily as other activities. The long-term benefits of nutrition activities, however, will be mutually reinforcing with other health interventions.

The most prevalent types of malnutrition in developing countries, or those that have severe consequences and yet are amenable to prevention and treatment are: protein-calorie malnutrition, vitamin A deficiency, anemia, and goiter. These will be discussed in the context of their causation, prevalence, consequences, methods of prevention and treatment, and program implications in a CBD setting.

PROTEIN CALORIE MALNUTRITION

Protein-calorie malnutrition (PCM) among young children is the most serious and prevalent form of malnutrition; it is also the most difficult to resolve. DeMaeyer (1976) estimated that nearly 10 million children under five years of age are severely malnourished (defined as less than 60 percent of the Harvard weight-for-age standard); and 90 million are moderately malnourished (60 to 75 percent of the standard). For both levels of malnutrition, this represents an average of 21 percent of children in Latin America; 31 percent of children in Africa; and 34 percent of children in Asia. The multifaceted causes of PCM relate primarily to the interaction between inadequate food intake and infection.

Preschool-aged children (under five years) in developing countries are most affected by PCM because of the high nutrient requirements of their age group, inappropriateness of foods commonly eaten, low frequency of feeding, and effects of infectious diseases. In order for young children with their small stomachs to obtain enough energy they must eat calorically dense foods frequently. Infections complicate the problem by: increasing nitrogen loss associated with the changes in metabolism that accompany fever; decreasing dietary intake because of associated lack of appetite (anorexia), or cultural patterns of withholding food from the child during diarrhea (DeMaeyer, 1976); and diminishing absorption of nutrients from the intestine during diarrhea. Mata (1978) and Black and colleagues (Black et al., 1982) observed in Guatemala and Bangladesh that an average child is ill one to two months a year, primarily from diarrhea and upper respiratory infections. Morley and Woodland (1979) estimated that due to such a high prevalence of illness, children aged 6 to 24 months have poor appetites one day in three and those aged 24 to 36 months, one day in every four. In order to compensate for this, they suggest that children eat 25 to 30 percent more food on the days when they are not ill.

Seldom is malnutrition seen among breastfed infants under four to six months of age since breast-milk generally meets the young infant's nutrient needs. Bottle-fed infants in developing countries, however, are at risk to malnutrition due to improper feeding patterns, such as: overdilution of formula or milk, bacterial contamination of the milk from unsterile bottles or nipples, and lack of refrigeration facilities needed to retard bacterial growth in milk. Malnutrition becomes prevalent during the process of weaning because of inadequate supplemental feeding, and associated bouts of diarrhea (Rowland et al., 1978).

Parasitic infections play only a small role in PCM, and only when worm burdens are extensive leading to diversion of nutrients or associated diarrhea and anorexia. The common parasites that may have some or all of these effects include ascaris, trichuris, and hookworm (Keusch, this volume). Heavy hookworm infestation can lead to substantial protein-loss (Layrisse and Roche, 1967; Layrisse et al., 1976). The peak incidences of ascaris, trichuris, and hookworm occur between the ages of 2 to 14, 5 to 10, and 16 to 30 years, respectively (Wittner, 1977). Because few children are heavily burdened with worms, especially under five years of age, and the likelihood of reinfestation is great, deworming programs are unlikely to improve nutritional status for most preschool children. There is also little evidence of a major impact for children over five years of age.

Consequences

PCM seriously affects mortality, morbidity, and intellectual capability. Kielmann and McCord (1978) noted a tenfold increase in risk of mortality for children aged less than three years with a weight-for-age less than 60 percent compared with normal chilren (weight-for-age above 80 percent). Chen and co-workers (Chen et al., 1981; Chen et al., 1980) identified a similar association in Bangladesh, noting a two- to fourfold increased risk of dying in severly malnourished children aged two to three years compared with normal or mildly malnourished children. Puffer and Serrano (1973), reported from studies in Latin America that PCM was an underlying cause of mortality in children aged one to four years in 9 percent of deaths studied and an associated cause in 47 percent.

Epidemiologic studies on the association of malnutrition and risk of disease are unclear; however, PCM appears to correlate directly with the severity and duration of diarrhea (Tomkins, 1981). Moreover, cellular immune response may be depressed under conditions of PCM and often major infections are masked (Taylor et al., 1979; Taylor et al., 1978).

Malnutrition has also been associated with impaired intellectual development. Brain growth occurs up to age two and inadequate nutrition has been associated with a reduction in the number of brain cells and in head circumference. The consequence of this response on intellect is less clear than the evident association between malnutrition and lack of environmental stimulation, which correlates directly with reduced intellectual capacity (McKay et al., 1978). Malnourished children spend more time in less stimulating activities, that is sitting or resting, rather than walking or running (Morley and Woodland, 1979). The effects of these environmental conditions and activity patterns may be more significant in determining intellectual function than the direct effects of nutritional deficiency.

Prevention and Treatment

As mentioned by Rohde (this volume), treatment of severe malnutrition is expensive and difficult within the hospital setting or within a nutrition rehabilitation unit. Costs in rehabilitation centers, using paramedical personnel and locally available resources are as much as $.10 per day (King et al., 1978). These approaches are obviously not feasible for the CBD setting or for most health programs in less developed countries. Referral to such treatment centers is often the advised approach, yet it is obvious that access to centers is severely limited and the costs to the families (in terms of transportation, lost wages, and time) make it unfeasible for most.

Supplementary feeding programs, including on-site and take-home feeding, have been used, but are also extremely expensive to operate because of administrative as well as food costs. The expense of providing 300 to 400 kcal/day is estimated at $15 to $25 per child per year (Beaton and Ghassemi, 1982). Additionally, the benefits of supplementary feeding programs on nutritional status have been limited by the small amount of food provided, substitution of previously consumed foods, and irregular participation in the program.

A number of activities of village health workers who have continuing contact with mothers have been shown to positively affect children's nutritional status. In Narangwal the length of breastfeeding was increased by five months in villages providing weekly visits to families of children under one year of age and monthly to trimonthly visits to children over one year. Nutritional status of these children (both weight and height for age) also increased, but the effects of growth monitoring, education, and food supplementation cannot be separated (Taylor et al., 1978).

In Kenya, village health workers who visited households in 92 communities every one to four months demonstrated an increase in families with kitchen gardens (27 percent in 1977 to 83 percent in 1980); an increase in children 0 to 35 months being breast-fed for more than 12 months (69 percent in 1977 and 93 percent in 1980); a decrease in bottle-feeding (34 percent in 1977 to 2 percent in 1980); and a decline in malnutrition (less than 80 percent weight-for-age, 18 percent in 1977 to 4 percent in 1980) (Were, 1981).

The Candelaria Promotora Program in Cali, Colombia used volunteers to promote family planning and provide health education. Through bimonthly home visits, information was given to families on nutrition, hygiene, and health services. Supplements were provided, weight and height measured, and illness cases were referred to the clinic on these visits. Malnutrition declined from 26 percent to 21 percent in six years. The need for continuous visits between health workers and patients, as well as improvements in mothers' knowledge, is demonstrated by the absence of differences between nutritional status of children born to families in control and experimental groups two years after the program terminated (Drake et al., 1980).

Unfortunately, few other programs have illustrated any benefits resulting from village workers' continuous involvement in growth monitoring alone or in combination with nutrition and health education. The major reason for this is that most projects do not report their evaluations. An American Public Health Association survey conducted in the late 1970's of 180 primary health care projects, found 30 projects that described nutrition related activities among their clinic-based health activities. These nutrition activities included weighing, distribution of food supplements, health education, kitchen gardening, and mother's clubs - however, none reported evaluations of their effects on nutritional status.

Aside from lack of evaluation, many programs illustrating improvements in health or nutrition included food supplementation or health care as components of the project (Gwatkin et al., 1980a; Gwatkin et al., 1980b). The effects of activities such as growth monitoring or home visits were not evaluated separately. This is true for Narangwal (Kielmann et al., 1978a; Kielmann et al., 1978b), Jamkhed (Arole and Arole, 1975), and the Kotter Social Services Project (Drake et al., 1980) where improvements in nutritional status were noted. Similar difficulties were evident with the positive results of growth monitoring seen in clinic-based studies, such as in Malawi (Cole-King, 1975), and Imesi, Nigeria (Morley and Woodland, 1979) where other health care was provided.

A third deficit in our knowledge of effectiveness of such nutrition activities is the lack of comparison groups. A Save-the-Child Project in Tangse, Aceh-Sumatra, Indonesia, staffed village health posts with volunteers (Drake et al., 1980). Children were weighed, mothers kept growth charts, and volunteers demonstrated food preparation and encouraged latrine building, home gardening, fish ponds, and immunizations. Weighings taken one year apart showed improvements, but since no comparison group was included, it was not possible to determine whether this resulted from aging or true nutritional improvement.

The prevalence of malnutrition declined from 37 percent in 1969-70 to 29 percent in 1972 as a result of using "under-five clinics" in Malawi. Child growth was monitored (with the objective of seeing the child six times in the first year and four times in the second year), nutrition education and cooking demonstrations were given, and immunizations were provided; some clinics demonstrated kitchen gardens and poultry clubs. Because of the absence of comparison groups of nonclinic attendees, it is unclear whether the improved nutritional status reflected in the clinic data resulted from clinic activities or extraneous factors (Cole-King, 1975).

Other programs attempting to improve nutrition through the use of village health workers have not been successful due to management problems including lack of supervision, training, logistic support, and community involvement. These factors are the hardest to overcome yet are an important prerequisite to any program's success.

Program Implications

The objectives of an optimal program for controlling PCM (DeMaeyer, 1976) include the following:

1. Improvement or maintenance of nutritional status by correction of deficient diets.
2. Control of infectious diseases, including diarrhea, by immunization and improved hygiene.
3. Minimizing effects of diarrheal disease by early treatment and rehydration.
4. Detection and treatment of severe malnutrition.

Depending on staff qualification, workload, and logistic support, CBD workers can be responsible for addressing some or all of these objectives. A minimal-level program would identify severely malnourished children by measuring arm circumference and focus nutrition education efforts on families of these children only. This approach can have more general benefits since it can serve to educate the community as a whole with respect to the existence of malnutrition. The next level of intensity would be to identify children at high risk to malnutrition based on biologic and social parameters. The third more in-depth approach would be aimed at monitoring the growth of all children. Variations and combinations of activities within each of these levels is feasible and appropriate depending on resource limitations.

Control of infectious and diarrheal diseases and the minimization of their effects are the important elements in PCM control programs. Since these efforts (including oral rehydration, immunization and therapy) have been described elsewhere in this volume (Cash; DeQuadros; Parker), this paper will focus on improving or maintaining nutritional status by promoting good dietary practices and correcting dietary deficiencies.

Manuals suitable for trainers of CBD workers providing more details on these topics include, Nutrition in Developing Countries (King et al., 1972), Guidelines for Training Community Health Workers in Nutrition (WHO, 1981), and See How they Grow (Morley and Woodland, 1979).

The high prevalence of malnutrition in a community may make it difficult for mothers or workers to determine which children are malnourished, since they may look like healthy younger children (King et al., 1972). For example, many 18-month-old children look "identical" to their six-month-old brothers, except they may have more teeth. Mothers may think that since their children do not look any different from other village children their children are not malnourished. The use of anthropometric measurement can be the first step toward sensitizing the community to problems of PCM. Measuring the child's arm circumference or weight also measures the effectiveness, intensity, and content of nutrition education messages given by the CBD workers.

Arm Circumference to Identify Severe PCM

Upper arm circumference measurements can be used to assess malnutrition among children aged one to five years because arm circumference does not greatly change during this period and even minor deviations may indicate cause for concern. It is a helpful screening technique since it has been shown to be as good a predictor of subsequent mortality as weight-for-age or height-for-age (Chen et al., 1981). Figure 13:1 illustrates the curve of arm circumference by age for children zero to five years. Even with kwashiorkor, though the lower arm will be swollen with edema, the upper arm will be thin (King et al., 1972). In using arm circumference measurements, it is important to exclude infants under one year of age and children over five years.

Various classifications in arm circumference measurements have been used to differentiate nutritional status. The World Health Organization (WHO) recommends the use of two or three categories (DeVille de Goyet et al., 1978). With three categories, 13.5 cm or more is defined as well nourished to mild PCM combined; 12.5 to 13.5 cm moderate malnutrition; and less than 12.5 cm, severe PCM. Two categories can be used, with 13.0 cm or more considered well nourished and mild malnutrition, and less than 13 cm as clearly malnourished. King and colleagues (King et al., 1972) suggest making 14 cm a cut-off point for malnutrition. The decision of which cut-off to use should be based on local patterns of malnutrition and resources of the program.

Arm circumference can be measured with a cloth or fiberglass tape measure, or a piece of x-ray film cut in a narrow strip (or some similar material that will not stretch) marked to indicate the cut-off points. Arm circumference can also be assessed by bangles, and other rings with a specified inner diameter. The cost is minimal, since cheap materials can be used and labor required to make them is low.

The CBD worker can visit children identified as being malnourished more frequently than normal children and at each visit discuss with the mother ways to increase the child's dietary intake. The measurement of arm circumference at each visit will focus on the problem. When the child's arm circumference no longer is below the minimum, the child can gradually be dropped from the worker's special surveillance. However, since such a child may be a high risk to future bouts of malnutrition, it would be optimal for the worker to continue monitoring the child's status whenever possible.

Although this is the easiest program to implement, it is unfortunately the least satisfactory because it cannot assess short-term changes in nutritional status or decreases in growth increments which can be accomplished through weighing. By definition, it does little to prevent malnutrition since it can identify only severely malnourished children. This approach can also lead to frustration for workers, since there usually exists a group of severely malnourished children who remain so, regardless of inputs of health workers. These children are often unwanted, and their nutritional status is based on sociological problems, rather than problems addressed by education.

High Risk Approach

In order to overcome some of the deficiencies of the above approach, the high-risk approach increases the number of children to be included for follow-up. Along with those identified as being malnourished through arm circumference measurements, this approach includes other biologic and social factors to further delineate children at risk. High-risk factors include low birth weight; twinning; high birth order; death of a sibling (especially if sibling died before the age of 12 months); history of measles, whooping cough, or severe or repeated diarrhea; death or separation of parents; unmarried mother; recent family migration; or general poverty (DeMaeyer, 1976; Cameron and Hofvander, 1976).

Such at-risk children should be targeted for the CBD worker's special attention. Children who are severely malnourished, or who have one or more risk factors, should be noted (with a red star for example) on the CBD worker's census. This will help the worker remember to visit the child more frequently than the other village children (Cameron and Hofvander, 1976). Being aware of these risk indicators helps to direct limited resources to those most likely to benefit; it is also important for focusing growth monitoring on those most in need.

Growth Monitoring

Growth monitoring is the largest preventive component, since it can highlight children who are slowly approaching malnutrition. Weight is the most comprehensive indicator in assessing nutritional status, but skill and expertise are required to decide from a single measurement, or even a series of measurements, if a child is growing satisfactorily (Cameron and Hofvander, 1976). A flattening growth curve is the earliest sign of PCM, and may precede clinical signs by weeks or months.

Growth monitoring has many functions. It facilitates the enrollment of children into the program, as well as continuity of care, by establishing a specified task to be accomplished. It also provides a research and evaluation tool (Griffiths, 1981).

The act of monitoring growth is obviously a necessary but insufficient task to promote adequate nutritional status. As stated by King and colleagues (King et al., 1972), "Weighing a child does nothing by itself. It is teaching the mother how to feed him that matters, not charting his weight." The growth chart is a tool to help the mother understand the importance of the child's diet to his or her health and shows her when changes in diet must be initiated.

As is the case with arm circumference, the utility of growth charts is hampered by the difficulty of knowing the child's exact age. Although one of the CBD worker's first tasks is to register births, it will take several years before all children are registered. Assessment of weight-for-age will therefore depend on an estimated age, using some type of local events calendar. Brown and Brown (1979) give a helpful chart to use in the initial estimate of a child's age (Table 13:1).

Table 13:1. Characteristics Used to Estimate Child's Age

Characteristics of the Child	Probable Age
No teeth Cannot sit alone	0-5 months
Has 1-6 teeth Can sit alone Cannot walk alone	6-11 months
Has 6-18 teeth Can walk Knows a few words	12-23 months
Has 18-20 teeth Walks well Starting to talk well	24-35 months
Walks and runs well Talks well Has not yet lost first baby tooth	36-59 months

Source: Adapted from Brown and Brown, 1979.

They suggest, for example, that children with three or fewer teeth are probably less than one year old, and those with four to 20 baby teeth, but no lost teeth, are probably one to five years of age. It is important not to estimate age by the child's size, since a malnourished child will be small and therefore appear younger.

The worker should be given simple directions to interpret the child's growth, such as how much weight should increase every month, including directions for months without gain or any month showing loss of weight. Directions that are too simple are risky, however, since a child may gain each month but still become malnourished. Table 13:2 gives the average expected increments in growth for specific age intervals based on the NCHS median values of weight and height for age (U.S. Department of Health, Education and Welfare, 1977).

Table 13:2. Approximate Monthly Expected Weight Increment

Age	Approximate Increase Grams/Month
1-3 months	800
4-6 months	600
7-9 months	400
10-12 months	300
12-36 months	200

Calculated for NCHS standard weight-for-age measurements for boys 1-36 months, U.S. Department of Health, Education & Welfare, 1977.

A village growth monitoring program can be accomplished in different ways. As in Indonesia, mothers can bring their children to a central location at monthly intervals where the measuring can serve as a social occasion or for other community activities (this volume, Rohde and Soejatni). The CBD worker will still need to keep record of attendees and make home visits to all children who do not attend so that those most at risk will not be missed.

In a population where cultural patterns restrict the travel of women outside their home areas, more localized weighing will be necessary. In Bangladesh, for example, children from several baris (homesteads surrounding a common courtyard) can be grouped for one weighing session. However, the inconvenience of setting up weighing stations in several different locations makes this method more difficult.

In some cases, it may be necessary to make individual home visits, although this is generally less advantageous. The involvement of the mother's peers can help her to learn new feeding techniques, while visiting each home isolates the experience to a one-to-one relationship. One of the most successful teaching methods used in Indoensia (Rohde, this volume) was the mother-to-mother system, where the mother of a well-nourished child was paired with one whose child was not growing adequately. The use of a locally available scale familiar to both mothers and workers is the optimum weighing method for a growth-monitoring program. In many cases, however, such scales may be unavailable or impractical for fieldwork. Several relatively low-cost scales are available, including the Salter Scale ($46.00), the CMS Scale ($40.00), and the AHRTAG or Super Sampson Scale ($10.00) (U.S. Department of Health, Education and Welfare, 1977).

The cost of growth charts ranges from $.03 to $.33 (U.S. Department of Health, Education and Welfare, 1977). The charts should be printed on strong cards and kept in a polyethulene bag, 10 cm larger than the card to prevent damage from handling (King et al., 1972). The Imesi Project in Nigeria had a recordcard loss rate of only 1 percent for those held by the mothers, compared with 5 to 10 percent for cards kept by the clinic (Morley and Woodland, 1979).

Potential CBD Nutrition Activities Associated with Monitoring PCM

Time limitations placed on worker training, and the generally brief and/or infrequent nature of contact with mothers make promotion of clear and simple nutritional messages essential. Breastfeeding should be promoted where its incidence is low or its duration short. Duration of breastfeeding varies by cultural context, but in general, for rural areas of developing countries, should be a minimum of one year, and preferably up to two or three years. Even in the third year of life, breast-milk has been shown to provide substantial amounts of energy and protein (Brown et al., 1982).

Complementary foods should be given to an infant from four to six months of age using a clean cup and spoon, rather than by hand or bottle which are easily contaminated. These "weaning foods" should include a cereal base (such as mashed rice or wheat gruel) mixed with legumes (lentils, beans) for protein and oil or sugar to increase caloric density. The child should be fed three to five times each day in order to provide sufficient calories. After an episode of illness, an additional feeding should be given each day for the number of days the child was ill.

As noted earlier, the involvement of village mothers in exchanging useful nutritional information may be of value in sustaining improvements. Finally, while the distribution of food to those severely malnourished is an often-used mechanism to gain the community's support, it is not feasible in a CBD setting.

Summary

PCM among preschool children is the most prevalent nutritional problem in the developing world. Programs designed to address it must focus on prevention, if at all possible, because treatment is difficult and costly.

The major emphasis of any PCM-focused nutrition project must be continuous contact between the CBD worker and the family, without which the project is likely to result in wasted resources. However, with ongoing monitoring of the child's status, and development of a rapport between the worker and the family, such a program can result in improvements in the nutritional status of the children within the community.

Growth-monitoring and other methods used to reduce the prevalence of PCM can often be hindered by the structure of some CBD programs. Training levels, logistic support, and large populations to be covered, can all reduce the effectiveness of the nutritional activities described above because of the need for frequent visits to observe declines in nutritional status and to subsequently encourage changes in feeding practices. The lack of medical backup for referral of severe infections also inhibits nutritional improvements since the cycle of malnutrition and infection is less easily broken. The larger issues of food availability and income limitation, which play a major role in malnutrition, are also beyond the scope of the CBD worker's activity.

Notwithstanding, CBD workers can be taught simple methods to assess the nutritional status of their communities and given the necessary knowledge and skills to encourage changes in feeding practices they can lead the way to improvements in nutritional status.

VITAMIN A DEFICIENCY

WHO estimates that 1 million children develop xerophthalmia each year and of these 100,000 become blind; the highest rates of vitamin A deficiency are found in Asia and the Near East (Solon et al., 1979; Sinha and Bang, 1973; Sommer, 1978; Sommer, 1982). An inadequate intake of preformed vitamin A (occurring only in animal products) or its precursor, provitamin carotenoids (primarily B carotene), leads to vitamin A deficiency. In developing countries, the majority of vitamin A intake comes from carotene-containing foods, such as dark-green leafy or yellow vegetables and fruits, or red palm oil.

In addition to low intakes of vitamins, certain physiological states, such as pregnancy and lactation, can lead to a deficiency by increasing requirements, or by decreasing absorption and increasing excretion, as in diarrhea, respiratory illness, and ascariasis (Bauernfeind, 1980). Measles has a particularly devastating effect on vitamin A status through systemic disruption of vitamin A metabolism, and through the associated sequelae of fever, malnutrition, and diarrhea. Where protein deficiency is a major problem, vitamin A deficiency has even more severe consequences due to a reduced synthesis of retinol-binding proteins necessary for transport of the vitamin A in the blood (Sommer, 1978; Sommer, 1982). Protein deficiency may also interfere with storage of vitamin A in the liver.

Xerophthalmia describes the syndrome of severe vitamin A deficiency, manifested by conjunctival xerosis (dryness of the conjunctiva), Bitot's spots, corneal xerosis, and keratomalacia (ulceration of the cornea resulting in corneal opacity). Secondary signs of xerophthalmia include night blindness, xerophthalmia fundus, and corneal scars (WHO, 1976b). Hypovitaminosis A is also associated with a reduction in the immunologic defense mechanisms and, in animals, with increased infections. Due to the difficulties of studying the independent effect of vitamin A deficit on infections, such an association has not been documented in humans (WHO, 1976b). Since vitamin A contributes to growth, deficiencies have been precipitated when body stores are low and PCM is diagnosed and treated. Studies in Indonesia and Sri Lanka observed a closer association between vitamin A deficiency and stunting than with wasting (Sommer, 1982; Brink et al., 1979).

Risk Factors

Young children exhibit more severe complications of vitamin A deficiency than older children, and preschool-aged children seem to be the most affected. Infants are usually protected by the vitamin A in breast-milk, which is generally adequate unless the mother's stores are severely depleted. However, infants who are not breast-fed have an increased risk of this deficiency. Sommer and colleagues (Tarwotjo, Sommer et al., 1982) noted that Indonesian children aged three years or less who had xerophthalmia were less likely to have been breast-fed in comparison to age-, sex- and village-matched controls.

In some areas, vitamin A deficiency has been noted to occur seasonally (Sommer, 1982; WHO, 1976b); moreover, it often peaks during periods of prevalent diarrhea, due perhaps to decreased intake of food caused by anorexia or food withholding, decreased absorption from the gut, or increased metabolism of vitamin A. Seasonal dry periods are also associated with vitamin A deficiency due to shortages of fruits and vegetables.

Consequences

In countries where xerophthalmia exists among children, the consequences are severe. In India, for example, when corneal involvement occurs, up to 25 percent of the children become totally blind and 50 to 60 percent partially blind. An Indian study showed that mortality also increases; one-third of those suffering from keratomalacia died within three to four months (Menon and Vijayaraghavan, 1980). In Indonesia, 40 percent of those treated for keratomalacia died within a few years (Sommer, 1982). These high mortality rates are probably not due to the vitamin A deficiency alone, but to its correlation with the severe PCM that occurs in this country. The effects of subclinical vitamin A deficiency are less clear, although it is likely that it decreases resistance to infection (Oomen, 1976).

Treatment and Prevention

The manner of addressing vitamin A deficiency has been described by the phrase: "First, the eye; second, the patient; third, the kitchen." (Sommer, 1982).

First, the Eye

Xerophthalmia should be treated as soon as it is discovered. WHO guidelines suggest an oil miscible dose of 200,000 IU of vitamin A on two successive days repeated in two weeks for children less than one year with 100,000 IU given to children less than one year (WHO, 1982). Generally, this approach has been used only in a clinical setting where skilled personnel have been trained to identify xerophthalmia. It is possible, however, that village health workers could be trained to identify such eye involvement and could, therefore, initiate this treatment in the field. WHO is currently testing a xerophthalmia recognition card for this purpose. However, where the occurrence of xerophthalmia is infrequent, it may be too difficult for a worker to maintain the level of diagnostic skill needed to recognize xerophthalmia.

Second, the Patient

Periodic mass dosage programs improve the vitamin A nutriture of children by treating those afflicted with the disease and preventing it in others. The usual oral dosage for children is 200,000 IU of ethinyl palmitate combined with 40 IU of vitamin E in oil every six months. Vitamin E is added to improve the storage of retinol in the liver and to reduce symptoms of toxicity (Bauernfeind, 1980). It is estimated that 30 to 50 percent of the dose is stored in the liver and is physiologically available for as long as four to six months (WHO, 1976b).

Most government programs give vitamin A supplements twice a year. However, several studies suggest that oral supplementation fails to maintain normal serum levels (Pereira and Begum, 1969; Solon et al., 1979). This supports the possible need for supplementation at intervals shorter than six months (Solon et al., 1979), although the approach may be infeasible within the CBD setting.

The most common of several ways to administer vitamin A is in a gelatin capsule which can be swallowed by older children. For younger children the capsule's tip is cut and the tasteless, oily solution is squirted into the back of the child's mouth. The National Program in India uses liquid orange-flavored syrup with measured amounts poured by spoon into the child's mouth. This solution is less costly than capsules but has some disadvantages: it requires the use of individual spoons for each child in order to prevent spread of infection; transferring the syrup to the mother's utensil can result in increased spillage; and administration from a spoon can result in more loss than when a capsule is given.

To prevent vitamin A toxicity in children it is important that dosage levels be carefully controlled. Because vitamin A toxicity may cause congenital anomalies, high doses of the vitamin should not be given to pregnant women (Bauernfeind, 1980). Although night blindness has been noted among pregnant women, it resolves suddenly upon delivery and xerophthalmia is rare (Oomen, 1976). CBD workers must be made aware of the adverse effects of vitamin A overdosing; this message can be conveyed through even minimal training. Although vitamin A deficiency among breastfed infants is uncommon, lactating women can be given vitamin A supplements to increase the amount of the vitamin in their milk (WHO, 1976b). Sommer (personal communication) suggests that within one month of delivery the child receive 50,000 IU and the mother 400,000 IU. Lactating women beyond one month of delivery should not be given massive doses of vitamin A in order to preclude the possibility of her being pregnant.

Adverse reactions to vitamin A observed in a minority of subjects included gastrointestinal distress and/or headache lasting up to two to four days (Oomen, 1976). In a Philippines study, 3.4 percent of children had reactions (vomiting, headache, or fever) that led to a 3.3 percent refusal rate at the second supplementation (Solon et al., 1979). Since no placebo was given, the reaction cannot be attributed with certainty to the high dose of vitamin A. However, symptoms of vitamin A toxicity that are transitory and not dangerous include reactions similar to these (Bauernfeind, 1980).

Third, the Kitchen

The massive-dose approach should be considered an interim measure until improvements in vitamin A intake through diet can be achieved (Vijayaraghavan and Rao, 1978). The most effective means appears to be through fortification of vitamin A in a commonly consumed food (Sommer, 1978; WHO, 1976b). Aside form this approach, educating the family on the necessary consumption of foods containing vitamin A is the most important step. Availability of such foods is usually not a major obstacle. An Indonesian study illustrated that 99 percent of all families consumed dark-green leafy vegetables at least once a week, although the children with Bitot's spots consumed them much less frequently (Tarwotjo et al., 1982).

Often, cooked vegetables are highly spiced and are thereby not suitable for young children. An important educational message is to encourage the separation of cooked vegetables to be fed to young children prior to the addition of spices. Overcooking is not a problem, since vitamin A is not destroyed by heat, nor is it water soluble and likely to be lost in the cooking water. The difficulty in feeding children vegetables they dislike should not be underestimated, especially when frequent morbidity results in prevalent anorexia. Adding small amounts of chopped leafy vegetables to a common weaning food, pap, or gruel might help. Consumption of fruits is easier to encourage, but those containing large amounts of vitamin A precursors, such as mangos, are seasonal.

Program Implications

A vitamin A supplementation program is suitable to a restricted number of CBD settings since vitamin A deficiency is geographically limited to a few areas. In locations where xerophthalmia is prevalent, the inclusion of a program to address vitamin A deficiency in a community-based health care system is advantageous. Although case finding and treatment eventually may prove possible for community-level workers, this approach has not yet been studied. The focus on educating families to increase consumption of vitamin A in children has not yet been shown to be highly successful (Solon et al., 1978), although some projects have led to an increase in home vegetable production (Were, 1981). Vitamin A supplementation programs, therefore, appear to be most appropriate in CBD settings; case finding and education are appropriate activities for the worker as he or she conducts the supplementation program.

Supplementation with vitamin A generally focuses on children between the ages of one and five. The CBD worker's list of families in the area will indicate the numbers and location of children under five, allowing an estimate of the supply of vitamin capsules needed, and the time required for administration. The guidelines of the National Program for the Prevention of Vitamin A Deficiency in India recommend concentrating the administration of capsules during particular months of the year, although this policy was often not followed (Vijayaraghavan and Rao, 1978). The seasonal nature of vitamin A deficiency would support the timing of such a supplementation program prior to the peak of the diarrhea season, or during the lean season when fresh fruits and vegetables are less available.

In order to ensure that all families are reached, visiting the home to deliver capsules is preferable to requiring parents to bring children to a central location. Even when home visits were used in a highly supervised research project in the Philippines, only 90 percent of the children were reached at the first visit (Solon et al., 1979). The second visit reached only 84 percent, and the proportion declined even further by the third visit. Other studies have illustrated that those most difficult to reach were also most at risk (Sommer, 1982).

The health workers' listings of all eligible children residing in the village are the most important means of determining who has not been supplemented. Additional lists should be made of children not reached during the program so that fieldworkers, at least once a month and preferably more often, can seek those children until they are reached. This obviously requires dedication and perseverance; supervision is an essential support to such follow-up. Thie worker's records are important in monitoring this process, as well as for subsequent evaluations of the program. However, such intensive follow-up may not be feasible in a CBD setting - even though exclusion of some children will limit the effectiveness of the program - and it should not be considered a prerequisite to the program.

A fieldworker should also be particularly concerned with children who exhibit severe PCM, as well as those recovering from measles, and others with chronic or severe infectious diseases. These children should have received a vitamin supplement within the preceding six months. The optimal program would combine treatment of PCM and vitamin A deficiency, but this will be possible only in programs that entail frequent household visits. Infants not being breast-fed should also be included for supplementation.

The inclusion of a vitamin A program in a CBD setting can have other benefits. The continuity of repeated home visits, even if only twice a year, can be the first step in monitoring child health, which can lead to the introduction of immunization programs and eventual growth monitoring. A home-retained health record, on which capsule distribution dates are recorded for each child, can be further refined to record other health promotion activities. The low cost of the program, each capsule being supplied by UNICEF at a cost of $.02 to the government, is an additional benefit. With a CBD project currently in operation, additional costs can also be minimal. The time required by the worker is small, especially when distribution of the capsules at home can be incorporated into scheduled visits. A village health worker responsible for a population of 1,000 would need to reach approximately 150 children per distribution period. Assuming a visiting rate of 10 households per day (with approximately two children per household), all 150 children would be visited in five to ten days.

In the absence of obvious clinical signs of vitamin A deficiency in the community, vitamin A supplementation is probably inadvisable. Although the population may suffer from a high incidence of hypovitaminosis A, it would be difficult to demonstrate health benefits from the program (Underwood, 1978), and the direct and opportunity costs would be better applied to other programs with more obvious health benefits.

Summary

Many governments (India, Bangladesh, Indonesia) have experienced some success with mass distribution of vitamin A over the last 20 years, assisted by UNICEF and other international agencies. These programs have contended with problems similar to those of most health and family planning programs (Underwood, 1978). The problems include:

1. Lack of personnel
2. Inadequate coordination
3. Poor record-keeping
4. Low coverage
5. High dropout rates
6. Lack of family cooperation
7. Migration
8. Symptoms associated with the dosage administration
9. Short supply of capsules
10. Low community awareness of program
11. Heavy workload for health workers.

Adequacy of training, supervision, and community participation are vital elements to consider in attempting to avoid problems with vitamin A distribution.

Because of the severe consequences of vitamin A deficiency together with the low cost of prevention, vitamin A supplementation programs provide a suitable initial step for CBD programs integrating nutrition activities with other health components. The infrequency of visits and the relatively low level of required worker training, particularly suit them to CBD projects that are less intensive, have greater population per worker ratios, or have other activities planned for delivery corresponding to the seasons of greatest vitamin A deficiencies.

ANEMIA

By WHO standards, half of all nonpregnant women and two-thirds of pregnant women throughout the developing world are anemic for a total of 58 percent in Asia, 40 percent in Africa, and 17 percent in Latin America (WHO Division of Family Health, 1979; Simmons and Gurney, 1982). Surveys in the English-speaking Caribbean illustrated 11 to 70 percent of children less than five years of age were anemic (WHO Division of Family Health, 1979; Simmons and Gurney, 1982; Simmons et al., 1982). Individual country levels of anemia in women are available in a recent WHO publication (WHO Division of Family Health, 1979; Simmons and Gurney, 1982). Table 13:3 summarizes some of the reported rates.

Table 13:3. Proportion of Nonpregnant Women Who Are Anemic

REGION	COUNTRY	YEAR	% BELOW 12 gm/ml
Africa	Tunisia	1978	31
	Mali	1973	58
	Nigeria	1978	36
	Togo	1977	35
	Botswana	1971	20
Caribbean & South America	Haiti	1970	33
	Guyana	1971	41
	Chile	1976	3
Asia	Turkey	1971	50
	Bangladesh	1975/76	70
	India	1973	67
	Indonesia	1970	55
Oceana	Fiji	1972	72
	Gilbert & Ellice Islands	1971	77

Source: WHO Division of Family Health, 1979.

Nutritional anemia, the most prevalent form of anemia, is defined when the hemoglobin concentration is below the normal level due to a deficiency in one or more nutrients needed for blood production (Baker and DeMaeyer, 1979). Table 13:4 gives the WHO (WHO, 1976a) standard hemoglobin concentrations at which anemia is likely to be present. Nutrients needed for blood formation include iron, folate, and vitamin B. Of these three nutrients, a deficiency of iron is the most common cause of anemia. However, deficiencies in folic acid, usually required only in minute quantities, can be precipitated by the increased physiologic requirements of pregnancy. Deficiencies of vitamin B are seldom seen under normal circumstances. This paper, therefore, will discuss only the anemias of iron and folate.

Table 13:4. Hemoglobin values below which anemia is likely to be present in populations

	mg/100 ml
Children 6 months to 6 years	11
Children 6 to 14 years	12
Adult males	13
Adult females (nonpregnant)	12
Adult females (pregnant)	11

Source: WHO.

Causes of Deficiencies

Factors that can lead to a deficiency of iron or folate can be categorized as increased losses, increased requirements, decreased intake in the diet, or decreased absorption and/or utilization (Baker and DeMaeyer, 1979).

Losses

Women are prone to loss of iron through blood lost during menstruation. Heavy parasitic infections, particularly with hookworm, also cause substantial intestinal blood loss. Necator americanus has been estimated to cause a total iron loss of 1.6 to 1.8 mg iron per day with a worm load of about 80 adults feces (represented by 2,000 eggs/gm feces) (Layrisse et al., 1976). Trichuris trichiura and Ancylostoma duodenale also can cause severe iron loss, as can blood loss due to shistosomiasis (Baker and DeMaeyer, 1979).

Increased Requirements

Because of menstrual losses, women have higher daily iron requirements than men (2.8 mg versus 2 mg, respectively) (WHO,

1976a). Since dietary iron is only partially absorbed, the recommended daily intake is 18 mg for women and 10 mg for men (National Research Council, 1980). With folate, on the other hand, requirements are 400 μg for both males and females.

Pregnancy is the major physiologic factor increasing women's requirements for iron and folate. Additional iron is needed for the increase in red cell mass that results from increased blood volume and the requirements of the fetus and placenta. The total requirement of iron during pregnancy is estimated at 1,000 mg, most of which is needed during the second trimester. An additional 30 to 60 mg of iron intake is suggested during pregnancy. Folate requirements double during the last two trimesters of pregnancy (Streiff, 1972). Thus, an additional 400 μg/day is recommended during pregnancy (National Research Council, 1980).

During the post-partum period, due to the need to replete iron stores (countered with the iron-retaining effect of amenorrhea), the recommended daily intake is 2.4 mg. Only small amounts of iron (estimated at 0.2 mg/day) are secreted in breastmilk (Baker and DeMaeyer, 1979). An additional 200 μg of folate is suggested during lactation to compensate for folate secreted in milk (WHO, 1976a).

Closely spaced pregnancies and high parity are associated in some studies with increases in the prevalence of anemia, due to increased demands associated with these physiologic states (Johnson et al., 1982; WHO, 1979).

Iron requirements for children are also increased during growth with the result that young children are prone to anemia.

Intake and Absorption

Normal subjects absorb 5 to 10 percent of the iron in their diets, while anemic patients absorb 10 to 20 percent (Finch, 1976). Although cereal-based diets provide high levels of non-heme iron, the amount of iron absorbed is low (5 to 10 percent). Meat-based diets, on the other hand, provide the majority of heme-iron, and 10 to 20 percent more is absorbed (Moore, 1973). Vegetables slightly decrease the absorption of heme-iron, while vitamin C enhances the absorption of non-heme iron, and meats nearly double its absorption (Layrisse et al., 1976).

Although folate is widely available in foods, it is destroyed by cooking. Meats, fresh fruits, and vegetables, the best sources of folate, are those most often lacking from the diet of women in developing countries. Folate deficiency results in megaloblastic anemia and is prevalent in malarial areas.

Consequences

Severe anemia of pregnancy is associated with increased maternal morbidity and mortality (WHO, 1975), and with an increase in premature births and fetal mortality (Baker and DeMaeyer, 1979). Folate deficiency during pregnancy has been associated with increased risk in some studies of abrupto placentae and fetal wastage (Pritchard, 1970). Studies in Narangwal (India) noted decreases in still-birth rates among women receiving supplements of iron and folic acid (Kielmann et al., 1978a; Kielmann et al., 1978b).

Some studies among anemic mothers have illustrated an increased risk of low birth weight infants (Iyengar and Rajalakkoni, 1975; Yusufji et al., 1973; Reinhardt, 1978), while others have not (Hemminki and Starfield, 1978; Sood et al., 1975). Infants born to anemic mothers appear to exhibit iron stores similar to those born to nonanemic mothers, both at birth and during their first year of life. The iron status of mothers appears to have little effect on the iron in breast-milk (Dallman and Siimes, 1979).

In adult studies, anemia has been reported to result in decreased work capacity and energy expenditure (Basta, 1974; Viteri and Torun, 1974). Susceptibility to infection is also thought to be associated with anemia, though epidemiologic studies to assess this association are difficult because of the need to control for numerous factors affecting infection.

In 1982 UNICEF cost per iron tablet (containing 200 mg ferrous sulfate equal to 60 mg elemental iron, and 0.25 µg folate) was about $.001 (UNIPAC, 1982). Costs for supplementing a pregnant woman during the last two trimesters (28 weeks) range from $.20, if one tablet per day is administered, to $.60 for three tablets per day.

Prevention and Treatment

Anemia of pregnancy can be prevented by supplementation with iron and folate. A large-scale study of the dose-effect of iron supplementation among Burmese women (22 to 28 weeks pregnant) indicated that the use of 240 mg of iron and 5 µg of folic acid daily resulted in an increase in serum ferritin levels nearly twice as great as that resulting from ingestion of 60 mg or 120 mg daily. Hemoglobin levels, however, did not differ statistically. The iron was provided in the form of ferrous sulfate taken after meals, six days a week for 12 weeks (Thane-Toe and Thein-Than, 1982).

Jackson and Latham (1982) conducted a similar study in Liberia in which large doses of ferrous sulfate were given to pregnant women in their third trimester. Women consuming 20 mg tablets of ferrous sulfate (supplying 60 mg of elemental iron) once or three times daily exhibited significant increase in hemoglobin four and eight weeks after onset of treatment. The addition of folic acid did not substantially alter the hemoglobin level.

The choice of a single daily iron dose, multiple daily iron doses, or combinations of iron and folic acid must be considered in light of: possible side effects with high single doses versus multiple doses of smaller quantities, compliance differences, the prevalence of folic acid deficiencies, cost, and availability.

Gastrointestinal disturbances have been associated with iron supplements. An Indian study noted fewer such instances among women given the supplement in combination with folic acid (Sood et al., 1975). While gastrointestinal disturbances decrease when iron is taken following a meal, the amount absorbed appears to be less. The discoloration of stools and constipation caused by iron intake may also be problematic.

The increased frequency of consumption of lower dose tablets may reduce compliance, but this could be countered by the worker's more frequent visits necessitated to replenish the tablets. Educating the mother as to the need for the iron supplement is important in improving compliance.

Program Implications

The village health worker or CBD worker should keep a register of fertile women in the area. This register should denote which women are pregnant, as well as the duration of their pregnancies. Optimally the worker should then visit the pregnant women every two weeks to one month in order to give them additional iron and folate tablets, and to serve as a reminder to comply with the drug regimens. Such home visits by the worker can also be the initial stage for promoting subsequent prenatal care. For example, tetanus toxoid vaccinations can later be incorporated into the worker's activities. Frequent visits, however, may be inappropriate in some CBD settings. Less frequent visits may be possible if more time is devoted during each contact to educating the mother on the need for iron consumption.

Even if a woman for some reason cannot be located during the second trimester of pregnancy, or if the pregnancy is not recognized early, iron and folic acid supplementation during the final trimester is important.

Aside form the use of iron supplements during pregnancy and lactation, the worker can be trained to recognize servere anemia in the general population by examining the patients' lips (the inside) and lower eyelids. A program of iron supplementation can then be instituted. The fieldworker should be especially concerned with assessing anemia in young children, although compliance with treatment among children is likely to be difficult.

Summary

Iron supplementation of pregnant women or of anemic children can be an important step toward including nutrition activities in a program. Because the community cannot see obvious results they are less likely to accept and appreciate iron supplementation than vitamin A supplementation, where severe sequelae to the deficiency are evident. However, for the individual, especially the severely anemic, an iron supplementation program can have significant benefits.

ENDEMIC GOITER AND CRETINISM

In 1960, an estimated 200 million people were affected with goiter. Due to government efforts in recent years, its prevalence has declined in many parts of the world (DeMaeyer et al., 1979), but the condition remains a significant problem in isolated areas of Africa, Asia, and Latin America (DeMaeyer et al., 1979; Medeiros-Neto and Dunn, 1980; Beckers and Benmiloud 1980; Kochupillai et al., 1980). Table 13:5 gives recent estimates for the prevalence of goiter in Latin America (Medeiros-Neto and Dunn, 1980). The number of people afflicted in India is estimated at 10,000,000. Endemic goiter is also common in Nepal, affecting up to 90 percent of the population of some villages. In the South Pacific a high incidence of goiter and cretinism is evident in Papua, New Guinea (Hetzel and Hales, 1980) and Fiji (DeMaeyer et al., 1979).

Table 13:5. Prevalence of Goiter in Latin America

COUNTRY	YEAR OF STUDY	TOTAL PREVALENCE	RANGE OF PREVALENCE WITHIN REGIONS OF COUNTRY	POPULATION STUDIED
Brazil	1975	15%	1-31%	Schoolchildren
Colombia	1973-74		1-42%	Schoolchildren
Guatemala	1965	5%		Schoolchildren
Honduras	1966	17%	3-31%	Schoolchildren
Peru	1975		0-50%	All ages
Uruguay	1970		21-24%	Schoolchildren

Source: Mediros-Neto and Dunn, 1980.

Endemic goiter, the enlargement of the thyroid gland, results from inadequate iodine intake. In some areas anti-thyroid substances in food (goitrogens) may also contribute to increased goiter prevalence. During periods of increased requirements for iodine, such as during growth in childhood, adolescence, pregnancy, and lactation, the prevalence of goiter may increase. Requirements for iodine appear to be less in men and in adults over 45 (Clements, 1976).

Endemic cretinism is caused by severe iodine deficiency during pregnancy. (Cretinism can also be caused by congenital hypothyroidism unrelated to iodine deficiency.) Endemic cretinism is a syndrome of irreversible mental retardation, accompanied by neurologic complications including abnormalities in hearing, speech, and gait, or hypothyroidism (referred to as myxedema) with associated impairment in growth (Pharoah et al., 1980).

Low dietary intakes of iodine are generally due to an insufficiency of iodine in the soil, which in turn results in low levels of iodine in food products. This is mainly a problem for those whose food is limited to locally produced foods in an area in which iodine content in the soil is minimal (Clements, 1976). Consumption of marine fish, because it contains a high level of iodine, is a protection against goiter. Sea salt, on the other hand, contains little iodine because the small amount of iodine in dissolved saltwater is lost in processing (DeMaeyer et al., 1979).

Consequences

Goiter does not greatly affect the individual's health until the age of 30 to 40 years since, even though the thyroid is enlarged, the gland is generally able to produce sufficient quantities of thyroid hormones. After this age, however, the progressive destruction of the epithelial parts of the thyroid gland may gradually reduce its ability to produce adequate thyroid hormones, and a subsequent slow onset of forms of myxedema may result (DeMaeyer et al., 1979).

Many goitrous individuals appear healthy, able to work, and are without signs of intellectual or physical impairment. Others with large goiters, however, exhibit symptoms of tracheal compression, trouble in breathing, or compression of jugular veins (Pharoah et al., 1980). In some parts of the world, goiter can have social and economic implications for those afflicted. In Bangladesh, for example, goiter can be a social stigma limiting the options for marriage. Conversely, in other areas such as Nepal, where the prevalence of goiter is high, the social stigma may be minimal.

In cases of goiter pertaining to pregnancy, the mother's hypothyroidism is associated with an increased incidence of spontaneous abortions and stillbirths. When the supply of iodine to the developing fetus is restricted, congenital malformations and cretinism may result, even though the mother is euthyroidic (McMichael et al., 1980).

The public health significance of goiter is primarily its association with cretinism. The mental retardation, deaf-mutism, and physical abnormalities have substantial negative effects on individuals, families, and societies. Mortality among cretins is high. Preliminary studies in a central Java community have associated lower mental performance in the general childhood population with the prevalence of endemic cretinism (Guerido et al., 1974).

Studies in Ecuador have reported improvements in intelligence of normal babies (by Stanford-Benet tests) when mothers were given iodine supplements prior to pregnancy, but not during pregnancy since it is likely that adequate iodine supply to the fetus is most critical very early in gestation (Fierro-Benitez et al., 1980).

Prevention and Treatment

The daily requirement of iodine is estimated at 200 mg; in practice, mean intakes greater than 50 to 75 mg of iodine per day are seldom associated with endemic goiter or cretinism (Trowbridge, personal communication). An otherwise normal food supply can be supplemented by four methods (DeMaeyer et al., 1979):

- Iodination of salt,
- Iodination of bread,
- Use of oral tablets containing potassium iodide,
- Administration of iodinated oil through injection or orally.

Iodination of salt is generally the easiest and most cost-effective means of preventing iodine deficiency. Based on national programs in Burma, India, and Thailand, the annual cost per person per year is estimated at $.003 to $.005 (Medeiros-Neto and Dunn, 1980). Since iodination of salt or other foods is outside the focus of a CBD project, the administration of oil or oral iodine should be considered in areas of prevalent goiter and where an iodination program has not reached the entire population.

Injection of Iodinated Oil

A single injection of iodinated oil reduces the prevalence of goiter and iodine deficiency be restoring normal thyroid function. It is not known for what length of time a single maternal injection will prevent cretinism in the offspring. DeMaeyer and colleagues (DeMaeyer et al., 1979) suggest that an injection of 1 to 2 ml of iodinated oil every three to five years can reduce the prevalence to less than 20 percent. This injection interval is likely to maintain iodine status above pre-injection levels in the majority of individuals. Riccabona (1980) states that 70 percent of a treated population will respond to 0.5 to 1 ml when treatment is carried out in the first 30 years of life.

Within three months of injection of iodinated oil, significant regression in goiter in a high proportion of cases is noted. In cases where the goiter has become fibrosed, the goiter may not disappear although the hormonal problem appears to be corrected (Kochupillai et al., 1980).

Thilly and coworkers (1980) reviewed several studies demonstrating that late administration of iodized oil during pregnancy can benefit thyroid function, psychomotor development, and infant mortality. Other studies did not find this association, however.

In order to prevent cretinism, it has been found necessary to inject women with iodinated oil prior to conception. With small children, injections should be given intramuscularly into the buttocks, whereas with adults it should be in the upper arm.

WHO recommends the use of .5 ml for children under one year and 1 ml for older children (DeMaeyer et al., 1979). Because of the viscosity of the oil, relatively large needles must be used and special care must be taken not to inject the oil directly into a vein. Some adverse reactions may occur, among them iodine-induced hyperthyroidism (jodbasedow or hypotoxicosis). However, in a study of 911 patients in Zaire, no secondary effects including cutaneous reactions suggestive of either iodism or incipient hyperthyroidism were observed following injection (Delange, 1974). In a study in Argentina, three of 94 patients receiving 0.3 to 1 ml of iodized oil intramuscularly developed jodbasedow, noted nine months after administration (Watanabe et al., 1974).

For purposes of storage, the oil is temperature stable and can be easily transported. Based on expenses in a government program in Central Africa, and similar figures from Peru, the cost of one ml dose of iodinated oil is \$.20, plus an additional \$.05 for syringes, sterilizing equipment, and registration forms (DeMaeyer et al., 1979).

Oral Intake of Iodinated Oil

In spite of the fact that a large fraction of oral iodine is excreted immediately afterwards, it appears to prevent goiter. An Argentine study comparing oral and injected iodized oil noted similar results in the proportion of cases whose goiter disappeared or diminished. The oral dose used was 1.4 times the injected dose (for subjects over six years, 1 ml injected oil, and 1.4 ml oral) (Watanabe et al., 1974). While 3 percent of the injected patients experienced jadbasedow, none of the patients receiving the oral dosage did. Since oral administration of iodized oil would decrease the cost of the program, more field testing has been suggested (Matovinovic, 1980a; Matovinovic, 1980b).

Potassium Iodide Tablets

Potassium iodide tablets taken at short intervals (perhaps once a week) have also been used to treat and prevent goiter. In the 1950s in Uruguay, schoolchildren were supplied with 2 mg tablets weekly. Despite irregular distribution, a decrease in visible goiter was reported (Salveraglio, 1974). Projects using potassium iodide tablets were successful in lowering the prevalence of goiter among schoolchildren in Guatemala, El Salvador, and Tasmania (Scrimshaw et al., 1953; Clements et al., 1968).

DeMaeyer and colleagues (DeMaeyer et al., 1979), however, reported that the distribution of iodide tablets has not generally been successful due to organizational difficulties and lack of patient acceptability. Tablet distribution carries the same difficulties as an iron distribution project, in that continued contact with the subject must be ensured.

Program Implications

In areas where goiter is evident, an iodinated-oil program can be a beneficial addition to a CBD worker's activities. It offers an excellent opportunity because it is one of the rare rural health programs that, although modest in scope and cost, can produce effects directly visible to the population (DeMaeyer et al., 1979). This program can have the success that other health additions to CBD projects have sought: that of gaining the confidence of the population while seeking their participation in other activities such as family planning.

For those workers already involved with giving injections (such as Depo-Provera), the additional training required for iodine injections is not excessive. For programs where this is not feasible, a mass campaign can be organized where the CBD worker locates appropriate subjects by means of a roster; then the supervisor, or a trained team member, can give the injections. The CBD worker's role would be to educate the community about the program and to encourage participation.

The population to be served should be defined in relation to funds, supplies, and logisitics. In highly endemic areas, the optimal approach is to administer iodine to all residents under age 45. If this is not feasible, all women of childbearing age at a minimum and those with palpable or visible goiters should be injected. In areas with lower prevalence, subjects with palpable or visible goiters should be diagnosed by the CBD worker, and given injections. The training needs of these various approaches obviously differ. With the mass campaign approach, a special short-term training session can be held which focuses on immediate learning rather than long-term retention.

The use of oral iodine tablets could be incorporated with the usual activities of the CBD workers. Various strategies to ensure consumption of these tablets should be tested. For example, tablets could be given at monthly intervals corresponding to the worker's home visits. The needed dosage and effectiveness of such tablets would have to be studied.

Summary

The inclusion of an iodine supplementation program is appropriate only in the isolated areas of the world where goiter and cretinism prevail. They are therefore applicable to a small proportion of health programs functioning in rural areas. However, for those specific programs, the effect of an iodine supplementation program can be substantial.

EVALUATION

Evaluation of the effects of nutrition activities in CBD projects is important to ensure program success and to communicate to policy makers the importance of such activities. As with many other health interventions, the multifaceted causes of malnutrition may make the effects of the program difficult to demonstrate. Process evaluations are therefore necessary, and when feasible, impact evaluations should be instituted as well.

Information needed to illustrate the effectiveness of the program process would include: denominator data on the number of children of specified ages or pregnant women, the number receiving treatment and at what intervals, the drugs received and distributed to each participant, and the timing of onset and completion of treatment (in relation to date, age of children, or months pregnant for women). Such information is needed for the population serviced by each CBD worker and should be contained in records kept by the worker; the same information will be needed to fulfill other job responsibilities.

Impact evaluation necessitates the inclusion of a comparison population that does not receive the services. A concurrent population in a nearby area not included in the program is the most appropriate group for comparison. Less advantageous but easier to obtain, are data on the population prior to service delivery or information on new participants to the program. Data for evaluation of program effects may in some cases be obtained from the worker's records, for example, measurements of growth or arm circumference. Laboratory measures or clinical assessment which are more expensive and require technically trained personnel, may be necessary to evaluate the effectiveness of some interventions.

Vitamin A programs can be evaluated by clinical assessment of the frequency of Bitot's spots or by laboratory analysis of serum levels of vitamin A. Changes in the prevalence of goiter depend on clinical determination of the frequency and size of goiters, or analyses of serum levels of protein-bound iodine. Analyses of hemoglobin or hematocrit can be used to evaluate the results of an iron supplementation program, but are less sensitive than more expensive and diffcult analyses of serum ferritin.

Process evaluations are the first step to any assessment or program success, since without delivery of services, no improvement can be expected. Every program should have some type of process evaluation built into it, and proper program management depends upon it. Impact evaluation can then follow, its extensiveness depending upon resources available to the program.

CONCLUSION

The choice of which nutrition interventions to include in a CBD program depends on the prevalence of the nutritional problem, its severity, and the feasibility of prevention and treatment given the operation and resources of the CBD program. Vitamin A and goiter programs are limited geographically, but in the areas where xerophthalmia or goiter are prevalent, they should be the first interventions to be included. Both are easy to implement and will give dramatic results that the community can observe. This is especially true in the case of goiter, and will be made more evident with vitamin A supplementation if the program is explained to mothers and the community in relation to its effect on reducing night blindness (which will be recognized in the community) and the prevalence of severe blindness among young children following illnesses (especially measles). The educational component is therefore more important with a vitamin A program which is more often a preventive measure than a curative one.

The prevalence of anemia and protein-calorie malnutrition is greater and more widespread than vitamin A and iodine deficiency. However, both programs are more difficult to implement and have less apparent positive effects. Of the two, anemia necessitates the least supplies, logisticis, and time to educate the community. Because it focuses on pregnant women, it can serve to communicate to the community that a CBD program is not only concerned with reducing births, but in promoting the health of pregnant women and their subsequent infants.

Discernible benefits of the program to the community will be few, except when the worker is able to treat severely anemic patients. A strategy to gain community acceptance to illustrate the potential of the program, would be to screen the community for severe anemia through home visits prior to initiating the supplemental program for pregnant women. Treating those cases found will convincingly demonstrate the effectiveness of the supplementation program for pregnant women. This could help to encourage participation in the program even though subsequent effects will be less evident.

Although a program to address preschool-child malnutrition is the most difficult to implement; it addresses the most prevalent problem, and one with great potential for the community. The result, however, is difficult to illustrate. Preventing PCM necessitates the greatest level of training and supervision of workers, the highest frequency of visits, and the most intensive participation by mothers and the community due to the multifaceted causes of malnutrition and the need to address these causes through various approaches. Because of these requirements, such a program is feasible primarily when a CBD worker serves a relatively small population (about 10 to 2,000), lives within the community, has established the community's confidence, is a persuasive communicator able to encourage changes in behavior, and has the ability to mobilize resources both from within and outside the community.

These characteristics may be difficult to find in many CBD settings. In those programs that can, however, the gain in terms of nutritional status and health of preschool children in the community can be substantial. This program focus should be the eventual aim of all programs where PCM is a problem.

The effect of malnutrition on mortality and morbidity in a population is great, making nutrition activities important additions to community-based health and family planning programs. However, the implementation of any of the above-described activities depends upon adequate training, supervision, and logistical support with community backing. Unless these are available at appropriate levels, as with other interventions, they should not be attempted, since the likelihood for success is small. Nevertheless, with the necessary resources, nutrition activities can play an important role both in promoting improvements in health and in paving the way for community acceptance of the program.

ACKNOWLEDGEMENTS

I would like to thank Dr. Robert Parker, Dr. Frederick Trowbridge, Dr. Al Sommers, Dr. Richard Osborn and Dr. Jerry Bailey for their helpful comments on this paper.

I also appreciate the support provided by the Agency for International Development, Office of Population, and the Ford Foundation, under whose auspices this paper was written.

REFERENCES

American Public Health Association. Health Information Exchange Project Capsules. Washington, DC: 1979.

Arole, R. and M. Arole. "Comprehensive Rural Health Project in Jamkhed, India." In Health by the People, edited by K.W. Newall. Geneva: World Health Organization, 1975: 69-78.

Baker, S.J. and E.M. DeMaeyer. "Nutritional Anemia: Its Understanding and Control with Special Reference to the Work of the World Health Organization (in Perspectives in Nutrition)." American Journal of Clinical Nutrition 32 (1979): 368-417,

Bauernfeind, J.C. The Safe Use of Vitamin A : A Report of the International Vitamin A Consultative Group (IVACG). Washington, DC: Nutrition Foundation, 1980.

Basta, S. "International Bank for Reconstruction and Development, Staff Working Paper." April, 1974.

Beaton, G.H. and H. Ghassemi. "Supplementary Feeding Programs for Young Children in Developing Countries." American Journal of Clinical Nutrition 35 (1982): 864-916.

Beckers, C. and M. Benmiloud. "The Present Status of Endemic Goiter as a Problem of Public Health: Africa." In Endemic Goiter and Endemic Cretinism, edited by J.B. Stanbury and B.S. Hetzel. New York: John Wiley & Sons, Inc., 1980.

Black, R.E., K.H. Brown, S. Becker et al. I: "Longitudinal Studies of Infectious Diseases and Physical Growth of Children in Rural Bangladesh." II: "Incidence of Diarrhea and Assocation with Known Pathogens." American Journal of Epidemiology 115,3 (1982): 315-324.

Brink, E.W., W.D.A. Perera, S.P. Broske et al. "Vitamin A Status of Children in Sri Lanka." American Journal of Clinicial Nutrition 32 (1979): 84-91.

Brown, J.E. and R.C. Brown. Finding the Causes of Child Malnutrition: A Comunity Handbook for Developing Countries. Atlanta: Task Force on World Hunger, 1979.

Brown K.H., R.E. Black, S. Becker et al. "Consumption of Foods and Nutrients by Weanlings in Rural Bangladesh." American Journal of Clinical Nutrition 36 (1982): 878-889.

Cameron, M. and Y. Hofvander. Manual on Feeding Infants and Young Children, 2nd edition. New York: United Nations, Protein-Calorie Advisory Group, 1976.

Chen, L.C., A.K.M.A. Chowdhury, and S.L. Huffman. "Anthropometric Assessment of Energy-Protein Malnutrition and Subsequent Risk of Mortality among Preschool Aged Children." American Journal of Clinical Nutrition 33 (1980): 1836-1845.

Chen, L.S., E. Huq, and S.L. Huffman. "A Prospective Study of the Risk of Diarrhea Disease According to the Nutritional Status of Children." American Journal of Epidemiology 114,2 (1981): 284-292.

Clements, F.W. "Endemic Goitre." In Nutrition in Preventive Medicine, edited by G.H. Beaton and J.R. Bengoa. Geneva: World Health Organization, 1976: 83-93.

Clements, F.W., H.B. Gibson, and J.F. Howeler-Coy. "Goiter Studies in Tasmania." Bulletin of the World Health Organization 38 (1968): 297-318.

Cole-King, S.M. "Under Five's Clinic in Malawi: The Development of a National Programme." Environmental Child Health 8 (1975): 183-191.

Dallman, P.R. and M.A. Siimes. Iron Deficiency in Infancy and Childhood. Washington, DC: The Nutrition Foundation, 1979.

Delange, F. Endemic Goitre and Thyroid Function in Central America. Monographs in Paediatrics, Vol. 2. Basel (Switzerland): S. Karger, 1974.

DeMaeyer, E.M. "Protein-Energy Malnutrition. In Nutrition in Preventive Medicine, edited by G.H. Beaton and J.A. Bengoa. Geneva: World Health Organization, 1976: 23-55.

DeMaeyer, E.M., F.W. Lowenstein, and C.H. Thilly. The Control of Endemic Goitre. Geneva: World Health Organization, 1979.

Deville de Goyet, C., J. Seman, and U. Geijer. The Management of Nutritional Emergencies in Large Populations. Geneva: World Health Organization, 1978.

Drake, W.D., R.I. Miller, and M. Humphrey. "Final report: Analysis of Community-Level Nutrition Program." In Project on Analysis of Community Level Nutrition Programs. Ann Arbor, MI: Community Systems Foundation and USAID Office of Nutrition, October, 1980.

Fierro-Benitez et al. "The Role of Iodine in Intellectual Development in an Area of Endemic Goiter." In Endemic Goiter and Endemic Cretinism, edited by J.B. Stanbury and B.S. Hetzel. New York: John Wiley & Sons, Inc., 1980.

Finch, C.A. "Iron Metabolism." In Nutrition reviews: Present Knowledge in Nutrition, 4th edition. Wasington, DC: The Nutrition Foundation, 1976: 281-289.

Griffiths, M. Primary Health Care Issues: Growth Monitoring. Washington, DC: Pan American Health Organization, 1981.

Guerido, A., R. Djokomoeljanto, and C. van Hardeveld. "The Consequences of Iodine Deficiency for Health in Endemic Goiter and Cretinism: Continuing Effects to World Health." In Endemic Goiter and Cretinism: Continuing Threats to World Health, edited by J.T. Dunn and G.A. Mediros-Neto. Scientific publication No. 292. Washington, DC: Pan American Health Organization, 1974: 8-16.

Gwatkin, D.R., J.R. Wilcox and J.D. Wray. Can Health and Nutrition Interventions Make a Difference? Washington, DC: Overseas Development Council, Monograph No. 13, 1980a.

Gwatkin, D.R., J.R. Wilcox, and J.D. Wray. "The Policy Implications of Field Experiments in Primary Health and Nutrition Care." Social Science and Medicine 14:121-128, 1980b.

Hemminki, E. and B. Starfield. "Prevention of Low Birth Weight and Pre-term Birth: Literature Review and Suggestions for Research Policy." Milbank Memorial Fund Quarterly/Health and Society 56,3 (1978): 339-361.

Hetzel, B.S. and I.B. Hales. "The Present Status of Endemic Goiter as a Problem in the Public Health: 6. New Zealand, Australia, Papua New Guinea." In Endemic Goiter and Endemic Cretinism, edited by J.B. Stanbury and B.S. Hetzel. New York: John Wiley & Sons, Inc., 1980.

Iyengar, L. and K. Rajalakkoni. "Effect of Folic Acid Supplements on Birth Weight of Infants." American Journal of Obstetrics 122 (1975): 332-336.

Jackson, R.T. and M.C. Latham. "Anemia of Pregnancy in Liberia, West Africa: A Therapeutic Trial." American Journal of Clinical Nutrition 35:710-714, 1982.

Johnson, A.A., M.C. Latham, D.A. and Roe. "The Prevalence and Etiology of Nutritional Anemias in Guyana." American Journal of Clinical Nutrition 35:309, 1982.

Kielmann, A.A. and C. McCord. "Nutrition and Health: Weight-for-age as an Index of Risk of Death in Children." Lancet (1978): 1247-1250.

Kielmann, A.A., C.E. Taylor, and C. DeSweemer. "The Narangwal Experiment on Interactions of Nutrition and Infections. II. Morbidity and Mortality Effects." Indian Journal of Medical Research 68 suppl. (1978a): 21-41.

Kielmann, A.A., C.E. Taylor, and R.L. Parker. "The Narangwal Nutrition Study: A Summary Review." American Journal of Clinical Nutrition 31 (1978b): 2040-2052.

King, K.W., W. Gougere, E. Ryland et al. "Preventive and Therapeutic Benefits in Relation to Cost: Performance Over Ten Years of Mother-craft Centers in Haiti." American Journal of Clinical Nutrition 31 (1978): 679-690.

King, M., F. King, D. Morley et al. Nutrition for Developing Countries. Nairobi: Oxford University Press, 1972.

Kochupillai, N., V. Ramalingaswami, and J.B. Stanbury. "The Present Status of Endemic Goiter as a Problem of the Public Health: 5. Southeast Asia." In Endemic Goiter and Endemic Cretinism, edited by J.B. Stanbury and B.S. Hetzel. New York: John Wiley & Sons, Inc., 1980.

Layrisse, M. and M. Roche. "The Relationship Between Anaemia and Hookworm Infection." American Journal of Tropical Medicine 16 (1967): 613.

Layrisse, M., M. Roche, and S.J. Baker. "Nutritional Anaemias." In Nutrition and Preventive Medicine, edited by G.H. Beaton and J.M. Bengoa. Geneva: World Health Organization, 1976: 55-82.

Mata, L.J. The Children of Santa Maria Cauque: A Prospective Field Study of Health and Growth. Cambridge: MIT Press, 1978.

Matavinovic, J. "Complications of Goiter Prophylaxis." In Endemic Goiter and Endemic Cretinism, edited by J.B. Stanbury and B.S. Hetzel. New York: John Wiley & Sons, Inc., 1980a: 589-596.

Matovinovic, J. "Recent Results in Goiter Prophylaxis." In Endemic Goiter and Endemic Cretinism, edited by J.B. Stanbury and B.S. Hetzel. New York: John Wiley & Sons, Inc., 1980b: 589-596.

McKay, H.E., A. McKay, and L. Sinisterra. "Improving Cognitive Ability in Chronically Deprived Children." Science 200 (1978): 270-278.

McMichael, A.J., J.D. Potter, and B.S. Hetzel. "Iodine Deficiency, Thyroid Function, and Reproductive Failure." In Endemic Goiter and Endemic Cretinism, edited by J.B. Stanbury and B.S. Hetzel. New York: John Wiley & Sons, Inc., 1980.

Medeiros-Neto, G.A. and J.T. Dunn. "The Present Status of Endemic Goitre as a Problem of the Public Health: 1. Central and South America." In Endemic Goiter and Endemic Cretinism, edited by J.B. Stanbury and B.S. Hetzel. New York: John Wiley & sons, Inc., 1980:3-30.

Menon, K. and K. Vijayaraghavan. "Sequelae of Severe Xerophthalmia - A Follow-up Study." American Journal of Clinical Nutrition 33 (1980):218-220.

Moore, C.V. "Section C- Iron." In Modern Nutrition in Health and Diseases, 5th edition, edited by R. Goodhart and M. Shils. Philadelphia: Lea & Febiger, 1973.

Morley, D. and M. Woodland. See How They Grow: Monitoring Child Growth for Appropriate Health Care in Developing Countries. New York: Oxford University Press, 1979.

National Research Council. Recommended Dietary Allowances, 9th revised edition. Washington, DC: National Academy of Sciences, 1980.

Oomen, H.A.P.C. "Vitamin A Deficiency, Xerophthalmia, and Blindness." In Nutrition Foundation: Nutrition Reviews' Present Knowledge of Nutrition, 4th edition. New York: The Nutrition Foundation, 1976: 73-81.

Pereira, S.M. and A. Begum. "Prevention of Vitamin A Deficiency." American Journal of Clinical Nutrition 22 (1969): 858-862.

Pharoah, P., F. Delange, R. Fierro-Benitiez et al. "Endemic Cretinism." In Endemic Goiter and Endemic Cretinism, edited by J.B. Stanbury and B.S. Hetzel. New York: John Wiley & Sons, Inc., 1980.

Pritchard, J.A. "Anemias Complicating Pregnancy and the Puerperium." In Maternal Nutrition and the Course of Pregnancy. Washington, DC: National Academy of Sciences, 1970.

Puffer, R. and C.V. Serrano. Patterns of Mortality in Childhood. Washington, DC: Pan American Health Organization, 1973.

Reinhardt, M.C. "Maternal Anemia in Abidjan - Its Influence on Placenta and Newborns." Helvatica Paediatrica Acta 41 suppl. (1978): 43-63.

Riccabona, G. "Treatment of the Individual Patient with Endemic Goiter." In Endemic Goiter and Endemic Cretinism, edited by J.B. Stanbury and B.S. Hetzel. New York: John Wiley & Sons, Inc., 1980.

Rowland, M.G.M., R.A.E. Barrell, and R.G. Whitehead. "Bacterial Contamination in Traditional Gambian Weaning Foods." Lancet (1978): 136-138.

Salveraglio, F.J. "Gaining Public Acceptance of Prophylaxis: Experience from the Campaign Against Endemic Goiter in Uruguay." In Endemic Goiter and Cretinism: Continuing Threats to World Health, edited by J.T. Dunne and G.A. Medeiros-Neto. Scientific Publication No. 292. Washington, DC: Pan American Health Organization, 1974: 198-204.

Scrimshaw, N.S., A. Cabezas, F. Castillo et al. "Effects of Potassium Iodate on Endemic Goitre and Protein-bound Iodine Levels in Schoolchildren." Lancet (1953): 166-168.

Simmons, W.K. and M.J. Gurney. "Nutritional Anemia in the English-speaking Caribbean and Surinam." American Journal of Clinical Nutrition 35,2 (1982): 327-337.

Simmons, W.K., P.J. Jusum, K. Fox et al. "A Survey of Anemia Status of Preschool Age Children and Pregnant and Lactating Women in Jamaica." American Journal of Clinical Nutrition 35 (1982): 319.

Sinha, D.P. and F.P. Bang. "Seasonal Variations in Signs of Vitamin A Deficiency in Rural West Bengal Children." Lancet 2 (1973): 228-231.

Solon, F., T.L. Fernandez, M.C. Latham et al. "An Evaluation of Strategies to Control Vitamin A Deficiency in the Philippines." American Journal of Clinical Nutrition 32 (1979): 1445-1453.

Solon, F.S., B.M. Popkins, T.L. Fernandez et al. "Vitamin A Deficiency in the Philippines: A Study of Xeropthalmia in Cebu." American Journal of Clinical Nutrition 31 (1978): 360-368.

Sommer, A. Field Guide to the Detection and Control of Xerophthalmia. Geneva: World Health Organization, 1978.

Sommer, A. Nutritional Blindness: Xerophthalmia and Keratomalacia. New York: Oxford University Press, 1982: 188.

Sood, K., K. Ramachandran, M. Mathru et al. "WHO-Sponsored Collaborative Studies on Nutritional Anemia in India: I. The Effects of Supplemental Oral Iron Administration to Pregnant Women." Quarterly Journal of Medicine 44,174 (1975): 241-258.

Streiff, R.R. "Disorders of Folate Metabolism." Disease a Month, 1972.

Tarwotjo, I., A. Sommer, T. Soegiharto et al. "Dietary Practices and Xerophthalmia among Indonesian Children." American Journal of Clinical Nutrition 35 (1982): 574-581.

Taylor, C.E., A.A. Kielmann, C. DeSweemer et al. "The Narangwal Experiment on Interactions of Nutrition and Infections: I. Project Design and Effect upon Growth." Indian Journal Medical Research 68 suppl. (1978): 1-20.

Taylor, C.E., A.A. Kielmann, C. DeSweemer. "Nutrition and Infection." In Nutrition and the World Food Problem, edited by M. Rechiegl. Basel, Switzerland: S. Karger, 1979.

Thane-Toe and Thein-Than. "The Effects of Oral Iron Supplementation on Ferritin Levels in Pregnant Burmese Women." American Journal of Clinical Nutrition 35 (1982): 95-99.

Thilly, C.H., F. Delange, and J.B. Stanbury. "Epidemiologic Surveys in Endemic Goiter and Cretinism." In Endemic Goiter and Endemic Cretinism, edited by J.B. Stanbury and B.S. Hetzel. New York: John Wiley & Sons, Inc., 1980: 157-184.

Tomkins, A. "Nutrition Status and Severity of Diarrhoea among Preschool Children in Rural Nigeria." Lancet (1981): 860-862.

Underwood, B.A. "Hypovitaminosis A and its Control." Bulletin of the World Health Organization 56 (1978): 525-541.

UNIPAC. Catalog Price List. UNICEF Packing and Assembly Centre, Copenhagen, Denmark, 1982.

U.S. Department of Health, Education and Welfare. "NCHS Growth Curves for Children Birth-18 Years." U.S. Vital and Health Statistics Series II, N. 165 (1977): 1-74.

Vijayaraghavan, K. and N.P. Rao. National Programme for the Prevention of Vitamin A Deficiency: An Evaluation. Hyderabad: National Institute of Nutrition, Indian Council of Medical Research, 1978.

Viteri, F.E. and B. Torun. "Anemia and Physical Work Capacity." Clinical Hematology 3 (1974): 609-629.

Watanabe, T., D. Moran, E. El Tamer et al. "Iodized Oil in the Prophylaxis of Endemic Goiter in Argentina." In Endemic Goiter and Cretinism: Continuing Threats to World Health, edited by J.T. Dunne and G.A. Medeiros-Neto. Scientific Publication No. 292. Washington, DC: Pan American Health Organization, 1974.

Were, M.K. People's Participation in Their Own Health Care. Dr.P.H. Dissertation, Department of International Health, The Johns Hopkins University, Baltimore, MD 1981.

Wittner, M. "Mycotic and Parasitic Diseases." In Pediatrics, 16th edition, edited by A. Rudolph, H.L. Barnett, and A.H. Einhorn. New York: Appleton-Century-Crofts, 1977.

World Health Organization (WHO). Control of Nutritional Anemia with Special Reference to Iron Deficiency. Report of an IAEA/USAID/WHO Joint Meeting. Technical Report Series No. 580. Geneva: 1975.

_____. Control of Vitamin A Deficiency and Xeropthalmia. Technical Report Series No. 672. Geneva: 1982.

_____. Family Formation Patterns. Geneva: 1979.

_____. Guidelines for Training Community Health Workers in Nutrition. Geneva: 1981.

_____. Nutritional Anemias. Technical Report Series No. 503. Geneva: 1976a.

_____. Vitamin A Deficiency and Xeropthalmia. Technical Report Series No. 590. Geneva: 1976b.

WHO Division in Family Health. The Prevalence of Nutritional Anemia in Women in Developing Countries. Geneva: 1979.

Yusufji, D., V.I. Mathan, S.J. Baker. "Iron, Folate and Vitamin B Nutrition in Pregnancy: A Study of 1,000 Women from Southern India." Bulletin of the World Health Organization 48 (1973): 15-22.

14
Community-Based Nutrition Programs

Jon E. Rohde

Nutrition activities in the community have in the past generally tended to be "distribution" programs long preceding similar efforts in the area of contraceptives, immunizations, or disease therapy such as oral rehydration for diarrhea. While a few programs have shown a modicum of success, the vast majority of nutrition interventions at the community level have been expensive failures, whether measured either by effect on nutritional status, morbidity, or mortality. Reviewed in considerable detail by several groups of highly experienced scientists, the consensus is generally that community nutrition programs are expensive and difficult to justify (Austin et al., 1981; Beaton and Ghassemi, 1979).

The design of a nutrition program based in the community which is aimed at fostering community self-reliance and utilization of existing local resources, leads to an entirely different approach from the traditional distribution concept of nutrition interventions. This new approach can be best described as nutrition promoted by and for mothers, focusing on the wisdom of child-rearing and the use of appropriate, understandable, and available technology. The major operational objective of such an approach is behavioral change, and the major program outcome is continued good nutrition. The participants themselves monitor nutritional status and this information forms an integral part of program motivation and evaluation. This paper describes experiences with such an approach in Indonesia and how it has been applied in certain other national and subnational programs. This does not propose to be a review of literature but rather an exposure to some extremely important, although apparently simple, principles that must guide the design of a successful and viable community-based nutrition intervention program.

STANDARD APPROACHES

A recent and extensive review of nutrition interventions in developing countries prepared for the U.S. Agency for International Development (Austin et al., 1981) discussed experience in the areas of: supplementary feeding, nutrition education, fortification, formulated foods, consumer price, food subsidies, agricultural production, and integrated nutrition programs in primary health care. The vast majority of programs show the relatively high unit cost of the intervention. Of particular interest were the food supplement programs which have been the basic nutrition intervention used in many countries since World War II. While definite improvements have been shown among extremely malnourished populations, the cost per child in supplement programs ranged from $10 to $50 per year and in rehabilitation programs, upwards from $75. Cost for four months' attendance of a child in a Haitian village-based nutrition rehabilitation program was $72. Cost-benefit calculations for those who showed any improvement in weight illustrate a cost of $100. For those who improved in weight in comparison to control children, the estimated cost was $600 per child. The cost per child of significantly decreasing third degree protein calorie malnutrition (PCM) compared with control groups was $3600. Even higher costs were found in other countries.

Another recent review for UNICEF (Beaton and Ghassemi, 1979) evaluated more than 100 reports of food distribution programs and concluded that such programs directed toward young children are rather expensive for the measured benefit. In fact most programs fail to even reach children in the ages most at risk of nutritional damage (less than 2 years) and in greatest need of feeding. Even for those children enrolled in the program, because of the leakage and loss of food to other family members or into the marketplace, the nutritional effect of the programs was surprisingly low.

The remarkable success of certain nutrition interventions has depended upon unique situations or highly focused input. Important examples are found in the distribution of vitamin A in populations showing a high prevalence of vitamin A deficiency blindness. The Helen Keller International Assisted Vitamin A Distribution Program in Bangladesh has substantially reduced this illness. Here a highly focused village distribution approach mobilizes virtually all health fieldworkers for one of each six months. Strong organizational incentives are provided to obtain a high degree of coverage (Northrup, 1981). Because of the nature of vitamin A capsule distribution, supervision and monitoring are relatively easy and the result is readily evident.

The INCAP (Guatemala) study of food supplements which increase caloric intake of pregnant women showed a 75 percent reduction in low birth weight infants and a concomitant reduction in early infant mortality. This study is an important demonstration of the potential effect of a nutrition intervention that could be applied at the village level (Lechtig et al., 1975a; Lechtig et al., 1975b). Unfortunately, this study has not been applied in a field setting and the targeting of such food supplements will be a critical issue. Significantly a clear trigger level was noted at 20,000 calories total intake throughout the course of pregnancy. Thus, any substantial leakage or diversion of food targeted at pregnant women can be expected to result in program failure.

Impressive results of mass feeding programs during famine or civil strife have been shown in the Beta Lifeline Program in the Bengali refugee camps of west Bengal in 1975 (Rohde and Gardner, 1973); in Companyganj, Bangladesh during the Bengal famine of 1974-1975 (McCord, 1980); in Rowmari, Bangladesh during the same famine (Dodge and Wiebe, 1976); and in certain targeted feeding programs in response to other disasters (Blix et al., 1971). However, the results of community-wide feeding programs, especially those based at a village level have been generally less impressive.

Recent prospective studies have indicated a clear cut-off point in nutritional status based on anthropometric measurements below which substantial increase in risk of death was noted. Both in Bangladesh (Chen et al., 1980) and in India (Kielmann and McCord, 1978) children of less than 65 percent of the Harvard weight-for-age standard appeared at substantially increased risk of dying. Interestingly, this level corresponds quite closely to the level at which derangements in the child's immune mechanisms can occur. Thus, at a minimum, nutrition programs should aim to reduce the prevalence or, better still, the incidence of this severe degree of malnutrition.

Nutritional status of a population is one of the best measures of its economic or development level. It is unusual to find substantial undernutrition in populations enjoying adequate but modest standards of living. Efforts at improving the quality of life through village-based nutrition programs have attempted to provide recipients with their basic food needs. Where a strong political commitment backed by major financial resources is made, such as in Sri Lanka, this approach can substantially improve the nutritional state and even life expectancy of a population. The commitment, however, is a massive one and, in any case, beyond the scope of this discussion. Any distribution system that cannot deliver a major portion of food requirements to an entire undernourished population is likely to fail. Therein lies the problem and inherent weakness of distribution programs, for nutrition is a daily life function involving habits, beliefs, and values, as well as knowledge and buying power. Efforts to distribute knowledge, food, new practices, and behavior have in most cases led to dependency, inappropriate use of input, and generally disappointing results. Observing this difficulty about a decade ago, Rohde and Hendrata embarked upon a new approach to nutrition at the village level in Indonesia (Rohde and Hendrata, 1981).

COMMUNITY-BASED NUTRITION PROGRAM

The goal was to find a pragmatic population-wide, community-based program replicable in cost, supervision, and administration that fostered self-reliance and behavioral change leading to improved nutritional status among young children. Inherent in this approach was the avoidance of input originating and controlled from outside the community or an organizational structure that excluded the community. Seeking a community-based forum, the first entry point became the traditional women's meeting in the village which was largely for social purposes. Women expressed their concern for the health of their children and an even greater desire for the ability to diagnose and monitor the state of their children's nutritional health themselves. The initiation of child weighing in the village came initially in response to the demand for information and an appropriate technology that mothers could use themselves (Rohde et al., 1975). Child weighing is not primarily a survey tool nor a measure of who is to receive a nutritional input. It is first and foremost an activity done by mothers to tell them on a regular and recurring basis of the progress of their child and the adequacy of the child's nutrition. The mothers are responsible for organizing the weighing and must do it themselves. Those who are literate help others weigh and mark the cards and interpret the growth of the children. It is growth that they are monitoring and not nutritional status.

Nutrition education messages are invariably based upon interpretation of scientific studies of malnourished populations, with the intent to formulate clear and practical advice for village mothers. Nutrition education messages aim to teach mothers so that their children may avoid or become rehabilitated from the fate of other children who show the lack of protein, calories, vitamins, etc. In contrast to this usual approach to nutrition education, we were struck, in even the poorest villages, not by the prevalence of malnutrition which surely was there, but rather by the existence of normally healthy, well-nourished children living in comparable poverty and deprived circumstances. Initial attempts to interview the mothers of such children, "the successful mothers," did not yield obvious explanation for such success. It became apparent, however, that these mothers could advise and guide their neighbors, providing clear, doable, relevant, affordable and culturally believable suggestions that resulted in effective growth when practiced in the village. The program adapted a pattern of pairing, asking a mother of a child who had gained weight to share her ideas with a mother of a child who had not done so well in the last month or two. Several basic messages common to most villagers were translated into a series of prescription-like messages used as a starting point to help mothers address the question of lack of growth between two monthly weighings.

The activity is self-motivating, self-evaluating, and provides immediate supervision through the results as measured by weight gain in the next weighing session. It is the dynamic measure of growth or weight gain from one month to the next that is the entire focus of the program and the results by which the program's success is measured. In contrast, the nutritional status of the child is both difficult to measure and to change. No child who is gaining weight is considered poorly nourished, no child who is not gaining weight is considered adequately healthy. Evaluation is immediate and done by the participating mothers. Responses to the adequacy of the level of weight gain are often spontaneously forthcoming from the mothers involved.

It does not take long in a monthly weighing program for mothers to realize that weight gain, the goal of the program, is related to regular adequate feeding. Participating villages can rarely afford to provide food supplements to the children. However mothers were willing to gather on occasion to cook locally available foods to feed to their children and to discuss their experience and different approaches to child feeding and child care. Interestingly, during these monthly or biweekly social feeding activities, which are predominantly educational experiences, mothers found their children ate foods they would otherwise avoid at home. The impression that peer pressure led to better eating particularly among the 2- and 3-year-olds led to pairing or shared eating experiences in the actual neighborhood on a daily basis in some communities. This overcame a common complaint of mothers throughout the world that "my child is a finicky eater; I try to offer him food but he won't take it."

The focus of this program is on the normal child. First, priority is given to enrolling children early in their first year of life when in almost all countries of the world, normal growth even by international standards is achieved by almost all children. Emphasis is on preserving this normal growth, initially through the encouragement of breastfeeding and peer pressure to continue breastfeeding well into the second year of life. The necessity of introducing weaning foods becomes obvious by faltering weight any time during the first year when breast milk alone becomes inadequate. This may be as early as the third month or as late as the tenth month and ideally is specifically adjusted to the individual child. The extensive literature in recent years arguing the adequacy of breastfeeding is unanimous on the decision that monthly weighing is the best indicator of when weaning foods should be started. The extensive focus on normality and continued growth is an important departure from almost all existing nutrition programs. The importance of this focus should not be underestimated. It is indeed difficult to offer a nutrition promotion program in a village to the young and well-nourished infants to the exclusion of undernourished older siblings. It is, however, an important aspect of a community-based nutrition program and within a short time (perhaps three or four years) all children having been enlisted as infants will arrive at preschool age in good nutritional health and the cry for rehabilitation will be diminished or gone.

Malnutrition is one of the most difficult medical conditions to treat; it is costly, fraught with failure, requires extensive staff time, and preempts virtually all other activities. Failure is so great that most nutrition programs are discredited in a relatively short time in the eyes of the community because of their inability to rehabilitate the obviously malnourished. Communities must accept the fact that nutrition promotion begins at or before birth and that while the community may be concerned about its malnourished children, a program that is to be effective must start early in the first year and continue regular surveillance throughout the subsequent years, usually to four or five years of age. This approach is often difficult to sell to health professionals as well. In the first instance, they tend to measure nutritional status by static nutritional status survey results. The weight approach measures nutrition by dynamic recurring surveillance focusing on growth rather than nutritional status. The difference, once again, is critical and central to a successful community program.

By promoting doable, home-based, self-financed activities, growth can be achieved and normal nutritional status preserved even in the face of frequent illness or relative food shortage. This is particularly true in populations such as those in villages in Java characterized by diets for the entire family which are marginally adequate. Small intra-family redistribution, greater attention to more frequent feeds and extra supplements at time of illness or in response to a measured weight loss are possible and result in rapid recovery of normal growth.

In communities where absolute food shortages are found, characterizing much of the developing world and particularly malnourished populations within these countries, food supplements have a definite potential role in such a program. They must, however, be introduced only after the program's emphasis on community self-help activities and continuing surveillance are well in place. Supplements are viewed as a therapeutic intervention in response to specific indications. It is not a rehabilitative measure nor should supplements be used over the longterm to assure continued good nutrition. If a participating child has shown over a period of several months that, in spite of advice and the mother's efforts at home, growth is inadequate, food can be provided for a period of four, eight, or even twelve weeks. The resultant growth will demonstrate the obvious importance of extra feeding for the child. In cases of extreme poverty, it may be necessary to supplement the entire family to assure that the necessary supplement is consumed by the index child. However, with the focus on the youngest child, this is generally less necessary, for the food can be provided in a form to be made into porridge and will not be consumed by older family members.

A further use of food supplements has been suggested by studies of the nutritional impact of common infectious diseases, particularly diarrhea. It is well known that among malnourished children given high caloric intakes (as much as twice the recommended daily allowance) that extremely rapid growth rates can be obtained. This appears to be the case for very much briefer periods lasting only several days, in the immediate convalescent period after acute diarrhea. Children eat more if offered extra food and their growth rates are more rapid than those of children of similar age and nutritional status who have not recently recovered from illness. Food supplements during this three to five days in convalescence may be one of the most effective means of reducing the nutritional effect of infections and assuring the continued nutritional health of the child (Rohde, 1981). This approach remains to be widely exploited in nutritional programs.

TECHNIQUES FOR COMMUNITY NUTRITION PROGRAMS

Scale

It is important to emphasize the use of appropriate and carefully developed technologies for village-based nutrition activities. For instance, a common Salter scale, widely used in nutrition programs, is a strange and somewhat frightening instrument that mothers in this program could not use easily. Fortunately, virtually all marketing in rural Indonesia is done by women and most sales are by weight, using a universally available, highly accurate, locally made beam balance. When one of these was borrowed from the marketplace, a dozen mothers unquestioningly slung their children under the scale using the scarf in which babies are often wrapped, and gave accurate weights of the children verified to within 50 gm. Three-quarters of these women were illiterate. The concept of weighing with this instrument is a part of their daily life. Thus, the dacin scale is an integral part of the Indonesian program, and comparable culturally adapted instruments should be sought in other countries.

Weight Card

The weight card is the primary educational, motivational, and evaluation tool of this program. It must be, from the outset, the possession and responsibility of the mother. It is remarkable how many programs throughout the world will not trust the mother with this simple piece of cardboard, all the while expecting her to take improved care of her living human infant. Mothers are responsible, and if they recognize the value of a weight card they will care for it better than a clinic will. Indeed, programs in which weight cards are often lost reflect the program operators' inadequate attention to the value of the card and its message to the mothers.

Indonesian mothers showed a great interest and understanding of weight cards, but after initial field tests with existing WHO models, it was obvious that they were substantially confused by the lines on the standard weight card (Rohde and Hendrata, 1978). Furthermore, they disliked the implications of nutritional status, which in the Indonesian language at that time were being described as "good nutrition," "poor nutrition," and "rotten nutrition." These value judgments were removed and in their place was printed a colorful rainbow with narrow channels of color paralleling the normal growth curve, none of which was considered "normal" or "abnormal." The emphasis on growth is displayed on the card with the simple explanation of a rising line being the desired monthly response, a flat line being a caution requiring added attention to feeding, and a falling line being a sign of danger to the child, in need of more food and probably medical consultation. The colors were carefully selected to encourage upward growth but at the same time to avoid adverse judgment of the smaller child who may grow at a regular rate but at a lower than standard median level. The card is decorated with the basic messages of the program, including a breastfeeding mother chosen from a large panel of women as the one whom rural mothers would most like to emulate. Messages on suggested foods, immunization timing, use of vitamin A capsules and the preparation of oral rehydration fluid from home ingredients are contained on the card. Mothers recognized this as a highly appropriate and valued tool. The more the card is asked for by health workers and the more professionals use and regard the card as a key measure of child health evaluation the greater is the perceived value of the card.

Nutrition Education

The third area of appropriate technology is the planning of nutrition education, including both the messages derived from discussions of successful mothers and those derived from village-based feeding activities organized and run by mothers themselves. The messages are uniformly oriented to behavioral change. This is a social marketing strategy in which the program is trying to sell patterns of behavior that are shown in this society to result in improved nutrition, as exhibited by regular growth. It is supportive of culturally accepted and useful activities, such as breastfeeding for two or more years. It is promotive of feasible and affordable activities. For example, frequent feeding of a child is promoted, especially in the second year of life, because children are unable to obtain enough calories at this time since commonly used foods are too bulky and the child's appetite becomes satisfied before he has obtained sufficient calories. The strategy uses a common goal, widely accepted, promoted, and easily measured - regular, monthly growth. By supporting growth as an ultimate and obtainable goal, any recommended activity can be interpreted by its effect on growth. Slogans and mass communication announcements have a common theme that can compete effectively with similar advertising and promotion in the commercial sector.

Program effectiveness is monitored by the mother herself, but at the same time a readily measured indicator of village-wide nutritional progress is also provided. Program goals of full participation and growth are easily recognized and plotted on a monthly bar graph. SKDN, a slogan based on Indonesian terms for various activities involving: total target children (S), those possessing a weight card (K), those coming to be weighed (D), and those gaining weight (N), forms a basis for village self-evaluation and intervillage comparison and even competition. These same data can be collated, collected, and processed quickly, reaching the national level within weeks. In Indonesia, this information on number of children weighed and number gaining weight in the past month in each of 15,000 villages is included in the monthly reporting form of the family planning system and is provided on a monthly computer print-out giving a sensitive index useful in a national nutrition surveillance system.

PROGRAM EXPANSION

What is the replicability of such a system? Its costs are low, representing the weight charts, scales, records, and educational materials required to put the program in place. In order to standardize the elements of the program, a self-instructional program text and a national manual for fieldworkers was produced in Indonesian, and initial field training was provided to workers in the health, family planning and education departments (Rohde et al., 1979). Training then followed departmental lines but is uniform in a packaged approach and illustrated by an attractive slide show. The logistics of this program are initially simple, involving weighing instruments, educational materials, and training manuals. In Indonesia, the logistics system of the family planning program was used for the initial distribution of materials as well as the training of the key fieldworkers. By avoiding the necessity of providing food supplements, cost as well as logistical problems are greatly reduced.

The step-by-step nature of the introduction of interventions at the community level is of critical importance to the success of such programs. In Indonesia, community-based contraceptive distribution came first. This was a logical and important addition to a community fieldworker distribution system which had recruited acceptors in such large numbers that the problem of resupply was virtually preempting all other program activities. Voluntary acceptors in each village agreed to accept, store, and distribute contraceptives to their neighbors, freeing family planning fieldworkers to manage the resupply and motivational jobs. Some 40,000 resupply posts were operative by 1978. Once communities had accepted the resupply function in family planning, fieldworkers found that an exclusive focus on family planning was narrow, limiting, and at times self-defeating. Then the recurring weighing program became a next logical step. From there further steps in primary health care have already been added. This approach of "sequential introduction of selective primary health care" is a simple and rather logical concept but one which is largely lacking in primary health care activities throughout the world. Often primary health care attempts to provide at the village level so-called simple services for every known malady with a stated emphasis on prevention while providing curative services for all. It is hardly a surprise that most such programs are failing or at least not accomplishing their primary objectives. The sequential introduction of individual activities grafted upon a sound village-based program of whatever nature is the logical way to introduce primary health care.

In Indonesia, the village-based contraceptive distribution program has provided the base and other interventions have been added sequentially including: village-based nutritional surveillance and nutrition education; and the introduction of six monthly vitamin A capsules in massive doses; iron and folate pills for all pregnant women in the community; packaged oral rehydration salts for diarrhea available at the village post; and in many villages, periodic deworming with piperazine. In malarious areas chloroquine distribution can follow the same system. Colleagues in Indonesia have attempted expansion to such activities as early treatment of pneumonia and the introduction of vaccination programs through the monthly weighing activities (Rohde et al., 1977).

The capacity of such a system to absorb increasing activities has been demonstrated in hundreds of villages in Java, which have now branched out into income-producing activities such as small dairy cooperatives, rehabilitation for the handicapped, improved housing, food production, home gardening, fruit production, small cooperative credit schemes, latrines, clean water, and more. In fact, a successful child weighing activity, even in the absence of statistically significant results, appears to be a motivating factor in community-based integrated development. According to the director of one large regency in central Java where more than half of the 275 villages are extensively involved in their own development, "a monthly weighing program provides a focus for the village's self-analysis and attention to its own priorities. A weighing program is the first step in integrated village development" (Haliman and Rohde, 1980).

To what extent can such approaches to behavioral change improve nutritional status? The nutritional impact of this approach has not yet been proven, although within a year it should certainly be possible to observe and measure nutritional differences in participating villages in Indonesia. The average weight of children participating in this program should rise by age 36 months in comparison with nonparticipating children, and concomitantly the severe and moderate degrees of malnutrition should fall. Yet it is obvious from the success and enthusiasm for the program both in Indonesia and where it has been tried in the Philippines and is now being initiated in Haiti that the approach is meeting important needs among rural mothers and has inherent value as a motivating and participatory tool.

One thing is clear: monitoring nutritional status has been viewed by pediatricians as their most critical assessment of child health, even in developed Western countries for the past century. Village-based programs bring this surveillance technology to village children at extremely low cost and in the process provide the first steps toward effective change in nutritional practices that can lead to an affordable, replicable, and self-reliant community-level program. Although unfortunately, the statistical proof of the efficacy of this program is not yet available, its measured high degree of replicability and participation are evidence of its operational success. It remains for careful evaluation and in-depth research (some of which is under way in Indonesia, but which must be done in other countries as well) to demonstrate the outcomes and long-range implications of such community-based, self-reliant nutrition activities.

REFERENCES

Austin, J.E. et al. Nutrition Intervention in Developing Countries. Washington, DC: U.S. Agency for International Development, 1981.

Beaton, G.H. and H. Ghassemi. Supplementary Feeding Programs for Young Children in Developing Countries. New York: UNICEF, 1979.

Blix, G., T. Hofvander, and B. Vahlquist. Famine: Nutrition and Relief Operation in Times of Disaster. Uppsala: Almquist and Wiksells, (1971): 200.

Chen, L.C., A.K.M. Chowdhury, and S.L. Huffman. "Anthropometric Assessment of Energy-protein Malnutrition and Subsequent Risk of Mortality among Preschool-aged Children. ACJN 33 (1980): 1836-1845.

Dodge, C.P. and P.D. Wiebe. "Family Relief and Development in Rural Bangladesh." Economic and Political Weekly (Bombay), May 29, 1976: 809-817.

Haliman, A. and J.E. Rohde. "Case Study of Primary Health Care in Banjarnegara." Presented at the Asia and Pacific Workshop on Development PHC as a Key Strategy for Health for All by the Year 2000. World Health Organization, Bangkok, 1980.

Kielmann, A.A. and C. McCord. "Weight for Age as an Index of Risk of Death in Children." Lancet (1978): 1247.

Lechtig, A. et al. "Effect of Food Supplementation during Pregnancy on Birth Weight. Pediatrics 4 (1975): 508.

Lechtig, A. et al. "Influence of Maternal Nutrition on Birth Weight." ASCN 28 (1975): 1223.

McCord, C. Price Subsidy During a Famine in Evaluation of Nutrition Intervention Projects. Washington, DC: Office of Nutrition, U.S. Agency for International Development, 1980.

Northrup, R.S. Bangladesh Blindness Prevention Program Vitamin A Distribution. Helen Keller International, 1981.

Rohde, J.E. "Therapeutic Intervention in Diarrhea." Food and Nutrition Bull 3 (1981): 34-38.

Rohde, J.E. and P. Gardner. Refugees in India: Innovative Health Care Programs in Disaster in Bangladesh, edited by L. C. Chen. Oxford, 1973.

Rohde, J.E. and L. Hendrata. "Measuring Weight Gains. Trop. Pediatrics Environ. Child Health 24 (1978): 3.

Rohde, J.E. and L. Hendrata. Development from Below: Transformation of Village Based Nutrition Projects and National Family Nutrition Program in Indonesia. New York: Plenum Press, 1981 (in press).

Rohde, J.E., D.J. Ismail, and R. Soetrisno. "Mothers as Weight Watchers: The Road to Child Health in the Village." Trop.Pediatrics Environ. Child Health 21 (1975): 295-297.

Rohde, J.E., D.J. Ismail, T. Sadjimin, A. Suyadi, and A. Tugirin. "Training Course for Village Nutrition Program." Trop. Pediatrics Environ. Child Health 25 (1979): 83-96.

Rohde, J.E., T. Sadjimin, and A. Suyadi. "An Approach to Village Self-help Health Programmes - Primary Care in the Village." Trop. Doctor 7 (1977): 123-128.

15
Nutrition and Family Planning: An Integrated Program in Bali, Indonesia

D. Soejatni

The Indonesian family planning program has evolved through several critical and overlapping stages with the addition of nutrition activities to the successful implementation of the family planning program. This paper discusses the process of integrating the two in Bali.

Prior to 1969 and 1970, limited family planning information and services were offered essentially through a privately funded and administered single-purpose program. Once the government became publicly committed to intervening in the population crisis - undertaking a nationwide program to promote the voluntary limitation of fertility - family planning services were channelled through existing health facilities, with the Ministry of Health providing a major portion of the services and support. The involvement of the Ministry of Health led to several early attempts to integrate the delivery of family planning services and information with maternal and child health care, the latter being recognized as a critical intervening variable in achieving a voluntary reduction of fertility.

During the first years an awareness grew that general acceptance of modern methods of fertility control cannot be treated solely as a health matter in which the Ministry of Health takes the primary initiative. Instead, it has been generally acknowledged that acceptance is based on a variety of factors resulting in an overall improvement of various other aspects of the individual's life, such as economic, social, and spiritual well-being in addition to physical well-being. Consequently, family planning has come to be viewed more as a general development issue. The degree to which the community accepts ultimate responsibility for managing its own program of fertility limitation and for reinforcing acceptance of a small family as the norm is an important determinant of success. Although such community involvement is not new - many villages on Java and Bali had already spontaneously undertaken activities along these lines - the government has more recently sought to systematize the transfer of program responsibility by implanting the program in the social, economic, political, and cultural institutions of the community.

BALI FAMILY PLANNING PROGRAM

The island of Bali, is one of the 27 provinces of the republic of Indonesia. According to the 1980 census, the population of Bali is 2.6 million. The population density (about 418 persons per square kilometer) is high, especially for an almost entirely rural population.

Most Balinese are Hindu. Politically the province is divided into eight regencies (kabutapen), and 50 subdistricts (kecamatan). Each kecamatan is divided into villages. Each of the 564 villages is further subdivided into banjars (community organizations or hamlets). There are 3,753 banjars in the whole of Bali.

Educational attainment is low among Balinese women, 65 percent have no formal schooling. Of the economically active male population, 73 percent are farmers. In terms of urbanization, income, education, and employment Bali might appear to be ill-suited for the successful promotion of family planning. However, the World Fertility Survey, conducted in April and May of 1976, shows that Balinese women had a total fertility rate of about 3.8 children per woman, compared with an estimated 5.8 in 1967 to 1971. Bali's fertility is now the lowest of any province in Indonesia.

The Banjar System

The province of Bali, has attained a high level of family planning use among its eligible couples. One reason for the high use rate is that a high proportion of Balinese women work outside the home performing labor intensive jobs, including construction and road work. This has led Balinese women to delay marriage and to desire smaller families. The implementation of the family planning program in Bali is based on the traditional banjar system.

An extraordinarily strong social and administrative group, the banjar is a traditional center for mutual aid and cooperative work, as well as a gathering point for recreation and ceremony. The contraceptive situation is discussed at each monthly meeting of the household heads. If an apparently fertile couple is not trying to conceive and also not using contraception, the husband is questioned.

During the banjar meeting, held every 35 days and attended by all banjar members, community problems are discussed. The meeting is led by kelian banjar or the traditional banjar leader. A kelian has a strong influence on the community and is chosen by the banjar members. The family planning program has built upon the prevailing sociocultural system in Bali. In the first semester of 1981 as much as 79 percent of total eligible couples were recruited as family planning acceptors in Bali. Family planning practice extends to more than 76 percent of the eligible couples in over 64 percent of the nearly 4,000 banjars in Bali.

FAMILY NUTRITION IMPROVEMENT PROGRAM

Children under the age of six years receive all or almost all of their nutrient intake at home. The family, especially the mother, is the center of all feeding and nutritional activities. As much of child malnutrition is caused by lack of knowledge, it is imperative to provide guidance and to deliver services below the lowest official health center level (the *puskesmas*) to the village and home level where all action must occur. It is only at this level that preventive measures can be successful in thwarting malnutrition among small children.

Family nutrition has always been a function of the food resources available in the home and community. This is especially true in Indonesia where the majority of families live in rural areas, and where more food is grown locally. The tradition of home gardening has long flourished in Bali and has provided a significant proportion of the food consumed by rural families. In conjunction with this tradition, the government has proposed to make the population more aware of the value of this resource so as to further encourage home gardening in villages.

In order for programs to be internalized at the family and village level, key persons such as village heads and community leaders must perceive a need for and understand the implementation of such programs. Indonesia has a long religious heritage with religion included as one of the five basic principles of *pancasila*, the doctrine of the Indonesian way of life. Religious leaders are quite influential in establishing and maintaining a social climate in the community based upon cooperation and mutual self-help (*gotong-royong*). As such, they play an important support role in preparing the community to accept good nutrition principles and in supporting action programs.

Description Of The Program

The Family Nutrition Improvement Program (UPGK) is a national intersectoral nutrition program supported by several governmental departments. The Departments of Health and Agriculture are the leading sectors. The program has been standardized and is administered uniformly by all agencies with the same objectives, messages, and materials. In this way, the communities and families themselves will perpetuate improved nutrition and not depend upon outside interventions. The use of village volunteers to guide village and home activities offers opportunities for the convergence of basic services as many of these volunteers are teachers, or health care, family planning or agricultural workers, or at least trained by other government programs. This program of multisectoral training assists in establishing a solid link between government-operated services at the subdistrict level and the families and communities which they are intended to serve.

The UPGK consists of several community-based activities which are carried out by trained village nutrition volunteers and the families themselves but supported by subdistrict (*kecamatan*) level services. These activities include the following:

- Monitoring the nutritional status of children under five years of age through monthly weighing and screening for nutritional deficiencies. These weighing sessions are the focal point of all UPGK activities and are associated with a community activity called *taman gizi swadaya* in which mothers learn to prepare food using local foodstuffs provided by the community itself.

- Nutritional first aid distributed in the form of vitamin and mineral supplements and oral rehydration solution dispensed to children, pregnant women, and lactating mothers at these sessions.

- Using nutrition volunteers to teach families, especially mothers, proper nutrition and child care, infant and young child feeding practices, sanitation, immunization needs, family planning, diarrhea management, and home food production and preparation. The educational aspects of UPGK are critical because the program is designed to be self-perpetuating by the villagers themselves.

- Referral by the village nutrition volunteer of mothers and children to the health center for treatment.

- Supplementary food support provided to children in those subdistricts (*kecamatan*) where a need is demonstrated. Children who do not gain weight satisfactorily are eligible to receive subsidized supplementary feeding. The village volunteer is trained to administer this aspect of UPGK under the supervision of the health center doctor.

- Home and village food production taught and supported through the UPGK. This will be carried out by village cadre with the technical assistance of personnel of the Department of Agriculture. In poorer *kecamatans*, seeds will also be distributed.

Intersectoral Approach

As an insectoral program it is important that UPGK coordination and cooperation be facilitated at all levels. In order to achieve this objective, nutrition (UPGK) teams will be formed at the subdistrict (*kecamatan*), district (*kabupaten*), and provincial levels. Members of the teams will be selected, where possible, from the regional nutritional improvement boards (BPGD). These teams will coordinate all activities at their respective levels and will be responsible for intersectoral training and supervising intersectoral teams at lower levels.

Objectives

The general objective of the UPGK is to improve the nutritional status of the community. The specific objectives are:

1. Program Participation
   a. All community members participate actively in the implementation of the program at various levels; at the subvillage level the implementation is the responsibility of the community members.
   b. The program is implemented by all subvillages.
   c. The program's targets are all children under five, and pregnant and lactating women.

2. Behavioral Changes
   a. All babies will be breast-fed by their mothers up to the age of two years or more, and will receive additional food according to their needs.
   b. All children suffering from diarrhea will receive sugar-salt solution or oral rehydration solution (Oralita).
   c. All pregnant and lactating mothers will eat one or two additional dishes of nutritious food daily.
   d. All pregnant women will take one ferrous sulfate tablet per day during the last three months of their pregnancies.
   e. All home gardens will be used to increase the family nutrition status.
   f. All eligible couples will understand and join the family planning program.

3. Nutrition Goals for Children Ages Zero to Five
   a. The weight of all children will increase every month.
   b. All children aged 36 months will achieve a body weight of more than 11.5 kilograms.
   c. No children will suffer from vitamin A deficiency-induced night-blindness.

The ultimate goal of the UPGK is behavioral change based upon improved understanding by the community of good nutrition for the family. While the ultimate effect of the UPGK program has yet to be measured, the objectives of the program have been formulated in such a way that the community itself can determine the achievement of their program down to the subvillage level. Since the program target is determined by the community, the hope is that they will feel that they own the program and will assume responsibility for the success of the program.

The achievement of the UPGK can be analyzed from the standardized reporting format, SKDN,* as an indicator of the achievement of the UPGK program at the village, subdistrict, and regency levels. Output of the program is evaluated by the ratio of the number of children whose weight increases divided by the number of children in the target area (N/S), an indicator which can be used by the program executor in measuring the achievement of the program in a particular working area.

Role of the Fieldworkers and Nutrition Cadres

Fieldworker

The daily function of family planning workers is to visit households. Before being employed as fieldworkers, they attend three week's training in a BKKBN training center. After the candidates have finished their training, they are assigned as fieldworkers and introduce the idea, goals, and benefits of family planning to individuals (husband, wife) as well as to the community.

Approaching the people personally provides the best chances for effective motivation for the acceptance of family planning methods. The fieldworkers belong to the local community for the simple reason that they are acquainted with and known in their neighborhoods and also known to local authorities.

Fieldworkers, nevertheless, are an enthusiastic and hardworking group. Their wage is modest by city standards, but they have the *esprit de corps* that goes with participation in a new and challenging enterprise. Over the years their responsibilities have broadened to include direct distribution of contraceptives and organization of discussion on the benefits of smaller families.

The fieldworker maintains the village family planning depots. Every fieldworker supervises two to five villages as well as the family planning volunteer. For the effectiveness of the family planning program they make a daily, weekly, and monthly work plan; and record their activities and the number of family planning acceptors. In the UPGK, a main task of the family planning fieldworker is to train the nutrition cadre and also maintain and supervise the nutrition activities, especially the baby weighing. They make monthly reports of the nutritional activities and provide technical guidance to the cadre as appropriate.

---

* SKDN is an abbreviation of:

S = Total number of children under five in target area.
K = Total number of children under five who receive growth charts.
D = Total number of children under five who attend weighing sessions.
N = Total number of children under five whose weight increases.

Nutrition Cadre

The village nutrition cadre is a group of volunteer workers who manage nutrition activities in the field. The village nutrition cadre have an average education of primary school from the local community. Some are members of the Family Welfare Education Program, others are satisfied family planning users, and others are local public figures such as an elected community representative (kelian), teacher, religious leader, or youth leader. The existence of the cadre reflects community participation and institutionalization of the activity in the community.

Each cadre member should possess the following qualifications:

- loyalty and a sense of dedication to the community.
- ability to read and write, and
- influence in community.

Program Coverage

The total number of children under five years (balita) in each banjar is approximately 50 to 120. Each cadre member is expected to supervise 20 balitas intensively, by counseling their mothers at the baby-weighing post or by home visits.

In giving nutrition information at the baby-weighing post or home visit, the cadre members relate it to family planning, health, sanitation, home gardening, and income-generating activities. When there are too many balitas the banjar can be divided in two groups or even more and the baby weighing can be held in shifts.

Table 15:1 outlines achieved and planned UPGK coverage in Bali.

Table 15:1. The Village Target

Bali Province	Target
1979/1980	231 banjars
1980/1981	465 banjars
1981/1982	461 banjars
1982/1983	1,300 banjars
1983/1984	1,278 banjars
Total banjars: 3,753	

SOURCE: The Bali Proposal: Projection of Nutrition Program for the Third Five-Year Development Plan (PELITA III)

Training

The UPGK activities in Bali began in Yogyakarta in 1979 with the training of the trainers of the Family Planning

Training Center and the section heads of the family planning council for the six provinces of Java/Bali.

The result of this training was to extend the UPGK by training the fieldworker and other family planning staff at the district and subdistrict levels. The group leaders as well as the Family Planning Fieldworkers, assisted by other sectors, conducted courses for nutrition cadres at the village level (see Table 15:2).

Table 15:2. Total Village Cadre Members Trained In Bali

	1980	1981	1982*	1983	1984
PPLKB (The Group Leader of Family Planning Fieldworker)	51	--	51 refresher course	--	--
PLKB (Family Planning Fieldworker)	231	56**	231 refresher course	--	--
Cadre	460	1,642	1,733	--	--

* Not implemented yet
** New replacement PLKB

Fieldworkers are expected to develop specific skills for each subject. For example, after the training on growth of the child, the fieldworkers are expected to:

- Understand that proper growth reflects good health and can be observed from regular monthly weight increases (children are weighed every month to monitor their growth and health);
- Be skilled in weighing children and recording the weight on the growth-chart; and
- Be skilled in counseling mother.

Preparation of the cadre includes training by the family planning field worker, health center staff, agriculture staff, and others. Village cadre are trained at the district level for three days including curriculum about: the growth of children; baby weighing; filling in the child's growth-chart; feeding patterns; eyes, health, anemia, diarrhea; recording and reporting; and referral.

Operational Activities

In Bali, children under five are weighed at the same time as banjar family planning activities. The family planning acceptors meet in order to obtain family planning information or family planning supplies for the following month, or to join integrated family planning and development activities such as savings club; cooperative; courses in sewing, cooking, embroidery, bamboo weaving, etc; as well as the UPGK. In every banjar that has UPGK activity there are one or two weighing groups.

The weighing post is equipped with: a flip-chart, bar-scale, growth chart, oral rehydration solution, vitamin A capsules, and ferrous sulfate tablets. The weighing post is organized by the community and coordinated by the family planning fieldworker who is responsible for the village.

The fieldworker and nutrition cadre member use the flip-chart to counsel the mother or to discuss nutrition problems and solutions with the community. The most practical messages for the people are described on the flip-chart. The messages are linked to the results of the weighing and specific dietary changes, for example, "As the healthy child grows older, his or her weight should increase."

The fieldworker's manual includes information and guidance on nutrition issues. For example, one exercise shows village mothers with healthy children but limited resources. In the group discussion mothers share their experiences in feeding their children. Their experiences are discussed and compared with other women's feeding practices and with the recommendation of the manual.

The field operational activities carried out by the village nutrition cadre include the monthly weighing of children under five years belonging to the acceptor's group or village contraceptive distribution center (VCDC).

At the baby-weighing post there are four activity stations. At the first station the child under five is registered and given a growth chart/card kartu menuju sehat (KMS). Children who have been weighed previously have merely to report their presence. The baby is then weighed using a bar scale at the next station, using either the weighing pants, a box, or a sarong to hold the baby. The baby's weight is then recorded on a piece of paper, and brought by the mother to the third station. Here the weight of the baby is recorded in the growth chart.

The nutrition cadre use the result of the baby's weighing as recorded in the growth chart (KMS) to motivate the baby's mother. The baby's weight can be a strong tool for motivation if the cadre interpret it correctly and give appropriate messages. On the growth chart, the baby's weight is recorded according to his or her age and month of weighing. Over time, these points are joined to form a trend line, that can be used by the cadre to counsel the mother about her baby's health. If the weight of the child does not increase, or decreases, the cadre will suggest that the mother feed the child five times per day with a basic staple such as porridge. If after three months the child's weight still does not increase, the child is referred to the local health center for medical care and rehabilitation.

In counseling the mothers of healthy babies, the cadre ask the mothers to continue feeding their babies more than usual. Thus, the monthly baby weighing and the child's growth chart are used to educate mothers about their infant's growth and health.

The fourth station is for consultation with the mother about the child's growth. These discussions can include information on other development programs such as immunization, contraceptive services for mothers, savings club, and cooperative. These other development programs, it is hoped, will strengthen community acceptance of the family planning program itself.

Nutritional First Aids

Nutritional first aids provided by the UPGK include vitamin A capsules, ferrous sulfate tablets, oral rehydration solution, and antihelminthics. The oral rehydration solution is given to babies suffering from diarrhea. A vitamin A capsule of 200,000 IU is given to each child aged one to four years every six months to prevent blindness. The ferrous sulfate tablets are given to pregnant women during the last three months of pregnancy. The antihelminthic tablets are given to children to combat worms.

These first aids are welcomed by the mothers since they are free. The program's comprehensive approach seeks to prevent as well as to cure diseases associated with malnutrition.

Referral To The Health Center

Referral to the health center of the child with serious diarrhea or other illnesses or a child whose weight has not increased after three monthly weighings is an area requiring special attention. To date the staff and facilities available at most health centers are not yet prepared to handle nutritional cases and the referral system is still weak. The health centers need improvements in order to manage the nutritional referrals uncovered by this new program.

The Village Nutrition Development

Long-term development of improved village nutrition is based upon intensification of home gardens, farming, and fish raising. This component of the UPGK is implemented with the technical guidance of the agricultural extension worker (PPL) or the *mantri tani* at the subdistrict level.

In order to provide local food for cookery demonstrations for the weighing groups, women are encouraged to cultivate their home yards intensively with vegetables or fruits, and to enhance animal husbandry (pigs, poultry, and goats) and/or fisheries. For families who have no yards but have skills for handicraft trades, home industries can be promoted using the capital available under the program to generate income.

Integration of the four components in UPGK support each other. For example, the Department of Health provides the primary health service; the Department of Agriculture provides technical guidance to agriculture groups and assists them in providing seeds; the Department of Religion provides information dealing with religious aspects or motivating the religious groups. The village land or temple land can also be used for seed gardens and its products can be distributed to the balita's mother as a member of the baby-weighing post.

EVALUATION

The progress, accomplishments, and problems of the integrated family planning-nutrition program are reviewed using the monthly report and monthly meetings from the central to subdistrict levels attended by all representatives from the components involved. To assess long-term effects of the program, a survey to collect basic nutrition data has been completed by Udayana University in Bali. The midterm evaluation of the UPGK in Bali will be conducted beginning in 1982. This evaluation will focus on process and programmatic input aimed at modifying the program to achieve the ultimate goals of the program. Table 15:3 gives program achievement during three periods.

The proportion of children who were registered and the proportion receiving growth charts increased substantially in the latter part of 1981. The program achievement for the proportion of children with weight gains over the several periods decreased slightly.

Cost-Effectiveness

Funds needed for the balita operational guidance can be seen in Table 15:4. The cost per banjar per month is Rp.27,046 (US$42.93) and the cost per balita per month, Rp.338 (US$0.53). The cost is minimal in comparison to the importance of improved nutritional status for the nation's children.

Problems and Issues

In the implementation of the UPGK in the field, some matters still need attention to ensure the success of the program such as:

1. Better coordination must be achieved among sectors coordinated by BPGD (Nutritional Improvement Board) in the implementation and the evaluation of the program.

2. Manpower and facilities must be developed to handle cases of malnutrition, especially for children who do not gain weight in three months.

Table 15:3. Program Achievement in Bali

ACHIEVEMENTS	FIRST 6-MONTH PERIOD APR.-SEPT. 1980(%)	SECOND 6-MONTH PERIOD OCT.-MARCH 1981(%)	5-MONTH PERIOD APR.-AUG. 1981(%)
Percent of children less than 5 who are registered (S)	20.3	21.0	55.3
Percent of children less than 5 receiving growth charts (K)	16.7	17.7	50.1
Percent of registered children receiving growth charts (k)	70.0	84.3	90.6
Percent of children less than 5 attending weighing sessions (D)	11.7	10.6	31.9
Percent of children receiving growth charts who attended weighing sessions (d)	70.0	60.0	63.4
Percent of children less than 5 with weight gains (N)	5.0	4.9	13.9
Percent of children attending weighing sessions who gained weight (n)	47.2	46.0	43.6
Children with weight gains as percent of total children (N/S)	27.3	23.0	25.2

Table 15:4. Cost-Effectiveness Per Banjar and Balita Per Month Bali Province The Village Program

1979/1980 (231 Banjars)	1980/1981 (456 Banjars)	Total for 2 Years (687 Banjars)
In Rupiah	In Rupiah	In Rupiah
Rp. 202,234,300	Rp. 243,700,900	Rp. 445,935,200

Cost per banjar/month = $\frac{\text{Rp. } 445,935,200}{687 \times 24}$

= Rp. 27,046,- = US$ 42.93

Cost per balita/month = $\frac{\text{Rp. } 445,935,200-}{687 \times 80 \times 24}$

= Rp. 338,-* = US$ 0.53

* The average number of balita per banjar = 80.45
NOTE: US$1.00 = Rp. 630

3. The system of distribution and accounting does not yet operate smoothly especially at the village level.

4. The communication strategy must be improved so the ultimate goal of the program of behavioral change in the community can be achieved. Education and communication materials still must be developed.

5. Supervision of the program, especially on the use of nutrition first aid, should be increased.

6. Since UPGK will withdraw after three years, there is a need to formulate how to institutionalize the program so the community can support the activity itself through home gardening, income generating activities, and the cooperative, to support the achievement strategy of a small, happy, and prosperous family.

CONCLUSION

The villages in which the family planning nutrition program has been implemented realize the benefit of the UPGK. Activities have already been standardized although the funds for this activity come from various donor agencies such as UNICEF, UNFPA, and USAID; in some areas UPGK is funded by the communities themselves. The program can be assessed through the SKDN feedback which reports the UPGK activities.

16
Nutrition, Family Planning and Health Components of the Guatemalan Program of Primary Health Care (SINAPS)

Aaron Lechtig, John W. Townsend, Francisco Pineda, Juan Jose Arroyo, Robert E. Klein, and Romeo de Leon

This paper describes SINAPS (the Integrated System of Nutrition and Primary Health), the result of the combined effort of the Ministry of Public Health (MOH), the Pan American Health Organization (PAHO), and the Institute of Nutrition of Central America and Panama (INCAP) to design, implement, and evaluate a program for primary health care in Guatemala. Its basic purpose is to increase the effective coverage of primary health care services delivery (Ministry of Health and Social Welfare, Guatemala, 1978; PAHO, 1980). SINAPS tests the hypothesis that it is feasible to implement an effective and efficient program based on services delivered by nonprofessional personnel with appropriate supervision and with the participation of the community (Lechtig and Klein, 1978; Lechtig and Klein, 1979).

NATURE AND OBJECTIVES OF THE HEALTH INTERVENTION

SINAPS was implemented in March 1980 in three experimental health districts of eastern Guatemala; total population was approximately 70,000. Activities are focused on the following areas: immunizations, food supplementation, oral rehydration, perinatal surveillance, family planning, encouragement of long-term breastfeeding, and promotion of health and environmental sanitation with the participation of the community. Specific objectives are:

1. To reduce by 30 percent infant mortality and the incidence of low arm circumference, both in newborns and in children under five years of age.
2. To reduce the incidence of neonatal tetanus and measles by 90 percent.
3. To decrease the incidence of and the mortality due to whooping cough, poliomyelitis, and tetanus by 95 percent.
4. To decrease the mortality due to measles by 80 percent.
5. To satisfy the demand for modern contraceptive methods. This would lead to an increase of 10 percent in the prevalence of contraceptive users.

6. To deliver motivational messages encouraging long-term breastfeeding, improved drinking water quality, better use of existing latrines, and installation of new latrines.
7. To develop and support community groups interested in the introduction of potable water and the installation of latrines.
8. To coordinate the implementation and supervision of potable water and latrine installation projects in communities designated by the MOH.

CRITERIA FOR SELECTION OF THE INTERVENTIONS

Most of the rural population covered by SINAPS suffers from prevalent malnutrition, illiteracy, infectious diseases, infant and child mortality, and short life expectancy. As in many similar populations of the world, this situation is produced by a complex set of social, cultural, biological, and environmental causes (Lechtig and Klein, 1978). The climate in the SINAPS geographical area is predominantly hot and dry. The terrain is rugged and arable land is scarce; most of the rural population is engaged in cultivation of corn and beans at a subsistence level. Estimated median family income in the rural population is about $400 per year. Most of the houses in the rural communities lack sanitary facilities. Children average two to three years of school attendance and adult functional illiteracy is high.

The main limiting factor in the diet of this population is energy, not protein, intake. About 80 percent of the children below five years of age suffer some degree of growth retardation (stunting). Infant mortality at about 100 per 1,000 live births and young child (one to four years) mortality at about 11 per 1,000 are both relatively high.

Main causes of death among children under five years in this population are dehydration due to diarrhea, lower respiratory infections, measles, whooping cough, perinatal-related problems, neonatal tetanus, and malnutrition. Since induced abortion is a major cause of maternal death, a great demand for modern contraceptive methods is expected in this population.

The authors' purpose was to design a selective approach to primary health care, replicable under the routine working conditions of the MOH.
As a consequence, the interventions had to be limited to the most cost-effective ones in terms of effect on health indicators, namely infant and child mortality.

Emphasis was placed on preventing and managing the main causes of infant and child mortality and disability and for which effective health interventions are available (SINAPS, 1981a) Those factors are grouped as follows:

1. Diseases preventable through vaccination (whooping cough, neonatal tetanus, measles, poliomyelitis, and tuberculosis),

2. Dehydration due to diarrhea,
3. Perinatal-health related problems,
4. Severe malnutrition,
5. Risk of early weaning,
6. Short birth interval and high prevalence of induced abortion, and
7. Poor environmental sanitation.

PROGRAM OPERATION

The rural health promoter (RHP) and the traditional birth attendant (TBA) are responsible for delivering the first level of health services with the supervision and support of the rural health technician (RHT) and the auxiliary nurse (AN), respectively. All health service delivery, training, and supervision activities of auxiliary personnel are the responsibility of the MOH through the corresponding chief of each health district.

In order to ensure maximum coverage and to address different potential barriers to the use of health services, SINAPS operations are based on two strategies: household visits and community meetings. Every two months RHPs visit all families assigned to them. At this time, routine services such as census taking and delivery of oral rehydration salts and contraceptive pills are performed. The estimated average time to perform this visit is about half an hour per day. In addition, follow-up visits are programmed for cases of malnutrition, dehydration due to diarrhea, severe infectious diseases, resupply of contraceptives, and emergencies requiring first aid. Other activities of SINAPS are implemented by means of frequent (about every two months) community meetings. Each community holds meetings regularly for vaccination and detection of malnutrition until the coverage is 100 percent.

The RHP is responsible for:

- mapping and census taking,
- vaccinations,
- detection of mothers and children at high nutritional risk,
- oral rehydration,
- distribution of food supplements and food orientation,
- primary curative care,
- encouragement of long-term breastfeeding,
- resupply of pills and condoms, and
- health promotion and environmental sanitation.

The TBA is responsible for:

- care of normal pregnancy, birth, and puerperium,
- referral of high-risk mothers to the health service,
- referral of all newborns and their mothers to the health service, and
- detection of newborns at high nutritional risk.

Medical Backup Included and Criteria for Referrals

Most of the activities performed by the RHP are of a preventive nature and are related to promoting active community participation in the delivery of health services. For example, the RHT immunizes the children and measures their arm circumference. Meanwhile, the RHP promotes the activities and informs the community to ensure high coverage. For each activity the RHP and TBA have clearly written indications describing when a patient should be referred to the health center. For this purpose a coupon for referrals has been designed and is presently used in all the experimental health districts. Preliminary data suggest that this referral system is being used and accepted by the physicians at the health posts and health centers in the experimental health districts.

EVALUATION

SINAPS is evaluated through two different approaches: the internal evaluation based upon MOH records of service activities, and the INCAP staff's external evaluation through surveys of random samples of households in the experimental and control health districts before and after the implementation of health services delivery activities. Most of the information for internal evaluation is collected by the RHP by means of the family health record and coupons for referral or coupons to assign malnourished persons to the food supplementation program. The TBA uses a birth coupon which includes a tape to measure the newborn's arm circumference to refer newborns and their mothers to the health services. The mothers turn their birth coupon in to the corresponding health center during their postnatal examination. Supervisors receive data monthly. Based on these data, the chief of the health district sends a quarterly report to the health area chief. Summaries of these reports are then processed through the regular MOH channels.

The criteria to select the experimental and control health districts were: (1) dispersed population; (2) each group of experimental and control districts approximating 70,000 inhabitants; (3) population predominantly non-Indian (ladino, 90 percent or more); (4) health districts not located on the border of any other country and without MOH hospitals; (5) one experimental and one control district selected from each of the three health areas; and, (6) if more than two districts in one health area fulfilled the above requirements, then adjoining districts should not be chosen (SINAPS, 1981b).

Based on these criteria, the following two groups of health districts were selected: (1) San Agustin Acasaguastlan, Rio Hondo, and Quezaltepeque; and (2) Sanarate, Cabanas, and Ipala. The SINAPS coordinating committee randomly selected group (1) as the control group and group (2) as the experimental group, and San Antonio La Paz as the pilot municipality.

Coverage of interviews in both the baseline and end-line (after services had been in effect) surveys was more than 95 percent and the total number of interviews was sufficiently large to detect the expected changes in prevalence of malnutrition and of contraceptive users. In addition, the survey team completed 226 quality control re-interviews in the baseline and 88 in the end-line to document the reliability of the survey data.

RESULTS

Total Population and Vaccination Coverage

With 93.7 percent of the RHPs reporting, the total population covered as of December 31, 1981, was 70,197 including 12,839 children under five years of age, 14,598 women between 15 and 49 years of age, and 1,012 pregnant women. Among children 2 to 60 months of age, coverage attained 93.1 percent for DPT, Polio first-dose and 95.7 percent for BCG vaccinations, and among pregnant women, 99.0 percent for first-dose toxoid. Coverage of vaccination against measles in children (74 percent) is not as high though still significantly higher than in the control health districts. But more important than trends were the large ranges in coverage among the experimental health districts (about 30 percentage points), an indication of need for better supervision.

The data collected through external evaluation surveys also clearly indicated a significant increase in vaccination coverage for all vaccines for children and mothers from the baseline to the end-line levels in the experimental health districts ($P < .01$). The results from these surveys were remarkably similar to those reported by the RHPs, a finding that suggests reliability of data collected through the internal information system.

Food Supplementation and Prevalence of Malnutrition

RHPs measured the arm circumferences of 85.6 percent of children 2 to 60 months old, of whom 14.3 percent were malnourished; and for 72.8 percent of pregnant women measured, 26.4 percent were malnourished. The finding that coverage was high for children and relatively low for pregnant women is similar to that for coverage of vaccinations because both activities were conducted during the same community meetings. As of December 31, 1981, 100 percent of the children and pregnant women identified as malnourished were receiving food supplements and food orientation through their local RHPs.

Data from the external evaluation surveys indicated no significant changes in the prevalence of malnutrition between the experimental and control health districts. No significant effect was expected in this area, as the food supplementation program was implemented five months before the beginning of the end-line survey, when effective arrangements between the MOH and CARE could be made.

Oral Rehydration

A total of 83.7 percent of the households with children under five years of age received bags of Supersuero (prepackaged oral rehydration salts) as well as information from the RHPs on how and when to use it. Equally important, 61.9 percent of the mothers receiving Supersuero knew how to prepare it and when to use it properly. Another 23.2 percent of the mothers knew how to prepare it but were not sure when to use it. In this sample 57.0 percent used the Supersuero received.

Table 16:1 reports mothers' responses to the question, "What did you do the last time your children under five years of age had diarrhea for more than two consecutive days?" Data from the baseline and end-line surveys in the experimental health districts indicate that use of Supersuero increased dramatically (from 0.5 percent to 37.8 percent) while the use of drugs from the pharmacy and the use of the health post facilities for diarrhea was reduced considerably. Data from the end-line survey indicated an overall increase in the use of MOH services of 9.1 percent in the experimental and 7.4 percent in the control districts during this same time period. Use of the health posts for the treatment of diarrhea remained high (18.3 percent) in the control health districts.

Family Planning

Table 16:2 presents the percentage of nonpregnant women in union between 15 and 44 years of age who used a modern contraceptive method at the time of the baseline and endline surveys. For all modern methods, the prevalence increased in both the experimental and control health districts by about 3 percentage points. However, for methods available within the SINAPS program (oral contraceptives, condoms, and female sterilization) the increment was of 4.3 percent (40 percent increase) between the baseline and endline surveys ($P < .05$) in the experimental health districts. A nonsignificant increase of 1.7 percent (13 percent increase) was found in the control health districts. The end-line survey was conducted from three to six months following the household distribution of oral contraceptives and condoms.

A comparison between users and nonusers of contraceptive methods indicated that users tended to be older (32.0 ± 6.7 versus 29.8 ± 7.8 years, $P < .01$) with more years in union (13.4 ± 6.7 versus 11.6 ± 7.7 years, $P < .01$) and more pregnancies (5.4 ± 2.7 versus 4.9 ± 3.4, $P < .05$). They also were somewhat heavier as evidenced by significantly larger arm circumference (1.8 cm larger). In addition, users tended to be more urban, (34.0 versus 16.4 percent, $P < .01$), more literate (56.6 versus 26.6 percent, $P < .01$), to have had more schooling (33.5 versus 13.8 percent, $P < .01$) and to work more frequently at income-producing tasks (27.4 versus 15.7 percent, $P < .01$). In general, the emerging pattern was that contraceptive users were a much more "modern" or advantaged group regardless of age differences (due

Table 16:1. Response of Mothers to the Question: "What Did You Do the Last Time Your Child Under Five Years of Age had Diarrhea for More Than Two Consecutive Days?"

	Used *Supersuero* Oral Rehydration Salts (ORS)		Used Drugs from Pharmacy (not including ORS)*		Visited Health Center or Post for Treatment		Did Nothing or Used Household Remedy	
	(No.)	%	(No.)	%	(No.)	%	(No.)	%
Baseline								
Control (n=490)	(1)	0.2	(349)	71.2	(107)	21.8	(33)	6.7
Experimental (n=630)	(2)	0.5	(424)	67.3	(134)	21.3	(70)	11.1
Post-Program								
Control (n=542)	(1)	0.2	(401)	74.0	(99)	18.3	(41)	7.6
Experimental (n=716)	(271)	37.8**	(331)	46.2	(83)	11.6	(31)	4.4

* Drugs commonly used to treat diarrhea are: antibiotics, mixtures of pectin and kaolin, iodine-based preparations, and popular products including bicarbonates and laxatives.

** The change in use of *supersuero* in the experimental health districts from the baseline was statistically significant ($P < .01$).

Table 16:2. Percentage of Nonpregnant Women between 15-44 Years of Age in Union who use a Modern Contraceptive Method

	Experimental		Control	
	Baseline (n=726)	Endline (n=700)	Baseline (n=536)	Endline (n=533)
Female Sterilization	6.3 (46)	7.7 (54)	5.6 (30)	6.4 (34)
Oral Contraceptives	3.6 (26)	4.6 (32)	7.3 (39)	7.9 (42)
Condoms	0.8 (6)	2.7 (19)	0.2 (1)	0.6 (3)
Program Total[1]	10.7 (78)	15.0 (105)	13.1 (70)	14.0 (79)
IUD	1.4 (10)	1.1 (8)	1.1 (6)	1.3 (7)
Others[2]	1.5 (11)	0.6 (4)	0.9 (5)	1.9 (10)
Total	13.5 (99)	16.7 (117)	15.1 (81)	18.0 (96)

[1] The difference between program totals in the baseline and endline surveys in the Experimental Area is significant $X^2 = 5.77$, df = 1, $P < .05$; The difference between baseline and endline in the Control Area is not significant.

[2] Other methods include, injections, foams, jellies, tablets, diaphragms and vasectomies.

largely to those selecting female sterilization) or location in the SINAPS area. Thus, despite the almost universal availability of oral contraceptives and condoms in the experimental health districts, it appears that contraceptive users remain a unique group.

In contrast with the relatively small changes in prevalence of contraceptive use, a large increment was found in the experimental health districts in the ability to recall or recognize the names of the contraceptive methods (from 59.5 percent to 71.2 percent). For program methods (oral contraceptives, condoms, and female sterilization), the increment was even greater, from 69.1 percent to 85.2 percent. Though it is recognized that the ability to name a method is quite different than being able to describe how to use it and where to obtain it, this increase in knowledge may be the first step in increasing overall contraceptive prevalence.

Mortality

No consistent changes in infant or child mortality were found either through the external evaluation surveys or the internal information system. Though there was a drop in child (one to four years of age) mortality rates in the experimental health districts from 11.4 to 4.9 per 1,000 children alive ($P < .01$), yearly fluctuations in mortality are common and additional data were being sought to interpret these results.

Cost of SINAPS Service Delivery Activities

Data in Table 16:3 indicate that the net additional cost per capita of SINAPS activities at the health district level is estimated at $0.99 the first year and $0.72 the second and subsequent years. The most expensive component of the program is the training and supervision of voluntary personnel due to the cost of per diem for their attendance at training sessions and the additional gasoline required per month for supervision. It should be noted that the administrative costs of managing the program at the health area level and above are not included (approximately 20 cents more per capita per year).

Per capita expenditure by the MOH for the SINAPS health districts in 1980 was approximately $2.00 (exclusive of hospital, central administration, and training costs). Costs presented in Table 16:3 may vary depending on the need for additional RHTs, the necessity of using CARE foods, previous vaccination coverage, and the availability of oral rehydration salts and contraceptives. The MOH usually allocates money within the regular budget for promoter training, vaccines, transportation of CARE foods, and other services which, when applied to a primary health care program, should reduce the marginal cost. The total additional cost of SINAPS for all rural populations in Guatemala is approximately $5.94 million the first year and $4.32 million in subsequent years, assuming national coverage of

Table 16:3. Net Additional Cost of SINAPS Activities at the Health District Level in Guatemala (1980)

ACTIVITIES	ANNUAL PER CAPITA COST (US$) First Year	Second Year	COMMENTS
Selection, training, and supervision of RHPs and TBAs	.66	.31	Costs of additional RHTs are not included since they are already included in the MOH projected budgets for the next five years.
Vaccination program	.09	.02	This corresponds to the 25 percent coverage additional to the MOH's present goal of 75 percent.
Treatment and referral of cases of diarrheal diseases, common illnesses, and obstetric risk	.14	.29	Oral rehydration costs are $0.02 and $0.16, respectively . About half of this cost could be recuperated by eliminating the use of kaolin/pectin.
Food supplementation program	.07	.07	This assumes the availability of CARE PL 480 foods.
Family planning program	.03	.03	This assumes continued collaboration between APROFAM and MOH.
TOTAL	$0.99	$0.72	

six million persons in rural areas. This amount represents less than 4 percent of the MOH national budget during 1980.

TRAINING

Every two weeks the RHTs train the RHPs during one-day sessions. After each session the RHP implements the corresponding service in the community. For example, during the training for detection and treatment of persons at high nutritional risk, this activity is implemented in the community. ANs train TBAs following a similar strategy, at monthly intervals (SINAPS, 1981d).

The district chief aided by the social worker when available, instructs the RHTs biweekly on the topic that will be discussed with the RHPs the following week. The district chief also trains the professional nurse once every month; the professional nurse then discusses the topic with the ANs during the same week. The district chief is also in charge of monthly monitoring of the training activities performed by the RHT and the AN.

A random sample of 135 of the 405 RHPs currently active in SINAPS revealed that the average age of RHPs is 27 years and about half are women. Approximately half are married or in common-law union, most had at least one grade of formal education, two-thirds are Catholic, and 20 percent had previous experience as RHPs.

As of December 31, 1981, there were 24 training centers for RHPs and 18 for TBAs. Usually, one RHT supervised and trained 24 RHPs and one AN supervised and trained 13 TBAs. In total, 405 RHPs participated in monthly training and supervision sessions with an attendance rate of 88.3 percent and a coverage of 93.7 percent of the families. In addition, 226 TBAs completed their first year of training during April 1981, with an average attendance rate of 85.8 percent.

SUPERVISION AND QUALITY CONTROL

Figure 16:1 presents the SINAPS diagram for supervision (continued lines) and coordination (dotted lines). It is clear from this figure that the district chief is the official channel for all information related to the health district. The maximum ratios of personnel recommended by SINAPS are as follows: The district chief supervises one social worker, seven RHTs, and one professional nurse.

The RHT supervises 25 RHPs in rural areas (35 promoters in an urban area or 30 promoters when the area is part urban and part rural). The professional nurse supervises 15 ANs and each AN supervises 20 TBAs.

The RHT supervises the RHP at two locations: the training center during the one-day training session every two weeks and in the community every two months. Supervision at the community level is more frequent during community meetings for vaccination

Figure 16:1. SINAPS Organization Chart

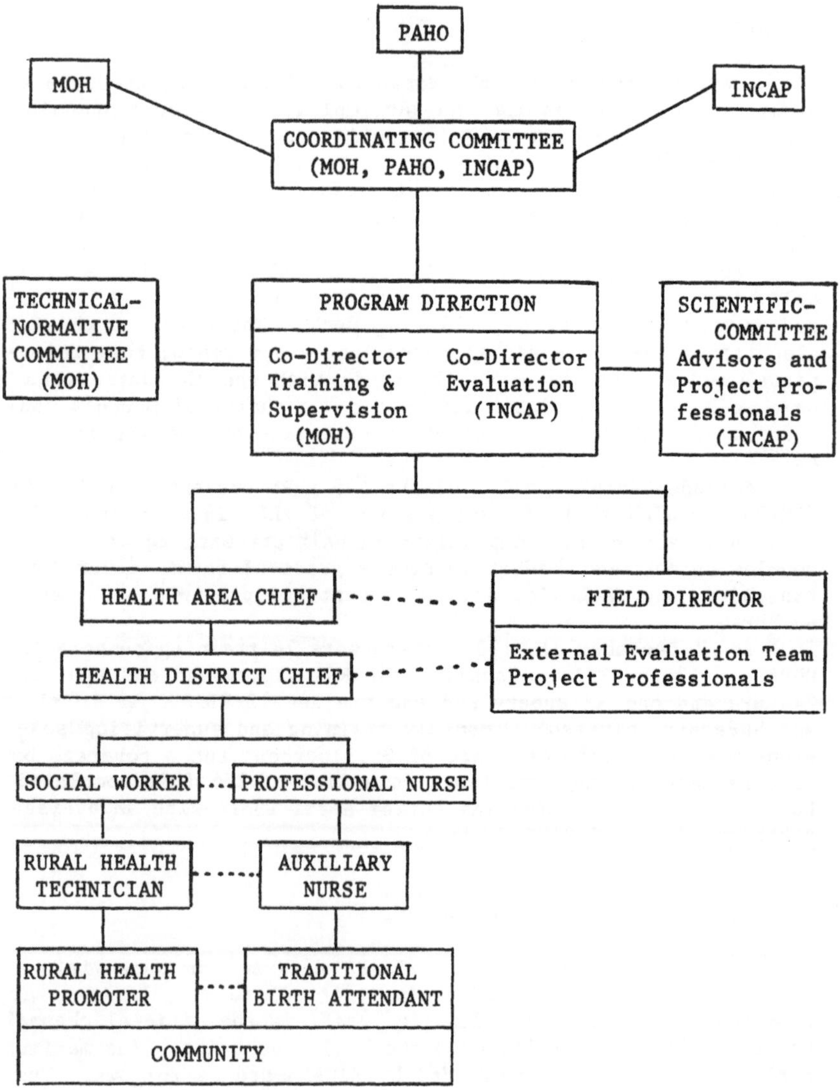

and detection of malnutrition and when the promoters have not completed their tasks or miss more than two consecutive training sessions. The AN only supervises the TBA at the training center simultaneously with the one-day training session every four weeks (SINAPS, 1981c).

ADMINISTRATION AND LOGISTICS

As mentioned, SINAPS is carried out through close cooperation between the MOH, PAHO, and INCAP. MOH is responsible for service delivery and personnel training activities while PAHO and INCAP are responsible for developing methods and evaluating programs. As presented in Figure 16:1, the coordinating committee - composed of three representatives from the MOH, two from INCAP, and one from PAHO - serves as the senior-level liaison and determines the policies for development of the program. SINAPS administration is performed by two co-directors, one for training and supervision (MOH functionary) and the other for method development and evaluation (PAHO/INCAP functionary). The coordinating committee meets quarterly to discuss all SINAPS activities and documents while the co-directors meet weekly to discuss program progress. Weekly meetings are also held at the level of health area and health districts on issues of coordination, training, management, supervision, and logistics. In addition, periodic workshops are held to review the implementation of SINAPS. As a consequence of this process, all levels of the MOH actively participate in decision-making, implementation, and evaluation of SINAPS activities.

SUMMARY AND FINAL COMMENTS

The Guatemalan Program of Primary Health Care's (SINAPS) main purpose is to increase the effective coverage of primary health care services in rural populations of Guatemala. SINAPS activities are aimed at controlling the most important immediate causes of death and disability in the maternal and child group - immunizations, food supplementation, oral rehydration, family planning, perinatal surveillance, and promotion of health and environmental sanitation with participation of the community. The RHP and the TBA have the main responsibility for these services at the primary level (community and household). The RHP provides services through periodic household visits (every two months) and through community meetings at two-month intervals.

The AN supervises the TBA. These nonprofessional personnel can provide effective and efficient health services; several methods developed in SINAPS are currently being adopted at the national level in Guatemala and in other Latin American countries as well.

The important characteristics that the SINAPS approach enjoys can be condensed as follows:

1. The number of interventions is circumscribed to those with the highest feasibility and potential effect.

2. Health services delivery, supervision, and training are performed by MOH personnel within the same previously existing physical and administrative infrastructure. PAHO/INCAP personnel are responsible for development of method and for external evaluation.

3. The training of volunteers is based on one-day sessions limited to a single topic, followed by service delivery. Initial training takes place biweekly over a period of one year followed by monthly retraining sessions. This approach permits continuous adjustment of the training program to solve service delivery problems.

4. The one-day training sessions are also used to carry out supervisory activities, simple tabulation of data routinely collected through the internal information system, monthly requests of needs for materials and equipment, and preparation of the quarterly reports to the health district chief. In this way training is integrated into supervision, data flow, and management.

5. The RHP is supervised by RHT, regarded as under-utilized in the MOH delivery system. In this respect, SINAPS addresses the frequent reluctance of traditional health professionals to carry out extensive fieldwork.

6. The service delivery provided by SINAPS, is carried out by means of community meetings (immunizations and detection of malnourished persons) and systematic home visits (delivery of contraceptives and oral rehydration salts). This approach addresses different barriers to the use of services at the community and family level.

7. The SINAPS evaluation model allows for comparison between results from external and internal evaluation approaches and provides information on validity of indicators and ways of data collection. Furthermore, the internal information system can be used to address a wide range of service delivery issues, beyond the external evaluation surveys.

8. A high priority is assigned to total coverage of the target population and to selective care of those at the highest risk of death or disability. As expected, the effect on health indicators after six to nine months of service delivery was relatively modest. However, the infrastructure developed and training carried out at all levels promises greater results as the program advances to the period 1983-1985.

ACKNOWLEDGEMENTS

The authors wish to express their gratitude to Dr. Roquelino Recinos Mendeze, Minister of Public Health of Guatemala, to Dr. Angel Paz Cojulun and Dr. Leonel Barrios, Director General and Deputy Director General, respectively, of the Health Services Bureau, Ministry of Health of Guatemala, for their valuable contribution to making this project a reality. The authors also thank Dr. Rudy Gutierrez, Dr. Salvador Baldizon, Lic. Rolando Duarte, Lic. Redi Deman, nurse Mercedes de Castillo, and Miss Marta Amanda Barrera, members of the SINAPS team.

Finally, the authors express their gratitude to Drs. Jorge Osuna and Carlos Hernàn Daza, Pan American Health Organization (Washington, D.C.) and to Drs. James Heiby, Jerald Bailey, and Duff Gillespie, Agency for International Development, Population Research Office, for their help and encouragement in this project.

REFERENCES

Lechtig, A. and R. E. Klein. "Estado Biologico de la Poblacion Guatemalteca: Definicion, Causas y Estrategias de Accion Para Mejorarla." Rev. Col. Med. (Guatemala) 29,3 (1978): 93-106.

Lechtig, A. and R. E. Klein. "Effect of Food Supplementation During Pregnancy and Lactation in Infant Mortality, Morbidity and Physical Growth." Arch. Latinoamer. Nutr. 29,4 suppl 1 (1979): 99-142.

Ministry of Public Health and Social Welfare. Republic of Guatemala, National Health Plan, 1978.

Pan American Health Organization (PAHO). Health for all by the Year 2000: Strategies. Document No. 173. Washington, D.C.: PAHO, 1980.

SINAPS, Evaluation Model. SINAPS Internal Document, Guatemala: SINAPS Program, INCAP, 1981a.

SINAPS, Model for Health Services Delivery. SINAPS Internal Document, Guatemala: SINAPS Program, INCAP, 1981b.

SINAPS, Supervision Model. SINAPS Internal Document, Guatemala: SINAPS Program, INCAP, 1981c.

SINAPS, Training Model. SINAPS Internal Document, Guatemala: SINAPS Program, INCAP, 1981d.

Part Six

Immunization in CBD Programs

17
Immunization*

Ciro A. de Quadros

The goal of this paper is to concisely assemble all of the major issues on immunization delivery pertaining to the prevention of childhood immunizable diseases in developing countries. The information as presented serves three purposes: (1) to present a summary of the components of immunization activities, (2) to assist decisionmakers in making more informed decisions on immunization delivery, and (3) to assist the planning of delivery of immunization services through community-based distribution (CBD) projects.

Much of this paper is based on field experiences. It has been written to raise major points on issues in immunization delivery. If matters are occasionally dealt with in a simplified manner, this is due to limitations of space rather than to a lack of appreciation of the many difficulties and frustrations that exist in the field.

IMMUNIZATION AS A COMPONENT OF PRIMARY HEALTH CARE

At the meeting on primary health care, in Alma Ata (1978) immunization against major infectious diseases of childhood was declared as one of the elements in attainment of health for all by the year 2000 (WHO, 1978).

The 30th World Health Assembly further emphasized the importance of immunization by adopting a resolution aimed at ensuring that by 1990 all the children of the world will be provided with immunization services. Since experience had shown that episodic mass campaigns are not effective, the Expanded Program on Immunization (EPI) was established by WHO in 1974 as an integral component of primary health care services (WHO, 1978).

EPI's long-term objectives are:

- To reduce morbidity and mortality from diphtheria, pertus-

* This Paper is a revised version of an unpublished document entitled "Issues on Immunization Delivery," by Ciro A. de Quadros, Howard G. Miner, and Alan Schnur.

sis, tetanus, measles, poliomyelitis, and tuberculosis by providing immunization services against these diseases for every child in the world by 1990 (other selected diseases may be included when and where applicable);

- To promote countries' self-reliance in the delivery of immunization services within the context of comprehensive health services; and

- To promote regional self-reliance in matters of vaccine quality control and vaccine production (PAHO/WHO, 1980).

The EPI seeks to establish permanent immunization services that reach a high proportion of newborns and pregnant women, as these target populations are constantly being replenished.

The EPI requires a long-term commitment to continued immunization activities and should be integrated within existing health care services as an integral part of primary health care (Mahler, 1977). The provision of immunization services is often the "entry point" for primary health care, especially for those living in remote communities. Additional primary health care services may be added to the immunization component after a schedule of routine visits and logistics has been worked out. Some additional services might include control of diarrheal disease, health education, nutrition education or assessment, treatment of minor illnesses, and prenatal, natal, and postnatal care.

Personnel

Since immunization activities take place at virtually all levels of the health infrastructure, it necessarily follows that personnel at all levels must be active to ensure adequate immunization coverage. Personnel can include both multipurpose primary health care workers and those responsible solely for immunization activities.

The most important point is that no matter which personnel are used, they must have the appropriate skills to carry out immunization activities. These activities include: transporting and storing vaccines, educating and vaccinating community members, planning, and supervising.

Vaccines

There are numerous vaccines of varying effectiveness and stability available to health workers. These presently include:

<u>Recommended by EPI</u>

1. DPT (diphtheria-pertussis-tetanus)
2. measles
3. polio
4. BCG
5. TT (tetanus toxoid)

Other

1. choleratyphoid fever
2. dt (diphtheria-tetanus)
3. influenza
4. meningitis
5. mumps
6. pertussis
7. pneumococcus
8. rabies
9. rubella
10. smallpox
11. typhoid fever
12. typhus
13. yellow fever

Which vaccines should be included in a country's immunization activities must depend on the epidemiology, morbidity, and mortality of diseases prevalent in the country, balanced by the sophistication of health services, availability of staff, adequacy of the cold chain, and logistics network. For example, measles, which has a high case-fatality rate in developing countries and strikes almost all children, would be a higher priority than in a developed country where measles is characterized by low mortality. At present, EPI recommends that six antigens - DPT, measles, polio, and BCG vaccines - be considered for inclusion in immunization programs as top priority.

Cold Chain

The "cold chain" is the logistics system composed of people and equipment that moves and monitors vaccines at acceptable temperatures from the manufacturer to the field. The cold chain is necessary because vaccines are sensitive to heat. The most organized field program, reaching a high percentage of the target population, is ineffective if the vaccine becomes impotent due to improper refrigeration or handling somewhere along the chain.

The essential elements of the cold chain are people to organize and manage the distribution of vaccines, equipment to store and transport vaccine, and the procedures used.

There are minor variations in activities connected with the maintenance of equipment or quantities of vaccine handled at the local, health center, district or regional, and central or national levels, as well as at the airport. However, the major areas of responsibility remain the same and include the following: obtaining and dispatching vaccine, maintaining vaccine, and maintaining equipment.

Obtaining and Dispatching Vaccine

Vaccine is obtained from the next level up. Before vaccine is obtained the responsible person must estimate the amount of vaccine needed, make sure enough cold-chain equipment is available to store the vaccine, make sure the amount of vaccine and dilute obtained is the same as that estimated as needed, and make sure the expiration date has not passed. Vaccines should be obtained and dispatched at regular intervals.

Maintaining Vaccines

When vaccines are administered to mothers and children at the vaccination sites, care must be taken not to expose the vaccine to heat and sunlight unnecessarily. The following activities are also necessary for the proper maintenance of vaccine: control vaccine stocks, monitor temperatures, retest vaccine potency, keep records of the amount and types of vaccine in storage, use vaccines with earliest expiration dates first, and keep records of receipts of vaccine, disbursements, and remaining stock.

Maintaining Equipment

If the cold-chain is to be effective, its equipment must be properly maintained. Detailed descriptions of cold-chain maintenance are provided in respective EPI manuals published and available from PAHO/WHO.

Levels of the Cold-Chain

Most countries have three or four major levels of the cold-chain - the central, regional, health center, and local (health post, clinic, or vaccination teams) levels.

The central store is usually located in the national capital or principal city and receives vaccine from the manufacturer, usually by way of an airport. It is designed for long-term storage of large amounts of vaccine. Necessary equipment includes a walk-in cold-room capable of maintaining temperatures of +4°C to +8°C, and a freezer adequate for -25°C temperatures or several large refrigerators and freezers with backup power supply, thermometers, thermorecorders, and an alarm system to warn if the temperature gets too high (PAHO/WHO, 1980).

Vaccine can be transported from the central level to the regional level in refrigerated vehicles or large cold boxes with sufficient ice packs to keep the vaccine below 8°C for the duration of the trip.

The regional-level store is usually located in a district, region, department, or provincial capital city. Facilities include refrigeration and freezers equipped with thermometers and possibly thermorecorders and alarm systems. Vaccines can be kept here up to three months. Vaccines are transported to the health center in cold boxes.

The health center is usually located in a large town, with or without electricity, and often supplies vaccine to surrounding subcenters. A refrigerator, capable of +4° to +8°C storage, is sometimes available but not always with freezing capability. A thermometer should be maintained here, especially since cheap liquid-crystal models can now be purchased. Storage should be one week or less. Smaller cold boxes or vaccine carriers with ice packs can be used for transport to the subcenter or local level.

Vaccines can be stored at the local level in the vaccine carriers they arrive in up to the limit of cold life of the container (usually 49 to 120 hours). Vaccination sessions can be planned to coincide with the arrival of vaccine from the health center. Excess vaccine can be returned to the health center, if possible, or destroyed.

Evaluation

An evaluation report of the EPI in Tanzania noted that an immunization program had been developed which could be regarded as one of the best in the developing world. However, one of their recommendations to the Ministry of Health mentioned the need for better training in vaccine storage procedures and preventive maintenance of cold-chain equipment (An Evaluation Report of the Expanded Program on Immunization, 1972).

A preliminary evaluation report on the national immunization program in Guatemala also recommended better maintenance of the refrigerators in the cold chain. (Brandling-Bennett and Jones, 1979). Recommendations for improved maintenance have also appeared in evaluation reports from many other countries. Such maintenance has been recognized as essential to the prolonged functioning of the cold chain, and thus of immunization programs themselves. While programs can be carried out in the short term, and even provide adequate coverage when maintenance procedures are being established or improved, in the long-term programs will be more efficient and effective if maintenance is adequate.

Experience in many countries indicates that the risks of damage to vaccine are greatest at the health center and local levels. Health center staff often have many duties and cannot continuously supervise vaccine storage equipment. (WHO, 1977). Yet the most important procedures of maintenance are the routine day-to-day and weekly checking and cleaning of equipment - chores often left undone by overburdened staff because they are tedious or seem unimportant, at least until the refrigerator or freezer breaks down.

Since maintenance of the cold chain is not very complicated, the most important aspect is the people. The challenge is to properly train, motivate, and supervise personnel who deal with the cold chain so they will realize the importance of the simple procedures and be able to carry them out.

Short cold-chain training courses for middle-level workers, providing the necessary knowledge and skills, should be routine. However, it also requires constant reminders, supervisory visits, posters, and continuing education to induce people to change their ideas about machinery and maintenance.

Simple maintenance procedures keep reappearing as the cause of cold-chain breakdowns. The more sophisticated the refrigerator or freezer, the less need of maintenance (although there might be more need of repairs). Given the power-source conditions in many developing countries, ranging from lack of electricity to intermittent supplies at fluctuating voltages, equipment must be kept technically simple, thereby requiring more maintenance.

Electric and propane gas refrigerators and freezers require the least maintenance, while kerosene models require the most. Unfortunately, electricity and gas are not available at most health facilities with cold-chain equipment in developing countries, so kerosene is the most widely used power source. Elementary maintenance procedures necessary for proper cold-chain maintenance are listed in Table 17:1.

Table 17:1. Procedure for Refrigerator/Freezer

	POWER		
	Kerosene	Gas	Electricity
1) Check and note temperature twice a day	X	X	X
2) Ensure secure electric plug-to-wall socket connection			X
3) Check and top up kerosene	X		
4) Check and clean wick	X		
5) Check and clean chimney	X		
6) Clean flue and baffle	X		
7) Clean gas nozzle		X	
8) Defrost refrigerator or freezer regularly	X	X	X
9) Make sure refrigerator is level	X	X	
10) Check and, if necessary, replace door gasket	X	X	X
11) Clean inside and outside of equipment	X	X	X
12) Properly keep records to show maintenance performed	X	X	X

ISSUES IN THE ESTABLISHMENT OF IMMUNIZATION ACTIVITIES

Tactics

Immunization activities should be carried out within the context of the established primary health care structure, whenever such care exists. Some alternate immunization tactics are: immunization in the health facility, outreach, mobile immunization team, reaching the hard-to-reach, and mass campaigns.

Immunization in the Health Facility

This is the most commonly used method of immunization. Health personnel assigned to a specific facility wait for children to be brought to them for immunization. As a rule, specific times or days of the week or month are established for immunization activities.

Advantages:

It entails no *per diem* or transportation costs for staff. All the medical services, equipment, and documentation are readily available at the health facility.

Disadvantages:

The outcome depends upon the motivation of the persons bringing the children to the center; only those living within perhaps a five-mile radius of the center may have access to the services.

Outreach

This approach requires health personnel to travel beyond a five-mile radius from the established health care facility to provide immunization services. The outreach community usually does not have other health services. The population served in the outreach community should be at least several hundred.

Advantages:

This approach brings immunization services to communities with little or difficult access to health services. Outreach visits can be used for prenatal care, nutritional assessment of children, and other primary health care activities, in addition to immunization activities.

Disadvantages:

There are costs of transporting staff and supplies, and *per diem* costs. Supervision may be difficult. This approach depends on a rigid adherence of staff to a fixed, previously established time schedule. If this schedule is not kept over a long period of time, attendance and confidence in the program will drop.

Mobile Immunization Team

A team of several health workers travels by permanently assigned vehicle to areas not served by existing health facilities to vaccinate and perform other health services.

Advantages:

This may be the only way to immunize children and pregnant women in rural areas or urban communities without health services.

Disadvantages:

The transportation and per diem costs are quite often prohibitively high. Supervision is very difficult.

Reaching the Hard-to-Reach

Certain sectors of the population may be hard to reach because of geographic or socio-cultural barriers. Geographic barriers may be overcome through a combination of house-to-house, outreach, and mobile team efforts. At some point the cost of immunizing the hard-to-reach may become prohibitive. Religious beliefs that prohibit or hinder immunization are examples of socio-cultural barriers. To scale these barriers requires a great deal of patience, understanding, imagination, and discussion with local religious leaders and other influential persons before immunization is accepted by the community.

Mass Campaigns

The health workers usually periodically discontinue their other routine activities in order to devote themselves exclusively to vaccinations for a short time (a week or a month).

Vaccination campaigns are a useful means of introducing vaccination into areas with no previous experience or where there are not sufficient personnel to cover the target population. They should be replaced by ongoing and continuous vaccination efforts as soon as such efforts are feasible. (Ambrosch et al., 1978).

Advantages:

With good promotion it is possible to elicit the interest and cooperation of the community and the health officials. Mobilization of volunteers from the community may lead to more extensive vaccination than would otherwise be possible with limited personnel.

Disadvantages:

It is usually not possible to keep the staff and the community interested. Coverage is often good during the first campaign but diminishes the following year. For this reason, many countries have begun to shift their efforts from campaigns to ongoing and continuous vaccination activities. Discontinuation of other activities during the days of the campaign disrupt other health programs (PAHO/WHO, 1979).

Implementation

After choosing one of the program ideas listed above, the personnel must decide on a method to carry it out: house-to-house vaccination, or collection-point vaccination.

House-to-house Immunization

Health personnel visit individual homes to locate and vaccinate infants and pregnant women. This tactic can be used as part of outreach, mobile team, and mass campaign activities.

Advantages:

It is possible to identify the children who run the greatest risk of contracting the diseases and to immunize them. The personnel and people in the area get to know one another. Health education and other health services may be dispensed at this time.

Disadvantages:

Vaccination in the home may be less cost-effective in terms of time required to visit each house and vaccinate appropriate members. This method involves displacement of health personnel and may involve per diem displacement costs. These activities are most difficult to supervise. The potential exists for vaccine wastage because of small numbers of children to be vaccinated.

Collection-point Immunization

Health personnel inform the public to come to one centrally located place, at a given time, where equipment and personnel are assembled for a vaccination session. Immunization offered at the health facility is one example of this approach, but it can also be used as part of outreach, mobile team, and mass campaign activities.

Advantages:

Personnel are used efficiently. All equipment can be brought in a vehicle (if not already at the facility) and set up for more organized vaccination sessions.

Disadvantages:

The outcome depends upon the motivation of the persons bringing the children to the collection point. Costs in time and money associated with getting to the collection point may be prohibitive. People who may not have heard of the session, or who hesitate to immunize their children, may not be served.

Major Factors in Tactic Selection

Although there are global EPI program recommendations encompassing vaccines against six diseases, the decision as to which vaccines to use and the geographic area to cover must be made individually for each country. In order to cover the entire target population, a combination of tactics rather than any one specific tactic may be best. WHO recommends that attention first be paid to immunizing children and pregnant women already using existing health facilities. Then outreach services from fixed facilities can begin, and finally coverage extended over the entire country using experience gained with static units (WHO, 1980).

To decide on the proper tactics - such as the use of mobile teams or programs based in static health facilities - data on the magnitude of the morbidity and mortality from vaccine-preventable diseases can be established from surveys or health service registers (PAHO/WHO, 1980a). For example, findings in many developing countries show that measles and whooping cough are major causes of morbidity and mortality while diphtheria is not.

With data on the health problems compiled, quantifiable objectives can be set for the reduction of disease-specific morbidity and mortality desired in the target population. The target population recommended by WHO is all children under one year of age and pregnant women, since the risk of morbidity and mortality has been found to be considerable from the vaccine-preventable diseases to children in this age group and the unborn. However, epidemiologic information for an individual country might show that the target age should be extended to two years or one-and-a-half, depending on what aged children con tract the disease.

After the target diseases and population have been decided upon, the next question is how to set about immunizing the target population most effectively and efficiently. Continuous immunization services have been found to be less expensive and more effective than mass campaigns and mobile teams. If static coverage were high enough, campaigns and mobile teams would be unnecessary. Otherwise, a mix of the two strategies might be required.

Equipment, financial resources, and availability of personnel must also be considered. Mobile teams are expensive. Are there enough funds and equipment to support them? Can personnel and static health facilities be used for outreach activities? Are health workers adequately trained and motivated? Is there enough equipment for extending the cold chain and immunization to the entire country, or should operations start in a small geographic area and be extended as possible? These questions must all be raised and answered before the establishment of immunization activities.

Delivery Characteristics of Each Vaccine

Vaccines differ in stability and refrigeration requirements. Tetanus toxoid (TT), DPT, and BCG are relatively stable and require only refrigeration at from +4°C to +8°C. DPT and TT can be stored for more than a year and a half at this temperature, while BCG can be kept for one year. However, DPT and TT must be kept from freezing. Polio vaccine is less stable than DPT and TT, while measles vaccine is presently the least heat-stable of the EPI vaccines. Both of these vaccines must be frozen at -20°C when stored for long periods, but can be kept up to two years for operational purposes. No vaccines should be kept more than one month at lower levels of the cold chain in a refrigerator at temperatures of +4°C to +8°C. (WHO, 1977).

Research is presently going on in the area of vaccine heat-stability, so changes in this information may be forthcoming in the near future. All vaccines used should be WHO-approved and of course not kept beyond their expiration date.

Cost-Effectiveness

Cost-benefit studies of immunization programs in developed countries have shown that immunization activities have a high cost-benefit ratio (Ambrosch et al., 1978; Kaplan et al., 1979; Ekblum et al., 1978). In one study in Austria, measles vaccination of all children under one year of age was shown to provide a 2.95 cost-benefit ratio over treating and caring for sick children (Ambrosch et al., 1978). Ratios would be higher for developing countries because mortality from vaccine-preventable disease is higher and prevalence greater.

While it is almost universally accepted that immunization programs are highly cost-effective when compared with the cost of treating the disease or the cost of time and productivity lost by morbidity and mortality, the question remains how to keep immunization costs to a minimum. This is especially relevant to developing countries where the amount of money available for all health programs is very low.

Estimates of the cost of running an immunization program vary greatly according to the geographic region and type of program established. WHO estimates that for the 1980s the cost per fully immunized child will be more than US $3.00, including developmental costs (WHO, 1980).

The cost of running a program in an urban area, with a high population density and ready access to health facilities, will obviously be less than that of a program in rural areas. Vaccinating from static facilities or through outreach programs is less expensive than running mobile vaccination teams in order to reach areas where there are few health facilities or widely scattered populations (WHO, 1977).

Taking into consideration the factors necessary for deciding on the strategies and tactics for immunization activities, plans of operations and coverage objectives can be set to establish the most effective system, given cost restraints. Trade-offs in percent coverage, vaccination schedule, and number of antigens to be included will have to be balanced against the amount of resources available.

For example, the minimum vaccination schedule can be arranged to require only three contacts between the child and health worker to immunize the child completely. With this schedule, BCG vaccination is delayed until the child is three months of age, and the third dose of DPT and polio is delayed until nine months, when measles vaccine is also given (WHO, 1977). Fewer contacts decrease the number of necessary staff, and also demand less time of mothers bringing their children for vaccination. If more resources are available, the schedule can be expanded to vaccinate infants at birth with BCG and give booster doses of DPT and polio. The cost must be kept to a minimum, but still meet the minimum vaccination requirements.

While the ideas of cost-benefit and cost-efficiency should be considered, the emphasis must be on effectiveness rather than cost. For example, an inexpensive vehicle, locally manufactured, may break down so often that it diminishes program effectiveness. On the other hand, the same vehicle may be easy to repair, and thus be more effective than an imported vehicle that sits idle for months while workers wait for the delivery of spare parts. The local conditions and availability of materials and personnel must be taken into consideration. The rule that cheaper is more effective (because it is more simple) seems to hold in developing countries.

Effective programs can be established in many areas even with limited funds. Using already existing health facilities, personnel, and equipment, adequate coverage can often be provided with only additional input in the form of improved management and supervision. The amount of money required to establish the central infrastructure, cold chain, and adequate services around existing health facilities is very little when compared with the benefits of immunization.

Selection and Equipment

Vaccinating a child is easy. It requires only a health worker with the proper vaccine, needles, syringes, and sterilization equipment. The major problem is logistics - how to get the equipment, potent vaccine, health worker, and accepting mother with child together in one place at the correct time. The challenge is to purchase the type of equipment that will function effectively in the given setting, with the given personnel, yet at the lowest possible cost, Cold-chain equipment for vaccine storage and transport includes cold-rooms, refrigerators, freezers, cold boxes, ice packs, vaccine carriers, thermometers, temperature alarms, time-temperature indicators, and vehicles for transport (with or without refrigeration capacity) (Ekblum et al., 1978).

Transport equipment for health workers might include bicycles, rickshaws, donkeys, mules, horses, landrovers, cars, minibuses, public transport, stout walking shoes, or plastic beach sandals. Other examples of equipment include colored pens to make posters, pens to fill in vaccination cards, kerosene stoves, boiling pans, cotton, and forceps.

Deciding on the necessary equipment is a surprisingly complex problem. A great number of variables and their interaction must be considered, and plans for backup emergency systems are needed if preliminary expectations are not fulfilled. Considerations such as the following must be answered and analyzed for each local situation:

1) How many doses and what types of vaccine are necessary?
2) Availability and quality of power sources (electricity, kerosene, or liquid propane gas).
3) Local availability of ice. How many ice packs must be frozen for cold boxes?

4) Availability of transportation and communication facilities from vaccine store to health facility. Distance?
5) Can the health facility be supplied with vaccine daily? At what intervals?
6) What are the average seasonal temperatures?
7) Geographic distribution of the target population.
8) Organization of vaccination system at health facility.

Once the quantity and type of equipment have been decided upon, the next question is: Which brands are most suitable? Again, pertinent questions must be answered for each country. A suitable piece of equipment in one country may be the worst possible choice in a neighboring country. Factors to be considered include:

1) Price of equipment.
2) Operating specifications of equipment:
   a) Equipment voltage - 120 or 220 v? 50 Hz or 60 Hz?
   b) Can it run well on impure kerosene?
   c) Is the refrigerator or freezer top-opening (which is much more efficient than a front-opening model)?
3) Reliability of manufacturer.
4) Availability of local maintenance personnel and facilities.
5) Familiarity of health personnel with different brands of equipment.
6) Equipment quality-control test results.
7) Advantages of beginning local production of some equipment.

Logistics

Along with a communications system, an effective and efficient transportation system is absolutely essential for the distribution of vaccines, supplies, and supervisory visits. In essence, supply and supervision are the two main uses of vehicles.

Supply

In order for health centers to function properly and deliver services consistently over a period of time, drugs, materials, and vaccines must be provided on a regular, uninterrupted basis. The employment of an adequate number of reliable, regularly maintained vehicles appropriate for the type of terrain is essential.

Supervision

The absence of regular supportive supervision tends to lead to complacency on the part of employees. Supervision, appropriately carried out on a regular basis, supports the continuation of quality services to the public seeking immunization among other primary health care services. In this respect, vehicles serve a twofold purpose. When questions of procedures or equipment breakdown occur, the health staff will be able to count on the regularly scheduled supervisory visit to resolve the problems. A radio communications system might also be used when questions arise.

Communications

The absence of a reliable communications system can raise havoc with any program. To rely on communications systems as they currently exist in most developing countries is to continue to deal with a high degree of uncertainty. These uncertainties cannot be tolerated when dealing with perishable vaccine shipments and fixed immunization session dates and locations. A reliable, constant system of communications can serve to avoid shortages of drugs, vaccines, and supplies; the loss of lives (medical emergencies); missed meetings; last minute correction and discussion of supply requests, accounting, or health care procedures; and delay in repair of stranded vehicles. A radio communication network will serve to improve program coordination, administration, surveillance and reporting, consultation, and continuing education.

EVALUATION

Evaluation may include monitoring activities by week or month, performing sample surveys to assess vaccination coverage, estimating the incidence of clinical disease, or carrying out serological studies (de Quadros, 1979).

Epidemiologic Surveillance System

Epidemiologic surveillance is concerned with the observations of the trend and distribution of cases and deaths attributable to the EPI target diseases (poliomyelitis, measles, diphtheria, tetanus, pertussis, and tuberculosis) in the population, in order to institute the necessary control measures on a timely basis (Ambrosch et al., 1978).

The activities of surveillance involve the collecting, recording, reporting, and interpreting of disease data. For each disease the following information should be known:

- How many cases are there?
- How many deaths?
- Who contracts the disease?
- Where did they contract the disease?
- When did they contract the disease?
- Were they previously vaccinated?
- How old is the patient?

The supervisor of vaccination activities at each level is responsible for ensuring that disease surveillance activities are conducted properly. The collection of this information should begin at the local (health center) level and be passed upward to the national level, where it will be used in the decision-making process leading to broader immunization activity improvements. Information collected at all levels will be used at those respective levels as circumstances dictate at the time of collection. Those responsible persons at the local level do not have to wait for surveillance information to be passed back down from the national level before acting.

Quality Control of Vaccines

A vial of potent vaccine held in the hand of a vaccinator looks and feels the same as impotent vaccine. Only through circumstantial evidence or tests after vaccination can it be determined whether the vaccine will protect the vaccinated child or pregnant woman. If a functioning system of quality control has been maintained, then the probability will be strong that the vaccine is good and will protect the person vaccinated. Without quality control at all levels, the vaccine must be suspect.

Quality control also serves as an evaluation mechanism. If the vaccine being used at the lowest field levels is tested and found potent, it is a good sign that the entire delivery system is functioning well. If quality control is maintained, it can serve as an effective mechanism to pinpoint trouble spots in a program which require attention. The alternative to quality control is to find that the vaccinated children are becoming sick with the disease they were supposedly immunized against. By then it is too late, since the harmful loss of public confidence has already taken place.

Monitoring quality control must begin in the country at the airport where the vaccine is received. Notation of the condition of the vials and storage temperatures must continue while the vaccine is in transit to the central stores and so on, down to the local level. If records of the vaccine show it has been exposed only to the proper temperatures for its entire lifetime, and the records are accurate, it is a strong indication that the vaccine is potent.

If a vaccine control laboratory is established in a country, it can carry out the dual function of checking the quality of incoming vaccines, and checking the quality of vaccines that have been distributed and handled within the country. Samples can be taken from all levels and checked within the country at the control laboratory (An Evaluation Report of the Expanded Program on Immunization, 1979).

CONCLUSION

The purpose of this paper is to outline the numerous factors involved in the operation of an immunization program. The importance of logistics, communication, the cold chain, training, supervision, and evaluation has been delineated. This paper should serve as the technical background for those considering inclusion of immunization activities in their programs. Aside from the technical issues outlined above, other concerns must be addressed, including: socio-cultural context, involvement of the community, health education needs, access to health facilities, and utilization of those facilities. These issues, as well as those discussed above, present significant areas of consideration in any immunization program.

REFERENCES

Ambrosch, F., G. Widderman, G. Harasek. "Costs and benefits of measles vaccination." Fortschr Med. 96,8 (Feb. 1978): 409-14.

An Evaluation Report of the Expanded Program on Immunization. A joint Ministry of Health/DANIDA/WHO/UNICEF Report, June 1978. Geneva: 3rd printing, October 1979.

Brandling-Bennett, A.D. and T.S. Jones. "Reporte preliminar de una evaluacion del programa nacional de immunizacion de la republica de Guatemala." U.S. Center for Disease Control, May 29, 1979 (unpublished).

de Quadros, C.A. "More Effective Immunization." Paper presented at the Royal Society meeting for discussion of More Technologies for Rural Health, London, Nov. 2, 1979.

Ekblum, M. O. Elo, J. Laurikain, P. Niemelo. "Costs and benefits of measles vaccination in Finland." Scand. J. Soc. Med. 6,3 (1978): 111-115.

Kaplan, J.P., S.C. Schoenbaum, M.C. Weinstein, and D.W. Frase. "Pertussis vaccine - an analysis of Benefits, Risks, and Costs." New Eng. J. Med. 301,17 (1979): 906.

Mahler, H. "Blueprint for health for all." WHO Chronicle 31 (1977): 491-498.

PAHO/WHO. Expanded Program on Immunization (EPI) Course on Planning, Management, and Evaluation. Washington, DC: 1979.

PAHO/WHO. EPI Training Workshop. Washington, DC: 1980a.

PAHO/WHO. Progress Report: Expanded Program on Immunization in the Americas. (CE84/16). Washington, DC: May 9, 1980b.

WHO. EPI Manual of Operations (EPI/G/77.1). Geneva: 1977.

WHO. International Conference on Primary Health Care, Alma-Ata, USSR, Sept. 6-12, 1978. A joint report by the Director General of WHO and the Executive Director of UNICEF, Geneva-New York: 1978.

WHO. EPI Global Medium Term Program, WHO document (EPI/GEN/80/2). Geneva: Feb. 1, 1980.

WHO/CDC. Expanded Program on Immunization (EPI), Mid-Level Managers Training Course. Geneva: 1980.

18
The Use of Tetanus Toxoid in a Community-Based Distribution Project in Rural Bangladesh

Shushum Bhatia

The family planning activities of the International Center for Diarrheal Disease Research, Bangladesh (ICDDR,B) in a village-based, integrated family planning/maternal and child health (MCH) project in the Matlab field surveillance area have been described in a separate workshop paper (Bhatia, this volume). This paper emphasizes the project's activities with respect to tetanus toxoid immunization for pregnant women.

HEALTH INTERVENTIONS IN THE FPHSP

Initially the FPHSP provided modern contraceptive methods and related family planning services exclusively. During the period, through training provided at weekly sessions, the FVWs gradually gained increasing knowledge about MCH care. Over time they were able to transmit added information about nutrition and hygienic practices during pregnancy, delivery, and breastfeeding, to the women in their work area. By June 1978, FVWs began to give tetanus immunization and iron and folate tablets to pregnant women.

The criteria for selection of the health interventions, and the sequence in which they were introduced, were based on results of social surveys and epidemiologic studies which identified priority areas. New topics were introduced gradually to enable FVWs to absorb and assimilate the new knowledge. This also provided FVWs time to test relevance and appropriateness of the knowledge in the field prior to its final implementation.

Tetanus Immunization

During the fortnightly visits, the FVWs informed all eligible women and their families about the advantages of tetanus immunization. By June 1978, when the FVWs were trained to deliver the immunization, those pregnant women who agreed to accept the vaccine were given a total of three doses on a schedule of 0.5 ml each during the sixth, seventh, and eighth months of pregnancy. On the recommendation of the World Health Organization (WHO), this schedule was modified to a two-dose schedule - the first 0.5 ml dose was provided any time after the fifth month of pregnancy, and the second at a minimum of four weeks later, preferably a month before the date of delivery.

The vaccine (an aluminum-phosphate-absorbed tetanus toxoid) was procured from the WHO office in Dacca. WHO guidelines on "cold-chain" procedures for storage, transport, and delivery of the vaccine were followed. The vaccine was transported to Dacca in specially designed cold-thermoses. From Matlab, the vaccines were sent to the subcenters in cold-boxes with refresher freezer packs. The FVWs collected the vaccine from the subcenters and took it to the homes of pregnant women where the dose was given using 1 cc disposable syringes. All unused vaccines left over at the end of the day were discarded.

Records for the pregnant women, with their immunization schedules and the dates on which the toxoid was given, were maintained by the FVWs in a register book.

Impact of the FPHSP

The effect of the tetanus immunization on neonatal death rates was calculated using data from the demographic surveillance system (Rahman et al., 1981). As some women in the FPHSP area had received tetanus vaccine during a double-blind trial of a cholera vaccine in 1974, comparisons can be made for neonatal death rates by age at death for infants born to three groups of women. The three groups to be compared are women who were never immunized, those immunized during 1974 and those immunized during FPHSP between September 1978 and December 1979. The results are given in Figure 18:1. The results suggest that the infants of mothers who had received full immunization during 1978-79 had lower death rates between days 5 to 12 and 6 to 15, respectively, in comparison to infants whose mothers had accepted no immunization either in 1974 or in 1978 to 1979.

Table 18:1 shows rates of neonatal mortality (0 to 28 days) and neonatal mortality on days 4 to 14, when tetanus is considered to be the predominant cause of death. The neonatal mortality rates of 42.8 (0 to 28 days) and 10.7 (4 to 14 days) were considerably lower for women who were immunized during 1978 to 1979 than they were for the other two groups.

An examination of stillbirths among these three groups and a comparison of the stillbirth ratios (per 1,000 live births) revealed findings shown in Table 18:2. The stillbirth ratios were lowest for women who were immunized during 1978 to 1979. The difference between this group and the other two was statistically significant.

On the whole, by mid-1979, the crude birth rate, the crude death rate, and the infant neonatal and postneonatal mortalities were lower in the FPHSP area than in the comparison area (Table 18:3). Although the lower crude death rate in the FPHSP may have been mainly due to differences in the age structure of the two populations (because of the reduced number of births in the

FPHSP area), the contribution of health services, including tetanus immunization, cannot be ruled out.

Table 18:1. Neonatal and 4-14 Day Mortality among Live Birth Cohort (September 1978-December 1979) According to Maternal Immunization Status during Nonpregnancy in 1974 or during Pregnancy in 1978-79, Matlab, Bangladesh

IMMUNIZATION STATUS	BOTH AREAS		FPHSP AREA		COMPARISON AREA	
	No.	Rate	No.	Rate	No.	Rate
Fully Immunized during Nonpregnancy (1974)						
Live births	956	-	436	-	520	-
Neonatal (0-28 days) deaths	61	63.8	28	64.2	33	63.5
4-14 day deaths	19	19.9	7	16.1[e]	12	23.1
Fully Immunized during Pregnancy (1978-1979)						
Live births	934	-	934	-	-	-
Neonatal (0-28 days) deaths	40	42.8[a]	40	42.8[c]	-	-
4-14 day deaths	10	10.7[b]	10	10.7[d]	-	-
Never Immunized						
Live births	7,237	-	2,379	-	4,858	-
Neonatal (0-28 day) deaths	567	78.3[a]	199	83.6[c]	368	75.7
4-14 day deaths	246	34.0[b]	82	34.5[d,e]	164	33.8

$P < 0.01$ comparison a, b, c, d
$P < 0.05$ comparison e
All other comparisons are not significant.

Figure 18:1. Neonatal Death Rates by Age of Death for Infants Born Between September 1, 1978 and December 31,1979 According to Maternal Tetanus Immunization Status, Matlab, Bangladesh

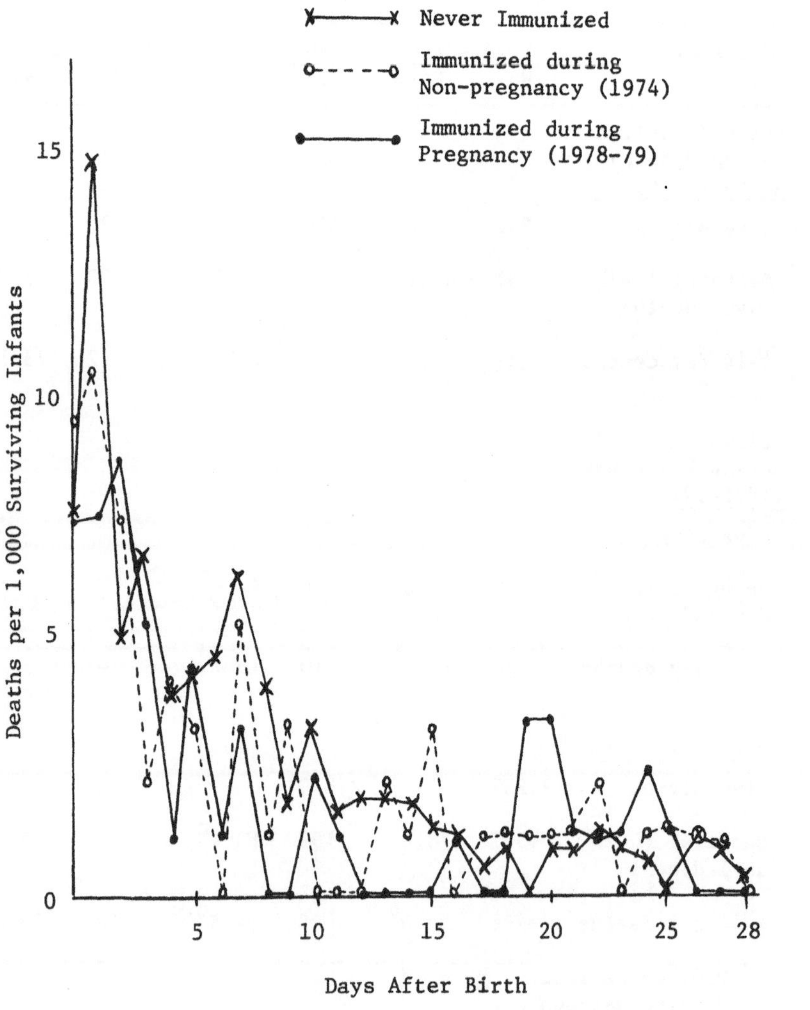

Table 18:2. Stillbirth Ratio (Per 1,000 Live Births) among Birth Cohort (September 1978-December 1979) According to Maternal Immunization Status during Nonpregnancy (1974) or during Pregnancy (1978-1979), Matlab, Bangladesh

IMMUNIZATION STATUS	LIVE BIRTHS*	STILLBIRTHS	
		No.	Rate
Fully immunized during nonpregnancy (1974)	956	44	46.0[a]
Fully immunized during pregnancy (1978-1979)	934	24	25.7[b]
Never immunized	7,237	313	43.3[c]

P < 0.05 comparison ab, bc

* FPHSP and comparison areas combined.

Table 18:3. Mid-year Population, Numbers and Rates of Selected Vital Events in Matlab, Bangladesh (1979) by Area

VITAL EVENTS	FPHSP AREA		COMPARISON AREA	
	No.	Rate*	No.	Rate*
Total population (estimated mid-1979)	90,134	-	86,649	-
Live births	3,131	34.7	4,061	46.9
Deaths:				
All ages	1,080	12.0	1,342	15.5
Infant	358	114.3	477	117.4
Neonatal	221	70.6	298	73.4
Postneonatal	137	43.8	179	44.1

* Crude birth and death rates are per 1,000 population. Infant, neonatal and postneonatal mortality rates are per 1,000 related live births.

A number of the findings in the project merit further consideration. The use of tetanus toxoid should not effect still births, nor lower death rates during the first two days of life (a finding for which there is some evidence in Figure 18:1). It is thus possible that other factors, such as client self selection may have been operating: women who were more motivated or who differed in other important characteristics may have sought antenatal care more readily. Nonetheless, the overall trend in reduction of death rates between days 4 and 14 suggests a positive effect of the tetanus toxoid.

Difficulties Encountered

A few difficulties were encountered early in the life of the service delivery. In the first year, only approximately 30 percent of pregnant women received the vaccine. Three possibilities were considered in discussing the difficulties in achieving full coverage. First, people may have mistaken the immunization for the injectable contraceptive Depo-Provera. Second, pregnant women may leave their husband's home to return to their own family for the gestation period. They are thus missed by the project. Finally, workers may not have been available, or may have had difficulty finding the woman at the time the vaccine was due.

The first possibility was considered unlikely, since no correlation was found between tetanus toxoid acceptance and post-use of family planning. (Knowledge of family planning, or use of Depo-Provera by relatives or neighbors was not controlled for.) The second and third possibilities may each have accounted for some percentage of women who were not immunized. However, they cannot clearly account for the entire large group not receiving the tetanus toxoid.

Matlab is currently considering mass immunization of all women of reproductive age as a means of overcoming the problem. In trials of mass coverage, acceptance rates reached 55 percent.

CONCLUSION

As had been its aim, the CBD program has not only reduced fertility, but has probably been responsible for reducing mortality as well. It should also be noted that the success in implementing tetanus toxoid was due in no small part to the fact that the Matlab CBD project is part of a well-organized program with many manpower and logistic resources. The tight organization makes it possible to organize an effective cold-chain and ensure that workers are available to deliver the immunization at the required times.

REFERENCES

Bhatia, S., W.H. Mosley, A.S.G. Faruque, and J. Chakraborty. "The Matlab Family Planning Health Services Project." Studies in Family Planning 11,6 (1980).

Rahman, M., L.C. Chen et al. Reduction of Neonatal Mortality by Immunization of Non-pregnant Women and Women During Pregnancy with Aluminum Absorbed Tetanus Toxoid. Scientific Report No. 41, Bangladesh: International Center for Diarrheal Disease Research, Bangladesh, 1981.

Part Seven

Other Therapeutic Interventions

19
Selected Health Components for Community-Based Distribution Programs

Robert L. Parker

Over the years, health services have been provided along with family planning in various health care settings. Only recently, however, has there been concerted effort to identify selected health interventions that can be combined effectively with family planning efforts for dissemination in community-based distribution (CBD) contraceptive programs. The purpose of this paper is to summarize the potential for CBD programs to distribute a wide range of health services that have as a common denominator their relevance to primary health care. A number of specific interventions (excluding those discussed in separate workshop papers) and a general framework for intervention selection will be discussed.

RATIONALE FOR INTEGRATION

The basic rationale for combining health interventions with community-based distribution of contraceptives can be considered from three somewhat different points of view.

First, when contraceptive use and its consequence on fertility are the primary concerns of a program, the inclusion of health care may be justified primarily on the basis that health services:

- May make family planning more acceptable to individual couples, communities, and countries; and,
- Increase the use of contraceptives.

These points depend on the selection of services which will not jeopardize existing family planning programs through negative side effects, whether related to the health interventions themselves or to the manner in which they are implemented.

Potential health effects and the community's perceived need for health services, are also important criteria for selection of health interventions to be combined with contraceptive distribution. In terms of the first rationale, however, the family planning effects remain a central focus for program organization and implementation. The measures of success in such projects include contraceptive prevalence rates, especially use by target segments of the population, and cost-effectiveness of the combined services in contrast to unipurpose family planning models.

In terms of the second approach, the combination of health and family planning is in itself the objective because of its theoretical potential to improve project efficiency. Program managers, often starting with unipurpose health or family planning programs, seek to provide both health and family planning services in order to make more efficient use of manpower and other resources. Unipurpose fieldworkers are often viewed as an underutilized resource capable of performing additional services at only marginal cost increases. A variation of this approach involves combining the functions of several unipurpose workers into the job description of one worker, and reducing the geographic area covered per worker. This is done to reduce travel time or time spent locating clients. Measures of success include cost per unit of service or cost-effectiveness where effect is measured using both health and family planning indicators.

A third approach assumes no predetermined difference in the priority given to health or family planning interventions. Under ideal circumstances, local communities working with health and family planning workers assess the health and fertility planning needs of their area and develop plans for a practical program of combined interventions. This combination should effectively meet the needs having the highest priority but take into account constraints on local resources. In areas with limited resources, the combination of services may consist of a very few basic health interventions along with simple family planning measures. Success would be monitored using both community-determined and professionally determined indicators of health services and family planning utilization and effect. Cost-effectiveness measures would be very useful in justifying the use of the limited resources.

SELECTION CRITERIA

When individual health interventions are considered from these three integration perspectives, differing values may be assigned to the intervention's efficacy, community demand for the intervention, and its enhancement of family planning practice. The first approach would weigh the enhancement effect more than efficacy or demand, although these latter are certainly considered. In contrast, the second approach would emphasize efficacy and enhancement more than community demand, while the third approach would probably consider efficacy, demand, and family planning enhancement equally.

In the subsequent consideration of health interventions an attempt will, therefore, be made to assess their efficacy (potential results significantly affecting health), the probable community demand for each intervention, and their potential for enhancing family planning practice. Other criteria will also be considered, as pointed out by Wawer (this volume), including the seriousness of the health problem to be treated in terms of mortality and disability, the extent of the problem measured by incidence or prevalence, the target group involved (age and sex), the cost, and the simplicity of the intervention in terms of manpower, skills, referral and supervisory backup, supply logistics, and required time frame.

SELECTED HEALTH INTERVENTIONS

Health interventions that might be combined with community-based contraceptive distribution can be categorized broadly into "specific" therapeutic interventions for a given condition or illness, and "combined" service interventions which simultaneously provide a number of services for a specific group, such as women or children. The former can be further subdivided into disease specific and symptom specific. Although general services usually include specific health interventions that are quite effective, their special consequences for family planning practice may be a phenomenon related to the general availability of multiple services and, therefore, greater than the sum of the individual intervention enhancement effects. Each of these categories is briefly outlined using the criteria listed above and then summarized in tabular form at the end of the paper.

Disease Specific

Four specific health interventions - oral rehydration, immunization, antihelminthics, and nutrition - are discussed elsewhere in the volume. Those considered here include pneumonia, pharyngitis (sore throat), otitis, conjunctivitis, skin infections, superficial injuries, genitourinary problems, obstetrical care, tuberculosis, and malaria.

Pneumonia

In general, pneumonia, or severe lower respiratory tract infection, is a major problem for the very young and the elderly. In developing countries it is often one of the more frequent causes of infant and child deaths. Studies in the Punjab, India (Kielmann et al., 1983) found that pneumonia was the primary cause in over 17 percent of deaths between eight days and five years of age, and it was a contributing cause in over 4 percent of other deaths. It was second only to diarrhea, which was the primary cause of 37 percent of deaths in this age-group. The mortality rate under one year of age was approximately 20 to 25 pneumonia deaths per 1,000 live births, and from one to three years about four to five deaths per 1,000 children. While lower respiratory tract infection as a disease, however, does not occur very frequently (annual incidence of about 180 per 1,000 children under one, and less than half that rate from one to three years), case fatality rates of 12 and 6 percent explain why mortality from this problem is so important in these two age groups.

In establishing a target population for a pneumonia intervention in community-based programs, concentration should probably be placed on infants and young children. Although many lower respiratory tract infections may be viral in origin, secondary bacterial infection makes the use of antibiotics in all cases of suspected pneumonia relatively straightforward. Early routine use of an injection of aqueous penicillin followed by a long-acting penicillin injection has been proven feasible for village-based auxiliaries to deliver (Kielmann et al., 1983). The treatment was very effective, lowering the deaths due to pneumonia by 45 percent within one year after its addition to the primary care interventions that the auxiliaries could provide. In this setting a good referral system to support the auxiliaries was already in place, but had previously only been moderately successful in dealing with pneumonia.

In terms of complexity, this type of intervention depends on a well-organized community-based health service that uses well-trained auxiliaries who are continually available in the community and can, therefore, detect early pneumonia and institute appropriate treatment. Adequate backup by a competent supervisor, and the resupply of syringes, needles, and penicillin from the area health center are needed.

Using the rule of thumb that a minimum of 12 cases must be seen annually by each worker to maintain competence, the community-based health worker would have to be responsible for the health care of a population of at least 800 (15 percent of the population being under five years of age, with an annual pneumonia incidence of about 10 percent yields 12 cases). From the experience in India the cost for this type of intervention in 1971 prices was estimated to be approximately Rs.7.50 ($1.00) per case identified and treated, or about Rs.150 ($20.00) per pneumonia death averted (Kielmann et al., 1983; Dept. of International Health, Johns Hopkins University, unpublished).* About one-third of this amount is related to drug costs. Because of the low incidence of pneumonia, however, the annual cost per child under five would be only about 9 cents, while the cost per capita would be a little more than one cent. Since this type of intervention can only be effective if provided as part of a program in which children are monitored closely, the cost of surveillance should also be estimated. In Narangwal this was roughly $2.00 per child per year or $0.30 per capita (Kielmann et al., 1983; Dept. of International Health, Johns Hopkins University, unpublished). Moreover, these surveillance costs should be distributed among all interventions included in a CBD program.

The community demand for this type of service is generally high in most rural populations that have had any exposure to modern medicine. Although pneumonia is much less frequent than diarrhea, children in respiratory distress generally evoke an

* These and subsequent cost estimates from the Narangwal studies are based on 1971 prices.

immediate health care seeking response by parents which is quite different from the situation with diarrhea. The potential link to community-based family planning programs is obviously dependent on the latter program being an ongoing effort in a specific community and not a single contact program or one based on widely spaced visits. Under the conditions of frequent interaction between the health worker and the community, evidence from the Narangwal studies (Taylor et al., 1983) suggests that this type of contact, involving both ongoing surveillance and early treatment of children, enhanced family planning practice in that rural community.

Sore Throat and Otitis Media

The type and complexity of interventions for sore throat and otitis media are very similar to that for pneumonia. Respiratory illnesses, especially of the upper respiratory tract, are often the most common illnesses seen by primary care workers. Various estimates indicate that they account for about one-fourth of all illness (Dept. of International Health, Johns Hopkins University, 1976; Institute of Medicine, Tribhuvan University, 1977). Most require only symptomatic care since they are minor and no specific interventions are available to treat them. (See treatment of fever under symptom-specific interventions.)

Sore Throat. Acute pharyngitis, although often of viral origin, is an upper respiratory illness that can be treated easily on those occasions when it is of bacterial origin (that is, streptococcal): signs indicative of the latter are relatively consistent, especially in older children and include redness and exudate. Little is known of the acute mortality or the long-term seriousness of streptococcal infections in developing countries. However, well-controlled outcome studies in the United States document the efficacy of identifying and treating streptococcal sore throat for reducing rheumatic fever and its complications (Gordes, 1973). Health authorities in Shanghai, China, have indicated that rheumatic heart disease was the first or second most common heart disorder among persons who were children before 1949, and that the occurrence of rheumatic heart disease has dropped dramatically since the availability of adequate primary care services (Gu Xing-yuan, 1981).

The incidence of sore throat sufficiently severe to initiate use of a health service has been estimated as approximately one episode per capita per year in the Punjab and Nepal (Dept. of International Health, Johns Hopkins University, 1976; Institute of Medicine, Tribhuvan University, 1977). The proportion of these episodes that could be clinically classified as streptococcal has been stated to be as high as 10 percent (Cecil and Loeb, 1959). With appropriate training, auxiliaries can recognize the signs and symptoms of an exudative pharyngitis and treat with either oral or long-acting injectable penicillin. The complexity of training, supervision, and resupply is similar to that required for pneumonia, but the frequency of contacts with the community would probably not have to be as intense, and the population required to maintain competence could be as small as 120 (300 if the target population is limited to children under 15).

Otitis Media. Otitis media is often a complication of upper respiratory infections and can be viral in origin, but frequently involves secondary bacterial infection. Ear infections are very common in young children. In Nepal and India (Dept. of International Health, Johns Hopkins University, 1976; Institute of Medicine, Tribhuvan University, 1977), an overall incidence of 0.6 episodes per person per year has been estimated, with children under five having at least one episode per year. In addition, as an indication of the potential seriousness of the condition, the prevalence of hearing disabilities found in children 5 to 14 years of age in Nepal, assumed to be mostly a result of otitis media, was around 2 percent.

The complexity of the intervention for otitis media is similar to that for sore throats and involves oral sulfa, penicillin, other antibiotics, or penicillin injections. The minimum population required to maintain competence would be about 200, again assuming 12 cases should be seen by the worker each year. Early detection would depend on teaching a simple set of signs and symptoms such as fever, ear pain, pulling at the ear, and irritability of the child. Use of an otoscope for more precise diagnosis can be taught to auxiliaries, but is much more difficult and expensive and would usually only be used to confirm a diagnosis already made through the fairly specific signs and symptoms. Later cases with purulent drainage would be obvious, but since many would be in a recurrent, chronic state, the outcome of their treatment is less certain.

The cost for treatment of a case of sore throat or otitis media will be lower than that for a case of pneumonia, based on the need for about half the number of treatments or follow-up contacts by the community-level worker. The costs related to training, supervisory backup, and the medicines involved would be only slightly less. Because otitis media and sore throat have a higher incidence than pneumonia, the annual costs per capita can be roughly estimated to be two cents for pharyngitis and five cents for otitis (Kielmann et al., 1983; Dept. of International Health, Johns Hopkins University, unpublished).

Community demand for these two interventions is believed to be fairly high since the associated discomfort is significant, although usually self-limited. As in the case of pneumonia, and for the same reasons, detection and treatment of acute pharyngitis and otitis media in children should enhance family planning efforts, but again under the conditions of a fixed community-based program requiring ongoing availability and contacts. Since it could involve individuals no longer of reproductive age, treatment of sore throats in adults would have a less direct consequence on contraceptive use. In this case, however, general acceptability of health workers could be indirectly helpful.

Conjunctivitis

Eye infections were found to be quite common among children in the Punjab, with an average of 3.1 episodes per year per child under one, and 2.3 episodes per year for children one to three years of age. Each episode lasted about ten days. The incidence across all ages in India and Nepal (Dept. of International Health, Johns Hopkins University, 1976; Institute of Medicine, Tribuvan University, 1977) was about 0.9 illnesses per person per year. In these countries, trachoma is still a problem, but long-term effects such as corneal scarring are being seen much less frequently, possibly due to the general availability of antibiotic eye ointment and drops.

Treatment of simple, non-trachomatous, eye infections is not complex and can be done by someone with minimal training, or taught to mothers or family members. Except for resupply of medicines, the intervention requires much less backup in terms of a system for referrals or supervision. Points which must be taught to household members are relatively few in number: the recognition of conjunctivitis, the correct method of instilling the medication, and the need to prevent contamination of the ointment or drops. In order to see 12 cases a year, the minimum service population would be about 50 if the intervention were provided mainly for infants and children. The general treatment of symptomatic eye infections using topical antibiotics is quite effective and seems to be well accepted and demanded by the community. (Topical treatment of trachoma is more complex, in that the duration of the therapeutic regimen is long and relapses are common.)

The simplicity of the treatment for non trachomatous conjunctivitis and the ease of instructing and supplying families makes it a potentially useful component of either a single- or multiple-visit CBD program. Its major strength is in reducing discomfort and the possible progression of the infection to a stage that might impair vision, although the extent of the latter progression is not known. The cost of such an intervention is not great if much of the responsibility of carrying out the treatment is shifted to the family. In India one small tube of antibiotic ointment, adequate for at least three eye infections, costs about Rs.1.20 ($0.16). If care were initiated by a health worker for half of all cases in children under 15, the cost per capita would be about 8 cents per year (Kielmann et al., 1983; Dept. of International Health, JHU, unpublished). The potential of this intervention to enhance family planning probably would be through increasing the credibility of the community health worker. This individual would be seen by the community as having an effective treatment for eye infections and could either apply the treatments or supply them to the family.

Skin Infections

Skin infections generally can be classified as bacterial, fungal, or scabies. Fairly specific and simple treatment protocols can be developed for each based on antibiotic ointments, Whitfield's ointment (6% benzoic acid and 3% salicylic acid), and benzyl benzoate, respectively. The detection of cases and correct therapy could be taught to almost any level of community worker who in turn could readily teach families to use them appropriately as each case arose. If treatment for all of these common skin problems is instituted in a project, it is preferable that the worker be the one to initiate treatment for each new case: the worker will have been trained to recognize the pathognomonic signs of each condition and select the appropriate medication. Treatment can be continued by the family. In situations where it is desirable that household members themselves initiate treatment, it may be preferable to limit the intervention to one of the more easily recognizable conditions, such as scabies.

Skin conditions are not generally sufficiently serious to require immediate therapy or frequent follow-up. Their treatment thus represents a suitable intervention even in those projects with a limited number of client-worker contacts. Less costly, but somewhat less effective, treatment of bacterial infections of the skin would involve the use of gentian violet. In all of the above conditions, the appropriate use of soap and water should be taught both as part of the treatment and as a means of prevention. Consideration can be given to including soap distribution as part of the intervention. The one CBD project where distribution of soap was attempted (in the Philippines) was unable to demonstrate an effect on family planning and did not determine how the soap was used or whether it had an impact on health. However, the idea is promising enough that it should probably be tried again, possibly in combination with the more specific curative skin therapies.

Skin-related interventions might include training workers to incise boils and abscesses. However, more technical skill and equipment are required: to determine the need for incision, to carry it out appropriately, and to accomplish any necessary drainage or other post-care. The knowledge and skills can probably be taught to community workers and when used should produce a very visible and gratifying effect (Rural Health Research Center, 1974), but only in well-organized programs with ready access to supervision. Referral of individuals with abscesses is probably more appropriate in most CBD programs. Because of their visibility and frequently associated discomfort, treatment of skin conditions meets a readily perceived need of the community and may positively affect acceptance of the health worker out of proportion to the seriousness of the condition.

In Punjab, infants on the average annually experienced 1.2 episodes of skin infection lasting about 10 days each. The population as a whole in Northern India and Nepal reported about 0.8 episodes per person per year, making it very easy for community health workers to maintain their skills in relation to this condition. Data from Punjab show that in that setting treatment of about half of all skin infections in children under 15 would cost an estimated $0.20 per child per year or eight cents per capita (Kielmann et al., 1983; Dept. of International Health, Johns Hopkins University, unpublished).

Superficial Injuries

Cuts, bruises, sprains, and minor burns occur frequently, with a reported incidence of 0.5 per person per year (Dept. of International Health, Johns Hopkins University, 1976; Institute of Medicine, Tribhuvan University, 1977). Many are cared for at home using traditional treatments. However, they do account for a significant proportion of demand for services, making up about 10 percent of conditions for which care is sought in government outpatient clinics in Nepal (Institute of Medicine, Tribhuvan University, 1977). Much of the care for injuries involves simple hygiene and first aid which can be readily taught. Although considerably less frequent, severe accidents are dramatic as well as life threatening, and when feasible, recognition and referral guidelines could be a part of the training for care of injuries. In general, because of their low frequency, community workers serving a limited population cannot be expected to maintain knowledge concerning the handling of serious accidents other than simple referral instructions.

In settings with even simple facilities where limited splinting and suturing equipment can be supplied and maintained, the ability to suture lacerations and splint simple fractures is a possibility. It should be noted that these tasks require a higher level of skill than is usually provided to a community worker, a reasonable supply system and an adequate level of supervision and retraining. In a rural hospital in Puerto Rico the incidence of such injuries was about 30 per 1,000 population per year (R. L. Parker, unpublished), indicating that a fairly large population is needed to maintain competence. However, as with incision and drainage, the procedures are dramatic and health workers who are trained to do such procedures may gain the respect of the community. The cost of therapeutic interventions for each case of superficial injury would be similar to that for skin infections. Although per capita cost would be lower due to the lower incidence of such injuries, the costs of additional training and supervision for workers have to be considered. The annual per capita cost of treatment can be expected to be approximately $0.05, based on data from Punjab (Dept. of International Health, Johns Hopkins University, unpublished).

Genitourinary Problems

A cluster of problems seldom considered in community-based programs includes urinary tract infections, especially cystitis, urethral discharge in men, and vaginitis in women. Cystitis, although not generally life threatening, is particularly frequent in women of reproductive age. Urethral and vaginal discharges are culturally important problems in the Indian subcontinent and possibly in other areas also. They are seen within the traditional belief system as evidence of losing vital life substances and, therefore, are doubly disturbing if one also includes their often irritating physical discomfort. Estimates from the Indian and Nepali (Dept. Of International Health, Johns

Hopkins University, 1976; Institute of Medicine, Tribhuvan University, 1977) surveys show that all genitourinary problems combined produce three to six days of illness per person per year, with an incidence of just under 0.5 episodes per capita per year, a fairly significant level of morbidity.

For most cases of cystitis, urethritis and vaginitis, signs and symptoms can be learned that indicate the need for sulfa drugs or another urinary tract antibiotic, with or without antiseptic (for cystitis and urethritis), or a broad-spectrum vaginal suppository. Injectable penicillin is indicated if gonococcal infection is suspected. The efficacy of these treatments is generally good, with rapid relief of symptoms. However, the problems all may recur frequently because of reinfection, anatomical abnormalities, or incomplete cures. They can also be relatively costly since they may require use of medicine over a number of weeks (the one exception would be male urethritis of gonococcal origin, which would respond to one injection of penicillin).

Based on experience in the Punjab, an approximate minimum cost per case for most of these problems would be about $0.60 (Dept. of International Health, Johns Hopkins University, unpublished). The maintenance of supplies and supervision to assure appropriate use and levels of skill would make this intervention most appropriate in a well-organized and stable community-based program with good facility backup. Under these conditions, it could significantly and directly affect men and especially women of reproductive age, raising the credibility of the health worker, increasing the acceptability of family planning advice, and providing evidence that the worker is someone who can be turned to if there are any problems or side effects of contraceptives, a particularly prevalent concern in Kenya (Parker, unpublished) and certainly common to some degree the world over.

Obstetrical Care

A significantly underrated problem in developing countries with traditional patterns of childbirth is mortality directly associated with birth trauma, intrauterine anoxia, and prematurity. This is true even excluding the contributions of prematurity to deaths classified as due to malnutrition or infectious diseases. In the Punjab (Kielmann et al., 1983), out of 104 perinatal deaths per 1,000 stillbirths plus live births, 39 were found to be associated with anoxia and birth trauma, while 34 were classified directly as prematurity. In addition, eight deaths directly due to prematurity after seven days of age per 1,000 live births were reported (Kielmann et al., 1983). In terms of relative importance, deaths due to these two causes almost equaled deaths due to diarrhea and pneumonia combined in children under three years of age.

Clear-cut, simple and universal interventions for these two problems have yet to be well worked out. One of the major difficulties is the wide variation in birth practices from area to area. However, there is evidence that some specific interventions could make a difference. In the Narangwal nutrition study, a 40 percent decrease in perinatal deaths was associated with simple antenatal care composed of dietary and health advice, routine provision of iron and folic acid, and voluntary food supplementation to underweight mothers. It is postulated that this intervention produced its main effect through reducing mortality related to prematurity or low birth weight.

Training of traditional birth attendants (TBAs) is probably the widest and best studied intervention related to improving the outcome of pregnancies (Simpson-Hebert et al., 1980). However, data to determine the overall effect of training TBAs on perinatal mortality and morbidity are either incomplete or inconclusive. The one exception may be the reduction of neonatal tetanus which has been demonstrated in Haiti (Simpson-Hebert et al., 1980; Berggren et al., 1980) and in Bangladesh (Bhatia, this volume). In Bangladesh one study estimated that up to 20 percent of maternal mortality could be eliminated simply by having adequately trained village midwives (Simpson-Hebert et al., 1980). In Narangwal, researchers estimated that almost 40 percent of deaths due to intrauterine anoxia were directly associated with intramuscular pitocin injections given by local practitioners at the request of the midwife. In addition, breech deliveries accounted for about 60 percent of deaths due to birth trauma (Kielmann et al., 1983). Assuming training of TBAs could stop the former and provide skills to deal with the latter (improved delivery techniques or early identification and referral), the researchers estimated the total perinatal death rate could have been reduced by 18 percent through these two specific program components.

Obstetrical interventions would require a well-designed training program for TBAs with continuing supervision and backup referral capability. This cannot be a one-shot program, but requires ongoing contacts between a health system and the community. Costs for such a program, including the initial training, would be relatively low if one used existing TBAs, although it would vary from program to program depending on the educational and literacy levels of the TBAs and their current practices. Such factors would influence length of training and the frequency of field supervision. Another important consideration in working with TBAs is that they have been used successfully to promote family planning (Simpson-Hebert et al., 1980). The potential for a link between maternal services and receptivity to contraceptive use which has been widely considered, remains one of the theoretical bases for integration of services and deserves further testing.

Tuberculosis

Active pulmonary TB is reported in over 1 percent of the population in many developing countries. Death rates exceed 1.0 per 1,000 where there are no adequate control programs (Benenson, 1970); Haiti has a cause-specific death rate of 0.8 per 1,000. Reduction of morbidity and mortality has been attempted through BCG immunizations (deQuadros, this volume) and through mass control campaigns. The relative efficacy of these approaches, particularly the use of BCG in developing countries, is not clear. In a primary care project in Haiti, Berggren and coworkers document a 50 percent reduction in TB deaths as a result of a TB control program which included sputum collection, and treatment and follow-up of cases. The entire project was targeted to a number of health problems other than TB alone, and cost an average of $1.60 per capita. In Punjab, the cost per treated case was $8.00, producing a cost of about eight cents per capita annually (Dept. of International Health, Johns Hopkins University, unpublished).

Any influence from larger programs, such as the National Tuberculosis Program in India, is difficult to document. China, as in many activities it has undertaken, is an exception, with reports of marked success in TB control based on the efforts of barefoot doctors (Han Jia-jing and Yang Sheng-ji, 1982).

Where such programs are carried out, they contain a number of simple activities which can be learned by community workers and which can be combined with other surveillance activities and contraceptive distribution. Community workers or auxiliaries are required to periodically visit families, collecting sputum from persons with chronic cough, and then referring and following up positive cases. A well-designed system that includes supervision, provision of supplies, examination of sputum slides, and referral and initial treatment at a facility is needed if such a project is expected to be effective. The main advantage of this intervention for contraceptive distribution is the frequent contact with the entire population. The perception that TB workers offer a positive service (have supplies, actually follow up and treat cases) may reinforce family planning practice. However, if they are perceived, as in many places, as a bother, coming around collecting sputum but doing little else, there is likely to be a negative effect on the acceptance of family planning advice from such a worker.

Malaria

Throughout the world, malaria is estimated to produce about 150 million illnesses and 1.2 million deaths annually (Walsh et al., 1979). In areas of high incidence both prophylactic suppression of malaria for selected groups and treatment of cases can be carried out within community-based health systems. As with other drug-related interventions, continued supply and reinforcement of the workers' skills and knowledge are essential. Although CBD programs based on a limited number of visits can provide treatment when a suspected case of malaria is encountered, any real curtailment of malaria prevalence and deaths would require that the community have continual access to services. The use of community-based depots that supply chloroquine to families who use it for prophylaxis or treatment is currently being investigated in Kenya (Kaseji, unpublished). If this type of program is effective, provision of contraceptives at the same depots might be considered.

Malaria control programs, apart from chloroquine distribution, offer another mode of linking a health intervention with family planning. In a manner similar to that of national TB programs, national malaria programs are based on routine home visiting, surveillance for fever, taking a blood smear of fever cases, giving presumptive treatment, and following up cases with radical treatment. This is also linked to the activities of spraying teams, depending on the phase of the control program. Program costs per household contact are quite low, amounting to about $0.02 each or $0.20 per household per year in the Punjab (Dept. of International Health, Johns Hopkins University, 1976). Estimates for a pilot primary care project or a state surveillance system yielded similar costs of about four cents per capita annually (Dept. of International Health, Johns Hopkins University, unpublished). A malaria control system has been shown to be highly effective under well-managed conditions, but as has been the case in a number of countries, can break down due to interruption of supplies, relaxation of supervision, and overloading workers with new tasks without adequate retraining and job planning.

Attempts to use malaria workers for family planning have produced mixed results. In the Punjab, attempts were made to add family planning activities to the responsibilities of malaria workers, but this reduced their effectiveness as malaria workers, prompting a cessation of the effort at integration. In this particular project, workers were expected to cover a very large number of houses on a tight schedule as part of their malaria surveillance activities, giving them no opportunity to introduce family planning messages, their main family planning responsibility. On the other hand, meeting fixed targets for referral of cases of IUDs or sterilization rapidly disrupted their malaria schedule. A more concerted effort at integration in Nepal, which included reducing the number of houses to be covered, produced better family planning results, but encountered criticism from the malaria program. A resurgence of malaria during the pilot study may have been linked to the integration attempt, but other factors such as disruption of insecticide supply could have been responsible (Thorne, 1975).

Although theoretically attractive and deceptively straightforward, combining a malaria control program with contraceptive distribution, like any attempt at integration, requires careful planning for realistic task assignments and may represent too complex a combination for most CBD programs. Treatment of individual cases of malaria as they arise may be more suitable in many projects (Wawer, this volume). Furthermore, acceptability to the community will be low unless they perceive that the health worker has something to offer beyond a hurried "does anyone have a fever," and a finger stick for those who complain.

Symptom Specific Complaints

Because of their high prevalence, three general complaints could be considered for possible symptomatic treatment as part of a CBD program. They are fever, musculoskeletal and joint aches and pains (for want of a better word they are lumped together as "rheumatism"), and abdominal discomfort and indigestion (GI complaints). Justification of treatment for these complaints using health outcome measures is difficult, but satisfaction of community demand and relief of symptoms may be valid reasons for providing health workers with some simple medications. In all of these cases, family planning efforts would probably be enhanced through improved rapport with individuals and the community.

Fever

Children under one in the Punjab (Kielmann et al., 1983) experienced 4.4 episodes and 16 days of fever per year. Between one and three years these rates were 3.7 episodes and 14 days, while the population as a whole averaged one episode and five days per year (Kielmann et al., 1983; Dept. of International Health, Johns Hopkins University, 1976). Besides relieving symptoms, a justification for providing nonspecific treatment of fevers in children is the control of febrile convulsions, a disturbing occurrence which can be dangerous. The majority of fevers are generally viral in origin, but treatment of more specific causes of fever, such as malaria, should be built into the capability of community workers who are expected to treat the symptoms of fever. Symptomatic treatment of fever should be linked to knowledge and skills necessary to determine that the problem is not complicated, and to making a referral if it is.

Treatment of fever consists of aspirin, sponge baths, and the maintenance of hydration. These all can be taught easily to both the worker and the mother and require minimal supervision, except for the monitoring of referrals to ensure that they are appropriate. This intervention requires very inexpensive supplies (aspirin). If care is sought from a health worker for about 60 percent of episodes (as has been shown in Punjab), the total program costs of seeing children under five would be \$0.25 per case or eight cents per capita (Kielmann et al., 1983; Dept. of International Health, Johns Hopkins University, unpublished). Because fevers are so common in young children, the intervention offers the opportunity of frequent contacts with families of reproductive age and, therefore, increase the opportunity to initiate and maintain the use of contraceptives.

Recent evidence in the U.S. would suggest that the use of aspirin in cases of influenza and chicken pox in children is contraindicated due to an association with the occurrence of a rare but serious problem, Reye Syndrome (Hall, 1982). Given the infrequency of this condition, the fact that a clear association remains to be proven, and the higher cost and other problems associated with aspirin substitutes, the use of this drug should probably not be stopped in CBD programs at this time. In the hot ambient temperature in many LDC's, aspirin's role in diminishing fever continues to be important in reducing febrile convulsions (mentioned above) and the risks of dehydration.

Rheumatism and GI Complaints

Rheumatism and GI complaints are discussed together since they are problems generally found in older individuals. Symptoms which are referred to by the term rheumatism have been reported on the average of 1.2 times per person per year, producing a yearly total of approximately two weeks of illness. GI complaints occurred an average of 3.2 times yearly, yielding 16 days per person per year (Dept. of International Health, Johns Hopkins University, 1976; Institute of Medicine, Tribhuvan University, 1977). Both are frequent enough to keep a community-based worker active practicing symptomatic medicine, but therein lies one of the problems of integration. Care must be taken to avoid overloading the worker with curative activities that do not produce demonstrable health benefits and potentially crowd out other more effective interventions, as well as family planning. There is justification in satisfying community demand and maintaining rapport by providing treatment for these problems, but only under conditions that permit time allocation to be monitored and reasonable controls instituted. This can be equally argued for other specific interventions when services with different potential health effects or priorities are provided by the same community worker.

Interventions for both rheumatism and GI complaints can be varied, but are most likely to include aspirin for musculo-skeletal conditions and an antacid or antispasmodic drug or mixture for the gastrointestinal complaints. These therapies could easily be provided by a CBD worker, and could be added to non-medicinal treatments including advice about application of heat, exercise, rest of the affected area, or appropriate diet. In some societies where manipulation and massage for problems such as low back pain are highly appreciated by the community, the linking of CBD activities with practitioners of this traditional treatment might be considered. Because of their high incidence and potential drain on health workers' time, estimates of per capita costs for these interventions would range from $0.20 to $0.60, with only 20 percent of the cost being due to drugs (Dept. of International Health, Johns Hopkins University, unpublished).

Workers who deliver these symptomatic services should be taught to recognize common serious causes of pain (particularly in the case of the gastrointestinal intervention) and to refer such cases. Algorithms can be developed to assist workers in deciding on referral: without such a precaution, workers may unnecessarily delay other care and also lose credibility.

COMBINED SERVICE INTERVENTIONS

The potential result of single health interventions on the acceptance and use of contraceptives has been mainly speculative. The studies that have suggested a positive effect, such as the Matlab project in Bangladesh or the Narangwal project in India, have involved multiple health interventions. Because the latter project provides the only data available that allow us to examine the potential effect of different combinations of major health services on family planning practice, the relevant findings are summarized here (Taylor et al., 1983).

1. When health services for women were provided in isolation from children's services, curative services were found to be more significantly associated with increased family planning practice than routine surveillance or preventive services.
2. When health services for women were provided in combination with children's health services, routine surveillance visits to women became significantly associated with increased family planning practice and curative services decreased in importance.
3. Both curative and routine preventive health services for children were consistently associated with increased family planning practice. This was true whether the children's services were associated with the complete women's services package or not. (In no case, however, were services for children provided independently from routine monitoring of women's fertility or prenatal care.)
4. General contacts with men limited to discussions of health and family planning, family planning motivation, referral for health care and family planning services, and distribution of condoms, were associated with increased family planning practice only in the early stages of the project. The effect was not seen when the entire project period was analyzed, possibly indicating that the consequences of these types of services are limited and short-term.

Costs for the combined women's and children's services, which included most of the specific and nonspecific interventions mentioned above, were about $2.65 per capita annually (Taylor et al., 1983). If one adds the estimated per capita costs of each specific intervention together, the amount is greater than this total, reflecting potential efficiencies in combining services.

It should be noted that the interpretation of data from both the Narangwal and Matlab projects is not easy because of the probable Hawthorn effect acting in each project, and because different services were instituted at different points in the projects, yielding unequal time periods for the analysis of each activity's impact. It has also proven difficult, especially in Matlab, to separate changes in contraceptive practice due to the use of project health interventions from those brought about by general improvements in the organization and infrastructure of each project. However, in Narangwal, analysis of the association of health services with contraceptive practice at different points during the evolution of the project demonstrated a consistently strong association between health services and family planning at each point in time (Taylor et al., 1983).

When reviewing the types of health services that have been combined with contraceptive distribution, community-level or environmental services are notably absent. Because contraceptive use is a personal practice, it is only logical that associated health services should be predominantly personal also. However, since overall community support is of value to a CBD program, community-level programs should not be excluded as a potential combination, particularly when demand is significant. A CBD project in Kenya is currently using volunteer community health workers to combine contraceptive distribution with health education, home-based oral rehydration, simple curative care, and a latrine building program (Parker, 1982). Other community projects could include improving water supplies and providing cooperative child day care. The last has proven especially useful for augmenting child health care at stressful seasons in certain cultures. In the Punjab, children of low-income women benefited at least in terms of improved nutritional status during the harvest season when they ordinarily would have been left in the care of siblings the entire day. Better care at day care centers prevented the usual pattern of weight loss during this time period (Dept. of International Health, Johns Hopkins University, unpublished).

As a part of comprehensive service, such community-level programs may benefit family planning efforts, but are time consuming, require a significant amount of long-term input from the community itself, and capable organizational and supervisory efforts. They are, therefore, unlikely candidates for short-term, limited-input CBD projects.

PROPOSED METHODOLOGY FOR DEVELOPING INTERVENTION SELECTION CRITERIA

Table 19:1 represents a preliminary attempt to summarize selection criteria for CBD projects semiquantitatively. It is based on data in the text, but interventions dealt with in other papers have been included for the sake of comparison. The characteristics of each intervention have been rated on a basis of 0 through 5 (0 = none, 1 = low, 2 = moderately low, 3 = moderate, 4 = moderately high, 5 = high). The characteristics include the mortality and morbidity (incidence, prevalence, or disability) of a specific problem as indicators of the need for an intervention (Table 19:2). Community demand or acceptability has also been estimated as a component of need. This latter estimate is based in part on studies showing the proportion of cases that seek care from primary health workers (Figure 19:1).

Interventions appropriate for the problem have been characterized according to their simplicity (a broad category estimating the level of manpower, technical, organizational, and managerial input required, as well as cultural acceptability), their relative cost (Table 19:3), and their potential efficacy under program conditions. This approach to setting priorities has been used in different formats for many years. The main innovation in Table 19:1 is an attempt in the last column to

Table 19:1. Illustrative Ratings* of Health Needs, Intervention Characteristics, and Family Planning Enhancement Potential

		HEALTH NEED		
Problem/Intervention Group	Target	Mortality	Morbidity	Demand
Disease Specific I				
Diarrhea	< 5	5	5	3
Nutrition	< 5 / Prenatal	5	5	2
Immunizable diseases	< 5 / Prenatal	5	3	2
Intestinal helminths	5-14	1	5	3
Disease Specific II				
Pneumonia	< 5	5	2	5
Pharyngitis	< 15	1	2	5
Otitis	< 5	1	3	4
Conjunctivitis	< 15	0	3	3
Skin infections	< 15	1	3	3
Injuries (superficial)	All	1	2	2
Genitourinary	15-49	1	2	4
Birth trauma, and anoxia	Natal	5	2	4
Tuberculosis	All	2	2	1
Malaria	All	3	2	3
Symptom Specific				
Fever	< 5	2	5	3
Musculoskeletal	Adults	0	3	2
GI complaints	Adults	1	4	3
General Services				
Women's	15-49	5	3	3
Children's	< 5	5	5	3
Combined Women's & Children's	15-49/< 5	5	5	3
Men's (limited)	> 15	0	2	1
Community/environment	All	5	5	3

*Rating: 0 = None, 1 = Low, 2 = Moderately Low, 3 = Moderate, 4 = Moderately High, 5 = High

Table 19:1 (Cont.). Illustrative Ratings* of Health Needs, Intervention Characteristics, and Family Planning Enhancement Potential

INTERVENTION CHARACTERISTICS

Problem/Intervention Group	Target	Simplicity	Low Cost	Efficacy
Disease Specific I				
Diarrhea	< 5	4	3	5
Nutrition	< 5 Prenatal	2	1	3
Immunizable diseases	< 5 Prenatal	3	4	5
Intestinal helminths	5-14	5	4	3
Disease Specific II				
Pneumonia	< 5	2	5	4
Pharyngitis	< 15	3	5	3
Otitis	< 5	3	4	3
Conjunctivitis	< 15	5	4	5
Skin infections	< 15	5	4	4
Injuries (superficial)	All	4	4	4
Genitourinary	15-49	4	4	3
Birth trauma, and anoxia	Natal	2	5	2
Tuberculosis	All	2	4	2
Malaria	All	5	4	3
Symptom Specific				
Fever	< 5	5	4	1
Musculoskeletal	Adults	5	3	0
GI complaints	Adults	5	2	0
General Services				
Women's	15-49	2	1	3
Children's	< 5	2	1	5
Combined Women's & Children's	15-49/< 5	2	1	5
Men's (limited)	> 15	5	5	1
Community/environment	All	2	2	2

*Rating: 0 = None, 1 = Low, 2 = Moderately Low, 3 = Moderate, 4 = Moderately High, 5 = High

Table 19:1 (Cont.). Illustrative Ratings* of Health Needs, Intervention Characteristics, and Family Planning Enhancement Potential

FAMILY PLANNING ENHANCEMENT POTENTIAL				
Problem/Intervention Group	Target	Need Rating	Intervention Rating	FP Rating
Disease Specific I				
Diarrhea	< 5	13	12	3
Nutrition	< 5 Prenatal	12	6	3
Immunizable diseases	< 5 Prenatal	10	12	3
Intestinal helminths	5-14	9	12	1
Disease Specific II				
Pneumonia	< 5	12	11	3
Pharyngitis	< 15	8	11	1
Otitis	< 5	8	10	2
Conjunctivitis	< 15	6	14	1
Skin infections	< 15	7	13	1
Injuries (superficial)	All	5	12	2
Genitourinary	15-49	7	11	4
Birth trauma, and anoxia	Natal	11	9	4
Tuberculosis	All	5	8	1
Malaria	All	8	12	2
Symptom Specific				
Fever	< 5	10	10	3
Musculoskeletal	Adults	5	8	1
GI complaints	Adults	8	7	1
General Services				
Women's	15-49	11	6	4
Children's	< 5	13	8	4
Combined Women's & Children's	15-49/< 5	13	8	5
Men's (limited)	> 15	3	11	3
Community/environment	All	13	6	1

*Rating: 0 = None, 1 = Low, 2 = Moderately Low, 3 = Moderate, 4 = Moderately High, 5 = High

Table 19:2. Rates Used to Estimate Need for Services

Problem/Intervention Group	Target	Mortality	Incidence	Prevalence	Demand
Diarrhea	< 5	14.0	5.0	30 Days	0.6
Nutrition	< 5	10.0-15.0	-	5-20% Under 60% weight-for-age standard	-
	Prenatal	40 Perinatal infant deaths per 1,000 births	1/3 of Pregnant women underweight	20% of birth weights < 2.5 kg	-
Immunizable Diseases	< 5	5.0-10.0	Measles 0.2 (others variable)	Polio: 7/1,000 limb atrophy or paralysis (5-14 yrs)	-
	Prenatal	4-20 Neonatal tetanus deaths per 1,000 live births	Tetanus = same as mortality rates	-	-
Intestinal Helminths	5-14	-	Obstruction: 2 per 1,000 infected children	Depends on type; Ascaris: 75-90% point prevalence	0.5

Note: 1. Estimates based primarily on data from the Naragwal projects. A dash indicates that data were not available on which to base an estimate.

2. Mortality = annual deaths per 1,000 target population; Incidence = annual episodes per target individual; Prevalence = annual days of illness per target individual; Demand = percent of cases seeking medical care. (Unless specified otherwise)

Table 19:2 (Cont.). Rates Used to Estimate Need for Services

Problem/Intervention Group	Target	Mortality	Incidence	Prevalence	Demand
Pneumonia	< 5	9.0	1.0	-	0.9
Pharyngitis	< 15	-	0.1	-	0.9
Otitis	< 5	-	1.0	2% Hearing disability (5-15 yrs)	0.9
Conjunctivitis	< 15	-	1.5	15 Days	0.5
Skin Infections	< 15	-	1.5	15 Days	0.5
Injuries (superficial)	All	-	0.5	-	0.4
Genitourinary	15-49	-	0.5	-	0.4
Birth Trauma and Anoxia	Natal	40 Perinatal infant deaths per 1,000 births	10% Births	-	-
Tuberculosis	All	0.8	-	1% Point prevalence	-

Table 19:2 (Cont.). Rates Used to Estimate Need for Services

Problem/Intervention Group	Target	Mortality	Incidence	Prevalence	Demand
Malaria	All	0.8-2.4	0.1-0.3	-	0.6
Fever	< 5	-	4.0	15 Days	0.6
Musculoskeletal	All	-	1.2	14 Days	0.4
GI Complaints	All	-	3.2	16 Days	0.5
Women's Services	15-49	80 Perinatal infant deaths per 1,000 births	See above estimates		
Children's Services	< 5	35.0-50.0	See above estimates		
Combined Women's & Children's Services	15-49/< 5	80 Perinatal infant deaths per 1,000 births; 35.0-50.0	See above estimates		
Men's (limited) Services	> 15	-			
Community/environment	All	See above related problems, e.g., diarrhea, nutrition, helminths			

Figure 19:1. Percent Distribution of Cases Presenting for Care in Children 0-14 With and Without Access to Community-Based Services, Narangwal, India

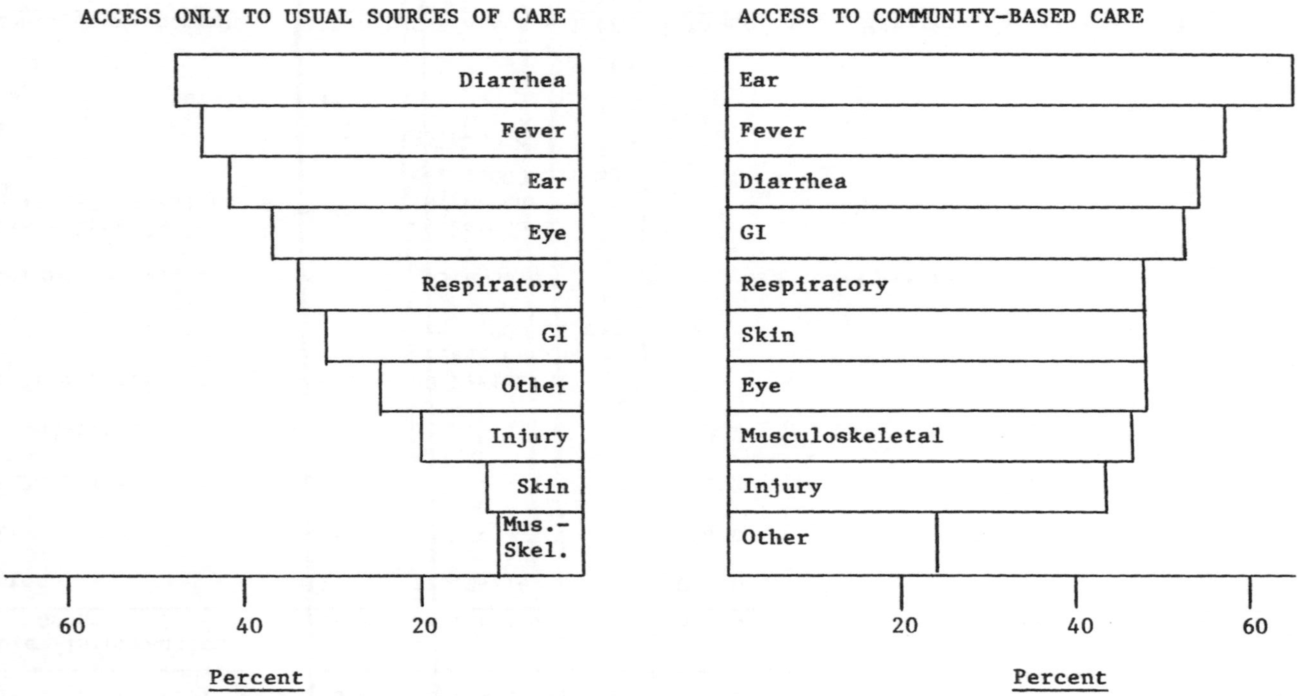

Table 19:3. Cost Estimates[1] for Different Interventions (in U.S. \$)[2]

Problem/Intervention Group	Target	Cost per Case	Cost per Target Population	Cost per Capita	Percent of Cost for Drugs
Diarrhea	< 5	Sugar & Salt: 0.20–0.70	0.40–1.40	0.06–0.02	< 1%
		ORS Packet: 0.40–1.80	0.80–1.80	0.12–0.26	15–60%
Nutrition	< 5	0.05 per Feeding 30.00 per Child-year	10.00	1.50	45–65% Food
	Prenatal	7.20 per Preg.	2.40	0.10	
Immunizable Diseases	< 5	3.00 per Child with completed immun.	0.60	0.09	15%
	Prenatal	0.50 per Pregnant woman	0.50	0.02	10%
Intestinal Helminths	5–14	0.25 per Treatment	0.12–0.25	0.03–0.06	15%

[1] Estimates based primarily on data from the Narangwal projects. Costs per target population or per capita take into account incidence or prevalence and demand for services.

[2] Average annual costs during 1969–1973 – Equivalent to 1971 U.S. $

Table 19:3 (Cont.). Cost Estimates for Different Interventions (in U.S. $)

Problem/Intervention Group	Target	Cost per Case	Cost per Target Population	Cost per Capita	Percent of Cost for Drugs
Pneumonia	< 5	1.00	0.09[3]	0.01[3]	32%
Pharyngitis	< 15	0.55	0.05	0.02	50%
Otitis	< 5	0.50	0.35	0.05	54%
Conjunctivitis	< 15	0.25	0.20	0.08	20%
Skin Infections	< 15	0.25	0.20	0.08 (Soap = 0.20)	20%
Injuries	All	0.25	0.05	0.05	20%
Genitourinary	15–49	0.60	0.12	0.05	43%
Birth trauma and anoxia	Natal	0.30 per Delivery	0.06	0.01	–
Tuberculosis	All	8.00	0.08	0.08	60–70%
Malaria	All	0.02 per Contact	0.04 (Surveillance)	0.04	–
		0.35 per Case	0.04	0.04	17%

[3] Cost of associated child surveillance program: $2.00 per child per year or $0.30 per capita spread across all included interventions.

Table 19:3 (Cont.). Cost Estimates for Different Interventions (in U.S. $)

Problem/Intervention Group	Target	Cost per Case	Cost per Target Population	Cost per Capita	Percent of Cost for Drugs
Fever	< 5	0.25	0.55	0.08	2%
Musculoskeletal	All	0.40	0.19	0.19	20%
GI Complaints	All	0.40	0.62	0.62	20%
		Cost per Contact			
Women's Services	15-49	Women's = 0.35 Maternity = 0.90	5.30	1.10	15%
Children's Services	< 5	Children's = 0.25 Surveillance = 0.07	10.30	1.55	15% Drugs 20% Food
Combined Women's and Children's Services	15-49 < 5		5.30 10.30	2.65	15% Drugs 20% Food
Men's (limited) Services	> 15	0.10 per Contact	0.10	0.02	-
Community/environment	All	(Note [4])	(Note [4])	(Note [4])	(Note [4])

[4] All estimates of costs depend on specific programs involved (e.g., rural water supply systems average $5.00 per capita yearly, 50% of which is annuitized capital costs).

rate the possible enhancing effect the intervention would have on family planning practice. As with the other ratings, the subjective element is large. Little firm evidence exists on which to base the strength of the specific health intervention-family planning link. However, some evidence of the relative effect of women's, children's, and men's health services on family planning, as well as the potential to use the service as an "entry point" based on the probable overlap of the health service target population with the potential family planning target population, provide the semiquantitative bases for the rating.

The entire rating exercise, including the summing of the "need" ratings and the "intervention" ratings, should be viewed as primarily illustrative. Very different results can occur depending on the rater's experience and assumptions. One might want to consider the use of a nominal group involving a number of individuals experienced in primary health care and family planning to reach a more universal consensus on the ratings for each of the interventions for any given program and cultural setting. In any case, this approach attempts to clarify the choice of interventions and should narrow down the choice for a specific project. Final selection will depend on the details of each problem and each intervention, as illustrated in this paper or elsewhere, and matching them to the resources available.

The problems in Table 19:1 have been divided into four intervention groups: Disease Specific I, those interventions reviewed in other papers; Disease Specific II, interventions considered in this paper; Symptom Specific interventions; and Combined Service interventions. Target groups for the interventions have been specified. This classification does not intend to imply limitation of the intervention to only one target group, but the concentration of a majority of services on this group. These targets certainly could vary depending on the need in a given area.

Using the overall objectives that interventions should meet major health needs, be effective and feasible, and have some potential to enhance family planning practice, choices for interventions might be limited, as an example, to those with ratings equal to or greater than eight for need, eight for characteristics such as feasibility, and two for family planning enhancement. This would suggest that six disease-specific interventions (diarrhea, immunizable diseases, pneumonia, otitis, birth-related, and malaria), one symptom-specific intervention (fever), and two general-service interventions (children's or a combination of children's and women's) deserve prime consideration in many CBD programs.

Interventions that have been used in some CBD projects but are omitted in this selection process include antihelminth programs and nutrition interventions. It is of particular interest to ascertain why this selection approach has omitted them. Antihelminth therapy has a reasonable rating for the frequency of the condition and a high rating for the intervention criteria. It has been rated low in terms of family planning enhancement, and, therefore, excluded from the above selection primarily on the basis that its main target population is school-aged children. This is certainly a judgment that needs further field testing: among the projects combining contraceptive distribution with antihelminthic treatment, there is little evidence to support or reject a link between antihelminthic services and family planning efforts. In contrast, the combined nutrition intervention, because it does target children under five and prenatal women, has been rated higher in its family planning potential. However, in spite of their high need rating, nutrition interventions are costly and require well-organized support activities, and their intervention rating excludes them from the illustrative selection process. One could argue that some components of nutrition, such as education about breastfeeding and appropriate weaning foods, and distribution of vitamin A, iron, or folic acid, would be much easier and less costly, and therefore should be considered separately.

CONCLUSION

The selection of appropriate health interventions for community-level family planning and health programs must be based on clear objectives for the initial consideration of the health interventions, and equally clear criteria for their selection. The current framework is designed to illustrate a possible method of selecting interventions and is not intended to provide all the information necessary for any given setting. It is apparent that variations in selection will occur, depending on factors such as the emphasis given to satisfying a health need or enhancing family planning. In either case, the need for relatively simple, easily managed services is a major limiting factor. When more than one health intervention is selected, the efficiency with which they can be combined is important. This is one reason the women's and children's general service intervention in Table 19:1 received such a high rating. It assumed a reasonable number of needed, effective, and efficiently combined components, a potential achievable with careful design and implementation. However, the relative complexity of this or other interventions may limit their application in many CBD settings. This example and others in the paper highlight one of the inherent dilemmas of current CBD programs: the trade-off between rapidly deployed, easily implemented programs, and programs combining more services over longer periods of time which are more complex and difficult to implement. It is an issue which operations research projects in health and family planning need to consciously address more adequately in the future.

REFERENCES

Benenson, Abram S., ed. Control of Communicable Diseases in Man, 11th edition. New York: American Public Health Association, 1970.

Berggren, W.L. et al. "Reduction in Mortality in Rural Haiti Through a Primary Health Care Program." New Engl J Med 304 (1980): 1324-1330.

Cecil, R.L. and R.F.Loeb, ed. A Textbook of Medicine, 10th edition. Philadelphia and London: W. B. Saunders Co., 1959.

Department of International Health, Johns Hopkins University, School of Hygiene and Public Health. Functional Analysis of Health Needs and Services. New Delhi, India: Asia Publishing House, 1976.

Department of International Health, Johns Hopkins University, School of Hygiene and Public Health. "The Narangwal Population, Nutrition, and Functional Analysis Studies." (unpublished data).

Gordes, L. "Effectiveness of Comprehensive Care Programs in Preventing Rheumatic Fever." New Engl J Med 289 (1973): 331-335.

Gu, Xing-yuan, School of Public Health, Shanghai First Medical College, personal communication, 1981.

Hall, W. "National Surveillance for Reye Syndrome 1981: Update, Reye Syndrome and Salicylate Usage." MMWR, 31 (1982): 53-56, 61.

Han, Jia-jing and Yang, Sheng-ji. "Tuberculosis Control." American J. Public Health 72,suppl. (September 1982).

Institute of Medicine, Tribhuvan University. Health Needs Study -- Tanahu District. Kathmandu, Nepal: Tribhuvan University, 1977.

Kielmann, A.A. and Associates, eds. Child and Maternal Health Services in Rural India--The Narangwal Experiment, Vol. I: Integrated Nutrition and Health Care. World Bank Research Publication. Baltimore, MD: The Johns Hopkins University Press, 1983.

Parker, R. L. "Family Planning Operations Research in Kenya. Unsolicited Proposal to U.S. Agency for International Development/Washington, DC." 1982.

Parker, R. L. "Kenya Trip Report, November 1981" (unpublished document).

Rural Health Research Center. Child Health Care in Rural Areas: A Manual for Auxiliary Nurse Midwives. New Delhi: Asia Publishing House, 1974..

Simpson-Hebert, M. et al. "Traditional Midwives and Family Planning." Population Reports (May 1980).

Taylor, C.E., R.S.S. Sarma, R.L. Parker, W.A. Reinke, and R. Faruqee, eds. Child and Maternal Health Services in Rural India--The Narangwal Experiment, Vol. II: Integrated Family Planning and Health Care. World Bank Research Publication. Baltimore, MD: The Johns Hopkins University Press, 1983.

Thorne, M. Personal communication, 1975.

Walsh, J. et al. "Selective Primary Health Care: An Interim Strategy for Disease Control in Developing Countries." New Engl J Med 301 (1979): 967-974.

20
Description of the Selection of Services for the Family Planning and Health Home Distribution Project, PRODEF, Bas Zaire*

Nlandu Mangani

The PRODEF project in Bas Zaire, begun in 1981, relies on home visits by trained distributors to deliver education directed toward improving the health of preschool children, and to provide a number of simple health services, as well as family planning information and services for women of reproductive age. Health services consist of the provision of an antimalarial (chloroquine, with aspirin for symptomatic relief), oral rehydration salts, and a broad-spectrum antihelminthic (mebendazole). Home delivery of family planning services is comprised of distribution of oral contraceptives, condoms, and foam, with referral for injectable Depo-Provera, IUDs, and tubal ligation. Tubal ligation, although not considered an integral part of the PRODEF program, is available through the establishment of a clinic in the largest local city, Matadi, and will be available from a smaller clinic-hospital following its renovation in the project's home-base village of Nsona-Mpangu.

SELECTION CRITERIA FOR PROJECT INTERVENTIONS

The severe lack of primary health care in the project area is reflected in high postpartum maternal mortality, and elevated rates of neonatal and infant mortality. It is estimated that only 25 percent of women are given prenatal and postnatal care and delivered in small rural maternity clinics: although complete statistics to quantify the problems do not exist, it is known that lack of adequate spacing between pregnancies contributes to both neonatal and maternal mortality, and infectious diseases such as measles and malaria coupled with malnutrition contribute to the elevated infant mortality rates. For these reasons family planning, as well as treatment for malaria, diarrheal dehydration, and intestinal helminths were chosen as priority interventions. Immunization, although potentially of great value, would require resources such as a cold-chain, thus rendering it an unrealistic intervention for a home delivery project of this type.

---
* Translated from French by D. Cebula and M. Wawer.

The integration of primary health and family planning offered certain advantages for the PRODEF CBD project. Since the population is aware of health problems and is interested in services to deal with them, it was believed that primary health care could provide an opening for the discussion of family planning. In addition, integration permits a two-pronged attack on fundamental health problems, in that it deals with the treatment or prevention of common childhood illnesses while encouraging the spacing of births with its concomitant effect on maternal and child health.

It should be noted, however, that integration can result in certain disadvantages for a CBD project. The project becomes substantially more vast in scope, which can lead to poorly defined objectives. Even if objectives are defined carefully, it may be difficult to attain them in the allotted time frame. The large scope of the project must obviously be supported by an appropriately large budget. Finally, workers need to cover a large geographic area and provide many activities. Work can become superficial if the project and its workers are spread too thinly (program activity in any one sphere becomes diluted) and the overall effect of the program may be reduced.

PROJECT MANPOWER AND SUPPORTS

Selection of Household Visitors

Household visitors in the PRODEF project are of an educational level equal or higher to that found in most CBD projects. Over half the home visitors have completed at least two years of nursing or health auxiliary training, and have easily mastered material about health problems encountered in the households. The remaining visitors are former elementary schoolteachers having at least three years of post-primary study. These workers have demonstrated good communication skills with clients. The level of personnel is, nonetheless, lower than that originally considered preferable to deliver the type and number of services offered by the project.

Although the level of previous educational attainment may influence job performance - individuals with nursing backgrounds having greater experience at patient assessment, etc. - the previous educational attainment does not necessarily guarantee the accuracy of the visitor's work. Each worker still needs to be instructed and tested concerning specific technical points of ORT use and other services.

Training of Recruited Personnel

Specific training of personnel, emphasizing those aspects of work peculiar to the CBD setting, is a necessity in a project of this nature. In spite of the limited duration of training

(12 days) in the PRODEF program, it was important to consider a number of different effects training had on the project.

Training represented a drain of project time and money. Funds had to be budgeted to cover the costs of both trainees and their teacher(s). However, the monetary and time loss was more than made up for by the quality of work and its efficient progression in the field which could have been seriously hindered, if not impossible, without adequate training of staff. In PRODEF, practical education was emphasized through role plays and field practice before home visits began.

Supervision

Supervisory personnel were trained by being included in part of the worker training. One of the goals of this phase of the supervisors training was to ensure that they would have appropriate technical competency concerning each intervention. This was particularly emphasized in the case of the field supervisor who would travel daily with the home distributors. Further training in supervisory techniques was provided to the field supervisor by the project coordinator, who herself had had supervisory experience overseeing the activities of home interviewers involved in the research aspects of the project. The field supervisor received a detailed job description and a copy of all project training manuals. In addition, the project director, who is a doctor, works jointly with the supervisor to oversee contraceptive and health service delivery.

Medical Backup and Referral Services

The household visitors are training village-level <u>matrones</u>, or traditional midwives, to whom female clients will come for resupply after the initial CBD visits. Women can also be referred, both by the home visitor and by the <u>matrone</u>, to dispensaries scattered throughout the rural area. These dispensaries are directed by nurses who have received an additional four days of project-specific training regarding family planning, selected health interventions and the philosophy of CBD projects. The area hospital serves as a final referral point for complicated cases and for surgical contraception.

Transportation

The large geographic area of the zone to be covered by the team poses a transportation problem. The necessity of a reliable vehicle became paramount, and this in itself posed other problems. The high cost of vehicles, fuel, and maintenance, and particularly the escalations in the cost of these elements are not easily budgeted. Spare parts are not only costly but scarce, leading to unforeseen unavailability of vehicles and thus delays for the project. The poor condition of local roads , especially during certain periods of the year, such as the rainy season, causes additional delays.

The availability of a project vehicle also affects the manner in which workers organize their activities. Their confidence in having access to a vehicle, with the implication of rapid transportation, may lead to inefficient use of time between travel periods. The same principle holds true in scheduling transportation for administrative staff.

Two vehicles have proven to be very important, as they decrease time lost due to vehicle breakdown and allow for more flexible scheduling of travel for all groups of personnel. With these issues in mind, the PRODEF project repaired an old Land Rover belonging to the local Mobile Public Health Team. Although PRODEF does not own the vehicle, it now has access to it when necessary.

Supply of Commodities

A program without stock resembles a vehicle without fuel. Two points can totally halt fieldwork - sometimes for several months: getting stock into the country (given various complications related to international transportation and to local customs regulations), and the difficulties of stocking and restocking local dispensaries. Early stock orders should be large enough to fill gaps if later shipments are delayed. It should be self-evident that a project cannot start without adequate supplies of stock being available: the PRODEF project has concluded it is preferable to delay startup than to begin and then run out of stock because initial supplies are too meager to ensure continuity.

Program Evaluation

The evaluation system provides a mechanism of measuring the progress of the program and of motivating program personnel. It must be planned and instituted from the inception of the program.

Household visits are evaluated by the field supervisor and occasionally by the project coordinator and project director, generally by observation using a checklist. In addition, both a baseline and post-treatment survey will assess the results of the project as to overall program goals (acceptance of family planning and specific health services). The latter form of evaluation is primarily research oriented and data will not be available in time to modify project services (if necessary). It will, however, provide valuable data for future activities.

SUGGESTIONS FOR OTHER PROGRAMS

The PRODEF program, despite its short duration, can propose some valuable suggestions for other new family planning and health programs that encounter similar situations or difficulties. In order to provide a program that will improve the level of health for the entire population, projects should consider the following aspects:

1. Health Needs. Survey the real health needs of the population to be served. If possible, the following should be considered and if found to be feasible incorporated into such a program:

- Popularization of oral rehydration among the people.
- Fight against malaria and parasites.
- Nutritional education, without which health progress is nullified.
- Fight against epidemic diseases, when infrastructure permits, for example measles, which ravage children.
- Family planning education.

2. Length of Training. The length of training is a factor that can improve the efficiency of the field team. In the PRODEF program, a training period of roughly one month would have been preferable. Emphasis on project objectives is important in training, as is field retraining.

3. Supervision. The supervisor must be well-versed in both theory and practice, and preferably be a nurse or a midwife capable of resolving certain health problems in the village. Supervision must be directly performed in the field by the supervisor, coordinator, or doctor.

4. Supplies. The stock of supplies must be adequate before work commences. A program should never be started without the assurance of an adequate supply-line.

5. Funds. Very often banking operations to transfer funds suffer from delays which can demoralize the team. Therefore, it is also necessary to attend to the smooth flow of finances through the program.

21
Community-Based Distribution of Low-Cost Family Planning and Maternal and Child Health Services in Rural Nigeria

O. A. Ladipo, E. M. Weiss, G. E. Delano, J. Revson, M. O. Onadeko, and O. Ayeni

The need for low-cost family planning and maternal and child health (MCH) services is apparent in rural Nigeria. These types of services either do not exist in the setting in question, or, due to the limited resources, only part of the population in need is being reached by existing services. There is, however, a strong commitment on the part of the Nigerian Government to improve and extend services in order to bring them within reach of all Nigerians. Recognizing the appropriateness of the CBD approach to service delivery, the current project will provide useful information to the government in implementing the national Basic Health Services Scheme (BHSS), which will contain CBD elements.

The health status of the rural population needs great improvement. Estimated health parameters for the rural area of Oyo state served by the present project can be summarized as follows: crude birth rate: 50/1,000 population; crude death rate: 20/1,000 population; infant mortality rate: 111/1,000 live births; annual rate of population growth: 3.0 percent; rural physician/population ratio: 1/60,000. While these estimates can not be exact because of unsatisfactory census gathering and vital statistics, it is clear that the rate of natural increase, fertility, and mortality are all extremely high. Even without further technological improvements and at the existing level of socioeconomic development, many of the infant and maternal deaths are unnecessary. One basic requirement is an effective mechanism for making MCH and family planning services more accessible to the population.

The broad consensus among national and international public health professionals working in sub-Saharan Africa is that family planning services can best be offered in an integrated health context. Some factors leading to the emphasis on integrated family planning, health service delivery are: the acuteness of basic health needs, the widespread ideal of large families, and low interest in family planning (FP) in terms of family limitation but a somewhat greater interest in contraception for birth spacing to promote maternal and child health (traditionally accomplished through prolonged breastfeeding and sexual abstinence during lactation).

The present project confronts these issues within the rural Nigerian context. Traditional birth attendants (TBAs), who conduct the majority of deliveries in villages, and other local community agents have been recruited from their villages. Working under the supervision of government nurse-midwives, they deliver basic MCH and FP information, supplies, and services to village residents at the household-level and make referrals for additional MCH/FP services to the local health/maternity center. This project marks a sharp break with the tradition of institutional care based on the Western model, moving toward extension of service delivery and community involvement. Thus, the training and reorientation of the nurse-midwives is a crucial step in creating and expanding the project. The training and supervision of TBAs in the provision of basic MCH/FP services in the household will greatly alter their job description. If the project succeeds, the implication for governmental midwifery training and for the entire medical system could be profound.

OBJECTIVES

The objectives of this project are to:

1. Develop and test the feasibility of a safe, effective, low cost, and potentially broadly replicable model (adapted to the social, cultural, political, and economic conditions of the region) for the door-to-door delivery of basic MCH/FP services in rural Nigeria through use of local community agents, such as TBAs and other nonmedical volunteers.
2. Develop and test appropriate training programs for both the TBAs and community agents, and for the midwife/supervisors.
3. Assess the individual contents of the service delivery package to determine community receptivity to each individual drug, contraceptive, or service provided.
4. Determine which individual or community characteristics distinguish effective from ineffective community agents.
5. Assess the community receptivity to and use of village agent provision of MCH/FP services at low, subsidized fees that can allow for greater self-sufficiency in the drug supply system.
6. Test the effectiveness of government midwives as the primary supervisory personnel of community agents and assess varying levels of the intensity of supervision.

PROJECT DESIGN

The project builds upon the existing network of government nurse-midwives and local health/maternity centers in an area with a population of approximately 85,000 in Akinyele North Local Government Area north of Ibadan. The rural midwives usually work singly in a small health/maternity center with the assistance of a female ward aide and a dispensary assistant. Services are limited, but include primary care for emergencies, prenatal and postpartum checkups, deliveries, and infant welfare clinics (including immunizations), with the referral of cases involving high risks or complications to the nearest government hospital or to University College Hospital (UCH).

Seven maternity centers have been selected to participate in the project while a total of 171 community agents have been selected and trained at the rural centers (18 to 32 agents per center). Given a kit with drugs, contraceptives, and first aid supplies, the community agents provide free information and education on health, nutrition, and family planning, but request a nominal fee (20 to 50 kobo, depending upon the age of the patient) for the treatment services from which the agents themselves receive a small commission. (No client is refused drugs because she cannot pay for them; 20 to 50 kobo equals U.S. $.32 to $.80.) Treatments are provided for malaria, cough, anemia (both childhood and prenatal), worms, diarrhea, cuts and abrasions, and other minor illnesses. One third of the agents are male volunteers, while the rest are female TBAs. The project in the seven selected areas began between February 4, and July 3, 1981, depending on the center. Centers have between 12 and 20 TBAs and 5 and 15 village health workers (VHWs).

PROJECT DIRECTION

Personnel of the Department of Obstetrics and Gynaecology of University College Hospital, Ibadan, direct the project and provide the design and supervision of training, backup medical support, project evaluation, and supervision of other project staff. Other UCH personnel include a biostatistician, a public health physician, and the senior nursing sisters of the family planning unit. The UCH nursing sisters have taken the main responsibility for carrying out the training of the community agents and for providing continuing UCH supervision. In addition, a senior nurse-midwife of the Akineyele project region provides field supervision and backup technical support for the midwives at the maternities. The project is funded by the Research Division, Office of Population, U.S. Agency for International Development, and technical assistance is provided by the Center for Population and Family Health (CPFH) of Columbia University (New York).

MIDWIFE ORIENTATION AND TRAINING

The UCH staff developed a specific two-week training course for the government midwives at the seven maternities in the project area and for their nursing supervisor. The emphasis of the training program (to be reinforced by in-service training) was not on theoretical instruction but rather on applied field experience. The basic topics included:

1. Assessment of child and maternal health and proper use of contraceptives and medication.
2. Techniques for selection and recruitment of agents.
3. Teaching methods for training agents.
4. Techniques for supervising, continuing training, and the resupply of the agents.

Other staff at UCH who would be involved in the project were also included in the training.

SELECTION AND TRAINING OF COMMUNITY AGENTS

Following the midwife orientation and training period, UCH staff and the midwives from the maternity centers met with community leaders to discuss the selection of candidates for the positions of community agents. The village leaders were encouraged to select representatives so that all of the villages in the area would have equal representation; 171 were chosen. The criteria for selection included:

- Present position: two thirds of the agents were to be TBAs (usually female) with the remainder to be VHWs. Only males, mainly farmers, were chosen as VHWs.
- Residence: agents must live in the village they are to serve and must be distributed throughout the project area.
- Personal qualities: agents must have the ability to communicate, hold a position of respect and acceptance in the community, and be available and willing to participate in the project.

Personnel from the Department of Obstetrics and Gynecology and the UCH nursing sisters, with assistance from the midwives, were responsible for training. Community agent training was conducted in each of the seven local health facilities. All agents were exposed to all parts of the training program, including delivery techniques. After an initial three-week course continuing in-service training is being provided along with three-day refresher courses on specific aspects of the services. The UCH staff's approach to the agent training program has been to build skills via modular field approaches. Required skills for every agent include the ability to:

1. Perform a simulated encounter with a member of the community, introducing the project and describing the services available.
2. Describe the importance of diarrhea in children, prepare a solution of Oralyte, and give proper instructions for its use.
3. Describe the importance of parasites and describe the appropriate treatment.
4. Describe the symptoms of malaria and its treatment.

5. Describe the major indications for cough syrup and the proper dosage.
6. Describe the indications for vitamins and the proper dosage.
7. Give the indications for use of an antihistamine and the proper dosage.
8. Give the indications for aspirin and the appropriate dosage for different age groups.
9. Describe the simple first aid and dressing techniques.
10. Describe the health and other benefits of family planning.
11. Describe oral contraceptives, including (a) how to take them correctly; (b) the proper procedure if one, two, or more pills are missed; (c) minor side effects and secondary benefits; and (d) contraindications to the use of oral contraceptives.
12. Describe the correct use of condoms and foaming tablets.
13. Discuss the contraceptive effectiveness of breast-feeding and folk methods of birth control.
14. Repeat the major nutritional concepts given in the course.
15. Give the major steps that each pregnant woman should take to promote the health of her infant.
16. Describe the benefits of vaccination and know how to refer for vaccinations.
17. Discuss the importance of environmental sanitation and the actions that can be taken to improve it.
18. Discuss the reason fees are charged for drugs.
19. Accurately record treatments and referrals on the tally sheets.

In addition, TBAs must be able to:

- Use the equipment provided in their TBA kits;
- Perform a simulated delivery using the equipment provided;
- Describe the major signs of an obstetric emergency and the appropriate procedures for these emergencies.

Given that most of the community agents are illiterate, specially designed oral and audiovisual training techniques have been employed. Pictographs have been developed indicating the different illnesses and the different services given by the agents. Pictographs have also been used to label the drugs and the tally sheet recording forms.

COMMUNITY AGENT MEDICAL KITS

The community agents have been given a locally produced metal kit containing drugs for treatment and first aid dressings. TBAs are also provided with delivery materials. The contents of the kits are listed below:

Drugs
Syrups: Benylin cough syrup, Nivaquine (chloroquine), multivitamins, Phenergan (an antihistamine)

Tablets: Nivaquine, Panodol (paracetamol), multivitamins, folic acid, Benadryl (an antihistamine), Ferrocal Plus (Prenatal), mebendazole.

Dressings
Iodine, Milton, Savlon, cotton-wool, gauze, bandage, strappings, scissors, soap dish and soap, hydrogen peroxide.

Contraceptives
Oral contraceptives, condoms, foaming tablets.

Delivery equipment (TBAs only)
Plastic sheet, plastic tubing (for removing mucus), scrub brush, spirits, distilled water, razor blades, ergometrine tablets, hand towel, Hibiscrub, cord ligature, and extra dressings.

LOGISTICS

Five points need to be considered in planning supplies and transportation:

- Procurement: Supplies for the project have been procured both locally and from overseas through low-cost bulk purchase. Contraceptives and initial supplies were provided by AID except for Oralyte which was provided by UNICEF, while the continuing supply of drugs and dressings is being met through local purchase.

- Distribution: Supplies are distributed from UCH in Ibadan to the local health facilities during regular monthly visits by UCH staff. The midwives in turn resupply the community agents at regular bimonthly supervisory meetings or as they use up their allotments.

- Storage: Supplies are, for the most part, stored at UCH. Smaller stores are kept at each maternity center.

- Accountability: A dual accountability system is used with the UCH staff having overall responsibility for supplies and the midwives having responsibility for storage of some supplies and the resupply of the agents.

- Transportation: While the agents work in their own villages, they also must visit nearby villages where no agents are in residence and go to the maternity center several times a month. They are given $10 reimbursement for their travel. The government midwives use either public transportation or their own vehicles for their supervisory and administrative functions. They are given a small monthly transportation allowance. A 4-wheel drive Land Rover is based at UCH and is used for transport to the project area by UCH staff.

RECORD FORMS AND DATA COLLECTION

Three types of records are being kept by the project to monitor the community agents' performance.

- Service statistics: The basic form for recording the community agent's performance is a tally-sheet with pictographs representing the different services given (rows), and the client's age and whether a new or old case (columns). The agent need only check the appropriate box. This form is turned in to the midwife every two weeks; she then reviews it with the agent. At the end of the month, the midwife summarizes the tally-sheets in a monthly report prepared for each agent which she turns in to UCH. UCH staff prepare monthly reports on the performance of the agents summarized for each service area.

- Supply records: The supplies (drugs and contraceptives) provided to the community agents are monitored in two ways. A duplicate receipt is filled out by UCH staff whenever supplies are brought to the maternity center. In addition, the midwife records the amount of drugs supplied to each agent. Supplies are usually distributed in standard amounts, for example, 50 Panadol tablets.

- Client forms: The agent can give a client a referral coupon (with pictographs) to take to the local maternity center or UCH. Reasons for referral may include an IUD insertion, vaccinations, or complications of an illness or pregnancy. The project plans to provide receipts to clients indicating the amount they have paid for the drugs given out by the community agents. Duplicate receipts would be turned in to the midwives indicating the amount of money collected by each agent.

EVALUATION

Inadequate census and vital statistics exist in the project area. In addition, it is likely that there will be only modest short-term changes in fertility and in maternal, infant, and child mortality and morbidity in the two-year duration of the project. These factors, plus the illiteracy of most of the community agents are expected to complicate but fortunately not to cripple evaluation. Illiteracy means that the system of forms and records must be kept simple. Much of the evaluation will depend upon routine service statistics and on the amount of health commodities and contraceptive supplies distributed. The fact that these carry a monetary value may be an effective check against the problem of over-reporting. Close supervision will provide another check. Periodic evaluations will be made by the midwife-supervisors and by UCH staff. Each midwife will hold twice-monthly meetings with the agents under her aegis in order to provide moral support, technical advice and in-service training, and to resupply drugs. The UCH staff holds monthly meetings with the midwives and the agents in order to assess their performance, to continue training, and to handle problems that may arise.

Health center maternity records and community agent service statistics are being supplemented by a household survey which was carried out prior to the initiation of services. This will be followed by a postsurvey during the later phase of the project. The presurvey has been used to assess health and nutritional practices, contraceptive prevalence, and fertility experience. A few knowledge and attitude questions were also included. Since the project emphasizes MCH/FP services, the primary target respondents for the survey were married women of reproductive age. However, a sample of husbands, whose attitudes may be relevant to the success of the project, was also interviewed. The postsurvey will be generally similar to the presurvey and will attempt to assess changes in health practices and contraceptive prevalence during the project period. It will also include items regarding the acceptance of and reaction to the community agents and their services.

Preliminary Results of the Presurvey

In 1980, a total of 441 married women, aged 15 to 49, and 500 married men were interviewed in the seven villages having a maternity center. While most of the women interviewed were between 20 and 40 years old, the men were older, over half being at least 40 years old. Only 14 percent of the wives have any formal education, while 35 percent of the men had been to school. The women were mostly part-time farmers and petty traders, as were the majority of the men. However, 16 percent of the men were craftsmen or artisans while 12 percent were teachers or other government employees. Two-thirds of the population were Moslem; most Christians belonged to the established Protestant denominations. Sixty percent of the men were monogamous (a single wife) while 48 percent of the women interviewed were in a monogamous union. The women averaged 4.75 live births.

Family Planning

Both women and men were very strongly pronatalist - they believed it important to have many children. When asked how many more children they wanted, 96 percent said they either wanted as many as possible or as many as God would give. Most disapproved of using a modern family planning method for preventing a pregnancy. Reasons given for objecting to family planning included the belief that childbearing should be left up to God, and fears that the woman could become infertile, that she could become promiscuous (according to the men), and that the husband would disapprove (according to the women). Only 10 percent of the women said they approved of family planning, but this proportion increased among those with any education and those over 35 years of age. Virtually none of the women had discussed family planning with their husband.

Knowledge of modern family planning was very meager. Only 26 percent of the women and 17 percent of the men could name any family planning method. Contraceptives most often mentioned were injection, the oral contraceptive pill, and the IUD. Use of the modern methods was minimal; 2.5 percent of the women had ever used a method while only 1.5 percent were currently using a method. Virtually all women, however, practiced postpartum abstinence, refraining from sex for an average of 23 months following the birth of their last child. Attitudes toward abortion and sterilization were also very negative: 99 percent of both women and men disapproved of abortion while 90 percent disapproved of sterilization. Both were regarded as dangerous and against "God's will" while some felt that abortion was "like murder." While much of the opposition to family planning is likely due to ignorance and confusion of modern methods (which are relatively safe) with traditional techniques (which are sometimes dangerous), one must recognize that many children are desired, and that the accepted technique of child-spacing is postpartum abstinence accompanied by breastfeeding.

Use of Health Services

Most women had not used a government health facility during the past year. Those who had done so used the child welfare services (19 percent) and the maternal health services (12 percent). About half (47 percent) of the youngest children of the mothers had had any immunization while 19 percent had had two or more rounds of immunization. The majority of mothers (68 percent) bottle-fed their infants, usually starting around three months of age. Among those who breastfeed, the practice lasted an average of 19 months. The women were asked where they delivered their last child. While a fourth (24 percent) delivered in a hospital, and another 30 percent delivered in a government maternity, nearly half delivered in their own home. Surprisingly, many of these women (33 percent of all women) said they delivered with no assistance from another person. Only 13 percent of the mothers said they delivered with the assistance of a TBA. The effect of the CBD project's upgrading of TBAs' skills on the number of TBA-assisted births and the utilization of the government health facilities will be followed closely.

EARLY PROJECT EXPERIENCE

The first few months of TBA and VHW services have generally supported the hypothesis that the community-based approach can be a viable one. The support of the village chiefs, elders, and other members of the communities has been very positive. This acceptance represents a great deal of spadework and effort on the part of UCH project staff. Even before the project was funded, UCH staff visited the villages in the area, explained the project, listened to concerns and questions, and met with both the political and traditional leaders. It was emphasized that the project was a cooperative one, and not something that would be placed in their midst by an outside agency. After funding, the communities organized themselves for the selection and recruitment of TBAs and VHWs. It should be noted that pre-implementation activities, while difficult to quantify, are critical to the success or failure of a project such as this in which implementation relies on voluntary participation.

At present, the communities have accepted the trained fieldworkers and are using them for treatment and preventative services. Each worker averaged about 8 to 10 treatments a month, as well as referring some clients to the local health center or UCH; several lives have already been saved by the agents bringing serious cases to UCH. The early success has been accompanied by administrative problems in developing an adequate system for the resupply of drugs and dressings for the large number of fieldworkers.

The first few months have thus witnessed adjustments in the logistics, reporting, and supervision systems as the UCH staff and the local government midwives experience the practical problems of running a relatively large rural health program: the accomplishment is, nonetheless, rather significant. Within a few months, the number of outlets for health services has expanded from 7 to 178. During the month of June 1981, with services established in five of the areas, over 1,100 persons were treated for illness by the community agents and over 50 persons became users of modern family planning (Table 21:1). The task for now is to maintain the enthusiasm of the volunteer VHWs and through supervision and further training to systematically improve the quality of their health services.

TABLE 21:1. Community Agent Services Provided: February to June, 1981, and June 1981*

Treatments	Feb. to June	June
Malaria	1223	591
Cough	445	295
Dressing of wounds	257	137
Diarrhea	82	54
Other illnesses	132	59
All illnesses	2139	1136
Antenatal anaemia (new cases)	119	67
Family planning (new cases)	107	55
Deliveries	62	32

* Services were only gradually introduced in different areas during this period. By the middle of June, six of the seven areas had services and 150 community agents were functioning.

Part Eight

Training Issues and Strategies in CBD Programs

22
Training CBD Workers for Family Planning and Health Interventions

Archie S. Golden,
Maria J. Wawer, and
Mary Anne Mercer

As part of the world-wide movement to expand family planning and primary health care to both urban and rural populations, auxiliary or village health workers represent an essential human resource. The use of such personnel requires the training of large number of individuals. Primary care and family planning represent complex activities, requiring the organization of supplies, logistics, and supervision, and it is enticing to assume that training is relatively simple in comparison. All too often, in fact, directors of community-based distribution (CBD) and primary health care (PHC) programs expect that training can be accomplished in a short time, with insufficient thought given to the consequences of inadequate worker preparation. In addition, evaluation of training programs is frequently incomplete and directors receive insufficient information to judge whether their programs are adequate. This paper discusses a set of principles for training CBD workers in family planning and health interventions.

TRAINING IN CBD PROJECTS: SETTING THE STAGE

Training CBD workers to deliver both health and family planning interventions entails certain difficulties. By definition, a CBD worker goes into the community to deliver program services and does not perform the bulk of these activities in a clinic. The supervision received by such a worker may be more sporadic than that offered to clinic-based staff, since personnel with supervisory potential are often based in health centers. The addition of CBD workers to an existing system may overburden the supervisory structure available. The CBD worker is thus in the position of performing an unfamiliar and complex role, often without benefit of regular support, assistance in problem-solving, or correction of errors.

An added challenge to CBD workers is their unique outreach role which requires continuous solo public contact - going into the homes of possibly uninterested neighbors in order to promote changes in life-style or habits. This is in sharp contrast with the more easily-recognizable, helper role assumed by workers providing curative services, particularly those in a clinic setting to whom patients actively come for assistance. In some programs, where it is necessary for the worker to cover several villages, the time spent with each client must be limited, making more critical the task of ensuring the effectiveness of every client contact. In addition, like all village-level workers, they have the task of instigating and maintaining clients' interest in diverse practices which may be preventive and not have immediate, tangible benefits (Bhatia, 1981). In the case of family planning, which may be considered a taboo subject in some communities, workers may face organized forces actively working against the service. Workers require preparation to handle their unique role in the community.

The integration of family planning and health may produce program benefits, including efficiency, as multiple functions are melded into the activities of one basic worker. It cannot be forgotten, however, that integration increases the burden on the worker who must master a larger number of curative and preventive functions. Recent trends to increase the amount of health care and other preventive measures delivered by CBD/FP workers must be reflected in training. The ability to assign priorities to activities becomes more crucial. Assignment of priorities implies the need for workers to comprehend program goals and tailor their activities accordingly, rather than being overwhelmed by activities that may be secondary to program needs.

Problem solving represents an important aspect of competency. No training course can cover all field situations and workers will, on occasion, have to react to new problems and make decisions without having previous training or experience with a particular problem. Identifying solutions does not necessarily entail the use of sophisticated reasoning methods and technology. Problem solving can mean that workers are familiar with their role, and know when to refer individuals with complaints outside the realm of what they have been taught. It is important that worker training address such situations.

In order to prepare CBD workers for their roles, there is a need for clear goals and careful selection of educational techniques. This is particularly important because courses are usually of short duration and teachers might not have ongoing contact with trainees once the latter return to their villages. Trainers seldom have recourse to relatively sophisticated teaching resources such as pretested materials or printed matter and audiovisual tools for students' ongoing retraining and self-learning. The problem has been compounded when project planners overestimate the amount of information students can absorb in a given time frame.

TRAINING ISSUES IN CBD PROJECTS

Training is an ongoing process wherein people learn to perform certain tasks in a competent manner. It signifies the attainment of specified skills, knowledge, and attitudes, and demands behavioral change on the part of the trainees.

It is important to look at training as a continuum (Figure 22:1), not as one short process which lasts, as it does in many cases today, from a few basic knowledge and skills of students and proceeds through training to continuing education, which should last throughout the health workers' entire career.

Figure 22:1. Training as a Continuum

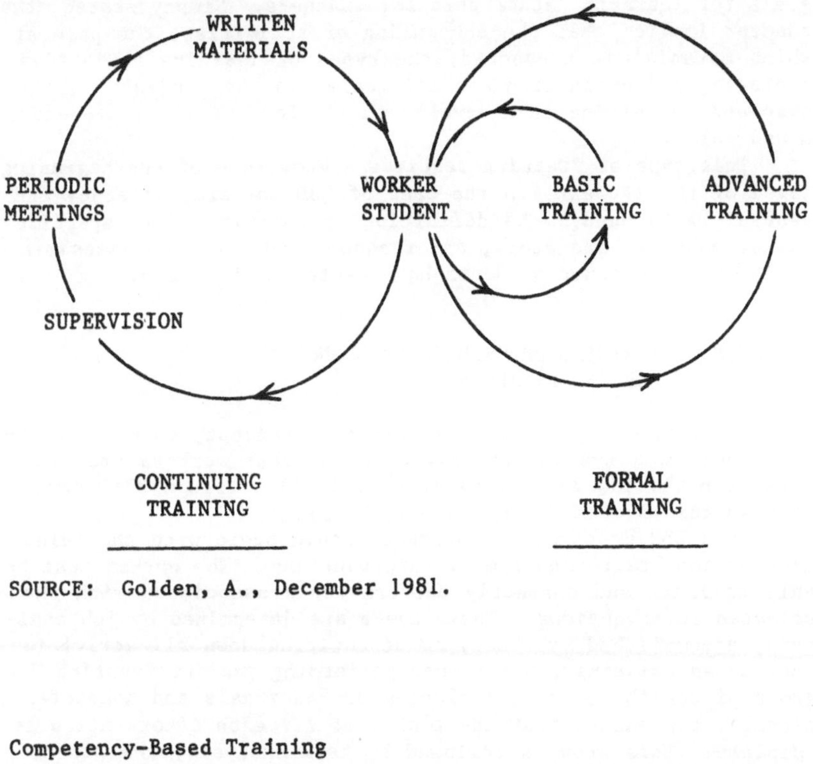

SOURCE: Golden, A., December 1981.

Competency-Based Training

Training for CBD workers has tended to be subject-centered. In such a system trainers decide that workers must know about a subject, without looking at the exact functions necessary to apply the knowledge. Students are frequently asked to study written theoretical material. All students study the same material in the same setting during the same time frame. Learning is divorced from the realities of the health care that people need.

In contrast, competency-based training programs are organized around specific functions or competencies. As McGaghie and Miller (McGaghie et al., 1978) have stated, "The intended output of a competency-based program is a health professional who can practice at a defined level of proficiency, in accord with local conditions, to meet local needs." Simkins has described what he calls nonformal education in terms that correspond well to the practice of effective CBD worker training. In a nonformal program, training is short-term and specific, and not oriented toward the acquisition of degrees or credentials. The content of training is skill-centered and practical rather than theoretical (Simkins, 1976). Wang has described such training as being tailored to performance specifications for a particular job (Wang, 1981). In addition, training centers are often community-centered and flexibly structured, and may be locally controlled (Simkins, 1976).

Competency-based training focuses on identifying training goals for learners rather than for teachers. Simply stated, the concept implies that the scheduling of activities, the pace at which material is presented, the types of learning activities employed, and evaluation are all geared to the students' abilities and to helping them develop skills for specific, predetermined roles.

This type of training requires a knowledge of the beginning level of the student (in the case of CBD workers, literacy and general background); the definition of functions into specific tasks, subtasks and steps; and frequent and thorough assessment to determine whether students have mastered the tasks.

A SYSTEM OF TRAINING PROGRAM (CURRICULUM) DEVELOPMENT FOR CBD PROJECTS

Using the competency-based training concept, courses can be developed in a systematic way, assuring that workers are prepared for the job to be done (Segal, 1975). Figure 22:2 demonstrates this system (Golden et al, 1981).

In a CBD program, the process should begin with the selection of the health and family interventions. The worker must be able to learn and correctly perform tasks associated with the selected interventions. These tasks are determined by job analysis, accomplished by observing and writing down all activities done by an existing practitioner performing the intervention. A group of health workers, including professionals and nonprofessionals, can ensure that the task list for each intervention is complete. This step is followed by task analysis, the process of analyzing the difficulty and complexity of each activity. At this point, one should consider whether the tasks are too complex. Subsequently the training planner decides exactly what the trainees are to learn - what they will be able to do at the end of training, referred to as the set of terminal competencies.

Guilbert (Guilbert, 1977), Segal (Segal et al., 1975), and others have outlined in detail the steps of moving from a job description to a curriculum that assures student competencies. The process, as applicable to CBD training, can be simplified as follows:

1. Describe the CBD job to be performed, taking into account existing job definitions, if any, and the needs and resources of the community.

Figure 22:2. A Model for Training Program Development

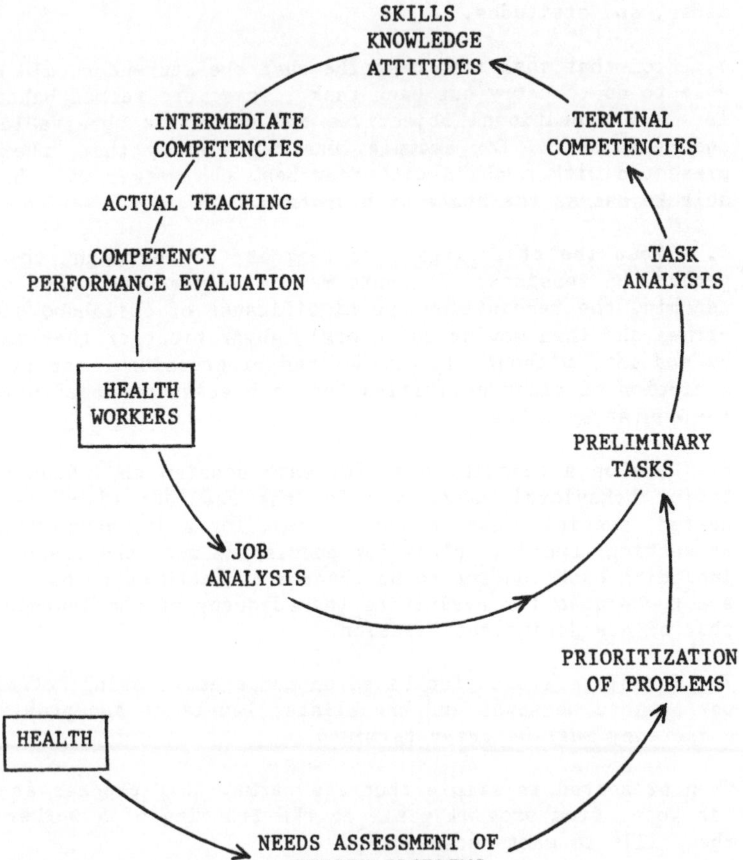

SOURCE: Adapted from Golden, A.S., D.G. Carlson, and J.L. Hagen. The Art of Teaching Primary Care. New York: Springer Publishing Co., 1981.

2. Analyze the job and separate it into its component tasks. Verify, if necessary, the validity of those tasks - are they really needed to perform the job?

3. Analyze each task in terms of specific behaviors needed to perform it, including requisite technical skills, knowledge, and attitudes.

4. From that analysis, describe what the student should be able to do to carry out each task. These are termed behavioral or educational objectives and should be observable and measurable. For example, one can specify that "when presented with a child with diarrhea, the worker will be able to assess the state of hydration."

5. Group the objectives into segments to be taught together, by sessions. Segments may be progressive, such as teaching the recognition and significance of childhood diarrhea and then moving on to oral rehydration; or they may be modular, without tightly-defined progression. The description of class activities for each session constitutes the course syllabus.

6. Develop a teaching plan for each session to include: topic; behavioral objectives for the session; time required; special requirements for teaching aids, personnel, or setting; specific plans for proceeding with the lesson, including both content to be covered and methods to be used; and techniques for evaluating the adequacy of the learning that occurs during that session.

7. Formulate evaluation based on competency, using actual performance measures and checklists; levels of acceptable competency must be pre-determined.

When presented in simple concrete terms, this process assists in going from program goals to the training of a worker with the skills to meet those goals.

An exact definition of points to be mastered is essential to any training program. It allows trainers to specify only that which is to be learned, minimizing superfluous content, yet including sufficient material for the worker to become competent in the intervention. From this step flows the determination of the skills, knowledge, and attitudes (educational domains) necessary to accomplish the terminal competency. The domains can be illustrated using the example of Oral Rehydration Therapy (ORT):

1. <u>Skill</u>: Show the mother how to prepare and mix the ORT solution.
   <u>Knowledge</u>: The contents and proportions of the mixture.
   <u>Attitude</u>: Value of carefulness in the measurements.

2. Skill: Be able to motivate the mother to use the preparation.
   Knowledge: Technique of motivation.
   Attitude: Belief in the utility of encouraging people to use ORT.

CBD projects sponsored by the U.S. Agency for International Development's (USAID) Research Division have varied greatly in the emphasis placed on tailoring training to field requirements. It is difficult to compare results from separate projects because a large number of variables differ in each situation. However, project success does appear to have been influenced by training strategies. This has been particularly true for projects at either end of the spectrum: those in which much effort was put into designing training to match field activities, and those in which this effort was minimal.

In the Peru PROSMIP Program, only 0.5 percent of the total time was spent on ORT, although this represented an important intervention on the program. In fact, only 17 percent of the total training time in this project was spent on material specific to direct provision of services, the rest of the course content being theoretical (Rosenfield, 1980). In the Nicaragua Partera program, an attempt was made to teach semiliterate traditional birth attendants to deliver oral contraceptives, condoms, ORT, vitamins, iron, aspirin, and mebendazole, and to use improved obstetrical practices, all in the space of five days. Even though there was time to repeat the 10 modules within the training course, the time frame appears inadequate to produce workers capable of the field duties demanded of them. In both these projects, workers experienced difficulties in fulfilling the field tasks in their job description partly as a result of the type of training received (Heiby, 1981).

The Sudan Community-Based Health and Family Planning Project designed training to equip workers for specific tasks. As described by El Tom (this volume), local midwives were trained for three weeks in home distribution of oral contraceptives, oral rehydration packets, and nutritional information. Techniques used included frequent repetition, role plays, and practice in the field. Results of field supervision indicate good results in retention of knowledge.

TRAINING METHODS FOR COMPETENCY-BASED TRAINING

How best to ensure that workers will be able to remember and carry out essential components of their task - communication, motivation, and application of technical skills? Both the literature and field experience provide some information. The present tendency is to train CBD workers using traditional lecture methods with little additional variation (Program Files, 1981). Although lecture formats can be useful in the introduction of general themes, CBD workers of various educational levels have demonstrated difficulty in taking notes and applying their content to the field (Heiby,1981). Different CBD projects have relied on illiterate, semiliterate, and literate workers. Many nominally literate students cannot effectively analyze the relevance of verbal information and record it selectively in note-taking. A primary school education of grade five or higher is generally required before a trainee can be expected to take classroom notes (Wang, 1981). Training methods not requiring literacy, or at least note-taking, are probably more effective in most CBD situations: a training program aimed at the illiterate or semiliterate level will reach all members of a classroom and can be expanded for those students who can absorb more information. Going in the reverse direction, that is simplifying complex explanations, can be more difficult, especially for relatively inexperienced trainers.

The general rule for training should be hear (or read) one, see one, do one; implying that supervised practice should follow theory and demonstration. Training rules include:

- Emphasize the practical and reduce the theoretical.
- Keep students thinking and active.
- Diminish passive learning, such as that which results from being lectured and spoken to in large groups.
- Use discussion based on real situations and cases.
- Demonstrate skills as often as necessary.
- Have trainees practice the skills and repractice them until they can perform them correctly using activities such as role plays.
- Repetition is necessary.
- Use the village as a laboratory.

Literate home visitors in the Zaire PRODEF project were able to remember and correctly recreate simulation of home visits three months after having been trained through participatory methods. These visits included contraceptive distribution and delivery of Oralyte, mebendazole, and chloroqine (Wawer, 1981d).

Self-learning in which trainees are given programmed booklets that cover and review project material may offer a useful adjunct to other methods used in a project. The Guatemala PRINAPS study (Aldana, this volume) describes one attempt to test the application of self-instruction in a CBD setting. One obvious criterion for the use of self-instructional material is that the student be literate. Materials must be written in a simple way and in a logical sequence, and their use supplemented by small groups or individual tutorial sessions and practical work under supervision. One objective of this method is to save trainer time and thus costs, but further data collection is necessary to test this assumption.

A comparatively new method of training uses protocols, algorithms, or decision guides. These guides aid trainees in learning what to do following each step in a specific sequence of activities and examinations (Figure 22:3). Protocols have proven to be helpful in the education of various types of workers, but must be very simple, explicit, and easy to use. Besides their training function, it would seem they could also be helpful as field guides. However, experience in various cul-

Figure 22:3. Decision Guide: Fever in Child Under Age 2

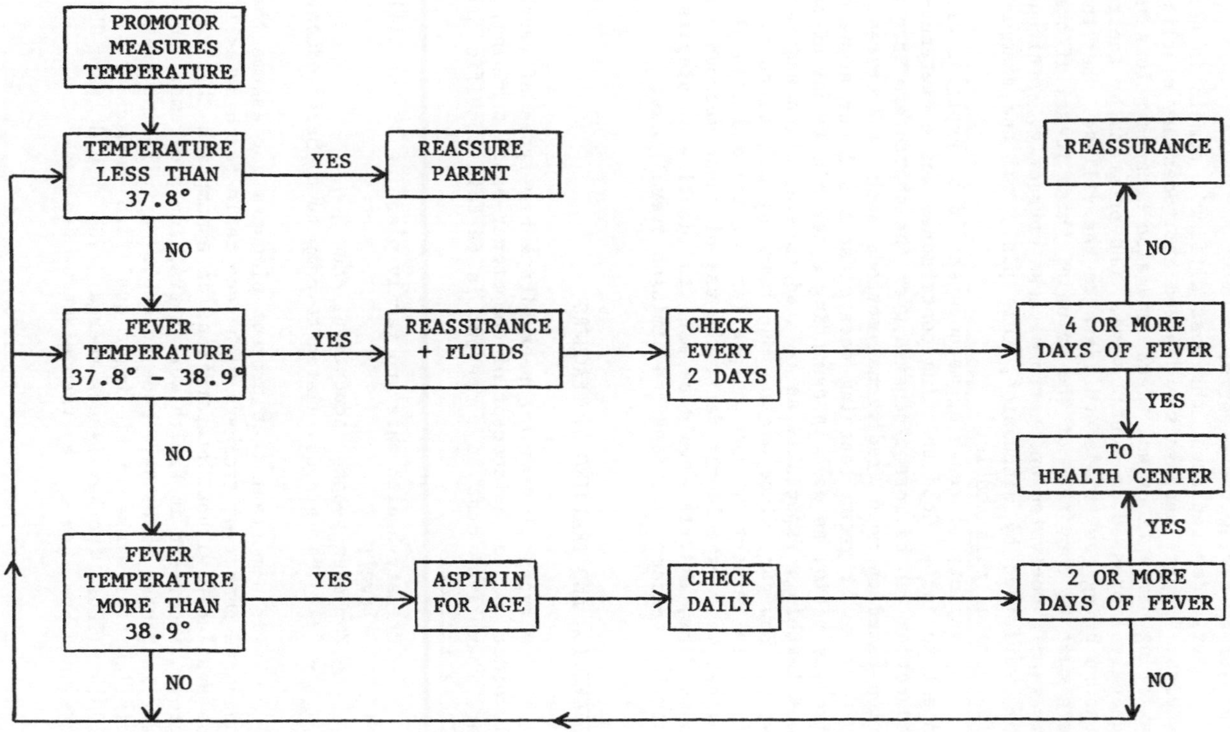

tures indicates that students use them during the course, but no longer refer to them once training is completed (Johnson, 1981). Most forms of these tools are inappropriate for illiterate workers, although literate family members can be recruited to help the worker review the material.

Attitudes represent the most difficult domain in teaching adults, in part because the desired attitudes may conflict with existing perceptions and ideas, and also because values are frequently expressed in subtle ways. CBD programs by their very nature bring new skills and ideas to the village. Health workers must be convinced of the value of these ideas, if they are to remain motivated and perform tasks correctly. Attitudes can be reinforced by discussion, role play, and the example of teachers as role models.

A variety of teaching methods should be explored with respect to cost. Good training costs money and competency-based education can be more expensive over the short-term than education based on more traditional methods such as lectures. The use of small group learning necessitates a lower student-to-faculty ratio, as well as demanding a certain amount of one-to-one teaching, especially as related to evaluation and remedial work. However, since small group learning is particularly helpful with respect to work on problem solving and role-playing, higher costs should not deter the use of these methods. At the same time, efforts should be made to identify strategies that stretch teacher resources and diminish overall cost.

SELECTION AND TRAINING OF TEACHERS

New types of training necessitate new types of teachers. In order to use the concept of competency-based training, teachers themselves must be competent in certain specific areas. These include:

- Primary health care and family planning at the village level,
- Competency-based education, and
- Training methods related to competency-based education.

It is important that project planners not assume that an adequate number of trainers with acceptable teaching skills will be available without preparation, an assumption that has been proven incorrect in health worker training programs. In Matlab, for instance, plans were made to employ a full-time trainer, but difficulties arose in finding a qualified candidates (Bhatia, 1981). Thus, two key issues emerge: Who should train CBD workers, and how should they themselves be trained?

Selection

Physicians and nurses, who have seldom been taught how to train, may not be the best trainers of CBD workers; in addition, they frequently lack direct experience in community-based care. The successful Taiwan FP programs recognized the need to combine the talents of technical and field experts with those of teaching and training specialists (Cesnada, 1970). In the past, however, many programs tended to rely on medically qualified personnel, specifically physicians and nurses, who may or may not have training expertise. Their most frequently reported error was the presentation of too much material at too fast a pace via didactic methods (notably lecturing), resulting in a lack of significant skill-acquisition by the trainees (Rosenfield, 1980; Cesnada, 1970; Garnier, 1969).

Researchers on the Narangwal project and others have found that effective health worker trainers, particularly in the later stages of training, are likely to be senior health workers of the very type being trained. The ability of the trainee to identify personally with the trainer (who often also functions as supervisor) has been considered a major advantage in the process of role integration (C. DeSweemer, 1981) and has been described in the Sudan Community-Based Health and Family Planning Project (El Tom, this volume).

Trainers should have experience in the tasks they are teaching. Practitioners such as the rural health technicians in Guatemala (Aldana, this volume) can become appropriate trainers having pre-existing primary health care and family planning experience. They have the added advantage of continuing contact with trainees, since they serve as the ongoing supervisors of the workers.

In Java, auxiliaries have been trained in a system that may be described as rolling: one group of trainers is selected and formed from the cadre of existing workers, this group trains a subsequent group of workers, and so on (Hendrata and Wardayo, 1977). A built-in weakness in this system is that there is never a continuous expert group of trainers with experience. Some countries now use experienced mobile training teams: a combination of mobile and local trainers can constitute the teaching team, connecting the training with local conditions and assuring continuity through expert input and supervision.

The extent to which a training program is decentralized can affect the choice of trainers, not infrequently resulting in the use of available local health personnel. Unless such individuals are trained to teach, worker competencies may vary greatly depending on the ability and pedagogical knowledge of the trainer (Golden 1981; Hurtado, 1981)

Training of Trainers

Methods of teaching CBD trainers are poorly documented. Issues are likely to be similar to those in PHC programs such as the SHDS program for West Africa. SHDS has established a regional teaching center for primary health worker trainers and its experience underscores the need to provide both technical and methodological content and experience for potential trainers. Candidates are required to take part in group discussion and other participatory kinds of learning throughout their training, with the intention of strengthening their abilities to effectively use such methods. Even so, the tendency to rely primarily on lectures is noted as a significant problem during the trainers' practice teaching session. Physicians and nurses often come to the center with a limited understanding of primary health care, making it necessary to include a module on its planning and implementation (Ericson, 1981).

Potential CBD trainers need to demonstrate competency at a number of levels. It cannot be taken for granted that a trainer, even if he or she belongs to a health profession, knows necessary details concerning the use of contraceptives or specific health interventions. The level of pre-existing technical knowledge must be ascertained and, if necessary, augmented. Trainers must be able to teach fieldworkers using a simplified, skills-oriented approach. They must also be capable of assessing the trainees' progress in meeting training goals, and adapt their pace and techniques to the needs of the group. Participatory techniques emphasizing pedagogical practice and acquisition of skills over theory are important in the preparation of trainers.

A final practical consideration is that of ensuring that trainers will adhere to the planned teaching activities rather than falling back into their own teaching styles, stressing content with which they are more familiar. As with the workers themselves, trainers who are introduced to nontraditional methods in their preparation will be more likely to use them comfortably later with their classes (Ericson, 1981). Some degree of standardized training content helps assure quality; the use of training manuals is one method of achieving standardization. In some projects, flipcharts have been developed to incorporate all the basic areas of skills and knowledge needed: their use allows the trainer to progress at an appropriate pace for the class, avoiding the temptation of teaching "too much" or neglecting important points. Further experience with such methods is to be encouraged, although too much faith cannot be placed in the production of a final "ultimate" training outline due to the different cultural and technical demands of every project.

TECHNICAL ASPECTS OF CBD TRAINING

Length of Training

The length of CBD worker training should ideally reflect the number of family planning and other duties to be performed. At present, however, the length of training allotted to teach the same number of skills varies considerably between projects.

A number of projects have provided information which may assist in determining how much training is necessary to ensure a viable CBD program; although the minimum time to train workers to provide family planning motivation and simple contraceptives appears to be three to five days (Kim and Ross, 1972; Gorosh and Ross, 1979; Bertrand et al., 1981). The trend for longer CBD training courses is growing, particularly as the number of project interventions increases. Current and recent programs frequently offer between a week and two weeks of training, in part to ensure sufficient time for worker practice: Zaire PRODEF, 12 days; Morocco VDMS Expansion, 8 days (both projects cover family planning plus several health services); and Brazil CPAIMC, 8 days (covering data collection and family planning) (Wawer, 1981c; Wawer, 1981a; Wawer, 1982). Workers in the three programs above were literate. The Sudan CBD project (El Tom, this volume) which employed some nonliterate workers spent a week each on ORT and contraception (primarily oral contraceptives).

Despite the trend toward longer courses, expense represents a frequent constraint in establishing the length of training programs. In addition, the Zaire PRODEF project (Mangani, this volume) and others (Labbok, 1981) have found that training sessions may need to be of limited duration - two weeks at the most - since most workers cannot be taken away from their work or families for longer periods of time.

The use of competency-based training can assist in indicating the necessary length of training. Training should continue until the student has mastered the required performance. This time will vary among trainees and will depend upon the level of literacy and other personal factors. Ideally, competency-based training demands a somewhat flexible program that allows certain students to finish early and others to keep learning and training until they attain the necessary level of competency. Realistically, however, time limits will need to be set; if students cannot master the material in the maximum time allowed, they may have to be removed from the program. As an alternative, the amount of material covered may require adjustment. As Heiby has indicated training for the specific competencies in the shortest reasonbable period of time remains the logical approach to determining program length, and "an explicit definition of the desired role of the volunteer is essential to this process" (Heiby, 1980).

Rate of Presentation

A major problem in CBD training which will increase with the addition of interventions is the presentation of too much material at too rapid a pace through the use of didactic methods; compounded, these factors result in a lack of skill attainment by trainees.

Attempts have been made to rationalize the rate of presentation of material. In Narangwal, only one new idea per two- or three-hour session was presented to illiterate or semiliterate workers (Rural Health Research Centre, 1975). In the Zaire home visitors program, one function (such as ORT) was taught per day with subsequent frequent repetition. Each function consisted on the average of 15 or more specific pieces of information (Wawer, 1981b). In Nicaragua, initial attempts to teach the parteras 300 discrete skills or areas of knowledge in five days proved impractical and the number was subsequently reduced to 130.

Relatively simple skills such as measuring temperature or arm circumference may take two to four hours, whereas more complicated skills such as ORT may take two to four days.

There exists no firm scheme for rate of presentation. In attempting to tailor training content to the time available for the course, there are two options. If a limited number of days is available for training, then only the competencies that the trainees can master in the specified time should be included. On the other hand, if the time period is flexible, essential competencies should be taught first and other activities added once the primary tasks are mastered. Training time should reflect the complexity of the competency to be learned, although many factors will also influence the length of basic training. These include age, trainee literacy and schooling, trainer experience and preparation, and the distance of the training site from the trainees' homes. Above all, the training program director as well as the health services director must understand the concept that learning is continuous and must not end after the basic program.

Centralization versus Decentralization of Training

Training centers may be centralized, decentralized, or be organized on a regional basis. The need for CBD training to resemble the situation in which workers will actually function suggests that the training be provided in or near their own communities and be decentralized, or at least regionalized. Decentralization may lower training costs and can increase the flexibility in the length of the training program even once the course is already in progress. It requires, however, that trainers travel to the training sites and be willing to live according to local standards during the training periods. Decentralization also demands the teaching of a greater number of classes since classes are generally smaller. This apparent inefficiency has been said to provide better trained and more effective workers, and thus may be more efficient over the long-term than the mass production of workers removed from their work setting (Wang, 1981). In addition, different levels of personnel can be trained at different levels of decentralization.

The relative merits of centralization versus decentralization have not been formally tested in CBD projects, although various patterns have been attempted. In the Moroccan Visites a Domcile de Motivation Systematique (VDMS) expansion, provincial training teams assembled in Rabat for centralized training. The teams then provided courses for field-level workers in their respective provinces, in the provincial capital, or in several catchment areas. The large number of fieldworkers to be trained (up to a hundred in each province) rendered the task of providing a decentralized course in each locality impossible, and at the same time, the numbers involved were too large to train in one central center. The compromise model of producing VDMS trainers who then trained smaller groups of workers close to their home regions offered a practical compromise (Nichols and Labbok, 1981).

As previously mentioned, a potential difficulty in decentralization is the lack of standardization among local trainers. In the Guatemala PRINAPS project (Aldana, this volume), training has been assigned to government-trained tecnicos de salud rural (TSRs) in their own districts. Preliminary results indicate the test scores of different groups vary substantially, indicating that the quality of training may have been uneven. One possible alteration being considered would be to provide the TSRs with a standardized course of their own, in order to decrease the potential for great variability in trainer ability (Hurtado, 1981).

Phasing of Training

The pace at which basic skills should be taught to CBD workers, whether in one initial training course or spread out over time, is another important question which has not been fully studied.

Experience and theory indicate that students may remember information and activities better if these are taught in discrete "chunks." The optimal size of each chunk will vary with the length of the training course and the literacy levels of workers. Phasing offers one model of learning in units. Workers learn only a few activities during any one training session and then work in the field for several weeks or months. They return periodically for short sessions to learn new tasks, each of which is applied in the field immediately after training. There are no direct data to indicate whether workers comprehend and retain information better when taught in a phased manner. However, experience with the opposite trend, where large amounts of information have been taught in a short period of time has generally not been positive (Heiby, 1980). Phasing, as practiced in the Sudan CBD project allows workers to absorb new tasks only when previously taught skills have been mastered and applied in the field (Wessley, 1981) and has been identified as an important training variable for workers in the Haitian community Health Program of the Albert Schweitzer Hospital (Bergren et al., 1981).

Another aspect of phasing merits further attention. As additional activities are phased into their job descriptions, workers may see their job as expanding in importance. Since the structure of many CBD projects provides little room for upward mobility or promotion, gradual changes and expansion in activities to be performed may have a positive effect on job satisfaction.

In-Service Continuing Training

Training is not an event lasting a few days or a month, but an ongoing continual process of which basic training represents only the initial event. Continuing training should include updating, clarification, and evaluation of existing skills, as well as the learning of new skills deemed appropriate for the CBD role. In fact, many programs that include both family planning and health interventions cannot cover all desired tasks and material in the basic training session. A system of continuing education takes the training program director "off the hook" since the pressure to include everything in basic training is lessened, and activities can be added as workers become ready for them.

Continued training should consist not only of educational activities but should be tied to regular supervision. Group meetings with the promotor, the supervisor, and the health center physician can serve as a means of retraining. The role of a supervisor should ideally be similar to that of a teacher, and the competency-based system should be maintained throughout all aspects of the training.

Materials

In any training program that is practical and emphasizes active learning rather than listening, training materials are important and should be based on technology appropriate to the situation. However, there is a need to avoid undue reliance on training manuals. Methods such as movies or slides should generally be avoided due to cost, the possibility that they will be misunderstood, and because workers will seldom be able to use similar technology when speaking to villagers. In general, ordinary pictures can do the job.

Discussions and role-plays do not require much in the way of sophisticated materials, and regular flipcharts, flannel boards, and a blackboard will almost always suffice to convey the required message. Once workers begin their practical training, they need access to all the types of supplies and medications to be used in the service program in order to practice their use. An example of such material would be mixing containers, measuring spoons, salt, and sugar necessary for the preparation of home-based ORT solution.

EVALUATION OF CBD TRAINING PROGRAMS

Training evaluation must be implemented early in the course to avoid the situation where deficiencies in worker preparation are not noted until fieldwork has begun.

Training evaluation relates to the process factors within the course (that is, evaluation of the course itself), the attainment of competencies, and ultimately to the outcome of the project as a whole. Purposes of evaluation include the quantification of training program effects, measurement of the degree to which goals were accomplished, and the identification of areas for improvement. Training objectives or goals must be explicit prior to evaluation, and should describe <u>who</u> will do <u>how much</u> of <u>what</u> by <u>when</u>.

Input Evaluation

Input evaluation serves to indicate the manpower and material resources included in the training program. Elements to include are the number of students starting in the programs and their characteristics, such as age, sex, literacy, schooling, occupation, and residence; trainers' background and experience; training materials; and cost of materials and of trainer and student expenses.

Process Evaluation

Process evaluation is concerned with the question of whether training is actually proceeding as planned; for example, whether trainers are using the designed approaches and methods, the number of hours students are attending the sessions, and whether both the time allotted and other resources are adequate. This evaluation component concentrates on technical aspects of the course rather than on what individual trainees have learned.

Process evaluation can utilize a number of methodologies. Both the trainer and students can be questioned regarding scheduling, resources, and program strengths and weaknesses. Attendance records and other applicable forms or paperwork can be examined. Evaluators can also sit in on class activities to observe teaching methods, and the level of trainee participation.

Process evaluation is important in that it can provide useful information if field performance by trainees is inadequate. In such cases, planners will need to know whether inappropriate or insufficient training contributed to the problem. Furthermore, it is essential to know which aspects of training must be modified - teaching methods, scheduling, the amount of material to be covered, etc.

Attainment of Competencies

Evaluation of attainment of competencies is concerned with changes that occur in the knowledge, skills, and behavior of trainees as a result of training (Golden, 1981). It should contain elements designed to evaluate student performance in situations that match, to the greatest extent possible, real-life situations. Prior to the evaluation, the trainer must determine the exact level of student activity and knowledge needed to satisfactorily fulfill the work requirements. Evaluation methods can consist of any combination of practical examination (including role-plays and field practice, both of which can be observed using a checklist), oral examinations, and project assignments.

In a CBD setting, oral examinations are probably best suited if they are centered around practical problem solving, although some objective questions regarding informational content may be appropriate. The evaluation of attitudes can be accomplished through discussion, oral questioning, or the observation of role-plays. In general, trainers should observe how workers perform required tasks and demonstrate desired enthusiasm or other characteristics, rather than rely on questioning them about their attitudes.

Ideally, there will be some alternatives based on the results of final trainee evaluations. Results can be used to make decisions about specific trainees, but can also serve to indicate where modifications are needed in the training content or process itself. The revised Bangladesh-Matlab project used written quizzes combined with field evaluation and applied criteria sufficiently stringent to result in the failure of 10 percent of the trainees (Bhatia, 1981). In the Zaire PRODEF program, field evaluation during the course was based on observation of worker-client interactions, using a checklist. The results of this evaluation indicated that workers in this particular program had little difficulty communicating with clients and explaining the basic use of contraceptives. However, they needed more assistance with the task of remembering simple contraindications, and in reassuring women about minor side effects. This observation led to greater emphasis on these points during the original training (particularly for workers having greater difficulties) and in subsequent retraining, and to the preparation of simple memory aids to be used in the field (Wawer, 1981c).

If the program is designed so that, for whatever political or programatic reasons, all trainees are allowed to finish the course, the evaluation criteria and methods may vary considerably from a project in which certain standards must be met for completion of the training program. Trainee evaluation results may be used to select individuals for specific activities within the overall project framework. In the Schweitzer Community Health Program in Haiti, peripheral-level volunteer health workers showing the most evidence of being effective community leaders were recruited for higher-level training, and thus rewarded with a salaried job (Bergren et al., 1981). If evaluation of trainees is to serve a useful program purpose, plans for its use will have to be made prior to its initiation: this will ensure that the planned evaluation is designed to provide the necessary information. A shortcoming of the original Nicaraguan partera training program was the lack of any individual evaluation documented for each trainee, making correlation of training effects with field performance impossible (Heiby, 1981).

The need to match evaluation to relevant aspects of fieldwork is illustrated by the Haiti/CPFH/DHF CBD project. Male trainers scored better on the final test (which evaluated basic knowledge), yet female workers were ultimately said to perform better in the field. An inverse correlation was found between test scores and performance (Allman, 1981). Although one must be careful not to generalize from this example (the number of trainees was small and it is unclear whether women may have been less confident than men in a test situation or were subsequently more effective in the field for factors unrelated to the training course), evaluation as it was executed did not measure factors essential to field activity and was thus of limited usefulness.

Evaluation of attainment of competencies includes data frequently referred to as output evaluation. This included student evaluation results, percentage of students who graduated, and the time needed for each student to achieve competency.

Outcome Measures

The last common type of evaluation measures program outcomes, such as the percentage of women using a family planning method after trained workers have been in service for some time. Accurate program output measures are notably difficult to quantify even when data are collected systematically, and poor project results may be due to deficiencies in areas other than adequate worker preparation. Thus, even though positive program results may be thought to imply that adequate training has been provided, program evaluation of outcomes should generally be considered a separate issue from training evaluation. A possible exception is the case of formal operations research projects, where two or more sets of workers are given different training courses. Even in such cases, however, the difficulties inherent in controlling for variables unrelated to training frequently render the interpretation of results very difficult.

POTENTIAL DIRECTIONS FOR TRAINING RESEARCH IN CBD PROJECTS

Two general types of training research are important for CBD programs. First, in selected situations, it is important to continue and expand the testing of various training strategies and methods through comparative quasi-experimental designs (for example, testing the effects of self-learning versus classroom-based work, as is being done in Guatemala). Second, elements such as the rate of presentation of information, the overall amount of information that can be absorbed in a given time frame, and differences in information acquisition among trainees with different levels of literacy must be examined.

Training is an important component of any program, but it is also a component for which strong data in essential areas are lacking. In general, there is a need to identify and test training designs that offer specific advantages with respect to cost, duration, enhancement of worker comprehension, retention and competency in the field, simplicity in preparation and use, and adaptability for use by relatively unsophisticated trainers.

CONCLUSIONS

The CBD setting provides unique challenges for the fieldworker, challenges that must be addressed in training and retraining. Training should be treated as a continuing process which is competency-based. An explicit definition of the desired worker role is essential, and training methods and phasing should be adapted to local conditions. Trainers must be prepared in primary health care, family planning, and competency-based training methods.

The development of instructional material for CBD projects has in general been left to individual programs. Although there are advantages to developing different methods suitable to each context, disadvantages also exist if projects repeat past mistakes. Thus, there is a growing need for better communication between projects regarding training methods, materials, and evaluation, in order to assist in the dissemination of successful strategies and to avoid previous problems.

REFERENCES

Bergren, W.L. et al. "Reduction of Mortality in Rural Haiti Through a Primary Health Care Program." N.E.F. of Medicine 304 (1981): 1324-1330.

Bertrand, J. et al. "Evaluating Distributors' Knowledge of Contraceptives in the Guatemalan CBD Program." Paper presented at Population Association of America Annual Meeting, March 1981.

Bhatia, S. "The Training of Community Health Workers: The Experience in a Rural Area of Bangladesh." 1981 (unpublished).

Cesnada, G.P. "Training Fieldworkers for Family Planning." In Taiwan Family Planning Reader: How a Program Works. Taichung, Taiwan: The Chinese Center for International Training in Family Planning, (1970): 45-65.

DeSweemer, C. Personal Communication, 1981

Ericson, S. Personal Communication, 1981.

Garnier, J.C. "Morocco: Training and Utilization of FP Fieldworkers." Studies in Family Planning 47 (1969): 1-5.

Golden, A.S. "Guatemala, PRINAPS Project Trip Report, March 22-April 3, 1981." Baltimore, MD: The Johns Hopkins University.

Golden, A.S., D.G. Carlson, and J. Hagen, eds. The Art of Teaching Primary Care. New York: Springer, 1981.

Gorosh, M.E. and J.A. Ross. "Community-based Distribution of Oral Contraceptives in Rio Grande del Monte, Northeastern Brazil." International Family Planning Perspectives 5 (1979): 4.

Guilbert, J.J. Educational Handbook for Health Personnel. Geneva: World Health Organization, 1977.

Heiby, J. "Peru PROSMIP Project, Trip Report, January 1980." Washington, DC: U. S. Agency for International Development.

Heiby, J. "Guatemala, PRINAPS Project Trip Report, January 1981." Washington, DC: U. S. Agency for International Development.

Heiby, J.R. "Low Cost Health Delivery Systems: Lessons from Nicaragua." American Journal of Public Health 81 (1981): 514.

Hendrata, L. and Y. Wardoyo. "Village Cadre System in Community Development: Regency of Banjarnegara, Central Java." Presented at the Symposium on Community Health Workers, Arlie House, VA, October 1977.

Hurtado, E. Personal communication, 1981.

Jen, E. "Alternative Approaches to Training of Trainers." Paper presented at NCIH Conference, Washington, DC, June 1981.

Johns Hopkins University. "Operations Research Family Planning Project, Program Files." Baltimore, MD: 1981.

Johnson, L. Personal communication, 1981.

Kim, T. and W. Ross. "Training." In The Korean National Family Planning Program, 1972.

Kozma, R.B., L.W. Belle, and G.W. Williams. Instructional Techniques in Higher Education. Englewood Cliffs: Prentice-Hall, 1978.

Labbok, M. Personal communication, 1981.

McGaghie, W.C., G.E. Miller, A.W. Sajid, and T.B. Telder. Competency Based Curriculum Development in Medical Education: An Introduction. Public Health Papers, No. 68. Geneva: World Health Organization, 1978.

Nichols, D.J. and M. Labbok. "VDMS Household Distribution of Contraceptives in Manakech Morocco." Project files Morocco VDMS Projects. Washington, DC: U. S. Agency for International Development, 1981.

Rosenfield, A. "Trip Report, Peru. PROSMIP, March 1980." New York: Columbia University.

Segal, A.J., H. Vanderschmidt, R. Burglass, and T. Frostman. Systematic Course Design for the Health Fields. New York: John Wiley and Sons, 1975.

Simkins, T. Nonformal Education and Development. Manchester Monographs, 1979.

Wang, L.V. "A Global Review on Training of Community Health Workers. Commissioned for American Public Health Association's International Health Programs." Washington, DC: 1981 (unpublished draft).

Wawer, M.J. "Morocco VDMS Trip Report, November 1981." Baltimore, MD: Johns Hopkins University, 1981a.

_____. "Zaire PRODEF Training Manuals, April 1981." Baltimore, MD: Johns Hopkins University, 1981b.

_____. "Zaire PRODEF Project Trip Report, April 1981." Baltimore, MD: Johns Hopkins University, 1981c.

_____. "Zaire PRODEF Project Trip Report, August 1981." Baltimore, MD: Johns Hopkins University, 1981d.

_____. "Brazil CPAIMC Trip Report, February 1982." Baltimore, MD: Johns Hopkins University, 1982.

23
Research Program for the Training of Rural Health Promoters (PRINAPS)

Danilo Aldana and
J. Romeo de Leon Mendez

Guatemala has many of the same health characteristics as do other developing countries. Of 1,000 live births, 72 die before reaching the age of one year; 42.5 percent of deaths occur in children five years of age or younger. Eighty percent of the births are not attended by health care personnel and of any 100 children only 17 ever attend an outpatient clinic. Malnutrition remains a substantial problem among children. According to the Gomez classification, 77 percent of children suffer from some degree of malnutrition. Attempts to expand health care and social services are hampered by the mountainous terrain, the rural dispersal of 60.5 percent of the population, and the fact that approximately one-third of the Guatemalan population does not speak Spanish.

PRINAPS Background

In order to improve rural health outreach, the Ministry of Public Health and Social Assistance has defined a number of new worker categories and has been testing different training programs for these workers. For example, in 1972 with the assistance of the US Agency for International Development, the Ministry initiated the Tecnico de Salud Rural (rural health technician) job category. A school specializing in training this group was simultaneously initiated and following two years of instruction, workers receive a Bachelor of Health Sciences. Training is designed to prepare the Tecnicos de Salud Rural to work with community personnel in the area of primary health care.

One important function of the TSR is the training and supervision of rural health promoters (RHPs), volunteers who receive no salary. Promoters are expected to provide basic social and demographic data regarding their community; a record of the immunization and health status of children under five; the number of pregnant women and the antenatal services they receive; basic morbidity data concerning diarrhea, upper respiratory infections, intestinal parasites, anemia, and minor trauma; and a mortality register. In addition, promoters can sell clients oral rehydration salts, iron, aspirin, and mebendazole; provide simple first aid; and are expected to provide selected contraceptives (oral contraceptives, vaginal tablets, condoms) and follow-up for women using them. Each promoter is responsible for approximately 50 families (250 persons). Criteria for RHP selection include that they be at least 18 years of age and live in communities having fewer than 2,000 inhabitants.

Promoter training provided by the local TSR lasts between four and six weeks. Personnel other than TSRs involved in RHP training include other members of the health team, doctors, nurses, or social workers. Training materials have been produced centrally.

Although RHP training is recognized to be an important element in ensuring competence in the field, perennial problems remain in identifying a sufficient number of qualified trainers, bringing promoters and trainers together for the course, and defraying the associated costs. In 1977, a similar dilemma was faced when 70 percent of the auxiliary nurses working in Ministry of Health stands (health posts) were found to have no formal preparation for their work. At that time, a system of directed auto-instruction, or self-learning, was developed to stretch training resources. Basically, such instruction included both the use of centrally prepared auto-instructional material and supervision by a professional nurse higher in the Health Service hierarchy. The system was designed to permit the auxiliary nurse to study an hour each day during service time and to meet monthly with the professional nurse for further instruction and clarification.

The Human Resource Division of the Ministry prepared the self-instructional material and was thus able to acquire experience with this kind of educational method. Given the difficulties inherent in training RHPs, it was decided to test the feasibility and cost of training this cadre with a similarly designed self-instructional course. The following sections describe the operations research project designed to compare the effects of a traditional training approach versus the use of self-instruction in the training of RHPs. PRINAPS operations research activities in areas other than training will be listed and described briefly where warranted.

PROJECT DESIGN

The Division of Human Resource Formation and Training of the Ministry of Public Health and Social Assistance, with the assistance of USAID, instigated the program to investigate training, supervision, and provision of supplies to RHPs. Given the difficulties inherent in conducting an investigation at the national level, a study of five health areas was proposed, with the idea of replication at the national level if warranted by the results.

The objectives of the study were:

1. To train 400 RHPs in five health areas. Of these 200 were to be trained along with their wives or any other female relative living in the same house.

2. To develop two educational models in the training of RHPs: the traditional, similar to the one actually used in the health services; and the modular, using directed and auto-educational material.
3. To establish a municipal sale of medicines in each of the five health areas in order to guarantee supplies for RHPs.
4. To develop a supervisory model for the RHPs that would apply to the health services as a whole.

The PRINAPS program will last a total of 36 months and will provide training and field activities for 400 RHPs. During this period, 200 of the RHPs will have been trained by means of traditionally designed four-week courses, while the remaining 200 will have received training using learning handbooks designed for modular self-instruction. Both groups of RHPs will depend on local TSRs for their training, although the self-instructional group is expected to use the services of the TSR primarily for review sessions and any necessary explanation. The bulk of this group's learning is designed to take place at home or at work using the manuals. TSRs associated with both program designs have been given a curricular guide. Each TSR is responsible for approximately 16 RHPs. Training was developed by the health district personnel with the help of the Division of Formation of Human Resources in the Ministry.

As indicated in the study objectives, the innovation being tested in the project consists of having 200 RHPs trained in conjunction with their wives or another female relative residing with them. These 200 couples have been selected from among RHPs receiving both the traditional and the self-instructional courses (50 percent from each group will have a female assistant). The female partner in the team is given instructions regarding community activities of the RHP and methods of assisting in this work.

After training, (alone or with an assistant) RHPs are to be examined in order to test their knowledge. At the end of the training, RHPs receive the equipment necessary to do their field work, including medicines and materials. Supplies are being made available to the project via the National Drug Store at a price that reflects the cost of production. Promoters will be allowed to sell the drugs at a commission of 30 percent in order to provide an incentive for their work.

Supervision

After the training, each TSR will supervise approximately 16 RHPs in the community. The district doctor and the TSR will organize continuing education activities for the promoters. It is planned that these individuals (RHP, TSR, doctor) meet every two months in the health center, with additional participation of District personnel. The TSR will present the doctor with a supervisory program for his approval and will also present a monthly report.

Evaluation

The design and evaluation plan of the investigation will consist of several elements:

- Tests of RHPs' knowledge, via pre- and post-training.
- Supervision reports and evaluation.
- An anthropological study to determine workers' activities and clients' perception of these activities.
- a contraceptive prevalence and project-related study of knowledge, attitudes, and practice to be conducted in five homes chosen at random in each community, both as a baseline and one year after the intervention is in place. The studies will determine the use of Western medicine and contraceptives in the community.
- Other evaluation elements apart from training include an assessment of supervisory activities and pharmacy sales.

Table 23:1 illustrates how information from the sources above will be considered in program evaluation.

The anthropological investigation will be carried out in 20 program villages. It is designed to provide information regarding the community's knowledge and perceptions of the promoter's job; community participation in his activities; cultural barriers to the effective provision of services by the promoter; whether municipal sales of medicines respond to the needs of the communities; and community perception about health problem priorities and the RHP's response to these problems.

Evaluation will stress measurement of the effectiveness of:

- Both education models,
- Promoters acting alone or with an assistant,
- The resupply system for contraceptives and medicines, and
- The supervisory system.

WORKER SELECTION, TRAINING METHODS, EXAMINATIONS, AND SUPERVISION OF TRAINEES

Selection

Individuals were selected for the RHP role by the TSR in each of the project districts. The TSR visited the selected rural communities (those having at least 30 houses, being accessible year-round, and not already having an RHP) and spoke to community members and leaders, who were asked to nominate candidates. Each proposed candidate was visited by the TSR, informed of the program, and questioned about his interest in participating. Selection criteria stipulated that the candidate be 20 years of age or older; in good health; literate; have community support and a good reputation; reside in the community; speak the local dialect; have fulfilled his military service; not be a political or religious leader; and not be involved in a business that includes the sale of alcohol, medicine, or groceries.

Table 23:1. Evaluation Plan*

	Home Survey	Anthropologic Survey	Promoters Supervision	Supervision Evaluation	Pharmacy Evaluation	Training Evaluation
1. Compare 2 Educational Models for the training of RHP (traditional and modular)	X	X				0
2. Compare the effectivity of promoters who are working alone or with a female assistant	0	X	X			
3. Determine the capacity of the promoters to modify the use of medicines for some health problems	0					
4. Determine the capacity of the promoters to improve the knowledge and use of contraceptives	0					
5. Determine promoter health activities in the field	0	X	X			
6. Determine community perceptions of the promoter's work	X	0				
7. Determine the community's participation in the promoter's activities		0	X			
8. Determine the cultural barriers to the provision of services by the promoter		0				
9. Determine the effectiveness of field supervision				0		
10. Determine supply problems in relation to the municipal sale of drugs			X		0	
11. Determine whether the volume of municipal drug sales is influenced by promoter activities			X		0	
12. Determine if the personal characteristics of the promoter influence his effectivity			0			
13. Determine the monthly income of the promoter			X		0	

* Principal Evaluation is indicated by 0;
Complementary Evaluation is indicated by X.

The district doctor and the TSR made the final selection, although social workers took a survey to assist in the final promotion in some districts. Over 350 RHPs have been selected thus far for the project.

Training Courses

At the end of the selection process, candidates are put into one of the two training courses. Necessary training materials for the two groups have been developed. Ministry personnel worked intensely on the elaboration and production of process rules for the RHP, and in effect delineated worker tasks. Resources used in the preparation of materials included the national health plan with its draft activities for RHPs; results of a PRINAPS survey carried out in 1978 to determine health needs and existing RHP activities; review of the existing RHP curriculum; surveys of personnel in existing rural health areas to garner their perception of the role needed to be fulfilled by RHPs; and others. (See Figure 23:1 and Table 23:2).

The approved curriculum contained five units:

1. The community
2. The gathering of morbidity data
3. Maternal and child health
4. First aid services
5. Community development

Materials for both the traditional and self-instructional modules were field tested to ensure that they were clear and appropriate for the literacy level of the average RHP. A standardized examination guide was also elaborated to test every student at the end of each unit and upon completion of the

Figure 23:1. Process for the Definition of the Curriculum, PRINAPS

1. Review of the National Health Plan
2. Evaluation analysis
3. Curriculum analysis
4. Survey of health personnel
5. Definition of tasks
6. Seminar to study the tasks to be performed by the RHP
7. Elaboration of educational objectives
8. Definition of teaching time and method
9. Structuring of teaching units
10. Elaboration of a curriculum guide for the teacher
11. Production of self-instructional manuals
12. Evaluation guide

Table 23:2. Training Activities

ACTIVITIES	PERSON IN CHARGE	ADVICE AND/OR PARTICIPATION
Community selection	District doctor	Area leader, social worker of area, TSR of district & PRINAPS personnel
Candidates selection	TSR of district	
Participants selection	District doctor	Leader of area, TSR of area or district
Organization of the course	District doctor	Social worker of area or district, TSR of district, PRINAPS personnel
Teaching of the course	TSR	Area team, district team, and PRINAPS
Final examination	Social worker of area	PRINAPS personnel
Continuous education	TSR	Social worker, district team

course. The test is not intended to fail students, but rather to detect areas where workers experience difficulties. The TSR is expected to formulate retraining and field supervision to improve these areas. Each specific activity or area of knowledge examined in the test is rated as being excellent, satisfactory, or unsatisfactory.

In the traditional model, the TSR conducts the training for approximately 16 RHPs over a four-week period. To accomplish this task, he uses the teacher's guide and is expected to produce his own teaching materials, such as posters.

In the modular model, students each receive a self-instructional manual. The TSR receives the teacher's guide and must meet with the student weekly to analyze learning problems and assess progress. The TSR has greater freedom in deciding upon the organization of his group of trainees to enhance both learning and convenience. For example, although some TSRs may elect to see each student individually, the majority choose to have trainees receive the weekly training in small groups of approximately four individuals at a time. TSRs in both groups are expected to visit the RHPs in the field to assess performance and assist in solving problems.

Post-training Supervision

After the end of training and the inception of field activities, RHPs receive supervision from their TSR. A series of supervisory instruments have been designed to assist in and standardize this task. These instruments include a supervisory schedule, use of family register cards and reference coupons, and planned visits to households in communities served by the promoter. The supervisor is expected to ensure that the promoter visits each of his 50 families at least once every eight weeks, and provides the family with preventive and contraceptive information and, on the first visit, treatment with mebendazole (a broad-spectrum antihelminthic) for children under the age of six. Mothers of children with diarrhea are supplied with oral rehydration packets and taught how to use the mixture. The supervisor is also expected to check that the RHP referred serious cases to the health service using the correct reference coupons and forms.

The TSR visits each promoter at least once every six weeks, reviews his records, and revisits some areas with the promoter. In addition, he visits five homes at random to ensure that they have been visited by the RHP. At the end, he gives the RHP an evaluation form indicating positive and negative findings. The RHP signs the document. The TSR is in turn supervised by a social worker who accompanies him on a monthly supervision visit (Table 23:3).

The district doctor meets with a group of promoters every two months in the health center, and discusses problems noted during supervision. He develops an educational activity to correct difficulties and discusses solutions to problems. District doctors inform the program director of the educational activities in their area (see Table 23:3).

Table 23:3. Supervision Activities

ACTIVITIES	PERSON IN CHARGE	ADVICE AND/OR PARTICIPATION
Supervision of HRP	District TSR	District doctor
Supervision of TSR	District doctor	Social worker of area or district
Supervision of district doctor	Area leader	Social worker of area

RESULTS TO DATE

Baseline Survey

Data available from the baseline survey indicate that the surveyed communities have not previously been serviced by RHPs (over 93 percent of households had never received a visit). In 67.4 percent of households that had received visits, a family member had received an "examination", 11.8 percent had been questioned concerning illness in general, 11.8 percent had received immunization referral to a health center, and just under three percent had received some form of contraception. Less than 1 percent of persons visited had bought oral medication from the promoter. Although diarrheal illness is a leading cause of childhood morbidity and mortality, frequently neither client nor promoter sought appropriate therapy. Indeed, 36.7 percent of children with diarrhea had received antibiotics, 27.5 percent other antidiarrheal medication and 3 percent purgatives. Such interventions are of questionable value or even potentially harmful in most cases of diarrhea.

The baseline survey was designed to also provide contraceptive prevalence data. Under the Guatemalan National Health Plan, medical examination is necessary prior to receiving a prescription for oral contraceptives. After the first prescription, however, users can be resupplied by RHPs.

Preliminary results from the baseline survey indicate that a large proportion of rural women are married (93.6 percent) and between the ages of 15 and 49 years (82.1 percent of the total are above age 15). Among women who know about contraception, the most common sources of information are radio (66.8 percent), health services (14.9 percent) and neighbors (13.4 percent). Among contraceptive users, oral contraceptives are used most frequently (47.2 percent), followed by sterilization (32.1 percent), breast-feeding (11.3 percent), condoms (3.8 percent), IUDs (1.9 percent) and other methods (3.8 percent). However, the total percentage of women using contraceptives is low. According to baseline survey results, 37.4 percent of nonusers reported no knowledge of family planning methods, of which 32.3 percent were disinterested in using them and 7.7 percent found methods difficult to obtain.

It should be noted that efforts are currently being made nationally to train all doctors, nurses, social workers, and TSRs about family planning, whether they belong to the PRINAPS project or not.

Observations and Preliminary Data from Training Courses

The PRINAPS program, designed to be carried out within the framework of the health system, has worked on strengthening the position of all members of the health team. In general, reports from RHPs, TSRs, doctors, and social workers seem to indicate that interpersonal work relationships have improved over the life of the project to date. After approval from the health services; program development had been discussed by small groups of workers in each health area. This was done to help personnel identify with the program and to aid in avoiding difficulties. Overall, project staff and worker retention has been high. Information from monthly meetings between RHPs, TSRs, and district doctors involved in PRINAPS are tabulated and analyzed: copies are sent back to participants, acted upon where possible, and have helped in motivating personnel. There are currently over 350 promoters in the PRINAPS activity, covering a population of 83,500.

Preliminary examination results are becoming available for RHPs completing their course. Although results have not yet been tabulated, and comparisons between groups of workers trained in the two systems are unavailable, early data suggest that female partners may have scored less well than their spouses in the self-learning system. Reasons for this (less time for study, lower level of literacy, lack of previous practice in how to study, less interest in the project) are as yet unavailable. Questions to which workers frequently gave faulty or incomplete answers included what advice to give pregnant women, and those concerning first aid and use of project forms and statistics. Workers have tended to score better in questions regarding simple treatment of diarrhea and intestinal parasites, and regarding correct methods of using contraceptives. As a group, RHP's trained by certain TSR's scored higher than did those trained by others. This may indicate some lack of uniformity in teaching ability between TSR's, although other factors must be considered. Once again, it should be noted that these results are preliminary and based on a small number of examination results compiled to date.

SUMMARY AND DISCUSSION

The majority of operational objectives of the project (selecting RHPs, elaborating training, etc.) have been achieved. The program is leading the way in gaining experience in the development of job descriptions for various levels of health personnel and training materials for RHPs. Data from the baseline survey and from the anthropological survey currently under way will provide information for project evaluation.

The provision of medicine and supplies to promoters has been established with no shortages reported. Support for the project has been excellent on the part of the Ministry of Public Health, the Health Services Directorate, the Health District, and especially the TSRs, who have developed into a strong cadre of trainers and supervisors for the RHPs.

24
The Sudan Community-Based Health and Family Planning Project: Description of a Training Course*

Rahman El Tom

In the Sudan Community-Based Health and Family Planning Project the selection of issues to be included in the training program was based on an assessment of national health problems and priorities. Top priority was given to preventive medicine with special emphasis on maternal and child health (MCH), family planning (FP) and immunization for children. Other national priorities include broader primary health care services and prevention of malaria, schistosomiasis, diarrheal disease, and malnutrition.

Not all of these could be dealt with in the project at this time. Activities selected were those in which the intervention was technically and operationally simple and inexpensive, could be performed by a primary health worker and had the potential for substantial effect on health. Thus interventions selected for this project were family planning, oral rehydration therapy (ORT), immunization referral, and nutrition counselling.

Once priorities had been identified, the problems had to be translated into program objectives and tasks. An initial step in this process was to identify available resources to include in a program.

RESOURCES

Resources were mainly human; they were identified according to the manpower categories of the health system in the area of the Sudan north of Khartoum. Such categories included frontline primary health care workers (PHCs), village midwives (VMWs), medical assistants (MAs), and community health workers (CHWs). Higher-level workers who could potentially serve as supervisors included health visitors, senior medical assistants, and certain community and religious leaders.

A primary task involved mobilizing these human resources to deal with the identified problems. The health infrastructure was surveyed to determine the numbers and distribution of various types of workers and their existing functions. Other data

---

* From Rahman El Tom's detailed description.

collected included their age, educational background, marital status, number of children, and their acceptance in the community. Based on this information, it was decided that VMWs were widely dispersed, well accepted, perhaps underutilized by the health system, and could serve as a valuable resource in reaching project goals. It was concluded that they could be trained for the role despite the illiteracy of many, especially the older ones (educational levels among VMWs varied from no formal schooling to approximately a grade-six education). Training was thus tailored to their needs, as well as to their potential trainers and supervisors.

CURRICULUM DEVELOPMENT

The curriculum was based on the tasks identified and was designed to use the skills of the available personnel. The design was competency-based and practical in nature: students learned by doing. A three-week timetable was developed to teach students oral contraceptive distribution, ORT, and immunization referral. Since there is heavy emphasis on retraining and teaching in the field, the original three-week course concentrated on the activities to be introduced first in the field (ORT and family planning). Additional project activities, such as nutrition, were to be added during subsequent training sessions, on the job retraining, and supervision. This sequencing of learning was thought to be useful in allowing VMWs to learn each activity well.

PREPARATION OF TEACHERS

Project staff decided that adequate preparation of trainers is essential for program success. Trainers were instructed as to the technical content of project interventions, project activities, and teaching methods stressing active learning and practical experience. Health visitors (HVs) were identified as the worker group best suited to provide the training. Some project staff resisted this scheme, thinking physicians and other high-level health personnel would provide better training. However, the question of project replication made using physicians as trainers impractical: Training costs would be too high on the national level.

Once training began, it became evident that HVs could provide training as well as or better than doctors. They had previous experience as teachers of illiterate VMWs, had long contact with and knowledge of the health service and the VMW role; were familiar with the psychology and vocabulary of their students, knew how to build on the VMW's role rather than compete with it; and gave simple and clear explanations using analogies. All in all, they were considered to be better communicators who were willing to repeat information in varied ways and took more time to explain than did doctors.

ORGANIZATION

Two training centers were identified for the VMW courses, one on the east and one on the west bank of the Nile. Both were located in midwifery boarding schools. This approach would clash the least with local conservativeness: the woman students were seen as being "taken care of" in the schools. As stated earlier, the courses were of three weeks' duration and alternated between centers. Dividing the VMWs into two groups resulted in teaching groups of a more manageable size, better accomodations, and because fewer students had to be taken through practice sessions, a shorter duration for any one course.

The program center on the west bank was generally newer and bigger than the one on the east bank, and had better records and immunization activities. In this center it was decided to use the school's MCH and FP program, and to stress these activities (particularly FP) in project work on the west bank. A family planning clinic was available for practical training.

The east bank center began by stressing ORT and nutrition. In addition to visiting the centers, it was decided that project staff would visit the different project villages once fieldwork began, and would meet with the VMWs and their local supervisors (described below) to provide ongoing training and to ensure project continuity.

TRAINING CONTENT AND METHODS

Maternal and Child Health/Family Planning

The course emphasized the learning of practical, relevant information and tasks. The religious point of view regarding health and FP was stressed, and discussions were held at length to overcome any resistance and to convince the VMWs of the need for an MCH/FP program. MCH principles, components and activities were described, and family planning was discussed in relation to MCH. The health benefits of family planning for mothers and children were emphasized. In order to ensure that participants understood and could explain this information, frequent repetition and active participation in the form of group discussion were worked into the program.

Individual sessions consisted of general presentations using different forms including talks, audiovisual aids (such as slides, films, tapes), demonstrations given by trainers in service settings, and practice for VMWs in performing actual tasks such as talking to contraceptive acceptors and users. Role plays were used generously throughout the training. In addition, VMWs were given practice in antenatal clinics. Evening discussions in the boarding school and informal sessions, sometimes out in the open air, were used for review and clarification. Such sessions were used for revision and consolidation of the day's material, with no additional information being given.

Role play deserves further mention. Each participant had at least one chance to play the role of the housewife and of the home visitor. This method was found to provide an enjoyable and useful experience which brought up practical points when dealing with potential acceptors. Role play teaches students how to respond to different situations, reveals gaps in knowledge and misunderstandings, and assists students in gaining experience and confidence. Students and teachers can learn from each other in a relaxed spontaneous atmosphere. Students appeared to be more alert, responsive, and emotionally involved.

Immunization

VMWs were taught to be village motivators for the extended program of immunization, particularly regarding the oral polio vaccine. Teaching methods used were similar to those above.

Oral Rehydration Therapy

An introductory lecture using slides and films was used to acquaint VMWs with this topic. Other techniques used included question-and-answer periods and discussions, practice in the preparation of ORT, and role playing. Role plays stressed not only the preparation of the solution but how to teach it correctly to mothers. VMWs were also given clinical experience in a hospital in the handling of dehydrated children. They learned to recognize the signs of dehydration and to see how ORT is administered. Finally, they had the chance to practice giving ORT to the children themselves, and could see its desirable effect.

Malnutrition

Teaching methods regarding malnutrition included slides and films of children with kwashiorkor and marasmus. VMWs were given hospital experience in handling cases of severe malnutrition. Apparently they were shocked to find out the significance of these illnesses. They had seen cases of kwashiorkor in their villages but had thought it was a skin disease. The midwives were taught about breastfeeding and the dangers of bottle feeding, and had some limited village practice involving actual preparation of weaning foods.

Records

Special training emphasis was put on service records to be used by the illiterate and semiliterate VMWs; record cards were color-coded. Training consisted of explanations of the records and their importance and frequent practice in their use.

Night Duties

Given that VMWs had no household or village responsibilities during training, they were asked to do some nighttime practice in the adjoining maternity hospital. This allowed them to brush up and update their knowledge and experience, and to participate in deliveries and infant care.

Evaluation

Training evaluated by means of a post-test and a checklist used when observing workers' activities. Questions testing problem-solving ability were also administered.

Ongoing Education and Refresher Training

One activity is being implemented at a time in the field. Before each activity is implemented, the MA in the health post (a senior nurse who has received basic project-related training in teaching and in well-defined supervisory functions) is expected to review the activity with the VMW using a checklist, demonstrate the activity to her, and observe her practice (again using a checklist). This retraining activity is further stressed during village visits by project staff who meet with each MA and his VMWs prior to the initiation of each new activity. Staff generally take part in the field retraining.

In addition, the VMWs were given notes on different project interventions. These were written in very simple, colloquial language, using the same vocabulary as used in the course. The notes were very specific and practical in nature, with no padding. It was intended that they be read weekly to the midwife in her home by her literate relatives or neighbors, or in the dispensary by the MA. The method has proven to be very useful and indeed, in a few cases sufficient in providing basic training for new service providers. MAs have generally been good teachers and supervisors for the midwives.

Weekly meetings with the MA and other VMWs constitute an important aspect of continuing education. The printed notes are read and discussed, question-and-answer periods are organized, and the MA and VMWs assess problems and achievements. Project staff members attend some of these weekly meetings, and give feedback to consolidate and correct knowledge. Teamwork has been high in this setting. In view of the need to communicate with all project personnel, a newsletter is circulated periodically to all workers. It discusses issues raised in weekly meetings throughout the two banks, and emphasizes important points.

SUMMARY

A few problems have been identified in the project. A number of personnel have transferred, necessitating the addition of new recruits which must in turn be taken into account in providing the new individuals with appropriate training. As well, a small number of very old midwives were found to resist change. They were not eliminated from the project, but are not expected to perform many activities.

Given the overall success of the VMW training program, thought is being given to expanding the program. As indicated above, new VMWs are already being trained to replace those who have transferred out of project areas. Extension is also being considered outside the project areas and thought is being given to using school children in propagating information about nutrition and ORT.

Part Nine

Evaluation and Research

25
Research Design in the Evaluation of Operations Research Projects—A Framework

Ronald H. Gray

Operations Research (OR) is defined by Heiby (this volume) as "any investigation concerned with the cost and effectiveness of a health delivery system." Such service oriented research is essentially evaluative in nature and the following framework summarizes approaches to evaluation which have been applied in the past, particularly in the area of family planning.

As in all research, it is essential to clearly define objectives, and with OR the critical issue is to first define the objective of the service or innovation so that the structure of the research design ensures the achievement of limited and realistic goals. For example, if the objective of a CBD program is simply to increase the prevalence of contraceptive use, then the research should properly focus on prevalence of use, but need not be concerned with issues such as demographic impact.

Service research is generally either descriptive or comparative in nature. Descriptive studies provide basic information on programatic features such as the number and characteristics of clients served, whereas comparative studies are aimed at showing whether or not a particular programmatic input has a desired effect. Comparative investigations may employ one of three strategies: either (a) a "before and after" design whereby a baseline measurement taken before a service innovation is compared to subsequent measurements taken after the innovation has been in place; (b) a comparison or control group design in which the innovation (treatment) may be implemented in one area or population subgroup, and the effects assessed by a comparison with another (control) area or subgroup with no intervention, or with other kinds of interventions; and (c) a combination of the above designs (see Figure 25:1), with before and after measurements in both treatment and control groups.

Although intuitively simple, experience with field research has shown that these designs are vulnerable to practical problems. The before and after approach (B-A) cannot account for secular trends such as generally improved family planning use independent of a specific program. It also is subject to "panel effects" which are measurable only through use of a comparison group. A comparison between treatment and control areas (T-C post treatment) or populations may be confounded by differences

Figure 25:1. Comparative Investigation using Before and After Measurements and/or Treatment and Control Groups

	Before	After
Treatment		
Control		

in basic characteristics which influence the outcome, and by the inability, for ethical or practical reasons, to keep a control area free of the intervention or of related activities. For example, one cannot, in many cases, deprive a control population of health services.

Many of these problems, if foreseen by proper planning, can be resolved in study design, site selection and careful analysis. However, there is an additional difficulty inherent to field research which arises from the fact that the effort put into observation and measurement such as repeated surveys or follow-up may influence the quality of service or behavior of the population - in other words, the act of observation alters the outcome observed. This has been recognized in other fields, for example as the "Hawthorn effect" or the principle of indeterminancy. Essentially it means that results from intensive research studies cannot be readily generalized to less-focused, large-scale programs. There is, therefore, often a need for phased evaluation whereby an innovation is first assessed in a restricted study population, and subsequently as part of a larger scale program monitoring.

A further problem is the duration of observation and frequency of events. Many OR projects are of limited duration usually under three years, and given often lengthy start-up times, there may not be a sufficiently long period for a service input to have measurable effects. Also, relatively rare events such as births or deaths are difficult to measure unless one is monitoring a large population for a sufficient length of time; more frequent events or continuing behavior or states such as diarrheal morbidity, contraceptive use, or immunization status are easier to measure, at least in their broader aspects. Therefore, the size and duration of the study will determine the types of events to be measured and the costs of investigation.

The following framework will briefly review the types of evaluation and their uses, the data requirements, and basic analytic methods.

TYPES OF EVALUATION

Program evaluation can be divided into four general categories each directed at different aspects of program operations and their effectiveness. These are not mutually exclusive, but rather complementary strategies which address separate issues.

Process Evaluation

Process evaluation is essentially a managerially oriented assessment designed to improve program operations by measuring direct program outputs. The program can be analyzed in terms of its functional components such as training, supply logistics, client recruitment, service provision, and continuity of care, and each component assessed by descriptive or comparative studies measuring program outputs. For example, training procedures might be evaluated by monitoring the trainees' acquisition of skills and knowledge, and the effects of new procedures such as role playing or inservice training. Recruitment of acceptors can be assessed from client registration data, and new approaches to IE and C evaluated by changes in recruitment.

Outcome Evaluation

Outcome evaluation measures the effectiveness of program outputs among users of services. In family planning, the output of interest is contraceptive use, and the outcome is usually measured by the number of new acceptors and the continuity of contraceptive use. The most rigorous procedure is the estimation of contraceptive use-effectiveness in terms of continuation and discontinuation rates using life-table procedures, but in many studies the percentage of clients still using a method after one year or more is a reasonable measure. Another outcome measure is Couple Years of Protection (CYP), which is the number of years the average couple is protected from pregnancy by contraception.

In other areas of Primary Health Care (PHC), outcome measures will be determined by the nature of the intervention. In the case of Oral Rehydration Therapy (ORT), the interest might be in the number of patients using ORT, the proportion of diarrheal episodes in which ORT was implemented, the number of packets consumed, and the number of patients requiring referral for dehydration. Similarly with immunization, the number vaccinated, and the completeness and timeliness of immunization schedules could be outcome measures.

The common feature is that the evaluation focuses on users of services rather than the population as a whole, and that service statistics provide the data for the outcome evaluation.

Impact Evaluation

Impact evaluation measures the effect of the program on the general population. In family planning the simplest measure is the prevalence of contraceptive use in the population estimated from sample surveys. More complex measures of demographic impact such as declines in birth rates or births averted are difficult because the necessary information is often lacking, and because one cannot fully account for substitution effects or predict the course of fertility in the absence of the program.

With regard to diarrheal disease, impact evaluation could imply measuring the proportion of the population using ORT or declines in diarrheal morbidity or death rates. With immunization, the proportion of children immunized, or declines in morbidity or death rates from specific disease such as neonatal tetanus can be monitored. Antihelminthic or antimalarial programs might measure such things as the prevalence of parasites in the population.

Cost-Effectiveness

Cost-effectiveness is a measure of program costs in relation to outputs, outcome, and impact. It is an assessment of the economic efficiency of the program and a managerial tool to determine how services may be provided less expensively (Sirageldin et al., 1983).

Cost-effectiveness evaluation is complex and the methodology is beyond the scope of this review. However, in general terms rigorous cost-effectiveness studies require the following:

- Subdivision of costs of program inputs into major categories such as training or provision of services.

- Disaggregation of these categories into component costs for personnel, facilities, and supplies. The personnel components are further disaggregated into the time devoted to activities such as administration, service, travel, or idle time.

- Expression of the costs of these inputs in terms of outputs (e.g., cost per client recruited), outcomes (e.g., cost per couple year of protection), or impact (e.g., cost per "x" percent increase in contraceptive prevalence; or per death or birth averted).

The proper derivation of direct and indirect costs, and the appropriate allocation of costs, e.g., as between overlapping programs, is very complex and beyond the scope of most projects. Usually, relatively simple measures such as cost per client or per couple year of protection are used, based on aggregated costs for the whole program.

SOURCES OF DATA

Process and outcome evaluation primarily depend on data from individual client records or other routine program statistics. However, basic recordkeeping is often defective, and to facilitate the maintenance of routine records, it is necessary to devise simple, brief forms which are relevant to the concerns of personnel using them from day-to-day, and which do not place too great an administrative burden on the staff. Clearly, where non-literate personnel are employed, one can only maintain rudimentary records.

Population based sample surveys are required for impact evaluation, even when service records are available. To minimize cost and logistic difficulties, the sample size should be large enough to meet objectives but not excessive. The study sample required can be readily estimated from the expected frequency of events and the anticipated changes resulting from an intervention. Simple graphic aids for sample sizes required to detect differences in proportions are given by Feigl (Feigl, 1978). In the interest of economy and logistics, questionnaires should be succinct, simple and readily analyzed. The interview should address in depth the major outcome variables, such as contraceptive use, and provide information on respondent characteristics (e.g., age, marital status, education, SES, pregnancy/lactation status) which are known or expected to affect the outcome variable.

The determination of both sampling frame and procedure in field studies is difficult because often one does not have census information, lists of households, or sufficiently detailed maps. Simple random cluster sampling and complete enumeration within readily identified clusters such as a neighborhood or village is a satisfactory practical compromise. Investigations of frequent events such as diarrheal episodes generally require follow-up studies with repeat home visiting. However, in sample surveys information can be obtained on illness or contraceptive use within one month or one to two weeks of interview which permits an estimate of incidence and prevalence without undue loss or misdating of event due to poor recall.

STATISTICAL MEASURES

Numerous statistical indicators can be used for program evaluations, and the list below briefly itemizes the more simple indices in common use.

1. User characteristics by age, sex, parity, marital status, prior use status, desire for additional children, etc., can be used as descriptive statistics of entry into the program.

2. Volume indicators, such as the number of new clients registered, and the number of discontinuations by category, can summarize the overall program activity. Usually it is useful to assemble such indicators with respect to relevant administrative geographic areas if the program is extensive enough to warrant it.

3. Coverage indicators, such as the percent of the population covered by services (.e.g, contraceptive prevalence) or percent of targets reached, measure the degree of program achievement. It is useful to cross tabulate indices such as contraceptive prevalence by population characteristics (e.g., age or parity), to more clearly define which subgroups are using

and which subgroups are in need of services. Also, contraceptive prevalence should be related to the population at risk of pregnancy (e.g., currently married or cohabitating non-pregnant women, aged 15-44). This makes the interpretation of levels, changes, or differentials in prevalence easier to interpret. Similar considerations should apply to incidence of diarrhea or prevalence of immunization in which the major population at risk is children under five years of age. Incidence rates may be expressed as episodes per unit of time, which allows for multiple episodes in an individual, or as persons per unit of time which does not measure multiple episodes.

Where necessary multivariate analyses can be used to adjust for differences in population characteristics or to estimate the correlation between characteristics and the outcome variable of interest.

4. Quality indicators, such as client satisfaction and knowledge or duration of training, may be used to assess the effectiveness of educational and information processes. Knowledge of the program, methods, or program personnel when related to actual or intended use can reveal the degree to which the program has "caught on."

5. Outcome or effectiveness indicators. In family planning contraceptive use-effectiveness is an important measure of both program and method performance. Simple life table techniques have been developed to estimate continuation or discontinuation rates over time (Tietze, 1973). To construct a life table, one needs to know the duration of use derived from the date of entry, the date of discontinuation for terminating subjects, the date of last observation for cases that cannot be traced (losses to follow-up), and for subjects continuing use at the end of the observation period. Information on reasons for discontinuation is complex and requires careful definitions of mutually exclusive reasons for stopping the method.

Couple Years of Protection is more complex and requires an estimate of mean duration of use derived from use-effectiveness data or assumptions about wastage for recurrent methods such as oral contraceptives, an allowance for the overlap between postpartum infecundability and contraceptive use, and information on the age distribution and numbers of acceptors (Gorosh and Wolfers, 1979). The objective is to provide a single index for recurrent methods (pills and barriers), semipermanent methods (IUDs) and permanent methods such as sterilization which summarizes the program achievement over a given year in terms of protection provided to those at risk.

REFERENCES

Feigl, P. "A Graphical Aid for Determining Sample Size When Comparing Two Independent Proportions." Biometrics 34 (1978): 111-122.

Gorosh, M. and P. Wolfers. "Standard Couple Years of Protection." In United Nations, Department of International Economic and Social Affairs. Methodology of Measuring the Impact of Family Planning Programmes on Fertility. Manual 9. New York: United Nations (1979): 34-47.

Sirageldin I., D. Salkever, and R. Osborn, eds. Evaluating Population Programs. International Experiences with Cost-Effective Analysis and Cost-Benefit Analysis. New York: St. Martins Press, and London: Croom/Helm, 1983.

Tietze, C. and S. Lewit. "Recommended Procedures for the Statistical Evaluation of Intrauterine Contraception." Studies in Family Planning 4,2 (1973): 35-42.

26 Operations Research in Primary Health Care

James R. Heiby

The large-scale delivery of virtually any set of health services requires the organization of a number of discrete activities into a system. A health delivery system includes interrelated functions such as training, supervision, logistics, and the collection of information. Each of these, in turn, consists of a number of components. The ability of a delivery system to provide the selected services effectively and at the lowest feasible cost is obviously central to the now familiar goal of universal primary health care (PHC), particularly in less developed countries (LDCs). Research on delivery systems is one approach to improving services (World Health Organization, 1978). Operations research (OR), as the term is used here, refers to any investigation concerned with the cost or the effectiveness of a health delivery system. OR is a strictly practical approach to addressing service delivery issues for which conventional management and evaluation techniques are inadequate. This does not imply any particular theory or methodology beyond the attempt to apply experimental design to the process of service delivery.

OR is widely applied in commerce, industry, and the military, but its application to health delivery systems is remarkably limited (Bristow, 1978). In contrast to the medical technologies that are delivered, health delivery systems are designed and operated largely on the basis of professional judgment rather than empirical data. In view of what is widely regarded as a pressing need for more cost-effective PHC, it is reasonable to ask why LDC ministries of health and private health organizations are not aggressively applying the findings of past OR and indeed conducting their own studies.

OPERATIONS RESEARCH EXPERIENCE

Without attempting to summarize them, it can be said that past studies have shown that a delivery system based on use of non-professionals is capable of effecting a substantial improvement in health status at a cost that is feasible for most LDCs (Gwatkin et al., 1980). Some would argue that such "demonstration" studies simply lend legitimacy to an approach that has evolved as a practical necessity, but a useful or even critical policy impact is still a likely outcome (Lewis, 1977). Other research has addressed broad strategies in PHC, such as the integration of family planning with other health services (Williamson, 1979; Taylor et al., 1976), the utility of systematic household canvassing to promote selected services (Gadalla et al., 1980; Lechtig and de Leon, 1981), and the effect of charging for the services provided (Ladipo et al., 1982). Only recently have studies examined discrete modifications of the elements of a conventional delivery system, such as the type of training provided for PHC workers (Aldana and de Leon, 1982) and the frequency of their supervision (Rodrigues et al., 1981).

These studies have been reported in a manner sufficiently consistent to allow some useful generalizations. This will help clarify the obstacles facing a ministry of health official who wishes to apply OR to his own program.

A common feature of past OR is the use of sophisticated population based surveys to measure the effect of the delivery system on health indicators, either directly, as with the infant mortality rate, or indirectly, as with the prevalence of contraceptive use or completed immunization series. Indeed, such surveys are often regarded as virtually synonymous with research, fulfilling an obvious need for objective measures of the ultimate effectiveness of the delivery system. But the use of refined surveys does not define OR (Osborn and Reinke, 1981). Because of the expense and the specialized expertise required, these surveys are likely to remain relatively rare. Furthermore, impact surveys leave largely unanswered the very questions such an official should find most pressing: Why did the delivery system produce a given outcome and what can be done to improve performance?

Without questioning the desirability, if not the necessity, of impact surveys, an official would still find it difficult to apply available OR results to his program, even with access to a relatively well-stocked library. Cultural settings are virtually always different, an obvious consideration for which researchers can only counsel thoughtful adaptation of their findings. The traditional approach to describing experimental delivery systems, however, constitutes a further and unnecessary obstacle to the effective application of the results of these studies.

A delivery system, even one that provides only a small number of services, consists of dozens of discrete functions that contribute to the observed outcome. Most reports describe the process of service delivery only in fairly general terms, while focusing on the relatively small number of elements that are innovative or experimentally varied. Whether or not the details of the delivery system have been defined in theory and described in practice by the original researchers, they are not generally available to those who may wish to replicate them. This is most obvious in the case of demonstration projects, which establish an entire delivery system de novo, but studies focused on specific variables are similarly problematic. A given research project may demonstrate that one pattern of PHC worker supervision is more cost-effective than another, but this finding also reflects the initial skills of the workers, the nature of the supervisory visits, the nature of second-level supervision, and a number of other factors. Similar considerations operate for the health official contemplating modifications of an existing program based on research findings or the initiation of new OR. The relative neglect of these seemingly mundane components of the delivery system undermines the wide application of research findings.

Any element of the delivery system that is not carefully defined becomes an uncontrolled variable of unknown influence. In order to permit the unambiguous transfer of the critical elements of a delivery system from one setting to another, the definition of the various elements must be expressed in operational terms - that is, in terms that are objectively measurable. Similarly, since actual practice may diverge from the original design, it is also essential to candidly describe what in fact takes place for each component of the delivery system. To some extent each project is a natural experiment with variables uncontrolled by the study director. Only with systematic, detailed documentation of the whole delivery system is it possible to interpret the effect of the components that are to be studied. If the process of systematically describing the delivery system reveals that some elements related to the issue at hand are problematic, it would, of course, be prudent to first correct these deficiencies. If, for example, field supervisors are found to use ineffective techniques, little would be gained from comparing different frequencies of supervision until techniques have been improved. The capacity to collect information on the effectiveness of each component of the delivery system, and then to take corrective action, is useful in its own right, whether or not there is a research agenda. But OR is not far removed from this process and is, in one sense, merely an extension of it.

RESEARCH NEEDS

The explicit objective of OR is to improve the way things are done, not to generate universal principles. Some useful generalizations may emerge with substantially more experience, but at present only a small fraction of delivery system components have been examined, and only to a limited degree. A greatly increased volume of OR will be necessary to study each of these components in even a preliminary manner. Such an increase is unlikely without a dramatic expansion of these research activities within ongoing conventional PHC programs. This expansion, in turn, will require attention to the ability of these programs to collect information on the effectiveness of different activities and to take the appropriate corrective action. The research needs in this area can be expressed not so much by an agenda of priority questions as by the new method that must be developed to respond to this agenda. In most cases, the first step will be assuring that a given delivery system is a favorable environment for applying OR techniques.

DELIVERY SYSTEM CHARACTERISTICS CONDUCIVE TO OPERATIONS RESEARCH

Systematic Definition

As indicated earlier, systematically defining the entire delivery system in operational terms is very useful. Although many PHC programs provide job descriptions for the staff, only rarely do they convey a detailed and unambiguous documentation of exactly how the delivery system is intended to function. This is obviously a formidable task, particularly for program directors who lack management training. A concrete definition of the individual elements of a delivery system also invites much more criticism than a more general definition. Few would take issue with, for example, directing the PHC worker to promote breastfeeding; but specifying the content of the relevant messages, method for contacting the target population, reporting requirements, nature of supervision, and so forth, is much more likely to provoke disagreement. On the other hand, open discussion of the details of the design of a delivery system, most of which is based on professional judgment, may in fact prove quite constructive and even essential.

The alternative to this approach - accepting a general definition or none at all - in effect transfers responsibility by default to the involved staff member, often the PHC worker himself. This is not to suggest that the contribution of lower-level personnel and, indeed, the community itself is not important, only that there should be explicit agreement regarding exactly what the delivery system is trying to do and how this is to be done. Unless these objectives and strategies are clear, systematic evaluation or monitoring is virtually impossible.

Monitoring Service Delivery

A systematic definition of the delivery system is the logical point of departure for the final step in creating a favorable environment for OR-establishing mechanisms to monitor the effectiveness of different components and to correct deficiencies as they are identified. It is difficult to imagine a delivery system that is capable of exploiting OR techniques, yet fails to carry out these more basic functions.

Virtually every PHC program collects information on service delivery on some regular schedule. This information is typically collected on standard forms, highly structured in that they ask for specific, usually quantitative information which is then summarized at higher administrative levels. Ideally, this information provides managers with an accurate impression of any major performance problems and leads to a specific response, often through the supervisory system. This cycle of monitoring and response can be impeded when the items reported provide unusable information. For example, a count of injections administered is well suited to quantitative reporting, but the results are virtually uninterpretable. Often, commonly included items illustrate the inherent limitations of a system based on easily quantifiable measures. Counts of health education talks, for example, reveal little about the effectiveness of this activity (McAlister et al., 1982). Of course, even a reporting format fully oriented toward monitoring the performance of the delivery system is not sufficient. The active utilization of this information by managers and supervisors, as opposed to the mechanical documentation of selected activities, is also essential to a complete information system. This requires specific training and supervision that is too frequently neglected (Evans et al., 1981).

Although the reports generated by traditional information systems are often referred to as process measures, clearly they do not actually describe the process of service delivery. Even if these reports were not limited to easily quantifiable measures, complete description of all the components of the delivery system on a monthly or quarterly basis is not practical for even the simplest program. In experimental as well as in regular delivery systems, many details of the service delivery process are known to managers only anecdotally, if at all (Danfa Comprehensive Rural Health and Family Planning Project, 1979; Heiby, 1981). This includes elements of obvious and even compelling relevance to the overall effectiveness of the delivery system, such as the content and style of the educational efforts of PHC workers, the quality of the care they provide, the effective coverage of services, and the content of supervisory visits. Knowledge of actual or potential difficulties in these service elements may escape the monitoring system. And it is not only problems that may be escaping the attention of managers and investigators, but also potentially useful local innovations.

The large-scale application of OR techniques requires the development of new methods for providing managers with detailed information on the process of service delivery. Among the properties desired in such an information system, the most obvious is the capacity to deal with the qualitative, descriptive information missing from conventional service statistics systems. Because the set of potentially reportable data is both vast and heterogeneous, flexibility and selectivity are also desirable characteristics. Among the resources common to most PHC delivery systems and potentially capable of providing these qualities in information collection, the supervisory system is the obvious choice. Certainly, observing and reporting these activities are legitimate, if rarely exploited, functions of supervisors.

Supervisors can produce detailed descriptions of the elements of service delivery based on direct observation and informal, in-depth interviews with PHC workers and members of the community. Supervisors are, in general, sufficiently disciplined to record their observations if appropriately trained. Through informal sampling, the volume of information reporting can be adjusted to the capacity of the supervisory system. Obviously, the basis of sampling will vary according to the function to be described, and might include categories such as a given group of PHC workers, specific services provided by that group of workers, recipients of specific services, or mothers of young children in certain communities. The sampling approach is also flexible with regard to frequency, and delivery system elements of lower priority or those that appear to be well performed could be sampled less frequently than elements that are more important or more problematic. The program director could also apply this technique to the administrative components of the delivery system, such as vehicle maintenance, the payment of travel expenses, and the ordering of supplies.

In contrast to a conventional service statistics system, the selective and flexible reporting of the process of service delivery requires active decision-making. Second-level supervisors and management personnel must not only receive and interpret reports, but must also decide which functions are to be reported and at what frequency. The need for decision-making could be minimized by establishing a fixed reporting schedule, but this would essentially eliminate the ability of the information system to adapt efficiently to changes in the program. Moreover, there is at present no empirical basis for designing such a schedule. Unfortunately, neither is there appreciable experience in the training and supervisory techniques best suited to the selective and flexible collection of process information.

The prominent role of refined surveys in public health research naturally leads one to question the validity of such an apparently casual approach to sampling. Even with training to minimize bias, a supervisor conducting household visits in a purportedly random fashion is unlikely to achieve a sample that is representative by conventional scientific standards. Similarly, the interpretation of findings from visits to a small number of children treated for diarrhea is limited by unforgiving statistical principles. The issue facing the program director, though, is not the desirability of sophisticated information collection, but whether or not this flawed but practical method is conducive to a more cost-effective delivery system. One obvious consideration is that supervisor sampling is intended to be an ongoing process. Particularly where results are unexpected, ambiguous, or suspicious, the director could request an additional, perhaps larger, sample, either by the supervisor herself or by her own supervisor. Similarly, the result of the sampling process will typically be a routine administrative action, not generation of a general principle. If, for example, the supervisor finds that four out of ten acceptors of oral contraceptives were inadequately instructed in their use, one response might be to provide specific in-service training for that worker. Whether the true proportion was, for instance, 28 percent, is irrelevant. If the worker was actually giving unclear instructions in only 10 percent of cases, one could argue that program resources were used inefficiently in providing additional training, but this must be balanced against the cost in supervisor time to accurately detect such situations. Issues such as this are legitimate subjects for OR, but studies up to now have not approached this level of refinement. A far more pressing need for the present is research directed toward the training, supervision, and evaluation necessary for this fundamentally qualitative process.

Even a delivery system that thoroughly monitors the process of service delivery may lack the flexibility to respond to weaknesses and innovations that it has identified. A program in which the level of performance has no consequences is in a poor position to improve its cost-effectiveness, with or without OR. Few would argue that substantive intervention in the service delivery process directed toward improved performance is a prominent feature of most PHC programs. To the extent that few programs generate substantial amounts of information on the process of service delivery, most program managers simply lack the resources for markedly improving the quality of such interventions. Any consideration of what range of actions is feasible where such information is available, is therefore rather speculative. The likely effectiveness of various management interventions is, if anything, even less certain, but evaluating the effect of a given measure would be relatively straightforward where detailed process information is collected routinely. Thus, after experience with this process has accumulated, it would probably be possible to list the specific actions most likely to resolve a given problem, such as poor acceptance of immunization services resulting from ineffective health education.

Among the resources under the direct influence of the program director, the activities of the staff probably have the greatest potential for change in response to an identified problem. Resistance to change is, of course, common to virtually all organizations, but there are specific methods for dealing with this phenomenon, largely focused on maintaining communication in the organization, particularly regarding the relation of the proposed change to the overall objectives of the organization (Lawrence, 1969). The willingness of the program staff to modify their routine activities is also germane to carrying out OR, and analysis of experiences in different LDC settings would facilitate future studies.

Many potentially useful responses to an identified service delivery problem involve financial resources. Interventions such as additional training courses or the payment of supervisor travel expenses may be virtually impossible because of a previously fixed budget. Few PHC programs provide discretionary funds for unanticipated activities, often reflecting a policy outside the control of the program director. There is, of course, no guarantee that any kind of research findings would influence policies such as this, but OR has never been used to assess the cost-effectiveness of providing increased budgetary flexibility.

INSTITUTIONALIZING OPERATIONS RESEARCH

In a program that routinely monitors the performance of each component of the delivery system and takes specific action, activities that can be regarded as OR are distinguished only by degree. For example, the testing of a new approach to promoting birth spacing is a more involved procedure than instructing a supervisor to retrain certain PHC workers in the program's standard approach to this activity. But the principles are clearly quite similar, as are the techniques of implementation and evaluation. In addition, while narrowly focused OR studies are reasonably straightforward within an appropriately functioning delivery system, even a very successful trial by no means establishes a scientific principle. A number of analogous studies in different settings producing similar results would certainly provide useful guidelines for other PHC programs. But there is at present no sound basis for predicting the degree to which the findings of one program can be productively incorporated into another. Nor is it prudent, therefore, to assume that a large body of OR will eventually define a model PHC delivery system which is suitable for a variety of settings. From the perspective of the program director, OR should be viewed more as a fairly routine problem-solving methodology than as a body of knowledge, at least for the foreseeable future. Thus, the appropriate orientation for research institutions in this field would emphasize method as much as technical results.

To the extent that a legitimate role for OR in PHC programs becomes widely accepted, the direct contribution of outside experts to a given program will necessarily be small, on the average. This suggests a need for increased attention to the role of the researchers themselves and the method that they develop. Simply documenting the contribution of outside experts in detail would represent a substantial advance. Despite its obvious relevance to PHC, the process of establishing an OR capability within a conventional service program is virtually undescribed. Beyond simply describing the nature of the effort required and its effectiveness, there is also a need to systematically test different approaches and levels of involvement for consultants. Different types of manuals, guidelines, and training programs for conveying OR techniques can be evaluated in much the same manner that is applied to service delivery itself. While a great increase in the number of traditional impact surveys is out of the question, it should be possible to give greater emphasis to the relation between survey findings and data from the program information system. In the event of a substantial expansion of OR activities, the common practice of simply by-passing weaknesses in routine information collection by conducting independent surveys, will rarely be possible. Most programs would be forced to rely on their own information systems, and occasional assessments of this type of information through rigorous surveys would be useful.

The degree to which health program directors will be motivated to pursue the substantial program changes necessary to conduct OR is unclear. The present dearth of such activities is hardly encouraging, but the technical obstacles outlined above have not yet been addressed in most PHC programs. Careful description of early experiences, both in terms of establishing an OR capability and of the findings produced, will certainly facilitate the spread of OR techniques, a process that is likely to be self-reinforcing with regard to both technical and motivational obstacles.

THE COST-EFFECTIVENESS OF OPERATIONS RESEARCH

Even in a program that is well prepared to conduct OR, a given study is not necessarily a good investment of resources. Alternative studies or even none at all could produce superior results. With justification, research directed toward establishing scientific principles or influencing policy is not usually subjected to such scrutiny. However, the prospect of widespread OR activities in programs of severely limited resources requires us to carefully consider the cost and effectiveness of these studies. A number of considerations provide grounds for optimism that most OR programs will produce overall improvements in the cost-effectiveness of service delivery. Since the design of most PHC delivery system components is intuitive, it is likely that there are more cost-effective alternatives that can be discovered through empirical testing, and the effect of these improvements is cumulative over time. The absolute cost of OR conducted by LDC service delivery programs will necessarily be low, and will probably produce indirect improvements in service delivery by focusing attention on performance and on detailed descriptions which permit process analysis. Setting the right priorities is also an important factor. Testing modifications that prove inferior to the established procedures or produce trivial differences contributes little to the program. Increased experience with OR in various programs should help identify the OR approaches that are most likely to be productive, another area where public health experts can make an important contribution. As PHC delivery systems become increasingly based on empirical observation, the opportunities for further improvement will become less and less obvious. The potential of this process, however, is limited only by imagination.

REFERENCES

Aldana, D. and J.R. de Leon. "Research Program for the Training of Rural Health Promoters (PRINAPS)". Presented at the Workshop on Family Planning and Health Interventions in Community-Based Distribution Projects, January 12-14, 1982, Charlottesville, Virginia.

Bristow, R.A. "Management of Health Services in Developing Countries." In Proceedings of the International Conference on Systems Modelling in Developing Countries, Bangkok, Thailand, May 8-11, 1978, edited by P. Adulghan and N. Shariz. Asian Institute of Technology (1978): 403-414.

"Danfa Comprehensive Rural Health and Family Planning Project, Ghana, Final Report." Accra: University of Ghana Medical School, and Los Angeles: UCLA School of Public Health (September 1979).

Evans, J.R., K.L. Hall, and J. Warford. "Shattuck Lecture - Health Care in the Developing World: Problems of Scarcity and Choice." New England Journal of Medicine 305,19 (1981): 1117-1127.

Gadalla, S., N. Nossier, and D.G. Gillespie. "Household Distribution of Contraceptives in Rural Egypt." Studies in Family Planning 11,3 (1980): 105-113.

Gwatkin, D.R., J.R. Wilcox and J.D. Wray. Can Health and Nutrition Interventions Make a Difference? Overseas Development Council, Feb. 1980.

Heiby, J.R. "Low Cost Health Delivery Systems: Lessons from Nicaragua." American Journal of Public Health 71,5 (1981): 514-519.

Ladipo, O.A., E.M. Weiss, G.E. Delano, and J. Revson. "Community-Based Delivery (CBD) of Low-cost Family Planning and Maternal and Child Health Services in Rural Nigeria". Presented at the Workshop on Family Planning and Health Interventions in Community-Based Projects, January 12-14, 1982, Charlottesville, Virginia.

Lawrence, P.R. "How to Deal with Resistance to Change." Harvard Business Review (January/February 1969): 4-13.

Lechtig, A. and R. de Leon. Integrated System of Nutrition and Primary Health Care (SINAPS). Fourth Biannual Report, Institute of Nutrition of Central America and Panama, July 20, 1981.

Lewis, C.E. "Health-services Research and Innovations in Health-care Delivery." New England Journal of Medicine 297,8 (1977): 423-427.

McAlister, A., P. Puska, J.T. Salonen, J. Tuomilehto, and K. Koskela. "Theory and Action for Health Promotion: Illustrations from the North Karelia Project." American Journal of Public Health 72 (1982): 43-50.

Osborn, R.W. and W.A. Reinke, eds. Community-Based Distribution of Contraception: A Review of Field Experience. Baltimore: Johns Hopkins Population Center (1981): 158-177.

Rodrigues, W., C. Valladao, and J.R. Foreit. "Piaui Supervisory Experiment." Sociedade Civil Bem-Estar Familiar No Brazil (BEMFAM), April 2, 1981.

Taylor, C.E., J.S. Newman, and N.U. Kelly. "Interactions Between Health and Population." Studies in Family Planning 7,4 (1976): 94-100.

Williamson, N.E. "The Bohol Project and its Impact." Studies in Family Planning 10,6 and 7 (1979): 195-210.

World Health Organization (WHO). Primary Health Care: Report on the International Conference on Primary Health Care, Alma Ata, USSR, Sept. 6-12, 1978. Geneva: World Health Organization, 1978.